AFTERNOON TEA

The Meals Series

Series Editor

Ken Albala, University of the Pacific, kalbala@pacific.edu

The Meals Series examines our daily meals—breakfast, lunch, dinner, tea—as well as special meals such as the picnic and barbeque, both as historical construct and global phenomena. We take these meals for granted, but the series volumes provide surprising information that will change the way you think about eating. A single meal in each volume is anatomized, its social and cultural meaning brought into sharp focus, and the customs and manners of various peoples are explained in context. Each volume also looks closely at the foods we commonly include and why.

Books in the Series

Picnic: A History, by Walter Levy
Breakfast: A History, by Heather Arndt Anderson
Barbecue: A History, by Tim Miller
Afternoon Tea: A History, by Julia Skinner
Christmas Food and Feasting: A History, by Madeline Shanahan

AFTERNOON TEA

A HISTORY

Julia Skinner

ROWMAN & LITTLEFIELD
Lanham • *Boulder* • *New York* • *London*

Published by Rowman & Littlefield
An imprint of The Rowman & Littlefield Publishing Group, Inc.
4501 Forbes Boulevard, Suite 200, Lanham, Maryland 20706
www.rowman.com

6 Tinworth Street, London SE11 5AL, United Kingdom

British Library Cataloguing in Publication Information Available

Library of Congress Cataloging-in-Publication Data

Names: Skinner, Julia, 1983– author.
Title: Afternoon tea : a history / Julia Skinner.
Description: Lanham, Maryland : Rowman & Littlefield, [2019] | Series: The meals series | Includes bibliographical references and index.
Identifiers: LCCN 2018042844 (print) | LCCN 2018044359 (ebook) | ISBN 9781442271029 (electronic) | ISBN 9781442271012 (cloth : alk. paper)
Subjects: LCSH: Afternoon teas—History. | Drinking customs—History.
Classification: LCC TX736 (ebook) | LCC TX736 .S54 2019 (print) | DDC 394.1/50942—dc23
LC record available at https://lccn.loc.gov/2018042844

♾™ The paper used in this publication meets the minimum requirements of American National Standard for Information Sciences—Permanence of Paper for Printed Library Materials, ANSI/NISO Z39.48-1992.

Printed in the United States of America

To Mom,
for teaching me that love and curiosity are the best guides

CONTENTS

SERIES FOREWORD

Custom becomes second nature, and this is especially true of meals. We expect to eat them at a certain time and place, and we have a set of scripted foods considered appropriate for each. Bacon, eggs, and toast are breakfast; sandwiches are lunch; meat, potatoes, and vegetables are dinner, followed by dessert. Breakfast for dinner is so much fun precisely because it is out of the ordinary and transgressive. But meal patterns were not always this way. In the Middle Ages people ate two meals, the larger in the morning. Today the idea of a heavy meal with meat and wine at 11:00 a.m. strikes us as strange and decidedly unpleasant. Likewise when abroad, the food that people eat, at what seems to us the wrong time of day, can be shocking. Again, our customs have become so ingrained that we assume they are natural, correct, and biologically sound.

The Meals series will demonstrate exactly the opposite. Not only have meal times changed but the menu has as well, both through history and around the globe. Only a simple bowl of soup with a crust of bread for supper? That's where the name comes from. Our dinner, coming from *disner* in Old French, *disjejeunare* in Latin, actually means to break fast and was eaten in the morning. Each meal also has its own unique characteristics that evolve over time. We will see the invention of the picnic and barbecue, the gradual adoption of lunch as a new midday meal, and even certain meals practiced as hallowed institutions in some places but scarcely at all elsewhere, such as tea—the meal, not the drink. Often food items suddenly appear in a meal as quintessential, such as cold breakfast cereal, the invention of men like

Kellogg and Post. Or they disappear, like oysters for breakfast. Sometimes an entire meal springs from nowhere under unique social conditions, like brunch.

Of course, the decay of the family meal is a topic that deeply concerns us, as people catch a quick bite at their desk or on the go, or eat with their eyes glued to the television set. If eating is one of the greatest pleasures in life, one has to wonder what it says about us when we wolf down a meal in a few minutes flat or when no one talks at the dinner table. Still, mealtime traditions persist for special occasions. They are the time we remind ourselves of who we are and where we come from, when grandma's special lasagna comes to the table for a Sunday dinner, or a Passover Seder is set exactly the same way it has been for thousands of years. We treasure these food rituals precisely because they keep us rooted in a rapidly changing world.

The Meals series examines the meal as both a historical construct and a global phenomenon. Each volume anatomizes a single meal, bringing its social and cultural meaning into sharp focus and explaining the customs and manners of various people in context. Each volume also looks closely at the foods we commonly include and why. In the end I hope you will never take your mealtime customs for granted again.

Ken Albala
University of the Pacific

PREFACE

This book is the story of afternoon tea, or the British midafternoon meal initially meant to stave off hunger until the late dinners of high-society Victorians. What I learned quickly, though, was that you couldn't talk about the history of afternoon tea in England without also understanding the beverage that serves as its namesake and the empire that moved the beverage and the meal around the world.

Through the story of tea, we can trace trade routes and empires and the histories of the companies that exported it around the globe. Tea's story is more than simply an economic or political-science treatise, though. Tea is the most popular beverage on Earth, and by tracing its journey we can reach all the corners of our world and learn the many preparations and rituals for tea, which are as varied as the countries they represent. Fully covering the depth and complexity of tea's influence on human cultures is well beyond the scope of this (or any) book. Instead, I've tried to convey one small slice of that complex history by covering a country whose culture has proliferated throughout the world thanks to its aggressive colonialism.

Many students of history are aware of the Boston Tea Party and the British East India Company, which are intertwined with each other but also equally entangled with the world's most popular beverage. What these students may not realize, however, is that this same interwoven complexity isn't reserved for tea (the beverage, that is). The British meal of the same name also traces the spread of colonialism, runs along the same trade routes, and ends up with as many variations as it has present-day homes.

Afternoon tea (different from teatime or tea, which refers to the evening meal, depending on where you are and whom you ask) has become synonymous with English culture to many tourists and some Britons, and its presence (or absence) in former English colonies tells of the rise and fall of English power and of which traditions were valued and preserved. Here in America (where this book was written) and throughout much of the world, we still feel the echoes of that colonial past through our own cultural traditions (although we Americans have largely abandoned our tea-drinking ways in favor of coffee). Afternoon tea is but one of those traditions, but it is a vital one. Through its story, we will venture into stories of war, conquest, and cultural suppression, as well as stories of human connection and stories of how our food traditions adapt to our larger lived experiences. If this book has taught me anything, it has reaffirmed the centrality of food to our experiences as humans: that what we consume has a past as complex as our own and that through the lens of food we can better learn about that past and our place in it.

ACKNOWLEDGMENTS

To use a tired (but accurate) trope, it would take an entire book in itself to properly thank the many people who have influenced me and my work, and without whose contributions this book would not exist.

My friendships and professional life often overlap, and there are many colleagues who have helped me become a stronger scholar, a better teacher, and a more curious and engaged person. Ken Albala has been a mentor to me since I first developed the itch to study food a decade ago and a tireless supporter who believes in me even at times when I doubt myself.

Michael Twitty fearlessly speaks his truth and helps others find theirs, and his devotion to tackling what can feel difficult or overwhelming for many is one of the greatest inspirations for me as an author and person. Many other food studies folks, either through conversations or simply due to the influence of their work upon my own, deserve mention here, including Rachel Laudan, Sandor Katz, Carolyn Tillie, Julia Turshen, Grace Bonney, Roy Choi, Anne Bramley, Yokoo Gibraan, Cheryl Day, Pascal Baudar, and many, many others.

Many more colleagues deserve endless praise and thanks, but I want to call particular attention to a number of colleagues (and friends) whose work is outside the realm of food history but who have still been an important influence on this work: Melissa Gross, my dissertation advisor, has offered countless hours of research advice and cheerleading over the years, as did other colleagues from my days as a timid doctoral student, included among them Gary Burnett, Don Latham, Michelle Kazmer, Richard Urban, Mikki

Smith, Warren Allen, Jonathan Hollister, Jisue Lee, and Lenese Colson. Without their guidance and support, I would not have learned to engage in a thoughtful and interdisciplinary research practice, which has taken me from the study of libraries to the study of food and everywhere in between.

I have countless other friends and colleagues to mention who have impacted my work (in its many iterations) and life for years, as well as newly introduced colleagues who constantly inspire me to keep learning and growing: Jessamine Starr, George Long, Karl S. Gorline Jr., Matt Marcus, Wendall Brown, Sarah Baker, Paul Westin, K. T. Blackmon, Michi Meko, William Downs, Fredrik Brauer, Philip Meeker, Anne Laros, Julie Leonard, Kathleen Kamerick, Patrick Resha, Taria Camerino, Logan Lockner, Emily Drabinski, Robert Williams, Kate Drabinski, Jaclyn Verbitski, Jessica Critten, Nicole Fonsh, Lauren Hall, Lauren Bradley, Richard Harker, Danny Davis, Ingrid Conley-Abrams, Heather Oswald, Annie Pho, Kyle Drea, Drew Kitchens, Matt Kohl, Anney Reese, Lauren Vogelbaum, Walker Brown, Carolynn Ladd, Katy Malone, Teresa Reeves, Justin Rabideau, William Lobb, Eric Long, Daniel Keith, Von Diaz, Armando Suarez, Christine Stevens, Lindsay Schettler, Dana Haugaard, Jennifer Koslow, Liz Shores Patel, Elli Marlow, Justin de la Cruz, Dana DeToro, Richard DeMontmollin, John Alan Grant, Katy Meyer, Elisa Rojas Cardona, Virginia Howell, Joy Butler, Bill Taft, Sarah Higginbotham, Codee Cook, Jesse Edmunds, JoyEllen Freeman, Adam Hanley, Lauren Harris, Matt Kohl, Matthew Harper, Justin Schoendorf, Shawn Averkamp, Hart Epstein, Daniel Davis, Sonia Martinez, Chelseigh Millar, Diana Symons, Jacob Engelsman, Liz McCoy, and many more.

I'd also like to thank my colleagues in the Foundation for Fermentation Fervor residency, whose deep passion for their work, love of community, and ability to create and hold space for others has absolutely transformed my world for the better. Sandor Katz deserves additional thanks here for being an incredible facilitator and for showing us that you can indeed be who you are, do what you love, and still impact the world in the ways you hope to. Thanks also goes to MaxZine, Meka, Leopard, Spree, and all the other wonderful people in Sandor's home community, as well as to the land itself. And finally, thanks go to my fellow residents: Mandy Hall, Alana Toro Ramos, Mike Powsner, Sarah Skinker, Mike Hrzic, June Jo Lee, Niki Cutts,

Flynn Harne, Jacob Kenna, Terry King, Lily Hu, Jillian Ross, and John Riepenhoff.

I'd like to thank my patient and gracious interviewees—Liz Holdsworth, John Kirriemuir, Paula Maiorano, Kataryna Leach, Grant Michalski, and Kathryn La Barre—who thoughtfully answered questions about their food experiences, bringing considerable richness and depth to this work.

A number of other friends have helped with everything from edits to support to offering comic relief or drinking the hundreds of pots of tea I made while writing, eager to "get it right." These include Katie Lapp, Jamie and Logan Shaw, Todd Kelley, Joann Brothers, Bethany Bennitt, Katrina Nelson, Joe Urban, Justin Denman, Sherry Pennypacker Meints, Ian Mott, Sean Crutchfield, Spike Mott, Kim McShane, Chad Cripe, Brittany McGee, Clint Deiva, Kellie Everett, Andy Rehm, John Randall, Jake Broderick, Lacy Doyle, Kristen Schreiber, Wes and Lisa, Matt Cooper, Michael Flippo, Novaria Gill, Tanisha Corporal, Yale Cohn, Charlotte Eléa, and Andy Sorensen. I have undoubtedly left many, many names off this list, but not for a lack of gratitude for your help (rather, from a lack of great memory on my part!).

Suzanne Staszak-Silva and the entire Rowman & Littlefield staff have been a lot of fun to work with, and their input has helped me polish this work to a far greater shine than would have ever been possible otherwise. My library colleagues at the many institutions whose collections I utilized through either digital holdings or the occasional in-person visit deserve my limitless thanks for all they do to make their primary-source collections available and, equally important, to help people find what they're looking for. In particular, I want to thank the folks at University of Iowa's special collections, whose Szathmary Culinary Archives served as the space where I first learned to research culinary sources and whose holdings have informed this project and many others. I'd also like to thank the Written? Kitten! platform (writtenkitten.net), which has served as a surprisingly effective reward mechanism for many of my writing projects and helped immensely whenever I felt stuck.

Longtime friend and colleague John Ira Thomas, who has known me since I was a nineteen-year-old kid working in a cafeteria, and everyone at Candle Light Press deserve special mention here for being willing to branch out into a new subject area to publish my first book and for creating a community that feels as much like family as a business. Nialle Sylvan, Logan, and Nierme at the Haunted Bookshop in Iowa City also deserve a special mention for offering a space that served as both refuge and classroom and for friendship that I know I can always return to and pick right back up, no matter how long the time between our visits.

Few of us in this life are fortunate enough to be part of a supportive and unconditionally loving friend group. I'm very fortunate that I feel that support and love from many areas of my life, but writing a book about a meal that is so much about togetherness, and particularly the gathering of women in private and safe spaces, brought home to me the power of those spaces in my life. I am a part of many groups of strong, supportive women (many of whom are mentioned elsewhere in these pages) but want to separately thank one community of women that has helped me grow immeasurably and is always there to laugh and cry with. There are hundreds of thank-yous to be given, but for this particular project I want to specifically mention Tricia Fetters, Rebecca Hutton, Shelby Jones, Ashley Waterstadt, Sara Anne Miller, Jessica Bergman, Sarah Rose Butler, Cara Zozula, Maeve Kate, Sami Fink, Korama Danquah, Darcy Aanning, Erin Rose Opperman, Kira von Sutra, Jamie Beckert, Audrey Provine, Melissa Schramm, and Michelle Burton.

There are several people who deserve special mention for being among my primary supports during the incredible time of personal and professional transition that I undertook in the course of this writing: Sarah Higgins is one of the most talented and intelligent people I know, and her thoughtful engagement with her work has helped me enter more deeply into my own, and her playful and curious attitude toward the rest of the world has helped me take myself less seriously. Daniel Holliday, possibly the most talented chef I've ever met and my ride-or-die friend, will jump into any situation big or small with me and always has my back and an encouraging word (and the best hugs). Stephen DeLorme has found ways to creatively build space for me to feel supported, to find my focus, and to have breathing room in my work life and my personal life, doing everything from bringing dinner over after a long day to letting me borrow his car when mine breaks down to driving a state away to pick me up after my travels. His presence brings a level of peace and joy to my life and enriches it very broadly and deeply.

ACKNOWLEDGMENTS

Ellen Ireland, a fellow food person and thoughtful researcher, can take any topic and, with her unique and curious wit, make it something interesting and exciting (and who is a rock star at helping me identify plants in my yard). Sarah Creel has dropped everything on more than one occasion to celebrate or commiserate with me and whose excitement for sharing knowledge in the classroom and beyond has stoked my own passion for teaching. Kimberly Coburn is always excited about whatever irons I have in the fire (and who always has lots of exciting irons in the fire herself) and reminded me at a critical juncture that my work is valuable and needed. Abby Phillips created space for my personal and professional triumphs (and occasional tragedies) in the midst of her own shifting life and work. Jeremy Fisher believed in my work enough to bring me into his kitchen and hand me a fermentation program, has spent countless hours with me discussing food and community, and helped me finally accept that I have earned and deserve the title of "chef." Jes Distad has created space for adventures both impromptu and planned and inspired me to live my life fully and curiously. And, of course, Scott Koranda has for more than a decade shared countless lengthy conversations about food, gave me a book that changed my life (McGee's *On Food and Cooking*), and continues to have a powerful and positive impact on my life as someone who lives and breathes a deep and curious love for the work they do and the people in their world.

Finally, I want to thank my family for unwavering love and support in my many and varied schemes over the years, and I want to include a long-lost arm of my family that I recently had the pleasure of meeting, and who were incredibly gracious in welcoming me. In particular, I'd like to thank Gwen Walker Cradle, Rosalind Lenoir-Zachary, and Joyce Lenoir. I'd also like to thank my cousins Jonathan, Jameson, and Jeremy Horton and my aunt, Janet Horton, as well as Dale and Ted Rosenfeldt, for consistently being supportive, deeply loving, and a joy to be with. Tim Meints built a life with my mom and welcomed her and me into his family. Few people are fortunate enough to have a father like Dave Skinner, whose insights, curiosity, and dedication to personal growth and to the people he cares for have crafted his role in my world into one of parent, mentor, and friend. Here is a good place to also mention a number of family members and friends who are no longer with us but whose presence is felt in this work, including Nicky

ACKNOWLEDGMENTS

Rahn, Margery Skinner, William Skinner, Eugene Sibbald, Emily Palmer, and David Huntley.

My grandma, Jean Sibbald, showed me through my whole life that age offers more opportunities than constraints, that love and learning are boundless, and that traveling the world (or dropping a kayak in the water close to home) is always a good way to throw your life back in perspective. She has always been a support for me and, as the other author in the family, an inspiration for every writing project I've undertaken, no matter how large or small. Her daughter's passing was enough to break her heart, and she unfortunately did the same not long after. While she did not live to see this work in print, she was extremely proud of it and of me and made me promise that I would write another book in the future to dedicate to her (which, of course, I will!).

There is one last, important person I want to thank: My mother, Margaret Huntley Meints, who passed away a week before this book manuscript was due, has been a constant support, a loving guide, and my biggest cheerleader. She was excited about this book, as she was about all my projects, and her enthusiasm and curiosity, alongside the space she created to ask me questions and encourage me, is a big reason why the final book is what it is. It's to her that I want to dedicate this work, and I want to take a moment to honor her in writing for all the incredible good she brought to hundreds of lives over the course of her own.

INTRODUCTION

The story of afternoon tea is as multifaceted as the seas the British East
India Company sailed to bring tea leaves to European markets. As
we move through the following chapters, we will learn about the English
afternoon meal associated with that beverage. We'll explore the birth of afternoon tea and see how it spread to England's colonies. I chose to highlight
a few examples of colonies to explore, as they offer some broad understanding of the different ways the meal might have appeared during colonialism in
different areas of the world. We'll also briefly explore tea itself as an agent of
colonialism, as tea exporters brought back more leaves to support the consumption of a beloved beverage as well as the practice of a cherished ritual.

We'll learn about how, as England's colonial powers waned, English food
traditions either themselves waned or held fast in former colonies, and we'll
conclude by learning about the state of afternoon tea today. I have used the
same examples from the colonial period to highlight and hopefully offer a
broad understanding not only of tea's introduction but also of its range of
iterations in the postcolonial world. Since so much of the world was under
English rule at the height of the empire, this is one way to begin to grasp the
meal's spread through the world without the impossible task of document-
ing it in every former colony.

Afternoon tea has a complex and fascinating history, making it perfect for
an exploration of English history. Because it is a tradition that developed
in tandem with colonial expansion—and is one that drew on the network
of colonial trade and labor practices to supply it (including slavery and

indentured servitude)—there are many avenues to explore and questions to answer. But before we delve into the story of afternoon tea as an English phenomenon, let's lay some groundwork by studying the drink itself.

TEA: THE BEVERAGE (A VERY CONCISE HISTORY)

According to Chinese legend, Emperor Shennong (2737–2697 BCE) encouraged his subjects to boil water before drinking it in order to keep from getting sick. As he boiled his water one day, the wind picked up and blew some leaves into the pot. Upon tasting the result, the emperor found the new beverage to be delicious and energizing.[1] Elsewhere, in Japan and India, Buddhist monks and scholars are situated at the center of tea's origin story.[2] No matter how it was discovered, the beverage has become a central part of human history.

The Tea Plant

Tea leaves come from *Camellia sinensis*, an evergreen shrub with attractive white flowers and bright, glossy leaves. There are three main varieties of the plant: China (*C. sinensis* var. *sinensis*, which has a more delicate flavor), Assam (*C. sinensis* var. *assamica*, with a more robust and earthy flavor), and Cambodian (*C. sinensis* var. *cambodiensis*, which is a hybrid of the other varieties and has a more balanced profile). Like wines, flavor is imparted by the soil and growing conditions, as well as hybridization, resulting in an endless variety of teas and an endless variety of flavor profiles.[3]

Harvesters only pick the most delicate leaves of the plant for tea (often the tea bud and the top couple of leaves) and leave the more developed ones behind.[4] Over the years, tea producers have continued to learn how to improve tea's flavor through cultivation and processing. Growers found that tea planted at higher elevations often tasted better. They also developed a number of treatments for the leaves to introduce a variety of flavors and health benefits. Unfermented teas (white, green, and yellow tea) are dried or steamed immediately after picking to prevent oxidization, and each type is a result of a slightly different treatment. Semifermented tea (oolong) undergoes some oxidization, while black tea is completely fermented, which was initially done to help it survive long journeys along land and sea trade routes.[5]

Our journey begins by following the *Camellia* plant through its discovery, proliferation, and eventual move across trade routes to Europe. There our story of English traditions can begin in earnest. *Camellia* is native to Asia, and it was initially discovered and consumed in China. The many variations on its name point to its Chinese roots. The word *tea* comes from the Chinese Amoy term *t'e* (pronounced "tay"). The Mandarin word for tea is *cha*, and from there we get other similar-sounding variations (such as *chai* in India and elsewhere). The European names for tea are derived from these earlier Chinese terms. For example, when tea was first brought to England, one term used to describe it was *cha* or *char*.[6]

There is no agreed-upon geographic origin for the *Camellia* plant, although the general region is likely the eastern Himalayan mountains or slightly southeast.[7] As with many older legends, it is also impossible to know with certainty who first boiled tea leaves in water. The tale of Emperor Shennong is often pointed to and, if true, would place the discovery of tea around 2700 BCE. Whether or not this story is factual or just a myth, we do know that the Chinese first cultivated tea bushes, popularized tea drinking nationally, and introduced the beverage to the international stage, although the secrets of tea's cultivation and processing were closely guarded for many centuries.[8]

In the Yunnan province, there is a long history of tea consumption, as well as tea bushes that are almost two millennia old. It is in this region that tea began to be cultivated, later spreading to the rest of China and throughout Asia.[9] The earliest reliable references in Chinese literature appear in the third or fourth century CE, as tea cultivation (rather than foraging) became more common. In the following centuries, the drink that had initially been used for a variety of medicinal benefits (from constipation to headaches) became a drink enjoyed for pleasure as well.[10]

Tea became central to Chinese culture and was named one of the seven necessities of life during the Song Dynasty (960–1297).[11] It also became central to Chinese commerce, as sales taxes were enforced to raise funds for the imperial government.[12]

Tea made its way into Chinese artistic expression as well. A poem by Lú Tóng (Lu T'ung) appears in many histories of tea[13] and is shared here as well for its beauty in describing tea as a food connected to identity and understanding (as well as a flowery description of heavy caffeine consumption):

The first cup moistens my lips and throat;
The second cup breaks my loneliness;
The third cup searches my barren entrails but to find therein some
thousand volumes of odd ideographs;
The fourth cup raises a slight perspiration—all the wrongs of life pass
out through my pores;
At the fifth cup I am purified;
The sixth cup calls me to the realms of the immortals;
The seventh cup—ah, but I could take no more! I only feel the breath of
the cool wind that raises in my sleeves.
Where is Elysium? Let me ride on this sweet breeze and waft away
thither.[14]

Tea was initially consumed for health benefits, but later Buddhist monks found it also helped them stay awake during long hours of meditation.[15] As the beverage was found to have more and more benefits, it became an increasingly valuable commodity and began to be traded at home and abroad.

Because of its value as a commodity, Chinese growers jealously guarded their crops, but by the ninth century some Buddhist monks had managed to transport seeds out of China and to Korea and Japan. Both countries began producing their own tea soon thereafter. Elsewhere in the medieval world, tea was typically traded for rather than produced. It often came in dense bricks and was a highly valued commodity, from Siberia to Tibet,[16] and along the Silk Road, south to the Middle East, where the earliest mentions of tea appear in the mid-800s.[17]

Tea Comes to Europe

The history of tea is the history of global trade and of colonialism. Its influence has touched every corner of the earth, making it the world's most popular beverage, and there are as many ways to enjoy tea as there are countries that drink it. As tea consumption spread through the Middle East, it continued west, eventually making its way to European shores. Records show that the Portuguese were aware of tea by the early 1500s, although it was not yet a regular import. The first printed account of tea by a European was in 1559, when Venetian author Giambattista Ramusio recounted a story about it passed along to him by Persian visitors. The Dutch became the first to import tea to Europe in 1610, and it was at this point that Europeans began to develop a taste for the beverage (and, eventually, a desire to participate in its import).[18]

By the 1650s, tea imported from Dutch merchants was being sold in London. In 1660, the well-known coffeehouse proprietor Thomas Garraway issued a broadside to draw in patrons to try the exotic new beverage: "The said leaf is of such known virtues, that those very nations so famous for antiquity, knowledge, and wisdom, do frequently sell it among themselves for twice its weight in silver."[19] Garraway then offered a laundry list of healthy benefits, from lustiness and increased energy to fighting colds and cleansing the liver.[20]

While tea was technically present in England, it was incredibly expensive and not particularly popular those first several years. However, in 1662, King Charles II married Catherine of Braganza, a Portuguese princess and devoted tea drinker. Her dowry included a small amount of tea, and the beverage was so heavily demanded by the court that the British East India Company began importing tea soon after the royal marriage.[21] By the dawn of the eighteenth century, the upper classes were hooked on drinking tea,[22] which was an extravagance that could be shared by both sexes in the home. Men had the luxury of enjoying other imported goods—such as coffee and chocolate—in London coffeehouses, where they talked politics, business, and other subjects off-limits to their female counterparts, who were not permitted in those spaces.[23] By 1717, tea moved into more public spaces as Thomas Twining opened the Golden Lion tea garden. Other teahouses and tea gardens popped up, catering to both men and women. This gave tea a firmer hold on English society than coffee, as coffeehouses were often male-only territory, and thus the beverage was less accessible to Englishwomen.[24]

Tea came to England through legal trade and through smuggling. The British East India Company brought in a significant amount of the tea consumed in England, although millions of pounds of tea were also smuggled into the country, particularly by the Dutch, who wanted to avoid paying the high import taxes on their goods.[25] About a century after its introduction, tea imports from China rose from hundreds of pounds a year to roughly nine million pounds in 1770 alone (this of course does not include the untold millions of pounds smuggled in to the country, which are impossible to account for accurately).[26] The flood of tea into England meant lower prices due to ample supply, and its affordability made tea accessible across class boundaries by the beginning of the nineteenth century.[27]

Tea became even more popular across Europe once physicians began to recommend it as a healthful beverage, which happened more often in the early years of its introduction (as we'll see in later chapters, it was later regarded as nonnutritious swill, in part because of its popularity with the working classes during the Industrial Revolution). Dr. Cornelis Decker, a Dutch physician, was named "Doctor Good Tea" because of his fervent support of the little leaves. Decker encouraged everyone to drink eight to ten cups a day, and while the good doctor was accused of being paid off by Dutch tea merchants, his advocacy resulted in increasing popularity for the drink. Many other doctors continued to sound the call, describing a wide variety of virtues the leaves supposedly would impart. As with any health claim, however, this belief was far from universal, and some doctors felt quite the opposite. German physician Simon Pauli felt that tea was healthful in Asian climates but became dangerous in European climates to the point that "it hastens the death of those who drink it, especially if they have passed the age of forty years."[28]

The way tea was consumed and served changed in the new continent as well. The Chinese had always served their tea plain, to allow the leaves' flavors to shine through, but their European counterparts added other ingredients—namely, sugar and milk—in order to cut its bitterness and give it a richer texture. These additions sparked further changes. While in Eastern cultures it was common to drink warm (not boiling hot) tea from a handle-less cup, Europeans served their tea hot in order to dissolve sugar and, as a result, created teacups with handles to avoid burning themselves while holding their drinks. Other household fixtures were born of the new drink as well: a teaspoon to stir sugar in to the tea, a saucer to hold the used teaspoon and to protect surfaces, a tea table to host tea gatherings, and a larger and more ornate teapot to serve as a centerpiece.[29] The saucer served an additional purpose, allowing those "of a less refined nature the option of pouring hot tea into the saucer to let it cool, then slurping it up—a procedure that gave rise to the phrase 'a dish of tea.'"[30]

The continued increase in tea consumption also meant an increased demand for tea-related goods like ceramics and silver, with Chinese porcelain pouring into European markets and silversmiths working like mad to slake the public thirst for teaspoons and teapots. These were often packed in chests surrounded by tea leaves to protect them during shipping, making efficient use of space in meeting Europeans' insatiable demands for Chinese goods.[31] The popularity of tea changed the face of global trade, as silk and porcelain relinquished their role as China's leading exports to Europe, particularly as continental producers of these commodities became more skilled and prolific.[32]

It also meant a demand for sugar, and in the British Isles in particular sugar was considered "the inseparable companion of tea,"[33] such that when the consumption of one rose, so did the other. The connection between the two may have evolved through the desire for sweetened tea, although there is also evidence that the link between sugar and tea (as well as coffee) was encouraged by European merchants and traders who dealt in the stuff, in order to increase the sales of sugar, which were lagging as its negative health impacts became more apparent in the latter part of the seventeenth century.[34] In the Caribbean and elsewhere in the British Empire, sugar plantations rose up to sweeten Europeans' tea. Most of the labor that went into this very demanding crop came from African slaves, and it was in part Europeans' love of tea that fueled the growing transatlantic slave trade.[35]

Sugar was so integral to the growing institution of slavery that it formed one-third of what is often referred to as "triangular trade," where people were enslaved in Africa and moved across the Middle Passage (the sea-lane across the Atlantic Ocean spanning from Africa to the Americas)[36] to the Americas and the Caribbean, where sugar (as well as tobacco and cotton) was grown using their labor and then exported to Europe, and European manufactured goods (such as textiles) were brought to western Africa and traded for more enslaved people, where the cycle would begin anew.[37]

Like sugar, the price of tea during its early years in England (and elsewhere in Europe) was high, and it fell rapidly, also like sugar, due in part to the labor practices employed in their growing, making both products accessible to the average English person. This development raised consumption and demand, thus increasing the demand for slave labor in the colonies for sugar and indentured or, at best, underpaid labor in tea plantations. Demand in Europe continued to rise, creating a trade built upon the lives and deaths of many generations of African people, based entirely upon tobacco, tea, and sugar—what Sheridan calls "those artificial wants that crept in and acquired the character of necessities."[38]

As the British Empire in particular grew into parts of Asia, the British were able to steal Chinese tea plants and begin establishing their own tea plantations,[39] run by exploited laborers whose living conditions were only marginally better than their enslaved or sharecropping counterparts in the Americas and the Caribbean.[40] Both the history of the empire's growth and that of the labor that supported it will come up again in this book, as they are necessary to understanding the context in which a meal became part of the imperial culture.

The history of tea and its prominence in European trade, colonial expansion, and the subjugation of workers has been the topic of many other texts, and these themes will crop up again in this book. The topic of afternoon tea has been covered elsewhere as well, but often as a subheading within pieces about English culture or lifestyle (such as that of the country gentry),[41] in a book about tea drinking or beverages in England,[42] from the perspective of a how-to book (etiquette, foods to serve, etc.),[43] or in travel guides (e.g., where is the best afternoon tea in Cape Town?).[44]

What has not been done previously, and what I hope this book will accomplish, is to pull these threads together: when we ask where Cape Town's best afternoon tea is, for example, we must also ask how afternoon tea got to Cape Town in the first place and, once it was there, how it became entrenched enough to stay after the colonial power that introduced it had left. The first chapter deals with the introduction of tea as a beverage to England and its evolving role in English society and mealtimes, resulting in the afternoon tea meal as well as its close cousin, high tea, and other tea-adjacent meals, such as elevenses and teatime.

Chapter 2 traces the spread of European colonialism across the globe and explores where and how afternoon tea followed. It turns out that afternoon tea in some form is ubiquitous across much of the former empire, whether as a special-occasion meal taken at a local restaurant (such as in America) or a simple snack meal consumed every day (as in India). To try to tease out some of the differences, I have included a few case studies that briefly explore the specific afternoon tea traditions and histories of a handful of colonies: India, America, Kenya, Australia, Malta, and South Africa.

In chapter 3, I revisit these same places as they exist in the postcolonial world and ask what the impact of colonialism has been on their present-day foodways. Does afternoon tea exist? Or, rather, how does it exist in this space now that English rule is over? Where appropriate—as in Kenya and India, where tea is still grown—I also explore how the beverage itself intersects with the country's culture and economy (for example, by looking at tea's relationship with the legacy of colonialism in the tourism industry).

Chapter 4 examines afternoon tea in modern Great Britain, exploring how the meal has changed in its birthplace and where it might go from here. In the conclusion, I offer a few thoughts about the future of afternoon tea as well as a (certainly not exhaustive) few recipes for commonly found afternoon tea foods, modernized from Victorian-era sources to reflect the cooking temperatures and ingredients of our current kitchens.[45] Studying afternoon tea, and tea itself, is an undertaking that has asked me to explore the entire surface of the globe, redefine my own understanding (when I started out, for example, I had no idea that low tea was the original upper-class meal and high tea was the working-class one), and face modern postcolonial practices reminding us that their legacy, and our own relationship to them, is not as far away as we might think. As one of my dearest friends once said, "Tea is leaves in hot water, and it's affected more of the human experience than almost any other commodity."[46] While afternoon tea may not have shaped worlds, it has certainly hitched a ride with the beverage and the imperial power that did, and this book is a road map to that journey.

1

A TRADITION IS BORN

TEA COMES TO ENGLAND

Most sources on afternoon tea will tell you that the meal of afternoon tea began in the mid-1800s when Anna Maria Russell, Duchess of Bedford, began partaking of small afternoon snacks and beverages to tide her and her guests over until their large meal late in the evening. However, as with most things in history, the truth is more complicated and requires us to go further back in time, and well beyond Russell's legacy. Russell's tradition of an afternoon snack and cup of tea, first alone and then with a small circle of friends, is certainly not the first instance of a cup of tea being drunk (or even a snack being eaten) in the afternoon. However, her promotion of the snack meal as both a social space and a new meal with its own etiquette and wares appealed to the Victorian sentimentality toward the world that demanded a place for everything and everything in its place.[1]

Tea gardens and shops were, by this time, already in place, cookbooks already offered recipes for small bites to serve while entertaining, and people had already become accustomed to tea as a daily drink and, in particular, a drink that allowed them to be social without becoming intoxicated.[2] All of this set the stage for Russell to codify the act of casually snacking into a meal with its own identity and social conventions. Russell was in the right place at the right time to set the ball in motion: the popularity of the beverage, combined with the opportunity for socializing and eating, may have been the key to the meal's successful integration into English society.

The choice of tea as the basis of the meal tells us about the larger contexts in which the duchess and her English peers existed. While the meal began to be called "afternoon tea" during the Victorian era, the English had been enamored of the beverage since the seventeenth century. Afternoon tea came into vogue when the influence of the British Empire was at its strongest, stretching across continents, from which the best wares were regularly imported back to England to profit the empire and fuel its continued growth. For nearly two hundred years these goods had been circulating back to England, ever the founding of the East India Company, which became famous for—among other things—its involvement in the tea trade and for popularizing tea in England in the early modern period.[3]

THE COMPANY

The East India Company became a giant, in terms of both global trade and its influence on English colonial expansion, and it built its vast monopoly on the trading activities and commodities introduced by earlier traders. Tea had first been introduced to Europe by Portuguese traders, who had reached China by sea in 1557 and established trade agreements to import tea and other goods to the European continent. The Dutch followed suit, and by the early seventeenth century both nations were bringing tea to Europe from the Portuguese trading post in Macao (on the Canton River) and the Dutch trading base at Bantam (on the island of Java).[4]

By 1611, the Dutch had also begun importing tea from Japan. And from 1613 to 1623 the British East India Company operated a trading post out of Hirado, an island in Nagasaki prefecture,[5] though the English did not export tea back home, having not yet developed a taste for it. But as contact with Europeans increased, so did Japan's alarm: fearing European influence would come to dominate their culture, in 1633 the nation sealed its borders to outsiders. For more than two hundred years, Europeans were permitted entry only into Nagasaki and the port of Hirado, putting a stranglehold on high-volume trade between Japan and Europe. Finally, in 1672, after the East India Company established a trading post on the island of Formosa (modern-day Taiwan), the English secured their importation of Chinese tea.[6]

The origins of the East India Company can be traced back to the Tudors, when Elizabeth I (r. 1558–1603) deftly exploited a new trade innovation in a move that would strengthen England's influence the world over for centuries to come. Her early rule had been marked by isolation from Europe, as the newly Protestant country was being shunned by the Vatican and, by extension, the very Catholic—and very powerful—Spain. The queen grew concerned that her small island nation, already suffering from trade embargoes, would be vulnerable to invasion.

Her options for alliances were limited: Antwerp, a major trading hub, had been sacked by Spanish soldiers in 1576,[7] and the ongoing Eighty Years' War between the Spanish and Dutch meant the Dutch were unavailable to partner with England in trade.[8] Elizabeth had also considered an alliance with the Germans at Emden, but this idea was quickly discarded as politically and militarily infeasible.[9] And so she turned to the Middle East, allying herself with Sultan Murad III of the Ottoman Empire, whose strength was great enough to counter even Spain's might. Hedging her bets, Elizabeth also reached out to the shah of Persia and the ruler of Morocco, stretching England's ties across the region.[10]

Borrowing the concept of joint-stock companies—in which investors would band together to back a trade venture and share in profits and losses[11]—Elizabeth signed trade agreements with the Ottoman Empire and other Middle Eastern partners—agreements that would be in effect for centuries. Among the trade groups affected by the treaty were the Muscovy Company, which traded with Russia and Persia and later served as a model for the Turkey Company, which traded with the Ottomans, and the East India Company, whose influence is better known but which could not have existed without its Middle Eastern predecessors.[12]

Elizabeth's maneuvering also influenced England's taste for Middle Eastern and Asian wares, as she chartered the trade companies that brought foodstuffs, silks, tableware, and decor to the country—and in large enough amounts that they were in the price range of middling as well as upper-class homes across the country. Thanks to her extensive treaties, English traders crossed through areas like Aleppo, Syria, and Mosul, Iraq, bringing Middle Eastern and Far Eastern wares to trading ports. Those traders were much safer in Middle Eastern and Central Asian countries than they were in most of Europe, where they were at risk of being captured by the Spanish Inquisition, which served the Spanish Crown and its trade interests as well as enforcing moral codes.[13]

At the end of the sixteenth century, the Spanish Armada was defeated, allowing English merchants more freedom to plan expeditions to the Indian Ocean and compete with other European merchants for imported goods. A group of merchants approached Queen Elizabeth with a petition to conduct an exploratory mission to locate more efficient trade routes, and in 1591, permission granted, they sailed around the Cape of Good Hope to the Arabian Sea. One ship continued on to the Malay Peninsula, with the mission concluding in 1594.[14]

These early voyages included costly false starts by English merchants as they were marooned or otherwise unsuccessful in their missions, but the English were determined to become a major player in international trade, in part because they saw the wealth it had brought to the Dutch and others.[15] Elizabeth granted a royal charter to George Clifford, Earl of Cumberland, giving him a fifteen-year monopoly on trade with all countries east of the Cape of Good Hope and west of the Strait of Magellan. Clifford (1558–1605) was a loyal member of Queen Elizabeth's court, with a reputation for being rambunctious and adventurous. His intrepidness seems to have been balanced by a talent for aptly calculating risk, which is, perhaps, what made him the perfect candidate to undertake a precarious new trading effort and contributed to the queen's willingness to grant him the charter.[16]

Clifford's new company was called the Governor and Company of Merchants of London Trading with the East Indies, which was often referred to by its shorthand names (the Honourable East India Company, the East India Company, the John Company, or sometimes simply the Company). The first East India Company voyage set sail in 1601, two years before Elizabeth I's death.[17] Her concerns over the Protestant country's isolation, which had initially driven her to aggressively build alliances and support trade efforts, did not outlive her. Soon after acceding to the throne, her successor, James I, signed treaties with Spain. However, Elizabeth left a legacy of investing in trade, and England's global trade presence flourished and grew along with the empire.[18]

In 1609, James I renewed Elizabeth's East India Company charter indefinitely, cementing a trade monopoly that would endure for generations.[19] The first years of the Company were marked by efforts to establish a foothold in the spice trade, then dominated by the Dutch and Portuguese. Slowly the Company began to establish trading posts around the Indian Ocean, and the three most important of these—Bombay, Calcutta, and Madras—grew into large towns. This allowed the English to eclipse their Portuguese competitors and to expand their trade across the Indian subcontinent.

By the following decade, the English East India Company, as it had come to be known, had sailed as far as Japan and was on good terms with the Chinese court, which positioned them to begin importing Chinese goods—including tea.[20] However, the Company's leaders, fearful of competition, grew distracted from their business efforts and engaged in a bloody power struggle with the Dutch over the spice trade to Europe. After four years of fighting, the Dutch were victorious and forced the English to withdraw to mainland India and the surrounding islands.[21] This meant English traders had no base in China, and the East India Company was not able to import tea to England until fifty years later, in 1669.

Even though the Company could not import tea, its agents, and increasingly the English people themselves, were aware of the drink's existence. In 1625, English cleric and travel writer Samuel Purchas, for example, used information from various sources to construct his own narrative about Chinese tea-drinking habits in a compilation of travel narratives by English travelers about different cultures around the world, which at the time was the longest work published in English. He writes in *Purchas His Pilgrimage*, "They used much the powder of a certaine herb called Chia, of which they put as much as a Walnut-Shell may containe, into a dish of Porcelane, and drinke it with hot water."[22] Purchas gained some of his travel experience through his work with English mercantile entities: he had joined the Virginia Company in 1622, formed to promote English settlement in the Americas, and the book itself had been written under the patronage of the East India Company; his pro-enterprise bent is evident in his writing.[23] His extensive work overseas, and specifically his work with merchants, would have given him early access to the beverage as well as firsthand insights about its consumption in China.

Fearing dilution of the market and loss of control over trade, Chinese trading restrictions on tea did not keep the Company from expanding their trade activities elsewhere: during the first half of the seventeenth century, Company merchants moved from dealing primarily in spices to marketing fabrics, dye, saltpeter, porcelain, and more.[24] Finally, when the Chinese lifted restrictions in the second half of the seventeenth century, the Company was able to import tea. They were eager to encourage the new trade, despite the beverage's expense. Their first order for tea, placed the first year trade reopened, was for a mere hundred pounds' worth.[25] Over the next twenty years, orders were increasingly placed for Chinese tea, which was then moved to the East India Company's various trading posts on the subcontinent and, from there, back to England. Tea was incredibly expensive, which meant early orders were small and infrequent, and which also made tea an inaccessible commodity for most English households. Despite this, demand for the beverage grew, and by the early eighteenth century merchants were bringing back tens of thousands of pounds of tea to meet demand.

The East India Company grew rapidly, with the East India House (a warehouse and wholesale market for imported goods) opening in London in 1648.[26] The Company later expanded its operations to spread across thirty acres of docks in east London (now appropriately known as Docklands, then called the East India Dock complex) in 1806.[27] Charles II granted a staggering list of rights to East India Company merchants in the 1670s and 1680s, including (but not limited to) the right to bear arms, command fortresses, acquire land, form alliances, mint money, and wage war or make peace.[28] This was done to protect the company's existing trade interests, but also to spur rapid growth, and gave the Company de facto power as the representative of the Crown throughout India. As we will see time and again, food and colonialism are deeply intertwined, and it is worth pointing out here that a company initially founded to move consumer goods from East to West was, less than a century after its creation, able to wage war, buy or take land, and even make its own currency as a representative of government.

This development, of course, had a huge impact on the foodways of England, because the Company, having many of the same powers as a government, now had the potential to exponentially increase the amount and variety of goods being brought in and access to a range of quality goods increases in England. Of course, the inverse was true for those living in the countries being colonized: land, food, labor, and personal freedom could be purchased or simply taken with little thought as to what it did to residents' food security, land, or lives. As we will see later, the sweeping power of the

East India Company also was a driver for the spread of English culture and traditions to the areas it colonized.

Although tea was often considered a feminine and courtly beverage in its early years in England, the earliest written account we have of its consumption in England is from a man. Samuel Pepys was a member of parliament and naval officer, often remembered for the extensive diary he kept from 1660 to 1669.[29] According to one entry, he and Sir R. Ford had a meeting during which Pepys "did send for a Cupp of Tee (a China drink) of which I had never drank before."[30] Pepys says nothing about his impressions of the drink, but this simple diary entry gives quite a bit of insight into the introduction of tea into English society.

Pepys's entry tells us a couple of things about tea in England at this time: First, he reveals that the beverage was available to high-ranking military officers in 1660, meaning that the beverage was popular enough at least among the elite to sometimes be available and requested in the homes and public spaces they frequented. The fact that Pepys had heard of, but had not yet consumed (or seemingly even encountered), tea before suggests that by this time tea was in the early stages of its introduction to elite English society but was not yet present at most or even many social and business gatherings. Further, the entry shows us that introduction to the new beverage was not only a social activity within a private home but also part of conducting official business.

The date of Pepys's entry is also worth noting: After the English Civil War had been waged (1642–1646[31]), the Commonwealth and Protectorate of England were established (1649–1660).[32] Pepys wrote only about five months after the English Crown had been restored—and only a few weeks after he'd sailed to The Hague to accompany the exiled King Charles II back home to be crowned.[33] This meant that tea was introduced to a country in turmoil, and in particular a country where political and social loyalties were shifting and where the future of the elites' wealth and stature was uncertain. This is an interesting mix in which to throw a new and expensive consumer product (the Dutch only began bringing small tea shipments to London about three years before Pepys's entry), which initially might sound like a disaster for cultural acceptance of the new product.

However, tea had a critical point in its favor: it was the preferred drink of Catherine of Braganza, the Portuguese princess who married Charles II and became queen of England.[34] As is the case with many other new commodities, the popularity of this new product was at least partially dictated by who was consuming and advocating for it. Products that evoke an ideal of wealth and class and have strengthened associations to desired social and political connections are often thought to have a better chance for success in new markets,[35] which aided the introduction of tea to the English market.[36] Tea may have also benefited from the timing of its introduction, as the newly reinstated monarchy undoubtedly benefited from offering symbols of national identity that demarcated a new era in England while connecting it to its history: tea not only served as a status symbol for the elite but also was introduced to the country by a member of the royal family and, as such, served as a symbol of loyalty to them.

Several years later, Pepys mentioned tea again, this time extolling its health benefits rather than its novelty, although his description leads one to believe that the beverage was still not common in his home, as he felt the need to describe its purpose: "I went . . . home and there find my wife making Tea, a drink which Mr. Pelling the pothecary tells her is good for her for her cold and defluxions."[37]

Another change in English foodways in the early modern period was the proliferation of English cookbooks, thanks to advances like the printing press, which spurred vast increases in publication. This resulted in the transmission of written recipes, although receipt books (as they were called at the time) did not contain much guidance on preparing tea until later on, when its price dropped and it became more widely popular. Published cookery books first appeared in English in the sixteenth century: *A Boke of Cookery* was published in 1500, followed in the mid-1500s by *A Proper Newe Boke of Cookery*, as well as books dispensing advice on diet.[38] These books were in some cases based on mid-fifteenth-century predecessors, which themselves drew from much older cookery and health traditions, and in other cases pulled heavily (and directly) from the sources they referenced.[39]

In these early modern books from the fifteenth and sixteenth centuries we begin to see a movement of English cookery traditions away from oral transmission to written and, with publication, the potential to share ideas beyond one's immediate circle increased exponentially.

The seventeenth century saw an accelerated pace for cookery-book publication. It also saw a greater variety of publications, such as Gervase

Markham's advice for rural middling households and Robert May's recipes geared toward wealthier and more cosmopolitan audiences.[40] Cookbooks during the first half of the century were often published by and attributed to men, even though they directly reference women's manuscripts as the source of much of their contents. By the end of the century, women's names began to appear on cookery books—for example, Hannah Woolley in 1661. This new tradition of written cookery books that went beyond the receipt book for an individual household (although those still existed as well) gives us a broad sense of what foods were available in England and, for those ingredients and dishes that appear regularly, what foods were actually being consumed. This includes foods for entertaining for, by and large, large-scale events like banquets but also—particularly as we move into the eighteenth and nineteenth centuries—begins to include smaller snack dishes with greater frequency, eventually including dishes for hosting afternoon teas as the meal became popular.

The Journey of Tea to England

The growing British tea trade was pushed along in large part by the East India Company, which had a vested interest in getting more Britons to consume the beverage. The Company's trade monopoly and its pushing of tea into British markets, as well as Company imports and the Dutch influence in the early American settlements, meant that American and British people in the mid-1600s took to drinking tea whereas much of Europe was warming up to coffee.[41]

The best-quality tea came from the first two spring harvests in China, and these were typically exported to international markets. Later harvests were lower quality and were usually kept by farmers for home consumption. The farmers would sell their spring harvests to local dealers, who would sample them and put together a "chop" (or a shipment that would blend together many farmers' harvests). The chop would fill between 620 and 630 tea chests, and these would be transported over the mountains to wholesale centers in the towns, where dealers from China and abroad would come to select the teas they wanted.[42]

From the wholesale centers, the chosen tea shipments would travel along a system of inland waterways to the main port at Canton, forty miles inland from Hong Kong. The journey from remote mountainous areas to the port city took more than six weeks and, depending on where in the mountains the harvest originated, could cover a distance of more than twelve hundred miles. Adverse weather could destroy a shipment, baking the tea in the hot sun or soaking it in downpours of rain, and many crops were lost in this way. The tea harvested in spring would often arrive in port by September, when agents from different European companies would engage in a second selection process. These agents, from the East India Company and other outfits, would then set sail with ships full of tea, silk, spices, and porcelain, reaching London in the winter or spring. This meant that the tea sold in seventeenth-century London, even when fresh from the supplier, was at least eighteen to twenty-four months old by the time it was consumed.

Both black and green tea were imported from the beginning of the tea trade in Europe. Initially, all teas were called "tea" or "tee," in keeping with early modern English's use of many variant spellings in written works. Later, the term "bohea" was adopted for black tea, named after an English approximation of the name for the Wuyi Mountains, where black tea is grown.[43] By 1700, English markets had access to more than a dozen types of tea, each with its own name. Merchants often published explanations of the different teas they offered to help customers understand what they were buying.[44]

Tea in China was taken without milk, and Britain initially adopted this custom. But eventually sugar and milk became popular, and by the reign of George I (1714–1727) it was common to find sugar bowls, teaspoons, and cream pitchers included in British tea sets.[45] Tea's high cost meant that it was purchased in small amounts and closely guarded during the first century of its use in England, after which the price began its decline. Tea was kept in locked caddies to which servants had no access and was dispensed by the lady of the house before being quickly tucked away again.[46]

Putting milk and cream in tea spoke to European tastes for rich food but had the additional benefit of covering the flavor of low-quality or adulterated teas. In time, "bohea" came to refer to lower-grade black teas, whereas "tee" or "tea" became the standardized English spellings to refer to the beverage in general as well as to higher-grade black tea.[47]

The quality of tea itself (even expensive, higher-grade tea) was often questionable. Not only would tea leaves be more than a year old by the time they arrived in a shop, but sometimes the "tea" being sold was made from reused leaves or mixed with nontea plant leaves like licorice, ash, or blackthorn. These fake teas were referred to as "smouch." To help these fake teas take on the desired colors and flavors, they were dyed, cooked, and dehydrated or mixed with colorants that would coat the surface of the leaves (one such infamous colorant and flavoring being sheep's dung).[48]

The problem of adulterated tea was not restricted to its early years in England but continued into the nineteenth century. In 1818, Friedrich Christian Accum's *Treatise on Adulterations of Food, and Culinary Poisons* first appeared, later being reprinted in America.[49] Accum's research showed that adulterated tea was being sold—sometimes unknowingly—by merchants around London, and he was the first to demonstrate how widespread the problem was and that it was not limited to inexpensive tea. His *Treatise* offered guidance on spotting tainted tea, but with the dizzying number of ways that tea could be cut, he admitted it was not always easy to spot counterfeits.[50] Accum argued for more government oversight, but others felt that high taxes were to blame for the fakery and pushed aside arguments for regulatory bodies in favor of instead focusing on import duties and sales taxes driving up prices, thus pressuring merchants and wholesalers to cut their product with other substances.[51]

Smouch was produced in England before being sold but was also produced in China before being shipped. In Robert Fortune's 1852 book on China's tea-producing regions, he describes the process of crushing Prussian blue coloring into powder and adding gypsum to create a light blue substance added to tea in the final five minutes of roasting.[52] Through accounts like Fortune's and Accum's, the public felt it was easier to adulterate green tea and so began avoiding it, purchasing black tea instead. This further solidified English preference for black tea, as tea consumption continued to rise but the amount of green tea purchased in the empire declined. The passing in 1875 of the Sale of Food and Drugs Act improved food regulation, and by the close of the century many of the questions surrounding the legal limits of food processing (does coloring tea leaves count as adulteration, for example, or does this only include cutting tea with non-tea items?) became a thing of the past.[53]

The Cost of Tea

England's early shipments of tea were an expensive commodity, due in part to the costly and time-intensive process of harvesting and transporting it within China and from China to England. Early tea shops—like Thomas Garraway's London coffeehouse, the first place in England to sell the beverage—offered tea for between sixteen and sixty shillings per pound.[54] When we look at account records from the time, it becomes clear how expensive tea was in relation to other goods and in relation to most salaries. In 1658, when the fifth Earl of Bedford presided over Woburn Abbey, wages for the entire staff of officials and servants[55] came to about six hundred pounds for the entire year. The lawyer's yearly salary was about twenty pounds, and each footman earned between two and six pounds. Considering that tea cost about sixteen shillings per pound on the low end and sixty on the high end, it very quickly becomes evident that the beverage was out of reach for everyone but the nobility; for most others, given that twenty shillings equaled one pound, purchasing even a small amount of tea would cost the equivalent of an entire year's salary.[56]

Tea drinking in England took about a century to catch on widely after the initial shipments reached English shores, but once it did, it was an unstoppable force. In 1711, tea consumption in Britain totaled about 142,000 pounds; by 1791, it had reached fifteen million pounds, and demand continued to increase.[57] Between 1789 and 1793, the value of tea traded into Britain by the British East India Company was nearly twelve million pounds, four times more than the next-most-valuable commodity at the time: calico. By the middle of the eighteenth century, tea-import duties accounted for 6 percent of the British national budget. These numbers, which do not account for revenue generated from tea smuggling, highlight the incredible rise of tea consumption in Britain over roughly a century.[58]

Most households did not embrace tea until prices started to drop, and even then it was slow to catch on outside of London. Many records of upper-class households show a very gradual increase in consumption through the later part of the seventeenth century, with significant increases not occurring until slightly later.[59] However, it is impossible to know the exact extent of tea consumption beyond noting a widespread, slow rise in the amount purchased over time. As Jane Pettigrew and Bruce Richardson say, "The absence of tea from most household account books for the late seventeenth century may not be entirely due to a complete ignorance of its existence outside London or a lack of interest in drinking it. Tea may have simply been such an expensive item that supplies were not bought as part of the list of everyday requirements, but were acquired separately by a superior member of the household staff or by a family member and the expenditure noted elsewhere in accounts that have not survived."[60]

Some advocates for the beverage focused on its health-improving effects, which included, by some accounts, plague prevention.[61] Ken Albala compares the marketing of tea, coffee, and chocolate to modern-day superfood marketing efforts: each is said to possess a staggering list of health benefits, and those making money from the commodities pull what serves them from the latest physiological theories. Teas were initially sold as medicinal herbs in apothecaries, although they were also sold in shops simply for enjoyment. Tension developed between shopkeepers and medical professionals, each looking to attract and maintain clientele. Physicians who prescribed tea laid out quality control, dosing, and preparation guidelines in order to keep prices high and maintain the public perception of tea as a medical product rather than a consumer good.[62] Proprietors of tea- and coffeehouses encouraged the beverage as a health tonic, but not a pharmaceutical one, adopting a "more is more" philosophy when advertising its benefits.

One of tea's most enthusiastic adopters was John Ovington, who served as chaplain to King William III, better known as William of Orange. Ovington's role in the court would have given him early access to the drink, and he spent a good bit of time researching different types of tea, how they were harvested and transported, and their health benefits and flavor profiles, all of which he shared in his 1699 *Essay upon the Nature and Qualities of Tea*. He also advocated for tea as an alternative to (and remedy for) consumption of alcohol, and as a clergyman this may have been where his interest in tea originated. "The last Remark which I shall make of this innocent lovely Liquor," he writes,

> is the Advantage which it has over *Wine*, and the Ascendant which it gains over the powerful Juice of the Grape, which so frequently betrays Men into so much Mischief, and so many Follies. For this admirable *Tea* endeavours to reconcile Men to *Sobriety*, when their Brains are overcast with the Fumes of Intemperance, and disorder'd with Excess of Drinking; by driving away the superfluous Humors that cloud the Rational Faculty, and disturb the Powers of the Mind. And therefore all those persons who have by this means lost their Senses, and have pass'd the Bounds of Moderation, ought presently to water

their Veins with this Liquor, and refresh themselves with its sober Draughts, if they are willing to recollect their roving Thoughts, and be Masters of their Faculties again.[63]

Shop owners, seeking to bring in clientele, also touted the beverage as a health tonic: Thomas Garraway, proprietor of Garraway's Coffee House, cited tea as a cure for a litany of complaints in a 1660 advertisement.[64] By 1700, tea was still an occasional drink for the wealthy, but its adoption by middle and working classes happened almost simultaneously in the 1730s and 1740s. By 1784, when William Pitt drastically reduced the customs duty on tea, making it more affordable, it already was embedded in English culture and had been recognized as a promising substitute for alcoholic beverages (a portend of its use by the temperance movement in the United States and England later on).

People continued to praise tea and recommend it as a health-improving drink in the 1700s, just as they had done a century before. Scottish physician Thomas Short, for example, recommended tea to "gentlemen of a spritely genius" who would "preserve the continuance of their lively and distinct Ideas."[65] King Louis XIV's physician, Nicolas de Blégny, published a tract extolling the virtues of coffee, tea, and chocolate. His royal apothecary was open to the public and stocked "properly prepared" versions of the beverages, as well as roasting machines and other equipment of his own design. While other authors certainly had pulled (selectively) from the available physiological theories to support their claims, Blégny went even further, and his writing effectively serves as an advertisement for his apothecary's products. Blégny delineates between type of tea (green and black) and origin (Japanese and Chinese) before moving into a discussion of medical properties that Albala compares to modern health-food marketing centered on free radicals and antioxidants, concepts the public grasps only marginally but that serve as effective marketing tools nonetheless.[66]

Those outside the medical field also joined the debate. French coffee merchant Sylvestre Dufour published the first widely read work on the beverages in 1685, and, while he proclaimed them to be healthy (and had considerable economic motivation to do so), he also based his claims on consultations with friends in the field of medicine and incorporated some understanding of the emerging field of chemistry into discussions of humoral properties.[67]

However, not everyone was in favor of the drink, including clergy. John Wesley, founder of the Methodist Church, was initially against the drink, proclaiming in his 1748 *Letter to a Friend Concerning Tea* that it caused nervousness, paralysis, and poor digestion, in addition to being expensive. Wesley, of course, would not stop drinking tea himself but urged others to do so[68] and complained that the drink made his hand shake.[69]

As with its proponents, many of tea's detractors in Europe were fueled by economic motives: Pharmacists who did not stock tea, for example, were quick to dismiss its benefits in order to push clients toward pharmaceuticals already on their shelves.[70] Those seeking to prescribe tea as a medicine had strong economic incentive to argue against self-diagnosis and point out the dangers of overconsumption.

In *Commentarius de Abusu Tabaci Americanorum veteri et Herbae Thee Asiaticorum in Europa novo* (1665), German physician Simon Paulli argued that there were perfectly serviceable alternatives to tea that were native to Europe (the sale of which, conveniently, would net him a nice profit).[71] Great debate raged in the medical field about the humoral properties of tea, coffee, and chocolate, with different medical authorities ascribing different properties to the entire class of beverages or to each individually.[72]

While in later years tea would be embraced by the temperance movement as an alternative to alcohol (just as it had been by Ovington), other authors at this time, like Wesley and physician Daniel Duncan, saw it as a beverage that required the same moderation (or abstention) that one would apply to alcohol. Daniel Duncan's 1706 tract advising against the abuse of various beverages warns that immoderate consumption of tea is dangerous to one's health, concluding that the body is like a lamp and our blood, like lamp oil: just as a lamp burns longer if we add water to the oil, so, too, does our body live longer if we add water to it.[73]

William Buchan, writing at the end of the eighteenth century, opposed tea for other reasons. He seems most concerned in his 1797 *Observations on the Diet of the Common People* that the working classes drink too much tea in lieu of other, more nutritious, food[74] and recommends the increased consumption of broths, soups, and stews, discouraging "that pernicious wash, tea, with which the lower classes of the inhabitants of this island drench their stomachs, and ruin their constitutions."[75]

The cost of tea fluctuated wildly in the early modern period, although it became more affordable overall as the East India Company imported ever-larger volumes of tea to satisfy growing public demand. Although increasingly consumed by greater swaths of the English population, tea still was inaccessible to poorer segments of the population until prices fell drastically toward the end of the eighteenth century.

A farm laborer employed twelve months of the year, for example, would earn between thirty shillings and two pennies per annum, which would barely cover food, let alone tea.[76] Laborers' wages, set by justices of the peace, were inadequate and rarely adjusted to account for cost-of-living increases. The justices sufficiently appreciated neither the difficulty of manual labor nor the fact that laborers were already living in dire circumstances, as the cost of living had doubled between Charles I's reign and one century prior, while wages had remained stagnant. Tea did eventually become accessible to, and popular among, working-class Britons, but it took continued drops in prices, such as the 1784 reduction of tea duties among others, to make this a reality.[77] In the middle of the nineteenth century, the tea duty continued to drop, and with it annual consumption rose from 1.22 pounds per person to 3.29 pounds per person over roughly a decade.[78]

Higher consumption and cheaper prices meant an end to the necessity of some tea-related household items—the locked tea caddy from which the expensive leaves would be sparingly doled out, for example. And less expensive versions of the beautiful cups and ornate pots and trays became available alongside their costly counterparts. As tea consumption became more ubiquitous in the Victorian period, it seemed to command less ceremony in many households, beyond the simple rituals afforded to daily activities: a simple teapot and cup, sometimes with company, sometimes with food. This transformation from costly luxury to daily necessity, and its ritualization, shifted tea from a beverage included within other meals to a beverage around which a meal was created.

TEA IN SHOPS

When in the mid-seventeenth century tea was first introduced into English culture by way of London, that city was already one of Europe's greatest metropolitan areas and home to more than 10 percent of the English population: it was the first market for new products and was the tastemaker for the rest of the country. From London tea consumption spread farther and farther out, northward and westward, into shops and homes. It first moved to fashionable resorts outside London—like Bath—then to the towns, and finally into the countryside. This whole process happened rather quickly, and within half a century tea had become an established part of the English diet.[79]

In laborers' households, tea increasingly replaced a range of other beverages, including milk and home-brewed beer. It also replaced infusions (what today we would call "herbal tea") of indigenous plants, as these became scarce as hedgerows and common land disappeared and land enclosures became common. In this sense, tea filled a niche for a warm, infused beverage, and by midcentury the price of tea was so low that it had become accessible to every social class.[80]

The first advertisements for tea were placed in *The Gazette* and *Mercurius Politicus* in the second half of the seventeenth century and show that tea was originally sold in London coffeehouses. Coffee had arrived in London a little more than a decade before tea, with the first coffeehouse opening in Oxford in 1650. As tea became more popular, it was sold in coffeehouses by the cup or dish, but for a heavy tax (4 pence for every gallon prepared and sold), making it quite expensive.[81] Sir Thomas Twining, whose name later became synonymous with tea, opened Tom's Coffee House in early 1706.[82] These early shops catered to a male clientele who would gather for beverage and conversation.

But Twining had the idea of opening his shop to women; to preserve accepted notions of modesty, he created a separate room in his coffee shop where they could buy and drink tea apart from the men, without drawing any public attention. In 1717, Twining opened the first Tea Shop for Ladies, separate from but modeled after the coffeehouse, a popular male space. Both the men and the women who visited these shops would have been in the upper classes: one hundred grams (3.5 ounces) of Chinese green gunpowder tea would have cost around $184 in modern currency.[83] Tea gardens also became popular around this time, the first opening in the old Vauxhall pleasure gardens on the south bank of the River Thames in the 1720s, after which the trend spread quickly.[84]

Residents living near these early coffeehouses were unimpressed, complaining about the smell as well as the "undesirable" patrons the establishments attracted.[85] Beer and wine merchants also raised concerns that coffeehouses would cut in to their sales. However, the overall reaction from the English populace was positive, and coffeehouses grew in popularity. As tea came into coffeehouses, either to be prepared and consumed there or to be purchased and brought home, it not only diversified the shops' offerings but also increased awareness of and demand for a range of tea options.

In order to stand out in the competition, shops created their own unique mixtures of teas, catering to different tastes and even to the time of day the tea was to be served, thus creating the celebrated tradition of English tea blends. Buyers were enticed to the shops by these myriad varieties of tea, as well as by the imported tea-related accessories—such as porcelain tea sets and tea trays—necessary to any respectable home's tea service. Those who traded for and purchased these tablewares and other accessories overseas did not always understand what they were getting and often misrepresented an item's country of origin to their sellers. However, accounts tell us that the consumers appeared to be more concerned with purchasing goods imported from distant lands than they were interested in which country had produced it (or whether the seller's assumption about the item's origin was accurate).

Through the eighteenth and nineteenth centuries, these imported goods were brought to areas outside of London by traveling merchants taking advantage of improved transportation and communication technologies. This signaled a significant shift not only for tea but also for commodities in general. Goods had previously been sold in a regional economy, where items were made, marketed, and moved locally. With railroads and other advances, a nationally integrated marketplace emerged, in which "large towns became commercial centers with shops of all kinds, legal services, medical practitioners, estate agents, theaters and public assembly rooms. Gentlemen and wealthy farmers traveled regularly to town, sometimes bringing their families to combine business and leisure."[86]

GENDER AND (AFTERNOON) TEA

Social historian Arnold Palmer says that from its adoption, the custom of afternoon tea was a gendered affair.[87] Women of the eighteenth and nineteenth centuries largely stayed at home, responding to the needs of the husband's changing schedule, impacted only by the world outside the domestic sphere when it wreaked havoc on her ability to prepare and serve timely meals without too long a distance between them.[88] While many scholars[89] tie afternoon tea's widespread acceptance to the advent of modern work schedules and commutes, Palmer goes further, calling the meal's advent a full-on cultural phenomenon, not just a pastime of the leisure classes, as afternoon tea was created entirely by women—though, of course, only by those women already admirably performing their duties in the home. Examining afternoon tea's gendered origins is an excellent vantage point from which to consider Britain's gendered social interactions, and specifically as they pertain to British tea culture.

A number of authors point to the central role women played in popularizing the beverage in England after its introduction in the 1650s, as they sought to emulate the queen of England whose Portuguese upbringing gave her a taste for the beverage. Many historians also credit the idea of the meal of afternoon tea to the Duchess of Bedford. In both cases, tea was associated with women and with entertaining[90]—unlike coffee, which was rarely associated with female drinkers (save for those in the American colonies protesting English tea duties).[91]

After the American colonies successfully revolted and gained independence from the English Crown, there were grumblings in Britain and especially in Ireland surrounding luxury goods, including tea. Published tracts insisted that luxuries eroded masculinity and thus martial capabilities: with these opulent goods, it was argued, were imported foreign notions of manhood that were too different, that threatened to weaken the populace, both physically and morally. Outraged about luxury goods and the mercantile systems surrounding them, members of parliament, journalists, and others decried the East India Company's corruption and monopoly.

And yet commercial interests were not completely forgotten; despite their many concerns, Irish MPs wanted a share in the company's profits and decided to become part of the monopoly they were so loudly decrying.[92] They were granted this right in 1793, to the chagrin of Irish radicals who felt that "the East India trade and associated abuses summed up all that was bad about the empire" and who "saw greater value in public disassociation from it."[93] In their minds, rejecting imported luxuries meant embracing a kind of masculine patriotic engagement that renounced effeminizing influences.

Despite the focus on masculinity, it was the actions of women that were called upon as a political example: American women had signed resolutions against tea drinking as a part of their patriotic engagement in the Revolution, which resulted in a greater loss to the East India Company than had the Boston Tea Party.[94]

And back across the ocean, British women also impacted company fortunes; in creating the afternoon tea meal, they negotiated accepted gender roles and societal restrictions to shape their public and private lives. Women, particularly wealthy women, were not regularly seen in public, which meant that social gatherings for women were, by necessity, held in the home. While escorted women were able to meet in public venues, the watchful eyes and ears of family members, spouses, and even restaurant personnel would necessarily quell discussion of any sensitive matters they might have been most eager to share with friends. And so gathering in private homes for tea and conversation quickly became a pastime for Britain's women. Before long, afternoon tea had developed into an established meal—and this not terribly long before other private gatherings of women resulted in the first stirrings of women's suffrage and the temperance movement.[95]

Many male and female authors write of women's private social gatherings as places for gossip,[96] but these informal gatherings were so much more, facilitating activist work as well as community building. They were perhaps one of the few places where women—unable to vote or hold property in their names—felt they were among equals and could speak openly. In some communities, where resources were tight, women pooled resources to form afternoon tea groups, using whatever creative means necessary, thus ensuring continued access to at least one space where they could privately engage other women. Nineteenth-century writer Marie Trevelyan explains that in 1893 Wales, for example, women in villages formed Tea Clubs, or Clwb Te, to which "One woman would bring tea, one a cake, another a drop of gin or brandy to put in it. They visited the homes of the members in turn."[97] As women defined this private sphere, and as mealtimes shifted and tea prices continued dropping, afternoon tea moved from an informal and perhaps infrequent gathering into an accepted daily meal, with its own name and its own related etiquette.

TEA IN HOMES: AFTERNOON TEA AS
LEGEND AND REALITY

In the 1830s or 1940s, depending on what source you consult, the Duchess of Bedford—suffering a pang of hunger in the long stretch between her noontime luncheon and her dinner, which the fashionable aristocracy would not serve until after 7:30 p.m.—called for tea and a snack to be brought up to her bedchamber. Pleased and sated, she adopted this as a daily habit to tide her over until her next meal, eventually inviting friends to share in a private midafternoon gathering of tea and snacks. This story, of course, is the commonly accepted origin of the afternoon tea. But while the duchess was undoubtedly central in popularizing the meal, it's actually acknowledged by many sources that throughout the eighteenth century mealtimes had already begun changing, and afternoon tea had already become something of an established snack meal, long before the duchess arranged her household repast.[98]

Anna Maria Stanhope, later Russell, was born in 1783, daughter of Charles, the third Earl of Harrington. While little information exists about her life prior to presentation at court, she seems to have come from a loving and involved family, which wasn't always the case for aristocratic children. She also benefited from mentors outside her home, including her godmother, the Duchess of Gloucester, with whom she maintained regular contact through her childhood and adulthood.[99] A good amount of information survives about Anna Maria Stanhope, and we know that in her day she was a central figure in the court. In 1808, she married the Marquis of Tavistock, who later became the Duke of Bedford, and accounts suggest that the duke and duchess were active in charitable work as well as in court life.

In 1837, with the accession of her friend Queen Victoria to the throne, the Duchess of Bedford was appointed Lady of the Bedchamber—a very powerful position for a noblewoman. In this post, she served as the queen's personal attendant and was privy to the innermost conversations in court. She and Victoria had been lifelong friends, and so, in addition to enjoying a reputation for kindness, the duchess was regarded as powerful within the court. Her visibility would certainly have made it more likely that her interests and habits would be widely regarded and thus more likely adopted. Indeed, the duchess was known as a trendsetter during her lifetime. She died in 1857, only about twenty years after her first bites of the now ubiquitous afternoon meal.[100]

Questions have arisen about the nature of Anna Russell's real impact on the invention of afternoon tea. In fact, the discussion has become such a controversy that some tea aficionados have begun referring to the tale of Russell's afternoon break as the Bedford Orthodoxy,[101] suggesting the story has become so rooted in our cultural lore that it is immune to challenge or modification.

There tend to be two different perspectives about Russell's role in creating afternoon tea. One side tells us that tea was already an established meal by the time Russell was born, meaning that saying she "invented" afternoon tea would require ignoring the historical record. The other side does not contest this, actually, but insists that her real contribution was not being the *first* person to consume an afternoon tea–like meal but instead being the first person to *codify* afternoon tea: what had been an informal activity was now formalized into a recognized and replicable meal tradition, with established boundaries, including appropriate foods and manners. Because of the Duchess of Bedford, so it goes, afternoon tea is universally understood to include tea, of course, plus sweet and savory snack foods, enjoyed amid a tone of casual socializing, often—at least initially—in the home.[102]

The historic record, as we might expect, reflects the complexity we see in the second interpretation. References to afternoon tea–like meals being consumed prior to Russell's birth in the 1790s are scattered and appear to be stand-alone occasions, a far cry from the ritualized meal we recognize today. This would support the assertion that afternoon tea was entrenched in English culture prior to Russell.

However, a meal, like many social phenomena, is not established overnight. We could look as far back as Pepys's 1660 tea with a colleague to find the first glimmerings of what would transform into quite a different repast. While Pepys's and countless other gatherings over tea and a snack do establish tea as an important part of English culture, they do not establish a set of stable, recognizable conventions, including when tea is served and how it is consumed, that would define tea in the same way we would define other meals (like breakfast being a morning meal, typically consumed in an informal setting, often in English culture including specifically defined "breakfast foods," like eggs and toast).

And so there is quite a bit of agreement between the two theories. The scattered early afternoon tea–like gatherings,[103] as well as the presence of tea in other social situations,[104] primed the pump for the standardization and widespread adoption of a meal, which was further helped by the promotion of an influential spokesperson. Tea parties, usually an after-dinner gathering, had already been in place prior to the mid-1800s. The duchess and her friends would have attended tea parties after meals in each other's homes, and these also set the stage by serving as a similar (although more formal) iteration of a tea-centric social gathering among the wealthy. Russell's tea gatherings built upon the evening tea party by offering a more informal and intimate afternoon gathering. The final piece of the puzzle was the changing workday, which had lengthened during the Industrial Revolution, meaning the entire family would not dine together until later in the evening when the head of household returned home.[105] This made gatherings like the after-dinner tea party less feasible and created a desire for other social outlets and an openness to new mealtimes across socioeconomic classes, all of which were impacted by the changing workday.

Thinking of the adoption of a meal as we might think of the adoption of a widespread social convention from our own time may be helpful for framing this idea. Often those ideas that are most successful within a certain society are the ones that feel new and innovative but still have some sense of familiarity.[106] Russell came along and publicized her daily ritual of tea and a snack—and its being publicized is key, because she certainly was not the only person requesting a snack and beverage in the afternoon. She made that ritual into a social event, and thus the process of widespread adoption could begin.[107]

Pinpointing the exact start of a meal tradition is difficult, of course, because most develop gradually and because a simple explanation glosses over the complex social contexts within which such a tradition evolves. Russell's afternoon tea gathering, as we've seen, did not happen in a vacuum but within the context of her social class (which gave her and her friends the leisure time and the financial resources to host regular afternoon gatherings), her gender (as women, Russell and her friends would not have had many options for meals or social interaction outside the home), and the emergence of the Industrial Revolution (which changed the nature of the workday, meaning evening meal times were already shifting to later in the evening).[108] This meant there were long, hungry stretches between the noontime meal and dinner. Having after-dinner tea with guests was no longer practical,[109] and so the gathering gradually shifted. In this case, Russell has been identified not as being wholly responsible for creating afternoon tea but as a flash point, moving an already-evolving meal tradition along more quickly.

In social science and business, this process of adopting a new idea (or technology, or food tradition, or what have you) often follows the pattern outlined by the theory of diffusion of innovation, envisioned as a bell curve where one end is the early adopters, who are the first to gravitate to and embrace a new trend, followed by the bulk of the population and, finally, at the other end, the late adopters.

This pattern of adoption is present within the history of afternoon tea as well and, as with any innovation, is reliant on any number of factors, including financial and social access to that innovation. In this case, the early adopters were Russell's aristocratic peers, who saw her as a trendsetter and influential courtier and who brought the trend into their own routines. From a socioeconomic perspective, afternoon tea, as a midafternoon snack meal, diffused through society in a top-down way, with those seeking to emulate the nobility adopting the meal. But it was also adopted as a response to larger scheduling changes. As we will see later, the emergence of the afternoon tea is related, but not identical, to shifts in meal habits among the working classes, whose high tea meal was in response to changes in their schedules.[110] The afternoon tea meal remained largely a middle- and upper-class meal for some time, but eventually it was adapted across all classes, and today it is enjoyed in rich and poor homes.[111]

How did Russell come to be identified with afternoon tea in British food lore? A number of letters were saved, written by her and others in the 1840s, describing the meals and offering a time line for the meal's development. In 1841, she wrote to her brother-in-law, "I forgot to name my old friend Prince Esterhazy who drank tea with me the other evening at 5 o'clock, or rather was my guest among eight ladies at the Castle."[112] A year later, actress Fanny Kemble wrote in a letter, "I received on several occasions private and rather mysterious invitations to the Duchess of Bedford's room, and found her with a 'small and select' circle of female guests of the castle, busily employed in brewing and drinking tea, with her grace's own private tea kettle."[113] Both letters suggest Russell's tea gatherings had begun to take place at least in 1841 and were a regular occurrence by 1842.

Author Georgiana Sitwell recollects that these gatherings were not happening in the 1830s but were in place by the end of the 1840s, confirming the above letters' suggestion that Russell and her friends made a habit of such gatherings beginning in the early 1840s. Sitwell also offers the insight that the structure of the leisure classes' afternoons made them amenable to the development of a private (and later communal) tea break: "There was no gathering for five o'clock afternoon tea in those days, but most ladies took an hour's rest in their rooms before the six or seven o'clock dinner, retiring thither with their books. . . . It was not till about 1849 or 50 . . . that five o'clock tea in the drawing room was made an institution, and then only in a few fashionable houses where the dinner hour was as late as half past seven or eight o'clock."[114] Fanny Kemble, writing in the same 1842 letter quoted earlier, says that Russell's gatherings were the first occurrence of "the now universally honoured and observed institution of five o'clock tea."[115]

By the 1860s and 1870s, afternoon tea began appearing in middle-class homes, and by the end of the century the meal or its slightly more filling counterpart, high tea, which emerged later, had been embraced by all social classes. Tea as a meal is hardly mentioned in diary entries from the 1850s but appears regularly in entries only ten years later.[116] Soon it had become so widespread that universities and schools offered instruction to women in how to properly prepare and serve the meal.[117] In 1872, Eliza Cheedle published *Manners of Modern Society: Being a Book of Etiquette*, which called these gatherings "little teas" because of the small amount of food served.[118]

Other later works, including Clara E. Anderson's 1912 play about an 1862 tea gathering, show that tea was entrenched within the middle classes by the mid-1860s. Anderson's work was published in and was about Ottawa, Canada, an early mention of the meal's appearance in English colonies.[119] Tea drinking, and the meal of afternoon tea, became common elsewhere in colonial England and former colonies around the latter half of the nineteenth century (which will be explored in greater depth in the next chapter). In America, for example, tea drinking surged in the 1830s, and the formalities of the meal followed in the 1850s, becoming firmly established in the following decades.[120]

Even when tea drinking and afternoon tea were established across socio-economic classes, there were still class-based differences in the meal's performance and purpose on a given day—for example, informal versus formal dress and table settings.[121] Austen and Smith argue that English patterns of tea consumption (as well as sugar and other imported commodities) weren't merely about emulating wealthier colleagues; rather, they dealt largely with "respectability," or acceptable codes of conduct in order to be seen as an upstanding community member.[122]

By the end of the nineteenth century, afternoon tea was being enjoyed throughout the country, from the smallest village to the center of London. Memoirs of afternoon tea abound from the period in both letters and published works. Summarizing the meal's social significance and its place within the private sphere, English novelist George Gissing wrote, "Nowhere is the English genius of domesticity more notably evident than in the festival of afternoon tea. The mere chink of cups and saucers tunes the mind to happy repose."[123] Flora Thompson's book *Lark Rise to Candleford* indicates that though the meal had by this point become conceptually separate from impromptu gatherings for tea alone, both would happen simultaneously, as neighbors would drop by for a cup of tea and conversation.

One episode in Thompson's book recounts the tale of a flustered vicar's wife who was trying to negotiate social proprieties in welcoming a new community member. "In the 'eighties," writes Thompson, "the schoolmistress was so nearly a new institution that a vicar's wife, in a real dilemma, said: 'I should like to ask Miss So-and-So to tea; but do I ask her to kitchen or dining-room tea?'"[124] Both the formal afternoon tea meal and the informal cup of tea were by this time so established within the village community as social activities that they were noted by name—kitchen tea or dining room tea—and anyone hearing would have understood the social etiquette and significance surrounding each.

The dilemma of the vicar's wife was where to place the schoolmistress within village society. Thompson indicates that the social standing of schoolteachers was peculiar and considered somewhat outside the conventional roles for women, referring to their standing as that of "neither lady nor woman."[125] The ambiguity and confusion suggests a level of exclusivity surrounding any who might be welcomed to the more formal afternoon tea meal, and it simply wouldn't have done to mistake the teacher's place.

AFTERNOON TEA ETIQUETTE

In wealthy households, afternoon tea moved from private boudoirs and small withdrawing rooms into larger drawing rooms and in the hall, the center of the Victorian home, where games were often played and parties organized.[126] Afternoon tea was a social occasion initially geared toward women, although in some instances it included eligible bachelors as well.[127] While tea became somewhat more relaxed later on, the arts of using the proper equipment and etiquette were central to the Victorian iteration of the meal. The Victorian tea set included separate bowls and jugs for sugar and cream, which are still a part of modern-day tea sets, and Victorians would always add cream after the tea, so each guest could decide the amount (or decline altogether, although cream in tea was quite common).[128]

An entire book could be filled with the proper etiquette surrounding the Victorian meal—and many etiquette and cookery books from the time do just that, outlining proper protocol in varying degrees of depth.[129] Invitations, for example, were to be either issued verbally or delivered in an informal note.[130] But generally the guidance appears to have been focused on middle- and upper-class homes; there was little in the way of publications on mealtime etiquette for the working classes, outside of what would have been included in the occasional tract on general manners.

Tea etiquette in England changed over time, and this shift was reflected in the specificities of what was expected at an afternoon tea meal. Earlier generations would have sipped tea from the saucer as well as the cup, but by the Victorian era it was no longer acceptable to do so. Other small mannerisms, such as laying a teaspoon across the teacup to refuse a refill, were incredibly contextual and among the many Victorian social cues that could be easy to overlook for anyone not intimately familiar with etiquette in that specific context. As they did with other meals of the era, the Victorians used a strict, yet sometimes subtle, inventory of proper manners that had been designed to include or exclude others based upon their engagement with those manners.[131] Some of the Victorian etiquette surrounding afternoon tea is still in place today. For example, at an afternoon tea gathering, the host pours tea into a guest's cup, at which point cream and sweetener are added according to taste; the host never adds cream and sugar first.[132]

And the Victorian obsession with complex etiquette didn't stop with tea-time protocols; they were as obsessed with the proper attire for social events. Tea gowns emerged as a fashion in the 1870s and were a relaxed yet attractive clothing option to be worn with other women, reinforcing the meal's location within the private sphere.[133] During a time when corsets were daily wear, tea gowns allowed women a clothing option that was flowing and comfortable and that flattered the body without a corset. Some women undoubtedly would have worn the gowns with a corset, but the afternoon tea gown, like the meal itself, offered women an informal, intimate, and comfortable option for socializing within the home. The gowns were considered too informal to be suitable for wearing in public, so this level of comfort continued to be restricted only to private, feminine spaces.[134]

Gloves were typically worn during the meal, and, of course, a number of etiquette directives guided when they should be worn and when they should not. The wearing of gloves necessitated that many of the foods served not have sauces, soft frosting, or anything that could soil them. If fried or sauced food were served, the gloves might be removed without breaking protocol, or else one could eat the finger sandwiches and other snacks with a knife and fork.[135] Gloves were typically worn before and after mealtime activities as well, but it was a suggestion rather than a necessity. That said, the suggestion was strongly made in certain situations: for example, "when receiving a large number of guests it can be especially nice if she [the hostess] has warm hands."[136]

Tea, and by extension tea-related gatherings like afternoon tea, were central to English culture as women moved further into the public sphere, sparking the activism movements of the nineteenth and early twentieth centuries. Many women in the suffrage movement also joined the temperance movement, whose chosen beverage was tea. This meant many meetings happened in tea shops and involved tea drinking.[137] Tea shops were less formal than expensive restaurants but more subdued than bars and gave young people an ideal meeting place that was in contrast to the stuffiness of a family afternoon tea.[138]

Afternoon Tea, Low Tea, High Tea, Tea, and Teatime

Modern afternoon tea is typically served between 1:00 and 4:00 p.m., slightly earlier than when served in Victorian times. Americans like myself might call a midafternoon snack meal an afternoon tea. However, to the British, "tea" can refer to any number of meals, and its meaning has changed over time. Consider low tea versus high tea. Counterintuitively, "low tea" has historically been for the upper classes the term used for afternoon tea, while "high tea" was initially the afternoon tea of the working classes. Many tourists to England have mistakenly spoken of "high tea" when the meal they are thinking of would actually appropriately be called "afternoon tea." Perhaps as a result of this confusion, "afternoon tea" and "high tea" are now often used interchangeably—at least in some countries. Meanwhile, "low tea" is no longer a regularly used term.

In earlier days, high teas were simple and hearty, with rustic dishes like potato cakes or haddock poached in milk to accompany the beverage. High tea served as a large, nourishing snack for artisans and laborers who were either finishing work in the afternoon or taking a break between shifts; it was quite conceptually different from afternoon tea, even though both meals were snacks occurring around the same time of day (although sometimes high tea was served a bit later, around the dinner hour). The differentiation between the two teas was heavily class-based, where the simple high tea of the working classes was more of a meal unto itself, built around the work schedules of those who consumed it, than a snack that had found its origins in the traditional social tea gathering.

Afternoon tea and low tea are, historically speaking, two different names for the same meal. Legend has it that Anna Russell and her guests would sit in low chairs and socialize while eating, thus quite literally enjoying a "low tea."[139] But "afternoon tea" would also have been used from relatively early on in the meal's existence. Today an afternoon tea might refer to the more formal and social meal, to a simple snack—say, of biscuits or a sandwich with a pot or mug of tea—and also to a larger meal in restaurant settings.

Nursery tea was a variant on afternoon tea, which took place around 4:00 or 5:00 and was a combination of the afternoon tea meal and the dinnertime meal. In wealthy Victorian households, children lived at the top of the house, under the direction and care of nannies who saw to the children's daily routines. If the children were of school age, they would have nursery tea upon returning home. Otherwise it was taken by younger children in the afternoon after clearing away toys and books from the day's activities. The meal often included simple dishes like soldier boys (boiled eggs with bread and butter); sardine sandwiches; pastries like muffins, scones, or biscuits; banana sandwiches; and sweets like gingerbread and fruitcake. Tea parties were reserved for special occasions when the children's friends could join them for a meal and snack to celebrate a birthday or holiday.[140]

High tea—as well as the term "tea" coming to refer to supper—emerged during the Industrial Revolution in response to changing meal times. Gas lighting was introduced in the 1830s, which meant that employers were no longer restricted to scheduling workers during daylight hours. Many company managers, of course, saw this as an opportunity to make some extra money and began to stretch their employees' workdays.

Longer work hours necessitated a shift in meal times, and breakfast began to be eaten earlier in the morning, with a snack lunch at midday to hold the worker over, and then dinner later on in the evening. However, high tea gradually replaced the later dinner, as many workers began to want something to eat right after coming home, around 6:00 or 6:30. And hence high tea was a late afternoon or early evening meal, whereas the midafternoon to late afternoon was when low tea or afternoon tea was taken. And unlike finger sandwiches and pastries, a plain pot of tea and simple but filling dishes were served at high tea,[141] along with a dessert. Many working families would not have had time for a leisurely afternoon tea break, although the beverage was often consumed throughout the day.[142]

Afternoon tea was usually consumed in well-to-do homes around 4:30. As workdays began to shorten slightly at the turn of the new century, the workers' high tea also moved to about 5:00 p.m., closer in proximity to its more affluent cousin.

Historian John Burnett suggests that high tea was first established later in the nineteenth century, in the full swing of the Industrial Revolution, in the north of England and in Scotland, a region full of industrial centers and blue-collar neighborhoods. Whether called "teatime" or simply "tea," the high tea always referred to the heavier evening meal.

And tea was taken in the southern part of the country as well. In *Lark Rise to Candleford*, Thompson recalls that high tea was "a substantial meal" intended "for the workmen" hungry from a day's work:

Bread and cheese and beer were at that hour taken to the forge for the men to consume standing. "Afternoon bavour," they had called it. Now a well-covered table awaited them indoors. Each man's plate was stacked with slices of bread and butter, and what was called "a relish" was provided. "What can we give the men for a relish at tea-time?" was an almost daily question in that household. Sometimes a blue-and-white basin of boiled new-laid eggs would be placed on the table. Three eggs per man was the standard allowance, but two or three extra were usually cooked "in case," and at the end of the meal the basin was always empty. On other afternoons there would be brawn, known locally as "collared head," or soused herrings, or a pork pie, or cold sausages.

As the clock struck five the scraping of iron-tipped boots would be heard and the men, with leather aprons wound up around their waists, and their faces, still moist from their visit to the pump in the yard, looking preternaturally clean against their work-soiled clothes, would troop into the kitchen.[143]

Longer workdays and limited financial resources meant that many working-class Britons packed a lunch to bring with them, whereas their middle- and upper-class counterparts did not.[144] Working-class diets were often simple: perhaps tea and potatoes or bread for breakfast, bread and cheese for lunch, and more tea and potatoes in the evening.[145] Their middle- and upper-class counterparts would often have lunch prepared for them in a social club.

For those who worked in fields rather than factories, it was customary to drink beer to quench one's thirst during the day. In 1878, this situation began to change when farmer T. Bland Garland wrote that beer was not a suitable drink in hot weather (he does not say anything about drunkenness). Instead, he would roll a cart into his fields with a large boiler full of tea with sugar and cream mixed in and urged other farmers to do the same. Not surprisingly, the farmers who replaced an alcoholic beverage with a caffeinated one said that the workers' performance was much better.[146]

The Industrial Revolution resulted in remarkable changes in English foodways, and the technological innovations developed helped food keep for longer and travel farther. In tandem with the continued growth of the British Empire, this development aided in the export of English foods and food traditions. It may also have aided in the homogenization of traditions within England itself. Twinings Tea, for example, would have benefited from the newly arrived railroads, which after 1848 facilitated efficient distribution of it and other goods across the country. Being able to move more goods more quickly also lowered costs on some commodities, making them accessible to the growing middle class.[147] Industrialization changed food access and, as a result, the way people ate. Afternoon teas began serving convenience products made in industrial settings.

Refinements were also made to existing products without drastically changing their packaging. The most well-known change came in 1861, when roller mills were introduced to Britain, facilitating the removal of the germ from the wheat to produce a finer, whiter flour—though even the finest white flour milled would have still had more germ than what would be considered "white flour" by modern standards.

By the 1870s, refined flour was available around Britain, largely replacing other flours.[148] This meant that the breads and cakes, always a part of afternoon tea, went from fairly dense fare, strongly flavored by the wheat germ, to something lighter and more delicate, giving us the baked goods still associated with afternoon tea today.

As the nineteenth century progressed, factory-prepared and -packaged products poured into the British market. Some of these were available to the poor, such as cheap American bacon or Australian canned meats that had been imported during an outbreak of cattle disease in the 1860s and offered an inexpensive solution to diets often devoid of protein. Cheap treacle and later a cheap jam made of colored fruit or vegetable pulp also became available.[149] The consistent availability of a sweet topping for bread and the reduced cost of meat meant that all but the poorest Britons could enjoy a wider array of toppings for afternoon tea pastries.[150]

However, many of the newly introduced convenience foods carried high price tags, largely restricting them to the middle and upper classes, at least initially. These included baking leaveners such as quick-acting yeast, self-rising flour, and baking powder and thickeners like blancmange powder—used for making a gelatin-based French dessert—custard powder, and egg powder. Bulk-produced cheese, sweetened condensed milk, dried milk, and margarine offered an alternative to farm dairy products. While many of these foods had sweet and savory applications, others largely served as convenience meals, like bulk-dried vegetables and soup packets, or as prepared replacements to sides and condiments, like pickles and ketchup.

Prepackaged biscuits were also introduced and became a staple in British households, including during afternoon tea. Biscuits were served at both luncheon and afternoon tea meals, and by the 1870s Huntley & Palmer's baking firm was selling thirty-seven million pounds per year, while competitor Peek Frean sold another seventeen million.[151]

The convenience of food delivery became typical for homes in urban areas, with bakers, milkmen, and fishmongers going door-to-door selling goods and wares. Besides going to the store to purchase convenience items, many middle-class urban women would have had all other groceries delivered to her home—except for meat, which she would purchase directly from the butcher.[152]

The latter part of the nineteenth century also saw new cooking technologies in home kitchens, such as gas ranges, ice chests, and refrigerators, giving cooks the ability to more easily prepare food and to store perishable food longer. This meant fewer logistical barriers for the preparation of all meals (including afternoon tea), when buying, storing, and preparing ingredients. This meant greater food variety and less food waste, which left room in the household budget for more goods—like more tea. As tea prices continued to fall, producers of kettles and teapots responded by making ever-larger wares to hold the increasingly affordable brew.[153]

All these sweeping changes in food packaging, the availability of prepared foods, and the availability of new kitchen technologies were adopted throughout English society at the same time Britons' daily routines came to include the afternoon tea. Those convenience foods were welcome to those serving only a quick meal to family or perhaps to close friends who didn't need to be impressed with the best homemade fare, making it easy to take a break with a snack and cup of tea for oneself or one's family without a great amount of effort.[154]

By the end of the nineteenth century, the formality of the private afternoon tea was becoming somewhat old-fashioned (in 1879, Mrs. Beeton wrote of a "veritable tea party, such as our Grandmothers delighted to give"[155]). And in 1890, a gossip column mentioned a new trend beginning to replace the intimate tea gatherings: "At-homes" and "tea receptions" were large events, still held in the afternoon, usually between 2:00 and 7:00, but for up to two hundred guests. Tea and some light snacks—cakes and bread and butter—would be set out on a buffet, and servants would hand out cups of tea and servings of food.[156] The at-home was an interesting phenomenon offering the simple foods and casual tone of the afternoon tea meal but on a much larger scale. These gatherings were very popular, we are told by such accounts as the *Tea and Chatter* column, but seem to have fallen out of favor after the Victorian period.

Afternoon tea and high tea slowly became adapted to the needs of different work schedules and budgets.[157] For example, while high tea in working-class homes might still include freshly made items, it was modified to suit the particular needs of middle-class households, whose families would take an evening meal of cold meats, cheeses, and other foods that did not require fresh preparation, as serving a leftovers-based meal meant servants could be released from work on Sundays to attend church. The equivalent of this Sunday high tea is still seen in Britain's modern homes.[158] The meals came to embody regional differences as well: in northern England, tea is still the meal taken in the late afternoon or early evening, whereas dinner is eaten in the morning and supper in the late evening.[159] Whatever the household, afternoon tea continued to be a relatively small meal taken in the midafternoon. Households with few financial resources might only have a cup of tea with any food going to the men and children (who were typically prioritized above women in poor households), or the food might be saved entirely for the family's dining for later in the day.[160]

However it was consumed, the tea-centered meal was firmly established in the English home. As the various teas had developed with the influences of the Industrial Revolution, they were also affected by the growth of the British Empire. The annexation of colonies worldwide, and the use of their resources (including labor), fueled English economic growth—part of the reason why tea became so affordable and could be so central to English life as to become a mealtime staple. This was particularly true once the English began to grow their own tea in India, Kenya, and elsewhere.[161] As the English imported goods and raw materials from the colonies, they also exported their cultural traditions. At the close of the nineteenth century, those in positions of power (such as colonial governors) would have been well accustomed to afternoon tea, consuming it in their new homes. And so the afternoon tea meal became a part of the colonial legacy left behind in many postcolonial cultures, and it continues to be consumed in both modified and unmodified ways to the present day.

2

THE EMPIRE
AND THE TEACUP

Some of the most trivial aspects at one level, most significant at another, of the so-called British national character—a nation of tea drinkers for example, with the highest sugar consumption in the world—result from the imperial experience. As Mintz puts it, "The empire . . . had an internal structure that had seen the creation of categories of plantation slave and (eventually) factory proletarian within a single political system, and had profited immensely from their provisioning one another under the imperial thumb." Perhaps as significantly, as Mintz shows, it was in the Caribbean—rather than in England—that the origins of the intensive factory production are to be sought. How then do we understand that central English experience, the industrial revolution, outside of empire?

—Shula Marks

It's impossible to fully consider the impact of a Victorian English food tradition without talking about England as a colonial power. The reach and scope of the British Empire regularly changed as more countries were colonized and, as the empire's influence waned, more and more countries fought for and won independence. Early modern colonial expansion in Europe was pioneered by the Spanish and Portuguese, and while many other countries colonized,[1] none expanded with the tenacity of the British.

At the height of its empire, Britain controlled about thirteen million miles of land, which is equivalent to a quarter of the Earth's total landmass. Of the world's 203 nation-states, Britain once ruled sixty-three and occupied about twenty others for brief periods though it did not bring them fully under colonial control (including Cuba, Greece, Senegal, and Vietnam). At least seven others are sometimes classified as part of Britain's "informal" empire, meaning that the countries were not formally ruled by the British Empire but had such a close relationship and were so heavily influenced by it that "Britain exercised a disproportionate influence upon the country's rulers and its economy."[2] These countries include Iran, parts of maritime China, Argentina, and Chile. Considering these three ways of exerting influence brings us to a British Empire that, over the course of its existence, controlled one-third of the world's nation-states.

Early accounts of faraway civilizations Europeans received played upon their prejudices, highlighting differences with an emphasis on the exotic or "barbaric." One author in particular, Theodor de Bry, who wrote in the late sixteenth century, based his works entirely on secondhand accounts and his own assumptions. While his works on the cultures of the New World were widely read, de Bry himself never traveled beyond Europe. In *Dritte Buch Americae*, for example, de Bry uses descriptions of cannibalism intentionally to create distance between European and First Nations cultures. Gruesome illustrations of human limbs and torsos over fires were included to highlight what he describes as barbaric practices.

During the early age of colonialism, literature and travel books were rife with similar attempts to make other cultures appear violent and barbaric, and their people unintelligent.[3] These works wondered at the brutality and savagery of other cultures, informing European attitudes toward other cultures during early contact. And so the colonial mindset was framed, as were the personal opinions of many Europeans making first contact with other peoples. Many of them shared de Bry's perspective that the new communities were to be conquered and exploited, or else redeemed (from a theological perspective) and civilized. Often in English colonialism, the two went hand in hand, as with Purchas's intertwined discussions of the benevolent good work of English corporations and the English church.[4]

A European desire to explore and discover new resources (trade routes as well as consumer goods), first initiated by the Dutch and Spanish, among others, set the stage for the British Empire. England was a formidable player internationally as of the Elizabethan period and began funneling many of its resources into empire building, maintaining a firm grip on its colonies through the Victorian period and beyond. However, as the empire spread across the globe, England's far-flung colonies paid a dear price. The impact on world foodways was profound: Not only did the English redesign the physical landscapes of colonies to grow crops for export, but they also imported English food traditions and preferences that shaped the meals and ingredients used across the colonies. Not surprisingly, one key import was tea, and, depending upon when a colony entered and left the empire, the meal of afternoon tea became a lasting part of the local culture.[5]

This chapter does not, and cannot, offer exhaustive coverage of all the former colonies; the history of an empire that stretched across much of the Earth at its height would span volumes. Instead, I've chosen to look at a sample of colonies, from large to small, that show the breadth of cultural engagement that can take place between colonizer and colonized—ranging from ongoing participation in colonial food customs, as we see in Malta, to many years of outright rejection of the former colonial power, as we see in the United States, and everywhere in between.

EMPIRE BUILDING

The rise of the East India Company was intertwined with the growth of British colonial power, with the trade of consumer goods, including tea, at the core of this expansion. The growth of the one would be hard to imagine without the growth of the other. The Company became a lumbering giant of a corporation with a monopoly on trade with China but that stretched its reach beyond business dealings to actively conquering lands and peoples in the name of trade and empire. With the strength of the government of the United Kingdom behind it, "the company was almost a country unto itself," writes Dolin, "having been granted the power to 'acquire territory, coin money, command fortresses and troops, form alliances, make war and peace, and exercise both civil and criminal jurisdiction.' As Edmund Burke, the renowned British statesman and philosopher, remarked, 'The East India Company did not seem to be merely a Company formed for the extension of the British commerce, but in reality of the whole power and sovereignty of [the United Kingdom] sent into the East."[6]

England's early forays into empire building began with King Henry VII, who sent the first overseas explorer, John Cabot, to find a new trade route to Asia. Cabot's journeys were unsuccessful, but his efforts laid the groundwork for English empire building, which Queen Elizabeth I picked up half a century later. It was during her reign that the Company was founded and that England began to establish colonies. Both the Company's ventures and the government's empire building were affected by a shift in language: it is much easier to pursue a national identity that you believe to be true.

The Ecclesiastical Appeals Act was passed in 1533 as legal groundwork for the English Reformation. But, equally important, the act denied papal authority in England, declaring itself too strong a nation to tolerate outside rule: "It is manifestly declared and expressed that this realm of England is an Empire, and so hath been accepted in the world, governed by one Supreme Head and King having the dignity and royal estate of the imperial Crown of the same."[7]

It was a short leap, then, for Queen Elizabeth's advisor, John Dee, to begin referring to the "British Empire" when advocating for England's early colonial expansion.[8] The empire began its spread during Elizabeth's reign, bolstered by her investment in building a formidable navy, which brought substantial military force to back trade dealings and control the colonies that were annexed to support them. The country lagged behind other colonial superpowers of the day, particularly Spain, which had dominated colonization within the Americas and with which England was involved in extended military conflict. However, England continued to make strides toward its colonial ambitions by hiring privateers[9] to raid slave ships off the West African coast[10] and by attempting to found a colony on the North American continent.

We have already discussed the East India Company's founding and growth, specifically in relation to trade, but here we explore how this trade activity cannot be fully teased out from colonial expansion. Modern textbooks typically refer to this period as the Age of Exploration, which frames European colonial expansion as an act of locating and inhabiting empty lands, which itself speaks to the perceptions that writers of history had (and often still have) about the humanity of the peoples encountered.

The East India Company's structure differed from our modern-day understanding of a company, where all the employees work toward the central goals of an organization and its shareholders and function within a direct reporting–based hierarchy where the heads of the organization oversee and guide company activities and delegate tasks and certain decisions.[11] The Company was certainly hierarchical, but its leaders did not always have control of every moving part (Tirthankar Roy uses the analogy of a head not having control of all the limbs of its body).[12] This was deliberately done so that the overseas branches were somewhat autonomous from domestic operations, which allowed those working overseas to engage in their own profitable trading partnerships and other activities that would build up their own wealth while also filling Company coffers.

Colonial tactics were central to the Company's identity and structure, used to gain and maintain a foothold in the areas where its goods and materials were produced, and leveraged to empower the Company like a state-supported entity to fight with any (like its Dutch equivalent) that might interfere with its bottom line.[13]

The empire's lumbering weight was often supported by the British people, first as taxpayers who paid for its expansion through the government's corporate subsidies and then as consumers who purchased Company products. Each of the many times the government bailed out the Company,[14] it was the people who paid, and later, during the Buy Empire Goods campaign, it was the people who bought. This campaign was waged in lieu of protective legislation that would favor imperial goods—say, through lower tariffs. The thinking went that generating pride and sentimental feelings about these goods would make them more competitive than nonimperial imports. This campaign was only somewhat successful, as protective legislation was enacted in 1933 that marked the end of the campaign by providing more effective measures for financing the Company, such as via reduced tariffs.[15]

Not surprisingly, in this context, other cultures were valued only if they offered something of interest or value to Europeans. Their cultures were discussed as commodities, and when the native populations were seen as a barrier to those commodities, their cultural practices were called "exotic" or "barbaric."[16]

This Eurocentric perspective on cultural exchange informed the East India Company's dealings and the British government's as both grew in global influence. From its inception the Company had not been directly controlled by the British government but closely intertwined with it. Its shareholders were wealthy merchants and aristocrats, and while it had been chartered by the Crown, it only answered to the Crown indirectly. As the two gradually became more intertwined, the government fiercely advocated for maintaining and expanding the Company's interests.

The Company continued to grow in the eighteenth century. It established more and more trading posts and factories in maritime east Asia, and its military swelled, made up primarily of men recruited from India and trained as soldiers to protect the Company's colonial and trade interests in India and elsewhere.[17] The Company's growing desire to rule foreign countries, rather than developing trade relationships as equals, became evident in the 1750s with the Company's military defeat of the royal army in Bengal and its spread across the subcontinent in less than fifty years. This meant that India's early experiences as a colony were not as a colony of Britain but a colony ruled by a private company.[18]

Gradually the Company came to have a larger military at its disposal than the English government and also grew more closely tied to government affairs. This meant that the resources of each entity were regularly leveraged in empire building, both through military dominance (with an army partially peopled by those forced to enlist from the colonies) and through the Company's ability to perform as a governmental agent overseas.[19] These efforts were directed toward areas with economic resources (e.g., landscapes either amenable to the introduction of agricultural practices or already including natural resources, and of course the countless people who were taken elsewhere in the colonies to work as slaves) or strategic value (e.g., Malta's central position on trade routes). In Kenya and in India, for example, whole regions of the colonies were repurposed to grow tea, while other colonies like Jamaica grew sugar and other exports to meet growing demand.

The increase in tea consumption in England and throughout Europe meant an increased demand for ceramics and silver, with Chinese porcelain pouring into European markets and silversmiths working like mad to satisfy public demand for teaspoons and teapots. In the colonies, tea and sugar were major drivers for export activities and for the development of plantations where slave labor was used to harvest crops to process and send to England or sell on the global market.[20]

Demand for tea and sugar went hand in hand: Europeans preferred the drink with cream and sugar, and as tea rose in popularity, so did sugar. Growing sugar, like growing tea, is backbreaking and intensive labor, but many Europeans in the mid-1700s were unaware of the human cost that went into their ever more affordable imported foods and beverages. This is not to say that no one was aware of the human cost, but rather that British consumers did not understand the explicit connection between their consumption patterns and British imperialism.[21] Instead, the records only show an ever-growing demand across Britain for the goods that eventually included all socioeconomic classes, which meant planting more tea and sugarcane fields and the labor of more slaves.

Camellia sinensis was the driver for colonial expansion beyond its role as a consumer product. Scientist Joseph Banks was a strong proponent of English colonial interests, in part because of his interest in botany and expanding botanical knowledge, although that certainly wasn't the only reason: Banks experimented with the transplant of plant species around the English colonies and was the first to promote the idea that tea plants could be grown in Assam.[22] His enthusiasm for the botanical possibilities he saw in colonialism resulted in the reenvisioning of entire landscapes and national industries, such as in Assam, where existing environment was scraped away to build tea plantations.[23]

However, building these plantations required access to the tea plant and the secrets to successfully cultivating and processing it. Tea bushes, along with the Chinese agricultural practices surrounding their cultivation and processing after harvest, were closely guarded by Chinese growers. To learn the process, then, Scottish botanist Robert Fortune completed a three-year spy mission into China's secretive tea-producing regions on behalf of the East India Company. From Canton, Fortune sent tea seedlings as well as manufacturing notes from Chinese workers, and the Company began experimental tea growing in the Himalayan foothills. Their efforts were successful, and this success gave Banks's idea for Assam tea plantations more weight. Of course, Company and government officials had a financial interest in expanding their tea-growing efforts, and the result was an entire region of the subcontinent altered to support a non-native monoculture, creating an industry that continues to this day.[24]

Dietler refers to tea in England as an example of "thoroughly indigenized foods with exotic origins," and the same could be said of sugar. In both cases, the commodities have become so commonplace within the culture that their faraway origins are de-emphasized and their centrality to English customs is placed at the forefront. Both of these commodities highlight the ways in which "the intimate links between food practices and the embodiment of identity and between commensality and politics have made food a central area for the working out of colonial struggles of various kinds."[25]

However, individual foods in and of themselves do not constitute an ethnic diet. "What is distinctive is 'the patterning of a whole cycle of combinations'—in other words, a series of menus and rhythms that structure their consumption or what is sometimes called 'meal formats.'"[26] It is here that afternoon tea and other English traditions surrounding tea consumption provide the structural undergirding to move tea from a popular commodity to a particularly *English* one, connected to cultural identity and regular, habitual practice. In this way, the afternoon tea meal serves as a driver to push those cultural traditions and commodity choices elsewhere into the empire.

By the middle of the nineteenth century, tea had become enough of a staple in the English diet that it was included among the goods affordable with the meager financial assistance provided to the poor. And in the 1830s laws were passed to make it available to those in workhouses. Although the politics of government assistance to the poor was hotly debated, no one seemed to take issue with the fact that now tea was almost universally affordable.[27]

In 1853, Chancellor of the Exchequer William Ewart Gladstone abolished duties on most foodstuffs, as well as reducing duties for many imports. This included nearly halving duties on tea,[28] which were reduced even further in 1865.[29] The steady decline in taxes was not universally favored within the government, and records from the period show heated debates. In 1884, Gladstone, then serving as prime minister, faced opposition from politicians who wanted to reduce duties on beer and spirits rather than on tea and sugar, although records from the time show that those in opposition later denied having ever taken that position.[30] Gladstone withdrew from his premiership, at which point Lord Salisbury[31] was brought in as a replacement.

Tea had been one of the divisive points between Gladstone and other government officials, but it also was a beverage of diplomacy and the beverage of choice when Gladstone, Salisbury, and several other government officials met to try to come to an agreement on how the government should be run moving forward.[32] The following year, Salisbury took over officially for Gladstone, after more hurried meetings and the appointment of a number of new officials.[33] Tea duties continued to remain stable and to occasionally decrease, except for during the Second Boer War, when duties were increased to generate revenue for the government. This was quickly reversed after considerable public backlash, but the increased duties would be brought back several decades later, at the start of World War I.[34]

As the nineteenth century closed, duties on tea imports were not the only thing changing in the global trade of tea. Not surprisingly, the exports from each colonial territory and imports from other countries were interrelated, creating a dense web of trade networks and commodities across the British Empire and beyond. Tea was a critical part of this web, particularly before it began being grown within the British colonies, as it was in high demand and had to be imported from China until the mid-nineteenth century. This made raw cotton and pepper, and later the opium that fueled a Chinese addiction crisis, important commodities that could be traded for tea. These products were all grown in India and brought to China in exchange for tea. The Opium Wars of the nineteenth century were caused in part by this exchange and the resulting opium crisis in China.[35]

By the dawn of the twentieth century, the origin of tea being imported into Britain had shifted dramatically. In the 1850s, nearly all the tea brought to London was Chinese in origin. Fifty years later, English tea's origin had shifted to teas grown in a larger number of places and under imperial control: 55 percent of tea was grown in India, 30 percent in Ceylon (modern-day Sri Lanka), roughly 7.5 percent in Indonesia, and only 7.5 percent in China.[36]

Nationally tea consumption quadrupled in the second half of the nineteenth century, because of reduced taxes, new sources of tea supply, and the rise of companies aimed at mass-market appeal, such as Lipton.[37] The temperance movement and a larger cultural shift away from beer and spirits to the consumption of other beverages, either in addition to or instead of them, also contributed. During this time, children's main beverage was tea taken with a bit of milk, and while weak beer was still sometimes consumed, pressure from the temperance movement as well as rising costs often discouraged this and pushed people—particularly women and children—toward tea instead. An added benefit of tea over other beverages was that it could be stretched further, as leaves could be reused to save on food costs.[38]

By 1900, tea was inarguably a drink of the working classes,[39] although there were occasional regional variations in consumption patterns, such as more coffee drinking in London. Indian-grown tea, initially unpopular in British markets, became more accepted, and tea grown in Ceylon was also becoming more popular on global markets.[40]

Foods served at afternoon tea from its inception through the twentieth century ranged in complexity, but even tea services that included finer dishes were still a lighter and simpler repast than luncheon might be—and certainly lighter than dinner was. *Mrs. A. B. Marshall's Larger Cookery Book of Extra Recipes*, published in 1902, lists a multitiered cake (the image shows five layers) interlaced with apricot jam and covered with a maraschino-cherry glaze under icing. This towering dessert could be served with dinner along with fruit compote but was to be served alone for afternoon tea.[41] Most of the intricate desserts for which the author provides recipes—save the pistachio-covered Norway cake—are not meant to be served at afternoon tea. For this meal, she suggests simple baked goods, like spiced bread, uncomplicated cakes, and cream buns.

Tea was still popular with the leisure classes in Edwardian Britain (1901–1910), who drank it at regular intervals throughout the day.[42] Employing servants had been common practice in middle- and upper-class homes a decade or two before but was becoming increasingly expensive and out of the reach of more and more households. As a result, labor-saving devices became popular so those in the leisure classes could enjoy creature comforts without paying for staff to provide them. One such device was the teasmade, a machine with a timer and alarm that would automatically heat water for tea so it would be available at the bedside first thing in the morning.[43]

Afternoon tea menus in English country estates during the early twentieth century varied considerably but often included a mix of sweet and savory items, which seems to be the same menu then imported with the meal tradition to the colonies. One sample menu from the interwar period includes cream cheese and pimento sandwiches, buttered crumpets, coffee éclairs, chocolate sponge roll, buttered date and walnut loaf, maid-of-honor tarts, and queen cakes. This menu is remarkably similar to those menus we see from a century before.[44]

Afternoon tea as a meal was complemented, and in some cases replaced, by quick-service meals in the twentieth century. For those who wanted a quick bite on the road or while at work, tea and coffee shops, as well as stalls catering to travelers on trains and ships, accommodated fast and inexpensive meals. In some ways, these meals differed from the leisurely afternoon repast enjoyed by the upper classes, but a similar desire for a simple bite to tide one over, and for conviviality and a chance to sit and relax (even if only briefly), meant the quick-service meals offered some of the benefits of afternoon tea—or at least similarities of foodstuffs and beverage—but on a tighter schedule.[45]

Tea consumption in Britain fueled continued demand for other imperial products in the twentieth century. British foods had been partially replaced by imported goods at this point (including sugar, but also tea, chocolate, coffee, and ham, among other staples), and sugar was more accepted a foodstuff in Britain than in continental Europe, where its use was largely confined to urban areas and considered an elitist food in rural areas.

This led to widespread sugar consumption at the dawn of the twentieth century, with British workers consuming twice as much of the stuff as their counterparts in France or Germany. By the outbreak of World War I, average sugar consumption in England was seventy-nine pounds per person, but this fell with the war's progression and the resulting upsets in global trade for many commodities (including tea).[46] The war and its aftermath resulted in the end of what Pettigrew calls "the Edwardian 'Golden Age' of elegance and indulgence," and the resulting changes in the lifestyles of the British leisure classes impacted everything from food habits (fewer servants to prepare food meant more automation, such as the teasmade, as well as simpler fare) to fashion (the popular Victorian tea gown was replaced by cocktail dresses and "afternoon frocks," which were more versatile).[47]

After the war, Britain continued to expand, colonizing areas of Africa, the Middle East, and the Pacific. By this point, the British government ruled five hundred million people (or one-fifth of the world's total population).[48] The British Empire was a massive force to be reckoned with, not only in size and population but also in political clout and economic power, and it maintained this position until the breakout of World War II. This war accelerated existing global trends in which aggressive colonizing and large-scale nation building were seen as anachronistic, and in the wartime and postwar world, Britain's colonial dominance hurt its standing on the world stage by making it seem old-fashioned, inflexible, and heavy-handed. In 1945, the empire began to rapidly shrink as colonies, feeling empowered by shifting global rhetoric surrounding colonialism, pushed British colonial forces out and began establishing new—or at least newly independent—countries.[49]

Shula Marks's quotation at the start of this chapter shows how English food traditions were built on the back of the colonial beast and reminds us that colonialism is so central to English history that it's hard to consider any modern English tradition without taking colonialism's influence into account. And while many authors reflect on the central place colonialism occupies, others remind us that its centrality does not mean an explicit awareness of cultural transmission or adoption on the part of those participating.

Ronald Hyam concedes that of course tea and sugar are a part of the colonial experience but asks how many modern tea drinkers actually realize this. "Might not people be affected by Empire," he asks, "without knowing anything about it?"[50] Troy Bickham asks, "When a woman in Edinburgh drank a cup of tea, or a family in Bath sat down to a meal of Indian curry, did they consider the cultures they might be mimicking, or how these products reached Britain?"[51]

It is worth noting here that the lack of awareness of colonialism's influence is a privilege afforded to those who are citizens of the colonizing country, particularly because colonial powers go to considerable lengths to frame themselves as benevolent and concerned stewards of the colonies they rule. Those within the countries that are taken over are certainly very aware of colonialism's influence, both on their individual lives and on their societies and governments as a whole.

In the British colonial period, just as in any other time, people in England were focused on daily living and were most likely unaware of how their day-to-day lives translated to or intersected with the lived experiences of those elsewhere in the British Empire. In the nineteenth century, the English considered eating out at a restaurant a necessity for urban workers whose commutes and changing schedules prevented their going home for a meal (similarly, rural agricultural laborers brought their meals with them rather than going home for lunch). What in earlier times was "primarily the provenance of royalty and landed gentry—to have other people cook and serve you"[52]—was increasingly available to people across the socioeconomic spectrum by 1880. More and more shops popped up to accommodate this new trend. For those eating their afternoon meal away from the home, a number of tea shops opened, including Kate Cranston's famous chain of shops in Glasgow.

In the industrial era, it wasn't a universal experience to enjoy daily family meals eaten by all family members sitting together. This would have required regular working hours as well as a steady income, along with adequate cooking and eating facilities, utensils, and so on—conditions not all working families enjoyed at the turn of the century (or even today, for that matter). Often the working-class family would only eat together once during the week, and the rest of the time meals would be eaten as individuals were available: One family member might eat breakfast before their early morning shift, while another might start later and not eat until the sun had risen high in the sky. Many workers did not come home to eat lunch, although schoolchildren often did. Teatime was, as Anna Davin puts it, "a 'running series of untidy meals,' as members of the household returned at varying times from school, work, and the pub."[53]

Initially the purview of women in the home, and designed to satisfy both hunger and a desire for fellowship, teatime eventually found its way into the public sphere, in politics and business as well, and there was transformed from a meal of togetherness to a tool of colonialism. Afternoon tea was one of the many cultural rituals exported to the colonies, brought by English people likely more interested in continuing their own familiar habits rather than using the meal to explicitly replace local traditions, although in many cases afternoon tea seems to have been incorporated into those traditions when not replacing them.

THE COLONIES: A FEW CASE STUDIES

While tea and tea traditions were popular throughout the British Empire, here we examine how the empire's spread and its increasing influence across the continents affected several colonies. Tea played a critical role throughout the empire, with popular tea spots and the afternoon tea tradition itself taking root across areas as diverse as Canada, Hong Kong, and Singapore. And in the following pages we'll examine how English influences profoundly impacted foodways and redrew political boundaries in colonial India, the American colonies, Kenya, the Australian colony, Malta, and South Africa, leaving an impact long after English rule itself had ended.[54]

Colonial India

India's location on global trade routes made it a prime target for Europeans seeking to wield global power, intermingling its history with European colonialism as well as with the trade of tea and other Asian imports. Indian history includes periods of colonization by several Western powers, but none shaped the country's identity and foodways more completely than England.

India's first experience with European colonization was with the Portuguese, who landed in India in 1498 while exploring trading routes. In 1502, the Portuguese established a trading center in Kollum, quickly followed by other posts, setting up local governing bodies and forcefully conquering cities over the following decade. Portuguese settlements were mostly located on the western coast, and the Dutch and French slowly established settlements on the eastern coast during the seventeenth century and on into the eighteenth. The English, of course, had established the East India Company in the early 1600s as a speculative venture to gain a foothold in the region's trade routes and trading posts, and this later caused friction with the Dutch, who had done the same and had similar hopes of dominating trade between Europe and Asia. In the 1660s, Portugal was at war with Spain and wanted to ally with England. To do this, Princess Catherine was married to the English king Charles II, and a part of her dowry included land in India, which helped further formalize England's presence there.[55]

The empire's presence in India continued to grow and spread, and the English were thoroughly entrenched in India by the mid-nineteenth century. English control of much of India was secured in 1757 after the Battle of Plassey—which, it is worth noting, was a military battle that took place between the Nawab of Bengal and the British East India Company, *not* simply the British government. This is but one example of the East India Company's exercising its extensive powers in order to directly shape political outcomes on the global stage in order to best benefit its trade interests. English control over India grew even further, especially under Lord Dalhousie in the 1840s and 1850s, when other regions were annexed and brought under imperial control.[56]

During and after the Opium Wars of the mid-nineteenth century, the British were seeking sources of tea outside of China.[57] The British Raj—literally, British rule, referring to the colonial government in India—discovered that tea also grew in Assam. Plantations were quickly established, which effectively ended the seminomadic lifestyle of the region's inhabitants.[58]

In 1830, the British planted the colony's first tea plantations[59]—but here known as "tea gardens," which imparts a soothing, almost luxurious image of lazing about in the sun at an outdoor restaurant surrounded by gardens, much like the early tea gardens in London. Perhaps this was the experience of the English colonists running the plantations. However, just as with slavery in the United States, tea growing in India was a system of forced labor built around the dual purpose of catering to the plantation's white residents and harvesting large amounts of salable product at a cheap price.

Indentured servants were brought in to work the plantations. Though Britain had largely outlawed slavery by this point, the experience of Indian indentured servants, and even of unindentured laborers, was not much better than that of a slave. Even in the 1930s, disease and malnutrition were rampant among tea plantation laborers in India,[60] and infant mortality was high; one report from the 1930s found infant-mortality rates for tea plantation workers ranged from 42 to 256 per 1,000. Malnutrition led to further health complications, including blindness caused by vitamin A deficiency; according to the same report, "Below our peasantry, there is still another even more helpless working class whose diet is alarmingly inadequate and ill-balanced."[61] Most laborers lived almost entirely on low-grade rice and small amounts of vegetables or legumes. Dairy or meat were very uncommon, though sometimes fruit could be added when seasonally available.

Low wages and poor living conditions impacted older children as well. A third of the children on one plantation, it was found, died during childhood. In this instance, the plantation owners raised wages slightly for workers who had at least three children who were not working, which helped reduce the death rate. However, there are no data available regarding how widespread these measures were or whether any other improvements were offered to better quality of life.[62]

The strenuous labor and poor working and living conditions physically and mentally broke down the workers, who often turned to narcotics as a solution. "There is an urgent need for special institutions for the treatment of opium addicts in India," found one report, "and it is hoped that the matter of their cure will be approached with sympathy and understanding; for in many instances the habit is formed among the undernourished agricultural labourers, coolies in the tea-gardens, and the workers in the mining areas, because opium stimulates physical energy and keeps their ill-clad bodies warm in the cold season."[63] While the British had been responsible for growing opium in India and sending it to China in exchange for tea and other goods, not all the opium produced was exported, and this report speaks powerfully to the impact opium had on working-class Indian lives and to the expectations of the wealthier ruling classes worried more about the quality of working-class labor than quality of life.

These tea plantations were largely based in Assam, and laborers were recruited on short-term contracts from Bihar, the United Provinces, Central Provinces, and Madras. Plantation owners specifically set up a system that provided a constant influx of new labor, which kept wages low. By the early twentieth century, the people of India were becoming more outspoken about these and other problems with British rule: While agriculture had been practiced in India for centuries, they argued, it was not until recently that it had come to be considered a vital industry, whereas historically it was used only to support local populations, not for export. Production had only been upscaled, they said, to offer raw materials that could bolster European industries, not because increased yield offered anything valuable to the Indian people: consider those who worked the land and depended on the industry to provide for them but weren't even having their basic needs met.[64]

But laborers on English tea plantations experienced violations more personal still than a collective lack of access to resources. On many tea plantations across Assam, as well as Ceylon, Mauritius, and Fiji, many of the planters who oversaw the plantations exercised *droit du seigneur*, a practice in which a landowner claimed the right to engage in sexual relations with a tenant or indentured servant on the first night of her marriage. While the servants and laborers of English plantations sometimes met these abuses with violent and nonviolent resistance, the mistreatment was widespread, as suggested by the power dynamics in play and by contemporary records speaking to the exploitation of power under long-standing English colonial rule in these areas.[65]

Modern-day India is a country that both produces and consumes tea. Tea consumption in India had, by the 1930s, risen considerably, and this in turn resulted in an increase in nationwide consumption of milk and sugar. While the beverage was produced and consumed in the country, it was not touted as having health benefits, as we see with its adoption in England. The 1939 *Health and Nutrition in India* report says that "tea and coffee are used rather for what is described as 'a mild cerebral stimulation' than for their actual food value. They contain no substances which are essential for nutrition."[66]

Tea estates in India were being established around the time that the Industrial Revolution was coming into full swing halfway across the world, with railroads being built and commodities being packaged and preserved in new ways.[67] The plantations were also being developed around the time that early records of afternoon tea gatherings by the English ruling classes begin to appear. English rule in the Indian subcontinent brought with it these cultural trends, and the meal of afternoon tea is one of those that still is pervasive today.

However, the English cultural impact on India and the other colonies cannot be seen as simply a top-down relationship, where the colonizer influences the colonies, which either willingly or unwillingly adopt whatever cultural behaviors are being presented. Modern Indian afternoon tea, for example, includes both elements introduced by the English (in the tea meal as well as the tea itself) and Indian elements (like traditional fried snacks). This was true with cultural exchange in other areas of Indian life as well, such as cross-cultural communication between Indians and Western missionaries and the resulting complex and varied religious communities and perspectives that emerged.[68]

The records are unclear about exactly when and how afternoon tea came to be practiced by Indians as well as English settlers. It could be that it was a cultural practice adopted by Indian elite interacting with English elite, or it could be that it also meshed with Indian workdays and existing cultural norms in a way that made its adoption more likely. But however afternoon tea was established in India, it had become part of the culture prior to the end of British rule in India and is still to this day, and the meal's coincidence with Indian-produced tea and falling prices meant that the region was shaped, even if tangentially, by the practice of taking afternoon tea and by the East India Company's continued responses to rising demands for tea.

The East India Company, of course, was central to British presence in the region. Initially founded to conduct trade via the Indian Ocean,[69] the Company, more than the government during early colonization, was a conquering and ruling force in India. Its first interactions were with the Mughal Empire in the north of India in 1608, whose leaders and merchants were invested in having European merchants in India, along with the resources they brought and new markets they opened.[70]

The Mughal Empire spread in the following years, eventually covering much of the Indian subcontinent, and worked with traders from other countries as well as England. The Company worked to maintain goodwill with the Mughal imperial family and court but still faced competition from the Portuguese, who also had a strong presence on the subcontinent. The Company set up a trading presence in Surat and several other areas, which gave it the ability to trade in the area but did not give its employees any sort of governmental control. This changed when Bombay (modern-day Mumbai) was transferred from Charles II to the Company,[71] and Bombay eventually surpassed Surat as the Company's most profitable trading post by the end of the seventeenth century.[72] Company representatives had a harder time establishing a presence in the southeastern part of the subcontinent, where the Mughal presence was weaker, but eventually did so, thus expanding their influence further.

Hostilities between leadership on the subcontinent and the East India Company heightened the longer the Company ruled in the subcontinent. In 1686, for example, tensions arose between the Mughal Empire and the Company after the Company sacked the Hooghly District in Bengal and was forced to close its trading post in the area. Its initial attempts to militarily seize Indian lands met with failure, but due to its increasing strength and the declining strength of the Mughal Empire, less than a century later the Company secured control over much of the subcontinent after the Battle of Plassey, mentioned above.

After this time, the Company served as the governing body as well as a commercial entity in India, and it remained so until 1858, when the British government abolished Company rule after the Indian Rebellion of 1857, assuming direct control.[73] Having a company that reaped financial interest from colonialism (while also supporting government coffers with those efforts) created an environment where corruption and abuse of local populations was rampant. The period at the end of Company tenure and the beginning of direct British rule is when tea plantations were established, with the many abuses and the dire living conditions outlined earlier.

This was certainly not the first instance of Company brutality in the region, and the Company's actions were openly discussed but not punished or restricted by the government until the middle of the nineteenth century. In the early 1770s, London newspapers had reported on the deaths of more than one million Bengali residents as the result of a severe famine. The Company was deaf to the plight of the Bengali, continuing to collect exorbitant taxes from people dying of hunger and hoarding stocks of grain to feed Company employees and officers without concern for what—if anything—the larger population would eat.[74]

There was outcry elsewhere in the colonies in response to the Indian plight, although it seems little was done in response. In America, the news added to the existing resentment of the Company, although this resentment did not translate into a direct concern for the Bengali people. Instead, the famine became part of a narrative about the nefarious rule of the Company and how Americans could suffer the same fate if they failed to separate from England—and, by extension, the Company.[75]

The plight of the Bengali people became a symbol of an extreme but—it was argued—plausible scenario that could happen on American shores.[76] This also points to the interconnectedness and disconnectedness of the different colonies: there seems to be no evidence that American colonists had regular contact with or concern for Indians outside of this incident, but the connection of a shared ruler stoked concerns about further mistreatment, and (for this moment at least) Americans described themselves as connected to Indians, suffering under the same oppressive rule (although I suspect those suffering from famine in Bengal might have a different perspective regarding the level of American suffering).[77]

The American Colonies

The American colonies were the first to become independent from England, making their foodways worth examining here, as they had many more years to create a separation between colonial and postcolonial food traditions. It is also perhaps the most famous British colony, at least as it relates to tea.

Tea arrived in America before English sovereignty. In the first half of the seventeenth century, much of what is now the northeastern United States was under Dutch control, known as New Netherland, and so it was that America's first shipments of tea were delivered by the Dutch East India Company to present-day New York State. Tea was already popular in Holland at that time and seems to have caught on in the Dutch colony at around the same time it was beginning to be served in England: records show tea was being consumed in New Netherland by 1647, when the Dutch East India Company's director, Peter Stuyvesant, arrived to serve as governor. The wealthy residents of New Amsterdam, the colony's seat of government, were as enthusiastic about tea as their peers back home: early records of the settlement show that tea trays and pots, sugar bowls, and other tea-service accessories were among the most prized possessions in Dutch colonial homes.[78]

In August 1664, the British forced Stuyvesant to surrender all Dutch settlements, and New Amsterdam was renamed New York in honor of the Duke of York, King Charles's brother. The largest borough in the colony was named Queens in honor of Queen Catherine. Under new British rule, the tea drinking remained popular, and the English replaced the Dutch as importers of the beverage.

The confluence of the burgeoning English interest in tea and the established Dutch tea traditions resulted in a colonial culture that was enthusiastic and prolific in its tea drinking, merging Dutch and English influences. In American cities, tea gardens and coffeehouses appeared, mirroring those found back in Britain. As in Europe, tea became more affordable in the colony, and as it did its popularity spread outward from the wealthy classes to the population as a whole.[79]

Once the British assumed control of the former Dutch colonies, all Chinese goods, including tea, that entered the colonies were supposed to come through the British East India Company, which by this time had a monopoly on Far Eastern trade across the empire. This monopoly was reinforced legally by the Navigation Acts, which first appeared in the mid-seventeenth century and permitted American trade only with England.[80] However, the distance between England and the colonies, plus the siren song of cheaper imports from elsewhere, motivated colonists and importers to find ways around these laws.[81]

Americans received many goods from privateers or pirates: heavily armed crews would leave America and travel beyond the Cape of Good Hope and into the Indian Ocean and Red Sea to bring back a variety of goods, including many that originated in China. While some amount of their bounty may have come from trade, most of it came from plundering other countries' ships.[82] English authorities were deeply distressed by the privateers, who were flouting both the Navigation Acts and the East India Company's monopoly and, in so doing, made a dent in their profit. The Crown fought back against privateers with its navy, which at the time was one of the strongest in the world. They coupled military strategy with legal strategy, creating new antipiracy laws, arresting offenders, and, in a few particularly high-profile cases, executing them. The Crown's all-out campaign against piracy was effective, and by the early 1700s privateers were practically a thing of the past.[83]

However, an even greater threat to the Company monopoly loomed on the horizon. Smuggling accounted for a considerable percentage of goods imported in to the American colonies. Unlike piracy, where an unchartered ship carrying plundered goods could be spotted, smuggling often happened quietly under the blanket of legal shipping activities. In the case of the American colonies, smugglers did not even have to necessarily hide their smuggling under the guise of trade, as the colonies offered thousands of miles of coastline, not all of which could be monitored by Crown representatives at all times.[84]

The Dutch were the biggest offenders, bringing loads of tea into the colonies without paying duties, although smugglers from other European countries did as well. The Navigation Acts' provisions that American colonists only trade with the East India Company was done not only to reinforce the Company's monopoly but also to put a damper on other European merchants' ability to access trade in the colonies. And yet the amount of tea brought in through smuggling was dizzying: one Philadelphia merchant's calculations in 1757 suggested that, in the two years prior, only about 10 percent of the tea consumed in the city had been legally imported through the East India Company. Of course, finding exact numbers for black market trade is impossible, but it is estimated that smuggled tea accounted for per-haps 75–95 percent of the total amount consumed in America at that time.[85]

Much of the appeal of smuggled tea was cost: The beverage had become much more popular in the early eighteenth century thanks to East India Company marketing, which saw the colonial market as a promising poten-tial revenue stream. However, measures like the 1765 Stamp Act and later taxes—such as the 1767 import tax, which was later repealed for all imports besides tea—led colonists to refuse to import English goods. While the East India Company appealed to parliament, the mounting duties led many colo-nists to boycott English goods on principle.

No matter who was bringing the tea, and whether legally or illegally, Americans relied solely on imports facilitated by others, as they had no direct trade connections to China. The closest they came was a 1770 letter published in a London newspaper under the pseudonym "The Colonist's Advocate"—likely either Benjamin Franklin or British Whig James Burgh. The letter first denounced the 1767 Townshend Acts, which taxed a range of consumer goods, including tea, and went on to suggest that Americans would be compelled to establish their own trade links rather than be sub-jected to unfair taxes:

> What will they [the British in favor of the Townshend Acts] say when they find, that ships are actually fitted out from the Colonies (they cannot, I sup-pose hinder their fitting out ships) for all Parts of the World; for China, by Cape Horn; for instance, to sail under Prussian, or other Colors, with Car-goes of various Kinds, and so return loaded with Tea, and other East India Goods. . . . The whole Navy of England, if stationed ever so judiciously, cannot prevent smuggling on a Coast of 1500 Miles in Length. Such Steps as these will soon be taken by the Americans, if we obstinately go on with our unjust and oppressive measures against them.[86]

It was not until after the American Revolution that the new country would develop a direct-trade relationship with China. And concerns over taxes, particularly on tea, were a central driving force behind that uprising. The Tea Act of 1773 was one of the most contentious instances of British taxation of colonists, although far from the only one. Essentially, the act was a government bailout of the East India Company, which, due to a number of factors,[87] had become insolvent.

The Company's enormous power had meant enormous profits, which meant enormous funding for the British government, and so the taxes the Company paid constituted no small percentage of the country's budget, leading lawmakers to aggressively seek a solution to keep themselves and the Company funded. Tea was a particular concern, both because it was so heavily taxed and because it was a desired commodity; as such, taxes and regulations related to tea became the focus of much of the outrage by colonists. About 90 percent of the Company's profits came from tea, but it had warehouses full of the stuff that it was unable to sell, partly due to the duties imposed by the Townshend Acts and partly because it could not compete with the more affordable tea provided to colonists by smugglers. The goal of the act was to revive the failing Company and help it get rid of excess product by offering that product to colonists cheaply. The government waived British export taxes, which dropped tea's price to about half of what was paid in Britain, allowing the Company to sell directly to colonists rather than through a third party—American merchants—who typically brokered these transactions.[88]

However, the Townshend tea tax was still in place, and the low cost of Company tea was not enough to assuage colonists' concerns about taxation without representation. Furthermore, American smugglers and the American merchants who legally imported tea were angered by the tea tax, as it cut deeply into both groups' profits. And so it was that Americans began pointing to the Company's heavy-handed tactics in India to illustrate what could happen to colonists. Tea became representative of corporate monopoly, and corporate monopoly became symbolic of state-sponsored oppression and a complete loss of autonomy. Protests broke out.

Every student of American history knows about the Boston Tea Party, perhaps the most famous tea-related event in Western history. On the night of December 16, 1773, several groups of colonists, each group containing about thirty to sixty people, boarded Company ships in Boston Harbor to throw the shipments of tea overboard. The tea rebellion spread to other parts of the Thirteen Colonies, including New York and Philadelphia.[89] After this, the port of Boston was closed and put under military guard on June 1, 1774. But, as we know, tensions continued to build between American colonists and the Crown, finally erupting into a full-blown revolution.[90]

Why such a tempest over tea? The beverage had, in the years leading up to the American Revolution, become a rallying point for colonists' concerns over increasingly high taxes from a colonial government that felt both geographically and culturally distant. The Boston Tea Party was significant to colonists not only as a form of protest against the Tea Act and other taxes but also because it demonstrated that an organized and determined group could pull off seemingly impossible feats.[91] This second point is what has led many historians to mark the Tea Party as the beginning of revolutionary action in the future United States, as it planted the seeds of revolutionary possibility within colonists' minds.

A large part of why there was such backlash to the Tea Act was the relationship that colonists had with the product that the act targeted. By the early 1770s, most colonists were drinking a considerable amount of tea. Some estimates place American tea consumption at 5.7–6.5 million pounds per year, which translated to more than a billion cups of tea per year, or at least one cup per person each day.[92] This familiarity with the product made it an ideal rallying point for revolutionary sentiment, because it was so identifiable and valued by so many.

Tea's centrality to the lives of American colonists, in tandem with the political significance after the Boston Tea Party, gave the beverage an almost mythological status as the revolution unfolded. As one historian noted, it became the topic of conversation itself rather than an "instrument in the creation of conversation."[93] While tea, and the taxes imposed on it, were critical to the revolutionary mindset, it was not, of course, the only log on the proverbial fire. Colonial Americans were upset with much of British rule, and this anger was fanned by the taxation dilemma, which was mixed up with tea. Thus tea became a central part of the early American mythos because it was a commodity being heavily taxed, not because of the beverage itself.

Colonial protest against English taxation included using locally produced commodities instead of anything imported by the Crown—and thus subject to high import duties. This included so-called "Liberty teas" made from local plants, ranging from barks and tree leaves (linden, sassafras, willow) to cultivated and foraged herbs (red clover, violet, parsley, rosemary) and dried fruits and rosehips. Newspapers began reporting that Liberty teas were an alternative for readers seeking to break away from bohea. In 1768, the *Boston Gazette* wrote of "tea made from a plant or shrub" that had been grown about twenty miles outside of Portland, Maine, in Pearstown and "was served to a circle of ladies and gentlemen in Newbury Port, who pronounced it nearly, if not quite, its equal in flavor to genuine Bohea. So important a discovery claims attention, especially at this crisis. If we have the plant, nothing is wanted but the process of curing it into 'tea' of our own manufacture."[94]

In an attempt to lure more of the American public into participating in the boycott of English tea, newspapers touted these Liberty teas as more healthful than imported bohea, which they sometimes even described as poisonous, Liberty teas became the drink to serve at social gatherings for those who supported the revolutionary cause. While many colonists continued to abstain from tea drinking during the revolution, not all did, including Abigail Adams, who mentioned her tea drinking in a 1778 letter to her husband, John Adams, who would procure tea for her when he could.[95]

Tea as Legend and the Consumption of Tea after the Revolutionary War

The Boston Tea Party did not take its place in American national identity until almost fifty years after the Revolutionary War. Prior to this time, Americans simply referred to the protest as the destruction of tea in the Boston Harbor. The act itself, while a catalyzing event leading up to the war, was not laden with the political significance we ascribe to it today. Until the 1830s Americans acknowledged but did not celebrate the Boston Tea Party, considering it a necessary act of vandalism and lawlessness but not an honorable, patriotic event. But its rechristening in the 1830s served as "part of a larger contest for the public memory of the Revolution."[96] Alfred Young argues that the choice of this particular name offered a lighthearted and frivolous reference to a serious event, making the lawless act more palatable and perhaps relatable to the average American. Young also points out that since by the 1770s tea was firmly considered a woman's beverage, calling an entirely male-led action a "tea party" poked fun at gendered social hierarchies and offered some acknowledgment of women's often-overlooked role within the revolution.

The Boston Tea Party had become a touchstone of American patriotism by 1873, when a special meeting of the Massachusetts Historical Society celebrated the protest's centennial. The speakers' remarks all point to the Tea Party as a critical turning point in American consciousness, and for the most part the remarks did not situate tea centrally within the narrative of the story, instead focusing on taxes and simply pointing to tea as the commodity that those taxes had been applied to. In doing so, they minimized the importance of the beverage to the colonists and glossed over the important point that these taxes were so infuriating and damaging precisely because tea was so important. By creating a distance, even if subconsciously, between American tastes and a beverage that at this point was very strongly associated with English tastes and English mealtimes, the speakers created a distance between the former colonizer and the former colonies.

This distaste for identifying with English cultural traditions—despite the fact that many of them have carried over from colonial times—is obvious in American's relationship to afternoon tea and to the beverage itself. Today Americans consume more coffee than tea, a relationship that some authors trace to the Tea Party and the country's revolutionary history.[97] But the truth is more complex. As in Britain, tea, coffee, and chocolate came to the American colonies almost simultaneously during the second half of the seventeenth century, but while tea was already a beloved staple for some living in former Dutch colonies, coffee was not. Many Americans were left disillusioned by the events surrounding the Revolutionary War and decided to turn to coffee rather than going back to drinking tea. However, tea was still the preferred beverage, or at least the more heavily imported one: while tea importation in the 1780s was low—and certainly much lower than in Britain (325,000 pounds per year)—coffee importation was lower (200,000 pounds per year).[98]

After defeating the British in the Revolutionary War, the young new country faced considerable financial obstacles, which may have also contributed to relatively low imports. The country faced both economic depression and rapid inflation; in response, the British closed off trade routes to Americans, in hopes of coercing the newly freed colonies to return to English rule. Members of the U.S. Congress considered addressing budget shortfalls in the same way their predecessors had: by imposing duties on consumer goods.[99]

The European wars following the French Revolution bolstered the American tea trade by collapsing the English-imposed trade barriers and allowing American ships to carry goods to Europe. Furs and sandalwood were in demand in Chinese markets, and these goods were easily procured by American business people, who then traded them for tea. This resulted in a booming American tea trade with China by the late 1780s, as well as an end to the British monopoly on the American tea market. Tea consumption skyrocketed in the 1790s, with Americans importing 2.5 million pounds of tea per annum, which increased by 50 percent over the following ten years.

Americans' efforts to distance themselves from English cultural habits often meant that few of these habits were adopted on a large scale—or were imported to America quickly. Afternoon tea is one such example: While it did seem to catch on eventually, it wasn't until a good deal later, and its popularity rose and fell just as it has in Britain. While afternoon tea itself may not have been an instant hit, functionally similar activities were held in America, although they were typically framed as tea parties or informal social calls rather than as meals unto themselves. We see evidence of these early tea gatherings in the American colonies before and after the revolution. One account of the early settlers of Schenectady recalls tea parties in the town remarkably similar to English afternoon teas.

The tea gathering was usually held by a group of women who gathered at 4:00 around a large, round table, which had been moved to the center of the room for the occasion. English custom was observed in offering the proper teacups and saucers and carefully preparing what was still a somewhat expensive commodity. As in early gatherings in England, tea at American tea parties was prepared and dispensed by the host, rather than set in a central pot to be passed around. However, the snacks on offer at these gatherings departed from purely English traditions: instead, they reflected the availability of local ingredients—using maple sugar instead of lump sugar, except for on special occasions, for one—and also acknowledged Schenectady's Dutch influence—with Dutch waffles and pastry—along with foods like pot cheese and butter that spoke to both nationalities.[100]

The earlier residents of the area were Mohawk, followed by Dutch settlers, and in the 1660s the English seized Schenectady as a part of the takeover of the New Netherland colony.[101] After this time, English colonists joined or pushed out existing Mohawk and Dutch residents, and the tea traditions that were just beginning to form in England joined them.

Tea drinking, and specifically gathering together for tea, had become common at least among the middle and upper classes by the mid-1700s, and the beverage itself was present across social classes, often as a morning drink. The timing of the American Revolution in relation to the rise of tea's popularity in England is particularly interesting, as it coincides with the broader appeal and lowering prices mentioned earlier. This means that many colonists were accustomed to drinking the beverage and to using it as a focal point of social gatherings—as we see in the account of the Schenectady tea parties. However, American colonists did not see how tea culture went on to development in the English culinary world, including the emergence of afternoon tea and the shifting and renaming of other meals.

The American Revolution did more than simply form a new country. Revolutionaries also used a foodstuff as a rallying point for that revolution and, in so doing, jump-started conversations about our food and food traditions, where they come from, and what they symbolize. It was that symbolism, rather than tea itself, that became critical and speaks to what parts of a country's past we accept and what parts we reject. In American cultural memory, tea holds considerable power to this day as a beverage that united a country in revolution. Sources vary on the particulars, but the one constant is the centrality of tea to the equation.[102] It is little wonder, then, that such an emotionally charged product would gradually fall out of favor, particularly as the emotions it evoked in the American cultural consciousness related to domination, unfair government, and restricted freedom.

However, this shift did not happen overnight. We've already seen that Americans continued to consume tea (and, in fact, consumed more of it) in the postrevolutionary period, particularly once they established their own trade relationships. We have also seen that some Americans eschewed tea in favor of coffee, having become disenchanted with tea after the war, and that both brews were imported into early postrevolutionary America.

The larger shift in Americans' relationship to tea seems to come a bit later, around the time Americans began referring to the Boston Tea Party by name. As noted above, the Tea Party's naming and the collective pride that swells around this act of rebellion did not take place until the 1830s, and the destruction of tea as a symbol of oppression, as much as the taxes and governing practices that symbol represented, became a critical focal point. While drinking tea was no longer considered unpatriotic, it was more common in America by this point to drink coffee, and creating a cultural discourse about the rejection of tea as a part of national identity helped solidify coffee as the American beverage of choice.

The afternoon tea meal is also built around tea, but in a completely different way. Afternoon tea situates tea at the center of what is meant to be a restful and social break—quite the departure from the Boston Tea Party. However, afternoon tea is as much about identity as it is about having a snack to tide you over until dinner. Partaking in afternoon tea is, for many people in England and former colonies, a long-standing tradition, and one that ties to collective identity in different ways.

While the meal was not brought to America as a part of the food traditions of a ruling foreign power, it did appear in some American shops and restaurants in the twentieth century, although in these cases it was referred to as an imported English ritual rather than one that Americans took ownership of. And, while the beverage had become less popular in the United States than coffee, it still continued (and continues today) to play a role in American life. Tea became a central part of the temperance movement in the United States and Britain. The movement itself encouraged drinking tea in lieu of alcohol and used gendered language to market the movement to women—for example, by claiming that "there is no error in the habits of Society, which female influence can go farther to correct, then the injurious practice of habitually using ardent spirits in the social intercourse of society, and at the private side board."[103]

Kenya

Kenya, like India, has undergone numerous colonial occupations by foreign powers, due to its strategic position along trade routes and in some cases (as during English rule) because of its value for agriculture. At the end of the fifteenth century, Portuguese explorer Bartolomeu Dias became the first European to round the southern tip of Africa; the information he brought back from his voyages helped Portugal set up naval bases that would help secure its control over the Indian Ocean, thus establishing connections with Asia and the spice trade. The Portuguese officially established a military presence in East Africa beginning in 1505. Two centuries later, and after a series of military scuffles, troops from the Arab nation of Oman defeated the Portuguese and took control of the ports along the Swahili Coast, which included the coast of present-day Kenya, and assumed complete control by 1730.[104]

In the 1840s, Sultan Seyyid Said moved the capital of his sultanate from Oman on the Arabian Peninsula into Zanzibar to better oversee long-distance trade routes to the interior of the African continent. The trade routes, as well as the physical presence of the Omani capital in Zanzibar, meant that the subjects along the Swahili Coast endured much closer scrutiny and stricter governance than they had before. The Omani government also viewed its subjects as a source of revenue, establishing plantations where its people were made to work cheaply, as well as sending some to be sold into the slave trade.[105]

In the latter half of the nineteenth century, the British became interested in the eastern coast of Africa and began applying political and military pressure on Oman. At the Berlin Conference of 1885, British colonization was codified as East Africa was divided into territories to be ruled by different European powers. In 1895, the British government took control of what they called the East Africa Protectorate, more or less present-day Kenya, gradually pushing its borders out to Uganda and encouraging white settlers to move to the area and establish tea plantations.[106]

The British preference for deeply colored and flavorful black tea led tea producers to seek new areas to establish tea plantations offering the right environmental conditions to produce bold, colorful tea. Finding the conditions in East Africa appropriate to the crop, they established many tea plantations up and down the coast by the mid-1920s, including in Natal, Nyasaland (modern-day Malawi), and present-day Kenya. Today, Kenya continues to produce staggering amounts of the crop, currently supplying more than 50 percent of the tea brought to the British market.[107]

In 1920, all but a small coastal strip of the East Africa Protectorate became Britain's Kenya Colony. Over the years, as the colony developed, British nationals living in Kenya enjoyed participating in British civic life, while African and Asian residents were denied direct political participation—which they didn't secure until 1944. Many Indian laborers were brought to Kenya to build the Kenya Uganda Railway Line and subsequently settled in the area with their families, one of the many ways the different colonies interconnected and the colonizer's influence created the (forced or voluntary) movement of people between them.[108]

With British rule in 1895 came rules about who could live where, and the new British residents decided that the Great Rift Valley, an area still critical to tea production and to tourism as a result of this, would only be inhabited by whites. The new residents began establishing coffee and tea plantations, ignoring existing residents' concerns about displacement, military-enforced resettlement, and quality-of-life issues. Wages for African workers were kept artificially low by white tea-plantation owners, who argued that this made their products more competitive in the global marketplace. Meanwhile, workers argued against plantation labor practices, which created many of the same concerns about health and access to resources afflicting workers on tea plantations in India.

During World War I, the colony served as a military base partly out of British concerns over the German colony to the south. After the war ended, many British military officers relocated to the colony, meaning that many of the colonial residents were aristocratic.[109] When Kenya finally won independence in 1963, many of these aristocratic settlers left, but their legacy of coffee and tea plantations remains, and even today it is seen in the country's tea industry and in the interconnection between tea plantations and Western tourism.[110]

The tea plantations made the beverage a central part of Kenyan life, and afternoon tea as a meal was imported to these plantations, although there are not records that show it being practiced by the Kenyan people during the colonial period. Tea drinking, at least, seems to have stuck, as we'll see in the next chapter, and the meal is still present in hotels and in tourist attractions, and it seems to be at least a special-occasion meal in some restaurants for Kenyan locals, although it is not clear from conversations or publications how widespread it is in Kenyan homes as a daily practice—if at all.

The Australian Colony

In 1786, a document titled "Heads of a Plan for effectively disposing of convicts" was presented to the British Cabinet, recommending that a new British colony be established on the eastern coast of Australia in New South Wales to house expelled convicts. The plan was proposed partially as an effort to free up space in jails on the British mainland and also was seen as an opportunity to use incarcerated labor to harvest raw materials from the island to be used for British ships in India.

The first shipment of people and goods, called the First Fleet, was a poorly planned affair, transporting 736 incarcerated men and women from England to Australia. Most were from London and had been convicted of property crime. Few of them had any skills that would prove useful to settling a new colony, which apparently had not been considered in the proposal.[111] The food supplies sent by the government were inadequate, and the early colonial farmers had little success in raising food to supplement them; food supplies and daily rations dwindled over the first few years of settlement. The ships' masters and military officers present during the colony's founding saw an opportunity to make money while addressing supply shortages and spread the word that merchants could make a profit by bringing cargo to the area.

The officers, who could work with merchants and had control over the colony's purse strings, brought in a range of previously unavailable commodities, selling them at a considerable markup. During this time, tea was seen as a luxury and was not given priority in government institutions (including, as one might expect, prisons). However, it was sometimes available, and the proximity of the Australian colony to the trading routes used by tea traders meant the commodity could be sourced easily.

At the beginning of the nineteenth century, a regular bank and currency were established, as well as a burgeoning grocery industry that catered to the growing population. However, the cost of tea fluctuated considerably during this time, as shortages would drive prices up, and traders, who rushed to Sydney to take advantage of high prices, would reach the port to find the market already flooded and the cost of tea at one-third of what it had been.

An 1823 report indicated tea was enjoyed regularly in the colony, and by the end of the century tea was a household staple.[112] This is something of a precipitous rise in popularity, given that it had not been listed as part of the First Fleet's official cargo in 1788. One woman among the first transported from England wrote a letter home bemoaning the lack of even basic amenities as well as a particularly beloved staple: tea. She says that many of her fellow convicts also missed the beverage but remained hopeful that a shipment would arrive from China.[113] Her letter tells us that tea was either unavailable entirely or at least unavailable to convicts at this time. Tea arrived soon after, with another letter in 1798 relaying news that the writer had been successful both in securing tea when traveling through Australian ports and in selling that tea to others.[114]

This swift adoption of tea into the culture of British colonial Australian settlers speaks to the spirit of the new colony and its willingness to adapt to new circumstances—and to seek the comforts of England when away.[115] This seems to be a driving force in bringing tea, and later the afternoon tea meal, to English colonial spaces worldwide. Australia's quick adoption of tea stands in contrast to England's, which took a century.[116]

As with other colonies, the new Australian settlements pushed out existing residents and used a range of governmental initiatives and the work of missionaries to share English norms and beliefs with existing communities. As with the residents of India, the British hoped to "civilize" and "save" the indigenous people by getting them to adopt Western ideals and behaviors. What emerged, of course, could never be called a purely English culture but was, rather, a cross-cultural exchange unique to the affected communities and cultures; however, that kind of exchange always has an impact, shifting the development of native cultures in large and small ways.[117] When exchanges are more casual, they are more likely to be genuinely cross-cultural, shaping both parties. However, English colonial power was maintained strictly and completely, and assimilation laws made it difficult for meaningful exchanges to include elements of indigenous cultures.

Parsing out the exact ways in which meals fit into this type of cultural exchange is difficult, making it challenging to pinpoint the exact moment or reasons that afternoon tea became a habit among Australians. Afternoon tea is documented within modern communities but does not always appear in records of cultural exchanges kept by native communities or even in most cases by English settlers. This is the case in understanding the meal in many former colonies, where records exist of tea being consumed among settlers and perhaps by original communities as well, but records of the meal, at least from early colonial days and often through the entirety of English rule, are scarce.

In Australia, however, there are a few clues that show where the native communities would have come in contact with afternoon tea. The concept of tea as a beverage would have been familiar to indigenous communities as well as to English settlers. Early English settlers observed Aboriginal communities drinking an infusion of another plant, referring to it as tea; from this we derive the name "tea tree" for plants within the genus *Melaleuca*.[118] While drinking an infusion meant indigenous communities had a similar food habit to that of the English settlers, it does not imply that they would have adopted tea as a beverage or that this habit would make them more interested in participating in afternoon tea (provided, of course, that they were welcomed at the table).

In the case of indigenous communities in Australia, we also have records of those who went through English educational programs, which taught etiquette and sometimes home economics or religious courses in addition to classroom subjects like language arts. Australian law mandated Aboriginal participation in these educational programs, which were largely overseen by missionary and other nongovernmental groups. In the late 1930s, assimilation policies were introduced to "bring the absorption of Aboriginal people into white society."[119] In 1987, Sally Morgan published a memoir about growing up disconnected from her Aboriginal heritage and her attempt to reconnect with her familial and cultural roots.[120] In conversations with her grandmothers, Sally learns of the assimilative educational programs they were forced to endure and how a seemingly innocuous cultural practice like afternoon tea could become something nefarious in a new community absent the appropriate context.

As part of her education into white British culture, Sally's grandmother Daisy Corunna was taught how to brew tea, cut crusts off dainty sandwiches, and make other preparations for afternoon tea. If we view the formalities of the meal through her eyes, the ritual becomes defamiliarized, and we understand how it all might have seemed awfully fussy and even nonsensical to Daisy: "We see, for example, how off the ritual of formal morning and afternoon teas must have appeared to her, transplanted as they were from the context of upper-class English life to that of colonial, suburban Australia and Indigenous people who had no idea of the original context and significance of English etiquette. It is only when Daisy sees this ritual enacted in an English film on TV that she recognizes the role that she had been trained to play; that is, she recognizes herself for the first time as a servant defined by a specific class etiquette."[121] Daisy was permitted to participate in the English cultural moment, but only in a peripheral way, as a servant. She is present and made culturally aware but is not given the same access as young white women.

Daisy eventually embraced the meal as a part of the identity she was meant to play. Formal English etiquette, dress, and relationships to food and meals, she felt, set her apart from her brother and others who were not desirable "blackfella." In her mind, being Aboriginal was shameful, but adopting white culture and identity markers to replace her Aboriginal heritage could absolve her. In this way, Daisy's proximity to whiteness became a status symbol and a source of pride—and it was afternoon tea specifically that gave her the proximity. This was true even though she understood her place in the pecking order: a carefully trained servant.[122] The relationship between white and Aboriginal Australians, and the relationship of both to afternoon tea, has continued to evolve and, as we see in the next chapter, continues to be a part of Australian culture in a form that very closely mimics its British predecessor.

Malta

As a crossroads for many cultures, the island nation of Malta lies smack-dab between Europe and Africa, exposing it to the conventions of those passing through and the cultures of its conquerors. As Christianity spread across the globe, Malta was one of its very first stops, as in 60 AD Saint Paul was shipwrecked on its shores. The island was later overtaken by Arab armies in the Arab-Byzantine wars before being absorbed by the Normans into the Kingdom of Sicily until 1530, when the Holy Roman Emperor gave Malta to the Catholic military Sovereign Military Order of Saint John of Jerusalem.[123] At this point, Malta became fully entrenched in Christianity. After Napoleon Bonaparte conquered the island while en route to Egypt in 1798, the Maltese requested English assistance in fighting the French, and the English, finding a toehold, took over in 1800. Each of these occupations left its mark on Malta's culture.

After the 1814 Treaty of Paris subsumed the tiny island into the British Empire, it was used as a shipping headquarters and way station. Malta became a critical asset to British trade after the Suez Canal in Egypt opened in 1869, as it was roughly halfway between the canal and the Strait of Gibraltar. It was also a critical stopping point for the many British ships en route to and from India, which meant that this small nation of only 122 square miles[124] was in regular, close contact with the colonial power.

We know afternoon tea was consumed in Malta by the turn of the twentieth century, although it is not clear whether it was being consumed by Maltese locals as well as the newly arrived English residents. A memoir published in 1908 by the wife of a military officer mentions afternoon tea being taken, but one gets the sense that it was the practice of English residents only: the memoirist mentions teas only at gatherings of military personnel and with other English people. That said, it is possible these are its only mentions because she had few other interactions.[125]

Unlike colonial India and Kenya, where tea was both produced and consumed, Malta's role in the imperial machine was as more of a stopover for tea making its way from colonial plantations to various global markets. But like all of the colonies, Malta was brought the same traditions England exported elsewhere.

During World War I the island housed many wounded British soldiers, and during World War II its strategic position next to shipping lanes meant that it not only staged Allied troops for multiple campaigns but also was heavily bombarded by Axis forces. Malta suffered devastating losses and was collectively awarded the George Cross by King George VI in 1942 after the Siege of Malta, after which the island continued to be used by the Allies as a listening post for radio traffic through the end of the war.

This is not to suggest that the relationship between the Maltese people and colonial forces was consistently peaceful or pleasant; in 1919, for example, several Maltese men were killed during a protest against higher taxes levied by the British government. Here, as across the empire, the colonized showed dissatisfaction with English rule. However, British influence has been enduring, and the country was not swift to remove all traces of its colonial past upon gaining independence in 1964 as the Republic of Malta.

British culture, and the meal of afternoon tea, is still very much a part of Maltese culture, which British travelers note feels more familiar in terms of customs and culture than in other former colonies.[126] In one memoir, we see that at least some Maltese residents were still practicing afternoon tea at home as of the 1960s: one Maltese nanny working for an American expat family would come by their house with her own tea service, preparing tea for the family and introducing them to the meal and its space to relax and socialize.[127]

Whether or not afternoon tea is a daily ritual in Maltese homes, its popularity worldwide since the early 2000s means that it is offered by hotels, including those founded on the island during the English colonial period.[128] British tour operators contractually oblige Maltese hoteliers to provide afternoon tea to their guests on package tours, which some argue could be an affirmation of national identity and traditions for British traveling away from home;[129] however, it's not the British alone who are being asked to participate.

South Africa

South Africa was a Dutch colony before it was an English one. Its location and the fact that it had few natural harbors meant it remained somewhat isolated for a good deal of recorded history; it was inhabited by hunting and herding tribes.[130] In the late fifteenth century, the same Bartolomeu Dias who was seminal in exploring the eastern coast of Africa, making way for eventual colonialization of Kenya, attempted and then successfully rounded the southernmost tip of the continent. Shipping routes had for some time gone through the Persian Gulf and the Red Sea, but after Dias's voyage the Portuguese began diverting European shipping around the Cape of Good Hope and into the Indian Ocean. By the end of the sixteenth century, Dutch, British, French, and Scandinavian merchant mariners were using this route, and strategic importance made the land at the continent's southern tip more appealing as a colony, despite its geographic isolation.[131]

In 1652, the Dutch East India Company took an expedition to occupy Table Bay (the area where present-day Cape Town is located), where they intended to set up a small fortified base to serve as a way station for their fleets using the trade routes. The early Dutch settlers were all Company employees and, in some cases, upon arrival were released from their work contracts and given land, which meant taking more space from the local peoples. The Dutch also brought in slaves to build colonial infrastructure (fort, roads, etc.) and cut off the local pastoral communities from fresh-water sources and rich pastures unless they agreed to work as servants.[132]

By the next century, the slaveholding activities of the Dutch burghers residing in the land near the Cape had grown significantly: while the majority had fewer than six slaves, twenty-five owned between twenty-six and fifty slaves, and seven of them had more than fifty.[133] Some of the slaves were freed, and this growing community of free black residents initially had the same rights as the whites. However, discriminatory laws began to be passed in 1760, with more such laws added later on. The Dutch originally colonized Southwestern Africa, eventually expanding into Southeast Africa by the end of the eighteenth century.

The Cape was later handed over to the French, and then the Dutch, and was eventually awarded to the British as a prize during the Napoleonic Wars. At this point, the colony's residents were a mix of the descendants of slaves, the descendants of the original Dutch settlers, and nearby indigenous communities. The region's nineteenth-century history is incredibly complex: The early part of the century saw the military expansion of nearby Zululand by a number of regional and colonial forces, as well as tensions between Dutch settlers and the English. Once the English gained control over the Cape settlement, some of the disgruntled settlers went further inland to escape the government's watchful eye. They formed independent republics, but their land became more appealing once diamonds were discovered in southern Africa and a massive diamond rush ensued.[134]

After 1870, the colony was an entirely different place from the isolated, rural spot it had been not long before: after discovering the region's rich mineral reserves, the British mined for gold and diamonds, which meant an influx of workers. And the annexation of African lands by the English continued, often bringing with it new and unfamiliar practices and systems: Africans were made to pay rent, surrender labor or part of their crops, or otherwise offer some sort of compensation for their continued existence on the land they had lived on for generations. In addition, discriminatory laws were introduced, and racist ideologies held by both new European settlers and longtime white South African residents began to calcify, creating a rigid boundary between white and black, laying the groundwork for additional discriminatory laws and practices, such as apartheid.[135]

The Anglo-Zulu War was waged in 1879 between the British and the Zulu Kingdom, who were fighting over contested border territory. The English eventually annexed Zululand several years later, folding it in to the larger Cape colony. Immediately after, in 1880, tensions between Dutch-speaking farmers—the Boers—and the British erupted into the First Boer War, which was won in 1881 by the Boers. Not long after, from 1899 to

1902, the Second Boer War was waged after the British developed a taste for Boer lands and the natural resources within them. The British were eventually victorious and later created a unified South African colony.[136]

These many influences made their way into the foodways of South Africa. The recipe for Dutch kockies included at the end of the book is an example of several layers of cross-cultural influence: It is a South African recipe originally adapted from a Dutch food and later published in a quintessentially English cookbook (*Mrs. Beeton's Every-Day Cookery*). As it is in Malta, the origins of afternoon tea in South Africa are hard to uncover, and when the practice does appear it is taken only within the ranks of the colonial powers. As we saw with the Americans in New York State, the Dutch also had afternoon tea–esque traditions, and so a similar meal may have already been in place elsewhere in South African society by the time the British imported their meal.

In any case, afternoon tea seems to have become a part of at least Boer and English settlers' rituals. One narrative from the early twentieth century relays a !Kung tribal member's experience working in Namibia, which is just north of modern-day South Africa; hired by a Boer farmer, the man "became in charge of the kitchen," where he "used to cook breakfast and prepare afternoon tea there." There's no record of what was served, and it's unclear whether a full afternoon tea was prepared or simply a cup of tea was brewed. We are told, however, that "the Boers cooked lunch and supper by themselves."[137]

In South Africa proper around the turn of the century, mentions of afternoon tea as a meal appear to be limited to the English. In one journal recounting battlefield experiences during the Boer Wars, the author says that the British government supplied its troops with free afternoon tea. In this case, the soldiers were given a hot drink, not the full afternoon tea spread, but even this abbreviated teatime pause is clearly an important, relaxing social break, which is what the full meal is all about, too.[138] Another soldier's recollections of the war include enjoying a full afternoon tea:

> In the morning a special invitation was sent from the corporals of the Sussex Squadron . . . requesting the pleasure of Seargeant Pullar's company to afternoon tea, parade order optional. We formed a table of biscuit boxes, which we covered with two recently-washed towels, and then I managed to

obtain a fine effect in the way of table decoration by taking the spotted red handkerchief from my beck and laying it starwise as a centre-piece. Then, having begged, borrowed, and otherwise obtained all the available tin plates, we covered the table with sardines, tinned tongues, pickles, condensed milk, jams, butter, and cake.[139]

This soldier's account shows how important community was to the meal's enjoyment, even when the spread on the table is scarce.

More than one hundred years after this soldier wrote his account, South Africans continue to enjoy a full afternoon tea, as is done in so many other former British colonies.

THE END OF THE COLONIAL PERIOD

After Britain established itself as the naval and imperial power of the world in the nineteenth century, for the better part of the next several decades it played global policeman and wielded a heavy hand in controlling international conflict—a period sometimes referred to as Pax Britannica, or "British peace."[140] At the turn of the twentieth century, Germany and the United States began to emerge as political and economic powers and a challenge to British dominance.

Tensions between England and Germany were one central cause of World War I, but though England suffered incredible losses in the conflict, the empire did not cease its expansion and continued to grow during the interwar period. However, the empire's colonies in Southeast Asia were occupied by Japan during World War II, and even though the Allies were victorious in that war, the compounded losses of lives and resources from the two wars had begun to signal the empire's decline. The country was nearly bankrupt and even had to take out a considerable loan from the United States to avoid ruin.[141]

The empire's reputation and resources diminished, its colonies began to demand independence, one by one. The postwar political climate was more favorable to decolonization, as the British had spent colony resources heavily as part of the war effort and now no longer had the means to stifle insistent calls for independence. India was the first to exit the empire, in 1947.[142]

The pace of departures accelerated, with dozens of colonies leaving midcentury. In 1997, Charles, Prince of Wales, formally handed Hong Kong over to China as a special administrative region.[143] Great Britain still maintains a handful of overseas territories, but the British Empire is no more.

3

AFTERNOON TEA IN THE POSTCOLONIAL WORLD

The British Empire affected so many countries in lasting ways and epitomized a period in which, all around the world, non-Europeans were dominated by Europeans. The Empire shaped the modern world, from place names and geographical boundaries, to racial demographics, economic networks, and international norms and laws.

—Ashley Jackson, *The British Empire*

In the modern world, depending where you are and whom you ask, "tea" can mean a lot of different things. There are commonly accepted variations on the term—tea as a snack and beverage taken in the afternoon or taken in the evening and, of course, simply the beverage itself. There are as many ways to have tea as there are stars in the sky, and each way has its staunch defenders. Opinions range for how the tea should be made, how and when it should be served, and what it should be served with. These opinions vary by geographic region, and sometimes even within families, making a comprehensive listing of all the ways to serve tea a dizzying prospect. This makes the afternoon tea a meal of endless variety to explore and to document, and as we'll see with the countries examined in the previous chapter, the ways that English colonial influence lives on (or does not) through afternoon tea are both varied and telling.

One of the first marked changes is the evolution of the name itself: "High tea" and "afternoon tea" are terms often used interchangeably by Americans (but not by Britons), even though in their early incarnations they meant very different things. Modern afternoon tea in hotels and restaurants is still very similar to what was served in Victorian Britain, although in many places it is still common practice to take afternoon tea in its simple form, often just a midafternoon break at home or work with a cup or pot of tea and a small snack.

Today afternoon tea outside the United Kingdom can be found at higher-end hotels, and an afternoon tea service is more common in countries that used to be part of the British Empire, such as Australia or Malta, where some residents still participate in the ritual as a holdover from colonial days. Afternoon tea service at hotels is incredibly common; when doing online research into afternoon tea in former British colonies, I found it easiest to get information on tea services in luxury hotels. This isn't terribly surprising, as they likely have more resources—search-engine optimization, professional graphic designers, trained photographers—all making their Web presence more noticeable and more visually appealing. By contrast, when looking into tea services provided in smaller establishments, I had trouble finding much information at all; I similarly hit roadblocks researching overall afternoon tea culture of different communities. Tourists—or even locals—searching for a place to enjoy afternoon tea might very well get the impression that luxury hotels are the only places—or at least the most common places—to enjoy afternoon tea, although this often is not true. Even in America, where the meal is not a fixture in many households, afternoon tea is still served in everything from tiny local shops to grand hotels.[1]

The afternoon tea offerings in small shops and restaurants vary considerably, but the services at large, upscale hotels tend to all include the following: tea (of course)—often chosen from a selection of at least a dozen options that include traditional black teas as well as herbal infusions, rooibos, and green teas—plus finger sandwiches (in great variety, but cucumber sandwiches seem to be the most popular), scones and preserves, and cookies. Often other treats are included—like petits fours and quiche—but it varies by tea service.

Most modern hotel restaurants try to upsell the afternoon tea experience by offering à la carte flutes of sparkling wine. Afternoon teas at fine hotels are often advertised as "the ultimate luxury,"[2] with decor, tableware, and every last detail carefully attended to, to create a fine-dining experience. In the end, going out to take a grand hotel's afternoon tea is a far cry from staying at home to enjoy a private, simple afternoon tea snack. This disparity between public and private is worth noting, as the meal first enjoyed by society's elite was a combination of the two: snacks prepared for guests in a somewhat casual setting in a private home.[3] And while hotels clearly cater their afternoon teas to tourists, locals also participate, although often for special occasions as opposed to part of a daily tea break.

Descriptions of afternoon tea service also create a temporal distance between the diner and the meal. It is often framed as an opportunity to travel back in time and enjoy the luxurious habits of previous generations.[4] This framing brings both assumptions about social class and assumptions about modern meal habits to bear: It is safe to assume that the working classes, in both previous and current generations, are unlikely to have regular access to tiered trays of small pastries, champagne, and imported teas. This realization focuses our understanding of who consumes the meal and how, giving the impression that it is the purview of social classes with more resources. People from countries without a regular afternoon tea tradition might buy the sales pitch, but someone living where the meal is common is more likely to understand that an elegant, high-end tea is only one version of a wide range of possible experiences—like choosing between having dinner at a Michelin-starred restaurant or at a taco truck.

Advertising afternoon tea as a "vintage" experience[5] suggests taking tea is no longer a popular, current, or relevant pastime. This couldn't be further from the truth. In the next chapter we explore afternoon tea as it is taken by many in the modern United Kingdom—usually as a simple, daily ritual enjoyed in the home, across the social spectrum.[6] While it's true that the popularity of both tea the beverage and tea the meal declined in the mid-twentieth century, afternoon tea is experiencing something of a resurgence: a growing number of establishments are once again putting it on the menu, and modern Britons, as well as people across the postcolonial world, express greater interest in enjoying both home-based and public teas.

INDIA

Indian discontent with British governance was palpable from the early days of the empire's rule and only grew along with imperial presence: as we saw in chapter 2, terrible living and working conditions, low wages, rampant disease, and British restructuring of the Indian landscape and economy to support European export interests rather than the health and economic well-being of Indians were all at issue.

Uprisings began almost as soon as the British colony was founded in the 1850s: Lord Dalhousie had established control over the Indian colony by 1856, and the following year the Indian Mutiny began in the Delhi area, soon sparking uprisings nationwide. The British focused their efforts on suppressing the revolt, and in 1858 they felt the population was under control. But British authorities continued to employ repressive and dehumanizing practices, like the zamindari system, which empowered absentee landlords and taxed peasants directly. Workers were overtaxed, and the poor found it almost impossible to get a foothold; without resources, the populace was easier to control.[7] Even though uprising had only just been repressed, the Indian people continued to demand reform.

The year 1858 marked the end of the East India Company's rule over India,[8] through which the British Crown had exerted its will. But now the Crown assumed direct control, signaling an important shift in the Company's direction: for one hundred years they'd been granted more or less free reign to colonize and rule India, making the fortunes of generations of Company men. So once the Crown withdrew this power, the Company's influence diminished considerably.

But for the Indian people, the change in governance did not mean improved living and working conditions. And so, over the subsequent decades, the early stirrings of the Indian national movement were felt: In Calcutta in 1875,[9] the Indian Association was founded, a forerunner to 1885's Indian National Congress, organized to represent the educated middle class of India and foster political participation. This development laid the groundwork for the nationalist movement in India; by the turn of the century, civic groups began reaching out to the laboring classes and displeasure with attempted political reform by the English had only grown,[10] all of which furthered interest in the cause.

After World War I, Mohandas Karamchand Gandhi became the leader of the Indian National Congress and went on to urge nonviolent resistance to British rule.[11] The desire for representation in government further galvanized the Indian independence movement, and after decades of protest—

and the split between India and Pakistan, and any number of other political happenings that could, and do, fill many books—in 1947 India gained independence from Great Britain. After two hundred years of British imperial rule, first by the East India Company and then by the Crown itself, India's landscape—physical and cultural—was forever changed.

England is largely responsible for tea's popularity today in India, as it was the empire that ordered the lands of northern India transformed into acres and acres of tea plantations. This legacy lives on in Indian meals, which include afternoon tea as well as the morning ritual of "bed tea," which is brought along with a small snack by a servant while the recipient is still in bed.[12] And British influence remains at the intersection of mealtimes and sport: Cricket, invented in medieval England, is wildly popular in India today. The rules and customs of the game apply not only to the wielding of the bat and ball, the scoring, and the play on the field but also to an entire decorum surrounding official matches,[13] including their long duration (often lasting the whole afternoon) and the break for afternoon tea between innings.[14]

Indian culture has in some ways cleanly divorced itself from its colonial past, but when it comes to food, some English traditions hold strong. Middle-class eating habits in India are Westernized, with many city dwellers sitting on chairs at dining tables adorned with Western-style cutlery. Those who can afford to do so eat lunch and dinner every day, along with breakfast and a light snack—sometimes called "tea" or "tiffin."

The foods themselves vary widely. One Bengali family living in Kolkata takes tea around 5:30 or 6:00 p.m., as they usually have a very late dinner around 10:00 or 11:00. For them, afternoon tea includes savory snacks (such as samosas, savory pastries that are stuffed and fried), Western- and Indian-style sweets, and tea served in the British style, with milk and sugar but rarely with spices.[15]

Blending British and local foods at afternoon tea is common across India, as the meal is becoming further removed from its British past and increasingly reflecting Indian regional differences.[16] Mirroring the ample portions served at tea and the meal's working-class origins, in India it is quite common to refer to high tea instead of afternoon tea.[17] Offering a more substantial meal and calling it high tea makes sense for restaurants and hotels around the former empire looking to attract the patronage of hungry tourists who may not know the difference in name anyway. (Ironically, there seems to be a perception, at least among the Americans I've spoken with, that "high tea" is somehow considerably fancier than a mere "afternoon tea.")

When Kathryn, an American academic, was visiting India for an extended research visit, she mostly ate at university canteens, which gave her a glimpse of afternoon tea within an institution. On the Mumbai campus where she lived, the meal was interchangeably called either "snacks and tea" or "afternoon tea" and very closely mirrored the British meal found in other colonies: hot tea accompanied by an assortment of cookies and cakes and sometimes small sandwiches or, often, savory local foods, like chaat (which can refer to any number of fried snacks, like potato or chickpea, often served with chutney and crisp unleavened bread). Kathryn says the meal was taken in the long break between lunch and a late dinner, as in the colonial period. And while tea drinking is common throughout India—in the morning and of course at afternoon tea—it is not ubiquitous: there are no tea or coffee stands or shops on campus, for example, as there are all over Europe or America, where you can get a quick drink between classes.[18]

As the postcolonial reckoning continues in India, examining the adoption of British-imported customs, afternoon tea has come under some criticism. Journalist Vir Sanghvi is "a bit of an agnostic" on afternoon tea's place in modern-day India. "I find it very difficult to get excited by a ritual that is so steeped in the British class system," he says, "and is—if you do it properly—so rigorously restricted in its specifications. Life is too short to cut the crusts off slices of bread (actually, life is too short to eat English white bread). Scones are possibly the most over-rated bakery item ever. And there are only so many cucumber or smoked salmon sandwiches you can reasonably eat without throwing up."[19]

Despite his misgivings, Sanghvi still has definite ideas about what the meal should be. There are only two forms of afternoon tea that are acceptable to his mind: One mirrors the traditional English meal—perhaps sweet and savory pastries served at a European diplomat's garden party, although presumably less exclusive gatherings would receive his blessing. The other form of properly taking afternoon tea, he says, is to fully embrace the Indian version of the meal.

Extended workdays and shifting priorities mean that many Indian families no longer have afternoon tea together at home. Several decades ago, when it was much more common, Sanghvi recollects, afternoon tea was a casual snack more akin to the daily British meal in most households than to the rigorously structured restaurant experience. The array often included pakoras—called Khopoli bhajias when he was a child, after the village that was a popular teatime stop on the Bombay–Poona road.[20] These savory fritters were made from chilies, potatoes, or sliced onions. Samosas stuffed with peas and French beans, batata vadas (mashed potato fritters served with cilantro chutney), and masala poori (spiced fried chickpea balls) were often served in Gujarat, where deep-fried snacks are popular. Some households served puri, an unleavened, crisped bread, topped with potato and chutney to make chaat, among other savory dishes.[21]

Restaurants in India, however, are much more likely to serve British-style afternoon tea dishes, like finger sandwiches. The meal remains a popular and enduring tradition in India, despite its contentious colonial past, even if it is not always taken in the home with family. To many Indians, teatime is considered so central to national food culture today that its Britishness is tossed aside and the meal is embraced as a tradition independent of its colonial roots. "Afternoon tea is a great institution," Sanghvi says, "but its true greatness lies in its Indianness. So, hold the cucumber sandwiches and throw away the scones. Bring on the batata vadas and the onion bhajias!"[22]

The legacy of British colonialism is cut into the Indian landscape and still shapes its economy. In Darjeeling alone, there are eighty-six operational tea gardens, which serve food and drink and often offer tours of the plantation fields, as well as roughly 160 tea gardens in North Bengal.[23] Afternoon tea is still popular nationwide, and while it draws rightful criticism as a colonial relic, its past seems less of a pressing concern to some than the legacy of tea itself. Working conditions on plantations, though improved from what they were under colonial rule, are not optimal, and the postcolonial tea garden is set up to give foreign tourists the experience of the white landowner rather than an opportunity to interact deeply with the people who live and work in the area.

THE UNITED STATES

America won independence before any other British colony, which gives it considerably more distance from English culture than more recently independent nations. Even so, tea has long been a popular beverage in the United States, even if coffee has become the caffeinated beverage of choice.[24] After the Revolutionary War, the United States managed to outmaneuver Britain to import its own tea directly from China,[25] at which point Americans continued to consume tea for the next century—though not at the rate the English did.

Scottish botanist Robert Fortune smuggled tea-producing secrets and plants from China not only for the East India Company, as we've already seen, but also for the United States, making his fourth journey into the country in 1858. He successfully brought back seedlings, but the plot in which he was to raise them was never used for that purpose. Changes in Department of Agriculture and Patent Office leadership meant that there was insufficient support for Fortune's work developing a program that would make tea an agricultural product stateside. Instead, many of the plants he'd brought back were sent by congressmen to their constituents in warm Southern climates, prior to the outbreak of the Civil War, which stopped American tea production before it had even started.[26] During Reconstruction, the Department of Agriculture tried once again to cultivate tea, building an experimental tea plantation in Summerville, South Carolina. But before long funding was cut, and the plants were eventually abandoned. In the 1950s, the Lipton Company[27] became interested in growing tea in America and took cuttings from Summerville to what is today the Charleston Tea Plantation.

American and British tea cultures experienced a considerable amount of overlap in the twentieth century: tea rose in popularity in both countries thanks to temperance, women's suffrage, and a growing number of tearooms as the century opened. While tea continued to be popular in Britain between the two world wars, in America it had come to be considered old-fashioned. By the second half of the century, tea consumption declined in both countries. Its popularity eventually grew again, at which point it became more common for Americans to drink iced tea.[28]

Americans' taste for hotel teas waxed and waned with the beverage's overall popularity.[29] Setting tea tables and having tea as a beverage, sometimes even with snacks, is mentioned in earlier records[30] but is not called afternoon tea until around the turn of the twentieth century. During this time, afternoon tea in restaurants seems to have been relatively common, appearing in a number of restaurant menus: one American-run restaurant that opened in

Paris to serve familiar food to American tourists initially only served afternoon tea before expanding their menu to include other meals.[31] Afternoon tea become so popular that in order to meet demand, New York's storied Waldorf-Astoria hotel extended its afternoon tea service, moving it from the Waldorf Garden into the Empire Room from 4:00 to 6:00 p.m.[32]

Afternoon tea, to many restaurants, referred to the light snack, but in American homes it often meant a cup of tea and socializing, perhaps with a snack, earlier in the day. According to Christine Terhune Herrick, author and housekeeping maven, American dinnertimes of the era tended to fall around 6:00 p.m., so the more substantial offerings of a high tea weren't as practical as pausing between lunch and dinner to take a hot cup of tea with some bread and butter and conversation. Herrick suggested that, in addition to afternoon tea, households stop for a brief half hour or so before dinner for 5:00 tea—a simple cup of tea and conversation, never served with food.[33]

When afternoon tea was served in American homes, the emphasis was on the beverage and rarely the food. Herrick declared dainty sliced bread and butter sufficient for most gatherings. Making a proper pot of tea was an essential skill to acquire before marriage, and many etiquette books stress the importance of setting a proper tea table.[34] Homemaking manuals published in the early twentieth century suggest setting the kind of simple table that would have been seen in the nineteenth century[35] and are similarly full of the proper decorum and ceremony that surrounded a proper afternoon tea.

Hosting an afternoon tea had its advantages for the middle-class American homemaker, as it was "the best method of entertaining guests on a larger scale, and with a minimum of expense," according to Herrick's 1915 manual on housekeeping. A tea was certainly less formidable logistically than a full dinner party and provided an opportunity to create an inviting and informal atmosphere for guests.[36] Herrick's advice on informal entertaining arrived at a critical juncture in American entertaining, just as the national relationship to afternoon tea was changing.

While one-quarter of all urban and suburban households employed domestic labor in the 1880s, this number dropped considerably prior to World War I and fell even further afterward. Faced with limited help at home, hosts were forced to simplify their entertaining, and afternoon tea fit the bill, offering a chance to gather informally at home among friends and catch up.

Gradually, afternoon tea in American society gave way to the cocktail party over the course of the 1920s, and by 1930 it was something of a rarity.[37]

Linda lives in the American South and can speak to the differences between American social-dining preferences and English, and to the preference for cocktail breaks over tea breaks, which remain a popular social activity in America to the present day. According to Linda, Americans are "more focused on getting a drink after work or on cocktails and appetizers to meet that hungry afternoon moment."[38] In her mind, American nine-to-five work culture does not allow for afternoon breaks—or, often, any breaks at all—which makes wedging afternoon tea into the middle of the work day unrealistic in a country where it is not already a national habit.[39] But Linda's comments suggest an important point: whether afternoon tea, cocktail hour, or something else altogether, a social gathering formed around a snack meal seems to exist in some form around the world.

Over time, home teas in America shifted in importance and style, but in the early twentieth century taking afternoon tea in a restaurant was still a popular pastime. One annotated menu from a Schrafft's in Manhattan offers a glimpse at how a restaurant catered to a wealthier clientele in 1929. Most of the dishes on the menu are small and purchased à la carte, costing between fifty and eighty-five cents—roughly the price of an entire meal in a humbler establishment. Included are the usual tea sandwiches and arrangement of desserts, as well as savory pastry (cold shrimp with tomato mayonnaise in a puff pastry shell, for example), a hot club sandwich, and creamed potatoes with lima beans. At first glance, the range of dishes appear heartier than the standard fare, but the annotations tell a different story: the creamed potatoes and lima beans, for example, are each portioned out in a single spoonful (of unknown size, but presumably a standard serving spoon). Compared to modern afternoon tea services, which usually provide a preselected array of delicacies, the Schrafft's menu is much more versatile, allowing each patron to select her own dish.[40]

Tea's popularity in twentieth-century America was fueled by the popularization of the automobile, the temperance movement, and, not least of all, women's suffrage. Perhaps because of its long-standing symbolism as a drink enjoyed with company, tea became a reliable stand-in for alcohol and was served at many temperance meetings. It also came to represent, albeit tangentially, women's financial freedom: many states would not allow women to own a restaurant until later in the century, whereas opening a "tearoom" gave women the opportunity to open and run businesses without raising the hackles of local government. These women-run spaces employed women and often were aimed at serving women customers. While tearooms are not strictly focused on serving tea alone—or even afternoon tea—their popularity at this period in American history is worth noting, as their existence in the public sphere and afternoon tea's development in the private sphere overlap conceptually.

Afternoon tea had long been a largely women-oriented gathering, which made it a safe space for women to be in community with each other in an era when such spaces were in short supply. In these private settings, women were often able to talk about the concerns and joys that shaped their worlds out of the hearing of male household members. And so, because afternoon tea developed in the private sphere, it allowed women to exercise some modicum of power and agency at a time when much of the rest of their world was heavily shaped by external forces.

Until well into the first decades of the twentieth century, the public sphere was considered the domain of men, both in Europe and in America, which meant "respectable" women rarely went out in public unescorted.[41] The tearoom, a public establishment run by women and catering to women, sat at the crossroads of the public and private worlds.[42] At the turn of the century, public eateries were still very male-oriented spaces, and women who were traveling often found it difficult to be served in most restaurants without a male escort (father, husband, or brother). Famed etiquette expert Emily Post recorded one instance in which she and a friend were denied seating at a restaurant in Omaha because they were unaccompanied by a man.[43] Tearooms were a rare exception and became a haven of sorts where women could expect to feel welcomed and to be served a meal.[44]

Tearoom proprietors gave other women an example of women business owners to look up to. In 1938, Virginia McDonald of Gallatin, Missouri, opened a tearoom, and her successful business inspired many women in other towns to do the same.[45] As the popularity of tearooms grew, businesses like the Lewis Hotel School's Tea Room Institute began to offer training for new restaurant owners.[46]

Tearooms offered another kind of freedom as well: Well into the 1960s, racial discrimination and legalized segregation in the United States made many public-dining spaces off-limits to African Americans. While tearooms felt welcoming for single women travelers, white-run tearooms served white patrons, and the welcome would not have felt as warm—if it existed at all—for women of color. But an African American–run tearoom could offer a welcoming space free of the discrimination that existed in other spaces, where patrons could enter and know they would not be turned away due to the color of their skin. Black-owned tearooms also hosted social events that included dances and community meetings, graduations, and live entertainment. In the 1920s and 1930s in particular, they became a community fixture, offering community activities and a gathering space in a way that white tearooms would not.[47]

American tearooms prior to the twentieth century were often hosted in private homes: a homemaker would put a sign in her window with a price for a meal and would welcome travelers—most often on weekends. Tearooms in rural areas were often rustic, without electricity and sometimes without running water or heat outside a central fireplace even after these utilities were available in cities. Many tearoom owners worked to update amenities when they were able, in part because publications of the time pointed to their correlation with a tearoom's success. By the dawn of the twentieth century, the tearoom became a stand-alone dining establishment or perhaps an addition on an inn or other structure, offering simple homemade meals.[48]

Midcentury tearooms opening in the United States were much more popular than their British counterparts. Unlike British tearooms, which served the hot tea and scones we still associate with afternoon tea, American tearooms were likely to serve iced tea and chicken salad. In an effort to speed up table service, American tearooms made tea balls in advance by wrapping small pieces of cheesecloth around the loose tea rather than letting it steep freely in the pot, which took time to clean. British travelers remarked on the poor quality of American tea made in this way; yet the tradition continued.[49]

British and American legislation made it increasingly expensive to run a tea shop in either country; as a result, tea culture nearly vanished from both between 1960 and 1990. During this time, the only tea a typical American would drink would be orange pekoe, a medium-grade black tea, served in a tea bag for efficiency's sake.[50] American tearooms' focus on efficiency was at odds with tea quality, prompting *The Tea Lover's Treasury* author James

Norwood Pratt to declare the tea bag an unacceptable adulteration for the modern tea drinker. His book, published in 1982, introduced his American audience to varieties of teas and nuances of flavor, and demand began to grow for more types of tea and better quality.[51]

Other discussions of tea were happening concurrently, and it became clear that tea preferences in America varied geographically. In 1983, a woman from Portland, Oregon, wrote a letter to the editor at the *New York Times*, complaining about the poor quality of tea she was served in New York, made from a tea bag and a cup of water. She decried New Yorkers' lack of understanding of tea: that to be made well it must be made in a pot and that an assortment of flavors should be available. In response to her letter, the editor spoke of the American ethos surrounding tea, espoused by "Coffee Bigots"—those who thought drinking tea was somehow un-American and making it too much trouble. Though Coffee Bigots seemed to be less vocal, if not less numerous, coffee remained the preferred drink in the United States of the 1980s. The editor closed with an anecdote from a tea-drinking friend that perfectly summed up America's relationship with tea: "Once, after lunch in a nice midtown restaurant," the friend recollected, "I got my tea, in a nice china pot. I poured it, lemoned it, sugared it and sat back, content. After a few minutes, with my cup now half empty, a solicitous bus boy came over and refilled it. With coffee."[52]

Despite their predilection for coffee, Americans have developed their own tea-related traditions. They are distinct from the meal of afternoon tea but are related—distantly—to British tradition. For example, recipes for tea cakes, a type of soft cookie typically served with tea, sometimes appear in recipe books of both British and American origin and are recommended as parts of afternoon tea menus.[53] Long ago in the antebellum homes of the American South, tea cakes were served in white homes and were considered a sign of gentility. After the Civil War, Northerners began to call them "cookies," an adaptation of the Dutch word *koekje* (also called *kockie*), the term for such treats. To this day, the term "tea cake" is still used in many places in the American South.[54]

The company whose tea was thrown twice into the Boston Harbor still ships to the United States and makes a Boston Harbour tea blend said to be similar to the blend that was thrown overboard at the Tea Parties in 1773 and 1774. Davison Newman & Co. Ltd. is the modern incarnation of an old firm that started in 1650 in London. According to the company's records, it petitioned George III for money to make up the losses from the two riots in Boston, and George refused. Around the end of the eighteenth century, the price of tea had dropped; the company's records indicate that Lapsang souchong was going for about three shillings a pound and pekoe for four shillings and sixpence. The company was also one of the earlier shippers of chocolate and scotch whiskey to the United States and kept a large sugar plantation, which became its claim to fame.[55]

Today in the United States, afternoon tea is typically reserved for the occasional hotel restaurant, tea shop, or café, although it is still enjoyed in the homes of some immigrants from the United Kingdom and former colonies. As in British establishments, American shops offer a range of choices. Dr. Bombay's Underwater Tea Party in Atlanta, Georgia, for example, has several afternoon tea options, and its name and its charitable work in India speak to the interconnectedness of tea traditions worldwide. Dr. Bombay's menu uses terms that might seem out of place for a Briton but do not raise the eyebrows of its American clientele: high tea refers to the full spread of snacks on tiered trays, while cream tea is close to its southern English counterpart and consists of scones, jam, clotted cream, and a pot of tea. Two other offerings unique to the restaurant—the Caroline tea and the Ivan tea—fall somewhere between the full high tea service and the simple cream tea. Like many afternoon tea services operating today worldwide, the tea offerings at Dr. Bombay's go well beyond traditional black teas and encompass herbal and fruit tisanes, rooibos, green tea, and other offerings sourced from around the world.[56]

Also in Atlanta is Tipple and Rose Tea Parlor and Apothecary, which blends American food with the more traditional snack foods found in a British afternoon tea. Afternoon tea menus in the United States are sometimes regionally inspired or otherwise developed around a theme—other than American perceptions of customary British tea foods, of course. Tipple and Rose, for example, has a Southern high tea service that combines food from the American South with the style of service and serving sizes found in the British meal. They also offer themed teas, like a Queen of Hearts/Mad Hatter's brunch tea, as well as the range of small bites typically associated with afternoon tea. Tipple and Rose departs from British tradition, however, in serving its meal much earlier in the day[57]—one more example of how meal traditions are often adapted to need, circumstances, and interest.[58]

Americans' relationship to afternoon tea may be best summed up by John, a British American who has lived in both England and the United States for long periods of time: "As much as I love the country and its people, the issues around tea [in the United States] were a problem. In many places, I am served a cup or mug of hot or boiling water, with a nondescript tea bag that I am invited to dunk or steep myself. The one occasion where something out of the ordinary happened was when a waitress called Darlene served me tea in a proper teapot and provided some sandwiches with the crusts cut off. This was startling, and I tipped extremely well, even though it took an age to come. I discovered later that, because of my English accent, she had looked up afternoon tea online, run home, got her mom's teapot, ran back, and prepared a pretty damned good afternoon tea."[59]

KENYA

Kenya gained independence from the British Empire in the twentieth century, as did most other countries under discussion in this chapter. As in other colonies, the people of Kenya had already registered displeasure with British governance before World War II, but after the war, in the 1940s and through the 1960s, the political protests intensified: it began in 1942 when members from the Kikuyu, Embu, Meru, and Kamba tribes took a secret oath to resist British rule.[60] Africans were able to be elected to Kenya's Legislative Council for the first time in 1957, and the country won independence from British colonial rule in 1963.[61] However, many markers of Britain's presence remained, including some of the rituals surrounding food.

As in India, Kenya's landscape is marked by the cultivation of tea, which serves as a reminder of how colonial power and traditions endure. An estimated 350,000 families in Kenya are smallholders—or family-farm tea cultivators—licensed by the Kenya Tea Development Agency (KTDA). Worldwide, tea factories are less numerous than farms, as many small farms grow the tea that is then collected and processed in bulk by a few factories. In Kenya, the KTDA is mandated to collect tea from farmers dotting the countryside and to process it in centrally located factories.[62]

The preponderance of tea in Kenya—both produced and consumed—has made tea tourism an important part of the country's tourism industry, particularly for visitors wishing to learn how the beverage is produced. As in England, afternoon tea is available in shops and hotels throughout Kenya, although what literature there is on the topic indicates that these meal services are geared more toward tourists than locals.

The Kericho Tea Hotel is located in the town of the same name, which was established in the 1920s and named in honor of English tea planter John Kerich, a nod to Kenya's colonial past.[63] Kericho is located in the Kenyan highlands in the western part of the country, some six thousand feet above sea level, which is considered the center of tea growing in the region.

The Tea Hotel comprises a series of cottages and a central building, surrounded by acres of tea crops, and offers tea-curious tourists any number of activities—from garden and tea-factory tours to tea tastings and afternoon tea service. None of the hotel's several online listings specify what foods are offered at the tea or even the times it is served, which could be happenstance or perhaps reflect a rotating menu and flexible schedule.

The hotel and surrounding plantation are one of many examples worldwide of the intersection between colonial efforts supported by and benefiting private companies: the Tea Hotel was built in the 1950s by the Brooke Bond tea company as "a kind of colonial clubhouse for expat executives in Kenya."[64] Brooke Bond is omnipresent in Kericho and employs around twenty thousand pickers to work its fields—many of whom live on-site. Hotel visitors rarely interact with any locals but those employed as staff in the Tea Hotel or as field hands on the plantation.[65] The cost of a stay at the hotel would be out of reach for most Kenyans: while the country's economy has grown in recent years, wages are still low, and nearly half the population lives in poverty.[66] And so the hotel caters to wealthy visitors, offering updated amenities and fine dining.

This pampering is worth noting, as the hotel also offers tours of the surrounding tea fields, which are farmed for PG Tips, Brooke Bond's signature brand launched in the 1930s. During the tea-field excursions, guests haul the same heavy harvesting basket that field hands carry and, after a quick lesson, help pick the tea (just the top, tender tips of the plant). When they tire of the work, they are free to set down the basket and return to their country club–style lodgings and fine foods.[67]

Tea picking is backbreaking, monotonous labor; yet experienced pickers can sometimes pick their body weight in leaves each day. The field tour could be an excellent opportunity for visitors to learn about and engage in the hard work and unpleasant conditions required to produce many of the foods we take for granted. However, the one travel-writer account of this experience I've come across focuses on tea picking as a novel diversion among travel excursions.[68] As seems par for the course in tea plantation visits elsewhere, the Tea Hotel's field trip appears to be a brief "Live like a local!" experience absent the important conversation about the tea industry or about Kenyan history. We in the Western world are often willfully ignorant of our food's origins and the human cost of the inexpensive prices we pay. For example, an English couple enjoys afternoon tea at their kitchen table, sipping a cup of PG Tips—and nibbling on any number of other imports along with it. In so doing, they are privileged to briefly enjoy something from that country without ever having to fully engage with that food's impact.

Afternoon tea is commonly offered at hotels and farms around Kenya, and these are primarily marketed to tourists. Kiambethu Farm, founded in 1910 by A. B. McDonnell, was the first commercial tea grower in the country. It remains in the McDonnell family to this day and continues to produce tea. Kiambethu Farm also offers its guests tours of the grounds and fields, but there is no tea picking on offer, and the tour is followed by a three-course lunch.[69] The comparatively recent founding of the farm is a testament to how quickly an economy, and the land that supports it, can change: in less than one hundred years, tea has become one of the primary drivers of the Kenyan economy, and it is becoming a draw in its tourist industry as well.[70]

But tea isn't entirely about tourism in Kenya: many families take afternoon tea at home, and tea is consumed throughout the day—always served hot, no matter the weather. Like the British, Kenyans usually brew a strong pot of black tea that they dilute with milk and sugar. And also like the British, afternoon tea is usually served in midafternoon with a selection of pastries, ranging from savory honey scones with rosemary and goat cheese to puff pastry tarts filled with cherries to marmalade bread.[71] Afternoon tea can sometimes be an event for locals, such as the annual Fashion High Tea, held at Zen Garden in Nairobi and showcasing Kenyan fashion while raising funds for local charities.[72] As in America, Kenyans occasionally use "high tea" to describe a high-end afternoon tea.

In many offices across Kenya, midmorning and afternoon tea are often provided by employers and are a welcome and expected break in the workday. In most workplaces, "afternoon tea" simply refers to a cup of tea, usually without any sort of snack. However, that cup of tea has become so entrenched in Kenyan work culture that going without is not an option, as the Family Bank learned in 2017. As a cost-cutting measure, the bank's executives dropped the afternoon tea service, so enraging employees that news outlets across Kenya picked up the story.[73] The memo announcing the cancellation was called a "PR nightmare" by one journalist[74] and shared widely across social media, eliciting disapproval from many Kenyans. Recognizing its misstep, the bank quickly backtracked and urged its employees to contact management with alternative cost-saving suggestions.

AUSTRALIA

Clarke describes Australia as a "paradoxical land": a "modern, industrialized, and technologically advanced nation on a continent that is largely unpopulated."[75] Its nearly three million square miles of space are inhabited by only about twenty million people.[76] Australia's path to independence from Britain progressed during the first half of the twentieth century. Britain had divided the Australian continent into six colonies, and in 1901 the Crown permitted them to form a single self-governing federation. The Commonwealth of Australia became a dominion of the British Empire, and after the British parliament passed a statute preventing the empire from making laws for its dominions, ties between the Crown and the commonwealth were further severed. However, Australia did not claim complete independence until 1986, when the Australia Act explicitly ended any British role in Australian government.[77]

Although the two nations are two separate entities, legally speaking, British cultural traditions still permeate the former colony. Cookbooks from the colonial period, as well as Australian foodstuffs today, show a striking resemblance to British dishes, with puddings, sponge cakes, meat pies, and roasts all making frequent appearances. While some Australian dishes drew upon local ingredients, it seems that most cookbooks from the colonial period only used British cookery techniques, which were applied to imported goods (like white flour), foods introduced to Australia (like lamb), or some-times native ingredients (like kangaroo). In some cases, adapting British tastes to the hotter climate and new ingredients created hybrid foods (like carpetbag steak, which is stuffed with oysters).[78]

Afternoon tea is still consumed in Australia, and tea itself remains a beloved staple. The meal appears where you would expect—on the menus of hotel restaurants, as part of public programming for social and cultural-heritage organizations, and in private homes. Paula, who is from Australia, doesn't regularly take afternoon tea, but many of her family members and neighbors do. In her experience, afternoon tea is a social activity and a gendered one, which involves "inviting people—mainly women—to your home midafternoon. It's considered a time to catch up and chat and doesn't involve alcohol." The afternoon tea of Australia looks a lot like the British one, in both composition and timing: served midafternoon and usually con-sisting of tea and coffee plus sweet and savory pastries or sandwiches. Some hotels and high-end restaurants also offer high tea, which Paula says is "an event" and, as a result, "is usually expensive and only happens on a special occasion." Just as in parts of England and elsewhere, afternoon tea in Aus-tralia is conceptually separate from teatime: "If you are invited somewhere for afternoon tea, the invitation to stay for a meal is not implied."[79]

The effect of colonialism specifically on the Aboriginal community of Australia was pronounced: Indigenous foodways were disrupted by as-similation laws passed in the 1950s and 1960s (as discussed in chapter 2) that were enforced through education programs and legal pressure. Further legislation was also passed restricting Aboriginal land rights and, with this, their ability to use the land to grow, hunt for, and forage food. Hunting and gathering were replaced by grocery stores, and those with limited financial resources were expected to grocery shop using food-assistance benefits rather than grow or hunt for their own food. This change was most marked in more populous areas, and while hunting and fishing continue to be im-portant in rural areas today, access to these resources is still limited.[80]

Aboriginals were included in the culture of afternoon tea, but as the servants—not the diners, who, it was implicitly understood, were white Australians. Present-day afternoon tea, however, has been expanded to include Aboriginal communities and is often a hybrid of cultures: consider the afternoon tea hosted by the Aboriginal Health Centre or the tea held in observance of NAIDOC Week.[81]

Today Australia is coming to terms with the damage done to the Aboriginal community by the assimilation laws. Some public schools serving communities with large Aboriginal populations intentionally create spaces for indigenous students to explore their heritage. In one classroom, students worked on independent projects focusing on a range of subjects from indigenous history, including foodways. These projects show a hybrid of Westernized and indigenous cultures. One child studying indigenous food made an afternoon tea for fellow students, using the timing and format of the English meal but serving traditional foods like kangaroo. The student intentionally patterned the tea on the work of the Yaama Dhiyaan Training Centre, a hospitality-training school for the indigenous community, whose owner, Aunty Beryl, of the Gamilaraay nation, uses modern kitchen appliances to create traditional Aboriginal dishes.[82]

MALTA

Malta gained independence from Britain on September 21, 1964, and has continued to operate as a sovereign political power since then, becoming a republic in 1974 and joining the European Union in 2004. In contrast to the United States, Malta's culture still centrally situates British cultural traditions within its own.

Afternoon tea is a fixture in many Maltese hotels. The menus bear a striking resemblance to their British counterparts: smoked Scottish salmon, smoked ham with mustard, raisin scones, and sweets dominate the menu served at the Hilton, Saint Julian's, for example.[83] One author of a travel blog posted photos of the Hilton's service, including the requisite tiered trays, stacks of sweets, and cups of tea that could be found in any number of hotel restaurant high teas around the world.[84] The author lives part time in Malta and part time in the United Kingdom but only writes about her afternoon tea experiences at upscale hotels. It seems that hotel restaurants in Malta stick to standard British fare, though Maltese pastries are served at some local shops offering afternoon tea. Elia Café in Hamrun,[85] for example, serves sinizza (a sponge cake decorated with chocolate, fruit, jam, liquor, and nuts, all encased in puff pastry) as well as qaghaq ta' l-ghasel (honey-filled pastry rings with citrus and spices).[86]

One journalist visiting the country in 2013 noted that while Maltese culture seemed slightly less British with each of his return visits, British influence was still evident in both the language and the cultural traditions—including the horse races that feature the very British interlude for cucumber sandwiches and tea.[87] This trend notwithstanding, the Malta Historical Society, which was founded in 1950 to document and share the history of the country, chose to host an afternoon tea to mark its sixtieth anniversary.[88] The use of a meal tradition imported by colonists is significant, as it shows how deeply British and Maltese cultures have become intertwined and how important afternoon tea has become to the Maltese people. In another instance, the 2016 World Summit on Arts and Culture included an hour-long afternoon tea break as a part of the conference activities.[89]

SOUTH AFRICA

Not long after the Boer Wars, in 1910, the British united the former Boer Republics with British South Africa to create an independent dominion that was self-governing but still technically controlled by Britain. Upon union, a number of harsh laws were passed targeting the black population, who were—and remain today—the vast majority in South Africa. Parliament passed legislation denying blacks the right to vote, and in 1913 the Natives Land Act prohibited the buying and selling of land between races, which meant that white people, who comprised only 20 percent of the population, owned 90 percent of South African land. But even white South Africa chafed under any remaining vestiges of British rule, and in 1960 a majority of white South Africans voted in referendum to leave the British Commonwealth and establish an independent republic.[90]

The country declared its independence during apartheid, an era spanning the second half of the twentieth century in which increasingly draconian legal measures were put in place to deny black South Africans legal and human rights. Attempting to pressure South Africa to end apartheid, the United Nations placed an arms embargo on the country in the 1970s and suspended their membership. Apartheid was finally repealed in 1994, but this turbulent period of the country's history, and the violence that black South Africans suffered at the hands of descendants of Dutch and English colonists, is all recent memory.

This discrimination continues to color South Africa's economic and cultural landscape to this day. For example, researching afternoon tea in South Africa mostly uncovers the experiences of white South Africans or else showcases venues like hotel restaurants accessible to only the middle to upper classes, and afternoon tea breaks are often still taken in universities, whose students are also primarily middle- and upper-class.[91] That said, some sources do discuss afternoon tea within the black South African community, framing it as a colonial cultural marker adopted as a status symbol and a way to identify more closely with those in power.[92]

As in much of the postcolonial world, afternoon tea in South Africa is enjoyed in private homes as well as hotels, restaurants, and cafés. Rooibos tea is very popular there and makes a regular appearance on menus and in kitchen cupboards, but many South Africans also drink more traditional black or Earl Grey teas.[93] Simple fare of tea and sandwiches or cake are de rigueur for home teas, just as they are in Britain and countless other places. And the meal serves the same purpose in South Africa as it elsewhere did in its earliest incarnations—a chance to gather together for a break and socialize before getting on with the rest of the day.

Author Jodi-Anne Williams-Rogers recalls afternoon tea with her cousin and grandparents in Eshowe: Her grandfather would pour his tea from his teacup into the saucer before drinking it—a colonial custom brought over by the English meant to cool the tea faster. Though in early modern English tea consumption it was customary to take saucer or dish of tea, eventually it was considered gauche in English custom to not use a teacup.[94]

Postcolonialism and postapartheid, South Africans continue to experience staggering disparities in wealth, and while there is a small and growing black elite, it seems that many of those with money, power, and property are white, while most black South Africans live in poverty. While simple afternoon tea in homes may be more accessible, and thus more universal, afternoon tea in cafés and hotel restaurants remains financially out of reach for many South Africans, reserved for white elites and for tourists.[95]

Afternoon tea in hotels in South Africa, like elsewhere, are all about luxury and ambiance. The Belmond Mount Nelson Hotel in Cape Town serves different teas throughout the day that reflect both British and local influences. Their morning tea consists of a simple beverage and breakfast-pastry option, whereas their afternoon tea includes savory snacks, like finger sandwiches, brought out on a tiered stand, as well as freshly baked scones and preserves. At their high tea, not everything is brought to the table; instead, the scones and savory foods are served individually, while the sweets are located separately on a buffet table, which might offer petits fours as well as local desserts like melktert (a milk tart) and koeksisters. The Belmond also has an evening tea service, but table service with bread and cheese replace the dessert buffet, making it something of a high-class—and high-priced—throwback to the high tea of old.[96]

The Belmond's tea service is more traditionally British in its offerings than are many hotel teas, in that the meals served mirror elevenses, afternoon tea, and high tea in their original forms (save for the dessert buffet). This is particularly interesting, as the Belmond company is an international hotel chain, with roughly fifty properties dotted across the planet. This includes several UK hotels as well as hotels in the Caribbean, Asia, and the Americas. However, its meal offerings are tailored to the clientele in each space, which suggests the importance of afternoon tea to travelers in South Africa—and perhaps to some South African locals looking to dine out.

Maybe ten kilometers down the coast from the Belmond Mount Nelson is 12 Apostles Hotel and Spa, part of the Red Carnation Hotel Collection, which has properties around the world, including in the United Kingdom and South Africa. This international chain was founded in South Africa in 1954 and later expanded after the founders relocated to the United Kingdom in 1975.[97] The Belmond hotel chain, by contrast, opened its first location in Venice, Italy, and is considerably larger than the Red Carnation chain. (It is important to note that Belmond does not have direct ties to South African or British cultural traditions as a part of its foundational framework.) The Belmond's offerings are location-specific, meaning it does not have one overarching company cultural identity (e.g., British or South African) that it tries to evoke in each of its properties. Instead, each Belmond hotel is tailored around local tastes and visitor demands. The Red Carnation hotels also tailor their offerings but still bring some version of the same meals—particularly afternoon tea—to visitors in each place, thus more explicitly highlighting the chain's cultural background.[98]

According to chefs at some of these hotel restaurants, afternoon tea is particularly popular with South African women, who prefer it to luncheon for their get-togethers, especially on the weekends.[99] Most afternoon teas in South Africa include a table service of tea and a tiered tray of snacks rather than a buffet; the Belmond is one of few including the buffet option. Afternoon tea, as it's usually called—although some do say "high tea"—may be served in small restaurants or occasional historic houses or museums, though usually it appears to be offered in higher-end hotels and restaurants, even more so than in the United Kingdom.

HOTEL TEA SERVICE

Afternoon tea service has become popular in hotels as an added service and luxury product, as well as an additional income stream. Afternoon tea fills the dining room in between the lunch and dinner rushes, and many of the foods can be either made ahead (such as pastries) or made per order with minimal equipment (such as finger sandwiches), which reduces interruptions to the workflow of tearing down and setting up between the more resource-intensive meals.

Some hotels build their reputations on offering a world-class afternoon tea service and as a result become pivotal in introducing the meal to new diners and helping others become reacquainted (or, for those who take the meal in the home regularly, helping them enjoy a more formal experience). The Fairmont Empress in Victoria, for example, serves between 110,000 and 115,000 afternoon tea meals each year.

When many travelers (and indeed some locals) in former colonies think of afternoon tea or high tea, it evokes scenes of hotel restaurants: three-tiered trays, ceramic teapots, white linens, and sometimes-stuffy decor accompanying bland finger sandwiches and a range of sweets in an experience billed as "traditional" or "luxurious." The tea service of international hotel chains offers a valuable window in to the role afternoon tea plays in each of the cultures where it is served, but always with an overarching theme of elegance and a return to tradition.

The 12 Apostles' afternoon tea service in Cape Town, South Africa, is given a bare-bones description on the website, compared to the pages of space dedicated to the Belmond's Mount Nelson hotel, which was discussed earlier. The 12 Apostles simply advertises "tea by the sea" with a few desserts and finger sandwiches and all-you-can-drink tea and coffee. Unlike afternoon tea in Britain, it is served from 10:00 a.m. to 4:00 p.m., creating a longer window of time to consume the meal than in most other places.

Other hotel locations have tailored afternoon tea to fit their clientele. Red Carnation Hotel Collection is the 12 Apostles' parent company, with locations worldwide. Its Palm Beach, Florida, location has a more formal afternoon tea service than "tea by the sea," which is also served at hours that are in keeping with the British meal (1:00–5:00 p.m.) and suggests a clientele that is either accustomed to the British-style of afternoon tea service or seeking a traditional British restaurant experience. Red Carnation's other hotels also offer afternoon tea, the descriptions of which vary wildly—the Geneva, Switzerland, hotel lists the ingredients in each of the finger sandwiches, for example, whereas other locations rarely list the included foods—but each one besides the meal at the 12 Apostles is billed as a traditional afternoon tea. However, the hours for each also vary—the Switzerland tea, for example, is served from 3:00 to 6:00 p.m.—presumably in response to the local pace of life and mealtimes and to demand (one would assume that afternoon tea is not as sought-after in Switzerland, where it was never a staple meal to begin with).

Not surprisingly, given the cultural variation in its different property locations, afternoon tea is not a staple at every Belmond hotel.[100] However, the places where afternoon tea is offered speak to the interests of clientele. For example, the Belmond chain's American locations offer afternoon tea, perhaps in an effort to market themselves as upscale, but many other locations either do not offer the service or do not market it on their websites.

The Belmond location in Oxfordshire offers breakfast, lunch, and dinner services but not afternoon tea, an omission that speaks to the role of afternoon tea within UK culture. While the restaurant's influence is French, the commentary about national meals goes deeper in this instance: Dining options at Belmond Le Manoir aux Quat'Saisons include a high-end restaurant attached to a cooking school for guests. This emphasis on fine dining in tandem with experiential learning asks the guest to be both more formal and more active than your average hotel dining experience. Afternoon tea, by contrast, is a meal characterized by casual gathering, conversation, and an opportunity to take a break from the day and relax rather than actively engage in a task. Not only is it a meal that takes little preparation but, perhaps most critically, the location's emphasis on French experience also underscores the Englishness of afternoon tea—so much so, in fact, that afternoon tea would have no place being served in a restaurant influenced by continental Europe.

How the hotels market their teas is also important, reflecting the history and cultural context of the chain: Red Carnation hotels, for example, always refer to their tea services as afternoon tea, showing the company's understanding of the difference between afternoon tea and high tea, but also perhaps creating some distance between the traditionally working-class meal of high tea and the experience the company wishes to give its clientele.

ELSEWHERE IN THE FORMER COLONIES

Afternoon tea is a regular institution across many of the British Empire's former colonies, and in the case of colonies like America, it is present (if not ubiquitous). In New Zealand, as with Australia, afternoon tea is a regular occurrence but "not religiously adhered to." Grant, an American who took part in afternoon tea traditions there for many years, spoke to the casual nature of afternoon tea in Kiwi homes. Afternoon tea was for him, and for many who enjoy the meal, something that was never overly structured. Instead of adhering to a strict mealtime or requiring a lot of preparation, the meal would naturally occur as the day unfolded and one felt called to sit down to it. He described the decision to have tea as "just a feeling as the afternoon drags on, or the occasion speaks to it" (e.g., just getting home after doing some shopping, you put on the kettle). This usually took place around 2:00–4:30 p.m. and would involve a simple pot of English tea (English Breakfast, Earl Grey, etc.) and a cookie or another small sweet.[101] In this way, New Zealand afternoon tea taken in the home is very similar to the modern English afternoon tea and, as elsewhere, is distinct from taking evening tea or having teatime.

As we will see in chapter 4 with John's experience, Grant's experience speaks to an almost universal adoption of tea among New Zealanders, whereas Paula's experience in Australia speaks to a gendered component in the adoption of tea. Kathryn's visit to India also shows the universality of the afternoon tea meal in that country, as do other stories elsewhere. It seems to be the case that many people regularly consume the meal, either as a private break within the home (with family or alone) or in a public setting (e.g., restaurant or hotel), and that this experience happens regardless of gender. Where the meal has a gendered component seems to be in its use as an occasion for a social gathering within one's home: just as with its inception, afternoon tea gatherings offer a space for women to connect and converse in a casual and intimate setting, and while the social conventions surrounding women in public and private spaces have changed considerably since the meal's introduction, it still does not seem to be as widely consumed by men.

Afternoon tea's preparations are as varied as the countries in which it's consumed. In parts of Canada that used to be under British rule, the afternoon tea tradition was popularized in the second half of the nineteenth century—not terribly long after its popularization in England. This is in keeping with its adoption in other colonies, which shows the quickness with which a food tradition can spread. This heritage is reflected today in afternoon tea's inclusion in tourist packages in Victoria, British Columbia. As elsewhere, many hotels in former British Canada serve a high-end version of the meal, which is popular with visitors and some locals.

Some chefs and restaurants worldwide have created a fusion afternoon tea, which combines the structure of the traditional meal with food and beverage from former colonies. In London, one Nigerian chef has hosted a series of meals with Nigerian food, including an afternoon tea: a 2016 event hosted by Lerato Umah-Shaylor included akara tarts, which she based on West African bean fritters; prawn suya rolls, described as an African version of the British summer rolls; and Lagos Angus pie, based on the meat pies that are ubiquitous in Nigerian homes. Scones were replaced with honey-butter rolls with strawberry and tomato jam, and sweets included a plantain and raspberry chocolate bark made with cacao from Ghana, as well as a mango mousse. The tea served at the event was all sourced from Africa and was accompanied by hibiscus lemonade and champagne.[102] Umah-Shaylor's interpretation of afternoon tea shows the interplay between colonizer and colonized: many of the foods are Nigerian-focused interpretations of traditional dishes, but the meat pies are a crossover dish between the two and hint at the British working-class origins of the UK iteration of that dish. Other venues' nontraditional takes on the traditional meal's component parts include replacing tea with whiskey and having dim sum as an accompanying food.

In India, the afternoon tea served with Indian snacks might not be best described as "fusion," as the blending of Indian and English cultures happened over centuries, but its resultant afternoon tea menus do speak to the cultural overlap that took place. The same is true of the Maltese or South African specialties offered during the meal service: each of these afternoon teas speaks to the host's own culture but uses the traditional structure and timing of a meal that was imported from elsewhere.[103]

Though Wales is a part of Great Britain, there is one story of a Welsh supper that for me sums up the purpose of afternoon tea in the commonwealth and former colonies. In the Evans household in Wales, eating is as much about gathering together as a family as it is about the food. Author Annie Levy writes about the Evans family's kitchen and their process of making the meal, and for me it touched on two important points I've found across the research I've done for this book. First of all, "tea" is a contentious term, and even differentiating "afternoon tea" from "tea" is not always the same thing to all people (in this case, the "tea" Levy describes in the Evans household refers to the evening meal).[104]

But second, and most important, "tea" for many people I've talked with is a term that embodies a state of mind as much as it embodies whatever form of eating and drinking the term might evoke. Afternoon tea was initially created as a light snack to tide people over until their evening meal, eventually coming to refer to the evening meal as well. However, both emphasize a slowing down and coming together over food and drink. The very essence of afternoon tea is taking time out of the day to do something relaxing, either to connect with others at the table or to take a moment to connect with oneself. This idea translates to the dinner table as well: for all the folks I interviewed, tea—as dinner—was a chance to gather with others, or at least a chance to slow down long enough to eat even a quick meal.

As an American, I'm accustomed to a world where it's not terribly uncommon for my peers (and me) to shovel a quick meal down while running (figuratively and sometimes literally) to the next place. Carving out intentional time each day to sit quietly alone with a snack and my thoughts, or to catch up with friends, is something that, to my American mind, sounds luxurious. But it also sounds doable. One of the greatest things I learned from researching this book is the mindset of afternoon tea and the value of carving out that small intentional space to slow down and enjoy.

THE LEGACY OF THE BRITISH EMPIRE AND AFTERNOON TEA

Postcolonial Great Britain, like the governments and peoples of its myriad former colonies, continues to grapple with colonialism's history and impact and the many ripple effects that have continued through to the present day.[105] Its presence is felt in our modern-day trade agreements, determining who labors for little and lives poorly so others may cheaply purchase goods, and in the presence, absence, or transformation of food traditions imported by colonial powers.

Colonialism's impact is also felt in meals in Britain and abroad, and Brits continue to engage with how they, like those living in former colonies, wish to engage with the English colonial legacy. This includes confronting the more tangible outcomes of the colonial world—for example, learning about versus ignoring where goods are imported from on the global market-place[106]—as well as how we frame the legacy itself. Afternoon tea is typically not connected to colonialism by many Britons and is usually seen as a purely British tradition, without an explicit line being drawn between its presence in other countries and how it got there. I could find little that expressly considered its reach as the result of colonial aspirations.[107]

In 2014, Sotheby's auction house hosted an Indian afternoon tea. The opening paragraph of the announcement speaks to a vision of imperial Britain as the height of greatness and frames the meal as a chance to participate in a sparkling vision of the past: "The British colonial rule in India may have concluded sixty years ago, but the fading memories of the British Raj can be relived at Sotheby's Café through the Indian Afternoon Tea service." Just as Indian afternoon tea combines the structure of the meal with Indian foodstuffs, this tea hosted by Sotheby's offers traditional English foodstuffs (scones and finger sandwiches) and adds in flavors from Indian dishes (coriander, cardamom, and curry, for example). The menu was introduced as part of the Indian and Islamic Week at Sotheby's—which, as one might expect, culminated in auctions of art and artifacts from India and the Islamic World—offering "a menu that is appropriate enough to have been served by the turban-clad attendants of the Raj to their sahibs and memsahibs, as they sit under the sweltering heat of the Indian summer watching their children play a game of afternoon cricket."[108]

The legacy of the British Empire can still be felt in our global trade systems, as well as the economies of postcolonial countries, the distribution of global wealth, and more. It also appears in our individual and collective values about food traditions and beyond—value systems both within Britain and in the colonies that prioritized and valued British culture over any other and emphasized the importance of assimilating to that culture and minimizing indigenous culture in order to be accepted into colonial power structures. In a postcolonial world, afternoon tea is indirectly symbolic of that power: created in England during its rise to colonial dominance, fueled by exported tea created through the empire's reshaping of colonies like India and Kenya, and spread throughout the world, afternoon tea powerfully demonstrates how a meal tradition is part of a larger, interconnected whole and is just as much about the larger culture as it is about what is served and when.

Part of the discourse surrounding life in a postcolonial country is awareness of what elements of the culture have been colonized and how the country's residents remove, adapt, or otherwise engage with that colonial influence.[109] Afternoon tea in India is a good example of how this navigation process has taken place in relation to the meal and shows the tension between embracing and rejecting a tradition that has at this point become a cultural mainstay. Many people in India continue to consume the afternoon tea, but it seems that outside of hotel restaurants the tea does not contain many of the hallmark dishes that accompany the British version. Vir Sanghvi sums it up well in noting that afternoon tea's power in Indian culture is its inherent Indianness, not its colonial legacy.[110] In this instance, the meal is being both enthusiastically embraced (as a meal with specifically Indian cultural markers, such as certain dishes, as well as in the casual tone of the meal) and rejected (in its English iteration, which is regarded as overly formal and includes ingredients and dishes not present in locals' meals).

Food ties us to our colonial pasts by offering an extension of tradition while also helping us examine that past critically, choose which parts to accept, and determine which parts no longer serve us within our shifting culture, as done in Sanghvi's consideration of Indian afternoon tea. Food is a powerful part of this collective reevaluation in large part because it is so accessible to outsiders, so ubiquitous, and yet so emotional and personal. Thinking of colonialism through the lens of food affords us the opportunity to sit with those emotional and community ties to colonial tradition, view them, and gently begin to break and reshape them or, alternately, keep elements that have become a part of our cultural identities, even if they originated elsewhere.[111]

The role of afternoon tea in the postcolonial world is as varied as its earlier incarnations. The meal is at once a beloved, comforting pastime as well as a vestige of colonialism and its difficult legacy. All of this, of course, depends on which former colony you visit and who you ask while you're there. In contrast to Sanghvi's call to embrace afternoon tea precisely because of its Indianness, elsewhere the meal is used as an identity marker specifically for the vestiges of colonial culture.

The High Tea with Elephants website, for example, bills itself as "a vision inspired by the African safari industry,"[112] which is an industry largely tailored to luxury travel for wealthy clients. The site serves as a lifestyle brand for wealthy travelers to Africa that compiles information about travel experiences and destinations as well as consumer products. High tea's working-class origins notwithstanding, it is pointed that the teas are advertised as "high" teas, which the average tourist is likely to interpret as meaning a luxury enjoyed by elites.

High Tea with Elephants and other luxury African-travel outfits offer experiences where travelers go "back in time" to encounter a wild and romantic vision of Africa, but implicit within this time travel is the legacy of European colonialism on the continent and European perceptions of African landscapes, people, and cultures. Add-ons to luxury-safari tour packages, "like the 'bush breakfast' or 'sundowner cocktails,' hanker back to an age when there were servants to cater to one's whims. If you wanted your breakfast on top of a mountain, you could damn well have it, and someone would carry your breakfast things up there for you, right down to the last teapot, napkin and tablecloth. In a high-end game lodge, this spirit is still alive."[113] These outfits use their teas as a marker for this type of experience to create a direct link between that colonial past and the African present, particularly as it relates to how tourists choose to encounter the African countries they visit.

This—how tea is used to shape someone's experience of another culture—more than nearly any other modern incarnation of afternoon tea, shows the power that a meal, and the concept of that meal, can have. Afternoon tea for many modern people evokes images of tea trays laden with sweets, fine china and silverware, and a formal setting. Placed within the context of former English colonies, this upscale version of afternoon tea, which has become synonymous with tourism and special-occasion outings for locals, speaks to dynamics of exclusion. In order to participate in this afternoon tea ritual, one requires economic access to it (for example, most South African afternoon tea services run about 330 rand, or about $30 US), making afternoon tea in many postcolonial countries a meal that is present but not universal.[114] In former colonies, particularly those with high poverty rates,[115] the snack meal between meals is not practical for people who have to stretch food budgets and may only eat one or two meals per day. This means that even though the meal is often found outside the white linen tablecloths of hotel restaurants and safari resorts, it still is not ubiquitous.

The business decision to name itself High Tea with Elephants, as well as high-end hotels and restaurants intentionally calling their services "High Teas" (often capitalized), is also significant. When we look at the etymology of the names of different tea meals in Britain, we see that afternoon tea was originally an upper-class meal called "low tea," later becoming more common and known as "afternoon tea," whereas high tea was a more filling meal taken later in the day among the working classes, and tea was simply an evening meal, depending on where you are situated geographically.

In the twentieth century, the dainty snack-laden restaurant meal began to be known popularly as high tea in areas outside Britain, perhaps due in part to a relationship between the more hearty fare of the original working-class meal and the variety and abundance of snacks served at these restaurant meals that are often more meal than snack. However, many Britons, when taking their daily tea, still often refer to it as afternoon tea (or sometimes just "tea"). Naming one's company High Tea with Elephants—or, more generally, marketing a meal as a high tea—targets outsiders who are tourists in the country and possibly also wealthy locals.[116]

The staff at High Tea with Elephants offer recommendations for their favorite afternoon tea services at safari lodges, and the focus is in keeping with the modern conception by non-British tourists of afternoon tea as a higher-end meal consumed during luxury travel. Like the Belmond hotels, emphasis is placed just as much on setting and ambiance as it is on food and beverage. The site pushes for experiences that are "decadent" and "luxurious"—anything evoking a sumptuous, plush experience.[117]

Other tour companies in the former colonies are more explicit about their colonial past in their marketing and use it—and its relationship to the tea industry—as a selling point, including the Tea Hotel in Kenya as well as tourism companies in India.[118] Heritage North East is an Assam-based tourism outfit offering luxury, boutique travel. The company tailors its offerings around India's colonial legacy, with properties on golf courses and tea plantations that offer some of the tea-tourism packages also found in Kenya (like touring factories and fields), with accommodations on colonial-era properties with original furnishings.[119]

This company, at least, hopes to attract customers by creating an experience that recalls the colonial era. According to its sales material, "Heritage North East provides boutique heritage hospitality, where we offer a colonial lifestyle and a tea holiday. Here one may step back more than a 100 years to savour the pleasures of a colonial past and feel the ambience of colonial days while relaxing in the period furniture and décor."[120]

Like High Tea with Elephants and the Kenya Tea Hotel, this marketing material focuses on area residents only insofar as they are service staff or provide part of the scenic backdrop. One of the marketing videos promises, "While staying in the heart of the Tea Estate, one can see the colourful women pluckers as they chatter and sing while meticulously plucking the freshest two leaves-and-a-bud from the bushes." The narrator continues, "Don't you just love the colours, the hats and the sound of the leaves being plucked?"[121] The video is of women working in the field, and the focus on their hats and colorful clothes reduces them to mere scenery: they are landscape for the tourist, a natural component of the tea field, there to render the service of picking tea and provide an aesthetic experience for the visitor.[122]

Tea tourism is found in other postcolonial countries as well. In Sri Lanka, commercial cultivation of tea began in the 1870s.[123] Books about the colonies that were published during the nineteenth century created a narrative of exotic and peaceful people living comfortably in lush surroundings under the benevolent, guiding hand of imperialism. An 1893 advertisement for Henry Cave's *Picturesque Ceylon*, for example, is described as "a pictorial—not a literary—effort: My purpose is to enable the friends of European residents in Ceylon, and others who are interested in the Island, to obtain a better idea of its charming features than is possible from mere verbal description."[124] Cave's book includes illustrations of local residents as well as glowing depictions of some of the physical marks of colonialism on the landscape, including Victoria Park (styled after European, and particularly Victorian British, aesthetics for outdoor spaces) and the Ruwanwella tea estate. Today, Sri Lanka's Ruwanwella area offers tea tourism to Western tourists similar to what can be found on Indian and Kenyan tea plantations.[125]

Afternoon tea's continued popularity worldwide may in part be due to its recent revival in Britain after decades of declining interest in a meal that was considered old-fashioned. However, the last couple of decades have seen a renewed interest in tea and in reconnecting with cultural traditions that offer a space to pause and rest, which has prompted a renewed interest in the meal. At the very end of the twentieth century, afternoon tea made a comeback, and it is now wildly popular in restaurants and private homes.[126]

This has been true elsewhere in the former colonies as well: In the United States, for example, tea culture nearly vanished in much of the country, only to reemerge around the same time that it did in Britain;[127] now it is not uncommon to see afternoon tea offered in a range of places from upscale hotels to small local shops. In Australia, afternoon tea has enjoyed a similar revival, and an increasing range of meal options are on offer (such as tea cocktails and dim sum) in addition to the more traditional fare.[128]

4

THE PRESENT AND FUTURE OF AFTERNOON TEA IN MODERN GREAT BRITAIN

Afternoon tea occupies a space in the British cultural landscape where it is at times considered traditional and outmoded but at others central to food and identity, either as an occasional treat out or as a simple daily ritual. For example, it has been described as a meal that "represents an experience that is now entirely heritage, but it is a heritage much pursued and regarded with enthusiasm and affection."[1]

In this estimation, afternoon tea as a meal in, say, an upscale hotel is a performance of British tradition that appeals to the expression of British identity by Britons and the temporary participation in that expression by tourists. The meal is thus purported to be beloved but an artifact rather than a daily experience. However, most other authors—myself included—would disagree that afternoon tea has faded away from the British daily experience. Every British person I spoke with in researching this book, and nearly every resource I consulted in both popular and academic literature, spoke to a meal still firmly entrenched within the hearts and stomachs of the British populace. For example, John, a British American, considers it an important break to punctuate the day, which has as much to do with a desire to slow down for a bit as it does with anything else.[2]

The difference may be that the quote above only considers the luxury version of the meal and, in so doing, connects it to its Victorian leisure-class iteration rather than to its more diverse modern iterations.[3] In this sense, afternoon tea is indeed a marker of an earlier age, but the meal as it has transformed in the twenty-first century is alive and well. This chapter shows afternoon tea's abundant presence in the simple pot of tea taken with a small snack to punctuate an afternoon at home, the brief work break enjoyed by colleagues in an office, an after-school snack, and the formal high tea service familiar to tourists worldwide.

Perhaps it comes as no surprise that the most battles about how to properly serve afternoon tea are waged in the meal's birthplace. In modern Great Britain, there are as many ways to serve tea as there are stars in the sky, but most all prepare tea the British way (with cream and sugar), include a light snack, and, most of all, provide a break in the day to relax before finishing with work and chores.[4]

English tearooms, hotel restaurants, and other establishments serve afternoon tea with tiered cake stands and fine table linens, but, just like any other midrange or fine-dining restaurant experience, this kind of meal is an occasional treat. The perception of afternoon tea upon which the restaurant version is based comes from the meal as it existed in wealthy homes in the Victorian period and immediately after. This type of meal, with three-tiered trays, silver tea urns, ironed table linens, and fine china, is described in both contemporary literature and modern scholarship.[5] Experiences of more relaxed versions of the meal, and particularly those in middle-class homes, can be easier to find in literature and memoirs, ranging from brief mentions of teatime in *Peter Pan* to several extensive recollections of the meal in *Lark Rise to Candleford*.[6]

Afternoon tea as a meal (rather than a quick break for a cup of tea) fell out of favor in the second half of the twentieth century but reemerged as the century drew to a close, with afternoon tea service in London hotels growing in popularity in the last decade as a counter to the many quick-service coffeehouses that had taken over the city in previous years.[7] In the new millennium, afternoon tea has become incredibly popular. Just as in the early decades of the twentieth century, hotels and restaurants have jumped on the trend, and the meal service often spills over from dining rooms into lounges and communal areas, with diners willing to pay decent money for a small meal that is simple for kitchens to prepare and brings in money during the slow hours between lunch and dinner service.

Afternoon teas at hotel restaurants in Britain can be pricey, often ranging from twenty to fifty pounds, and in some cases going north of sixty.[8] In London, as in hotels around the former colonies, guests are paying just as much for the ambiance as they are for the food. Hotels make sure that the ambiance—whether cozy-but-refined in a historic building or with stark-white tablecloths in a sleek, modern dining room—is almost a theatrical experience, with everything carefully crafted to make a small-plate meal feel worthy of the price tag. Some hotels elevate the experience with classical piano or other live music playing gently in the background.[9]

Hotel food-and-beverage managers in Britain design menus that emphasize variety, both in the foods served and in the types of teas available. In some cases, tea sommeliers are on hand to develop the tea menu, which typically is chosen to include a range of teas from diverse geographic origins.[10] The meal has become so popular that it has created fierce competition between dining establishments looking to stand out from their peers. This has led to attention-grabbing themed teas, often by celebrity chefs, for holidays (Mother's Day and Valentine's Day are popular occasions) or major events (like Wimbledon or the Chelsea Flower Show). Special occasions like the Diamond Jubilee celebrations for Queen Elizabeth II, which took place throughout 2012, created even more demand as Britons headed out for fancy meals to mark the occasion.[11]

Afternoon tea in restaurants continues to have some regional variation. Cream tea, which includes a dish of thick, clotted cream along with jam and scones, can be found all around the country but originated in southwestern England, where the rich pastures gave milk the high fat content necessary to produce clotted cream. In this area, it is more common to find a cream tea than not, and there are debates between proponents of Devonshire cream (from the county of Devon) and Cornish cream (from the county of Cornwall) about which came first and which is better.[12]

Kataryna[13] is a London-based artist who regularly goes out to afternoon tea in the city. She spoke excitedly about the topic, talking with me as she was on her way to have afternoon tea at the Wolseley, a café-restaurant in Mayfair, one of the many afternoon tea services she has enjoyed. Her enthusiasm about the meal is infectious (her first piece of advice to me when I started this book was to "Make sure you know the difference between afternoon tea, cream tea, and high tea. There is nothing more important in the world!"), and she talked at length about the meal and the kinds of foods and drink she expects to see when she goes out:

> One of my personal favourite places is Browns. . . . They are the peak [of] both traditional and contemporary and also offer healthy and even savoury afternoon tea . . . and the *best* jam in the world. They won't tell me what is in it, but I keep asking. . . . Afternoon tea is served as four layers, three on a cake stand, finger sandwiches at the bottom, scones—two plain, two fruit in the middle—and small petits fours and sweet cakes on top. With a separate plate of a traditional sliced cake on the side, such as lemon drizzle/Victoria sponge, etc. The sandwiches must be the width of two fingers, white and brown, with crusts off. Buttered with a range of fillings, I'm a veggy so I usually have cheese and chutney, cream cheese and thin cucumber, or hummus and peppers.
>
> My husband usually has ham and cress, egg mayonnaise, beef and mustard, salmon and cream cheese—that sort of thing. Scones must be served with strawberry jam and clotted cream separately. The petits fours can be a whole range of things, but I like macaroons, tiny lemon posset[s], mini éclairs, mini coffee Battenberg, tiny shortbread biscuits, etc. A large selection of loose-leaf tea must be offered, but I usually choose English Breakfast, Earl Grey with or pure Kenyon, all with milk. I prefer the teapots, milk jugs, cutlery, and strainers to be silver and the crockery to be very fine China.[14]

As with other people I talked to,[15] the central theme of afternoon tea for Kataryna is to relax and enjoy conversation as well as the food and drink. For her, it is also a marker of identity and social graces: "A statement that you are going for afternoon tea demonstrates that you have class, taste, and quiet sophistication but that you are relaxed, less formal."

This restaurant version of the meal evokes a sense of luxury and leisure but is only one of the meal's current iterations. Since the twentieth century, afternoon tea has come to encompass a range of meanings, from a simple beverage break with a small snack taken at home to the full restaurant experience Kataryna enjoys. Afternoon tea was still very popular in the decades after Queen Victoria's death: By the 1920s, 60 percent of all world tea exports were consumed by the British.[16] In the 1930s, radio broadcasters had to carefully consider the tea break when scheduling programming so that programs of possible interest to housewives would not overlap with the meal or the subsequent washing up.[17]

Afternoon tea's popularity does not seem in question today, but from the postwar period until a mere twenty years ago it was in danger of fading away entirely—or, put another way, of devolving into a quick beverage break in lieu of anything that might resemble a meal. In 1958, one study found that afternoon tea could barely be considered a meal at all, as only half the respondents had any food to go with their tea (and even then would often only have cake or biscuits).[18] Even though it could scarcely be called a meal, this new pared-down break was still somewhat popular and, whether including food or not, was referred to as afternoon tea.[19] It fell out of popularity between the 1960s and 1990s in part because changes in regulations made it difficult to profitably operate a tearoom.[20] Britons' tastes were changing, too: Caterers often relied on self-service coffee bars rather than on serving tea in order to meet the changing tastes of the public. Many of the finest hotels still begrudgingly served afternoon tea, but it was rarely anything more exciting than a tea bag in a pot with an equally thrilling piece of prepackaged cake to go with it.[21]

The tea services in most places were uninspired, where they existed at all, but traditional afternoon tea was still regularly consumed in some areas, particularly the West Country, Scotland, and Yorkshire. In the 1970s, the National Trust began to offer traditional afternoon tea to visitors at many of its properties,[22] and this helped gently nudge the country toward a renewed interest in afternoon tea.[23] Afternoon tea and the tea beverage still were not popular in many shops from the midcentury through the 1990s (both in England and abroad),[24] and tea bags, rather than the more flavorful loose-leaf tea, accounted for the lion's share of tea sales.[25] Tea drinking seemed to be of less interest in the postwar world where efficiency and productivity were prized and where coffee, a grab-and-go, highly caffeinated drink, seemed more appropriate than its somewhat more leisurely cousin.[26]

This situation began to shift slowly in the 1980s and 1990s, as people began to look for ways to slow down in a fast-paced world. Tea "slowly reclaimed its unique role as a communal beverage,"[27] and the art of properly preparing loose tea was talked about in news stories and tea was once again made and enjoyed at home and in restaurants. Even the lowly and oft-maligned tea bag got a face-lift, as Americans popularized premium beverages thanks to Starbucks and other coffeehouses, and with this came a desire for quality but convenient lines of tea.[28] Companies that specialize in herbal infusions helped popularize tea by either offering blends with a specific purpose (a famous example would be Celestial Seasonings' Sleepytime blend) or flavor profile (like lemon) that provided options to those not interested in black or green teas. These herbal infusions, and the variety of choice they offer, are often found next to teas on many modern restaurant's afternoon tea menus.

As people began to embrace tea as a beverage once again, they also slowly began to return to afternoon tea as a meal. By the early 2000s, afternoon tea had become a booming business and has continued to grow since then as more shops offer a greater variety of options, from the traditional to the eclectic. Hotels and restaurants continue to compete to provide afternoon tea services that will draw customers, and patrons' high expectations are often met, thanks to many options.

Kataryna remarked upon the ever-growing suite of afternoon tea options:

> Here in the UK it has always been popular, but there has been a massive cultural explosion in it since the early 2000s, and it has overtaken from lunch and dinner in many places, so much so that places like Fortnum and Mason have now devoted whole refurbished floors to it and expanded to include little outlets. There is a big growing trend in London not only for afternoon tea but for unusual types—like, healthy versions, vegan, savory-only, themed ones, chocolate-afternoon teas, et cetera. Lots of places and restaurants are also cashing in on the resurgence in popularity, but the best is still in the old traditional hotels or proper tea houses. . . . Champagne afternoon tea is also now very popular, where you also get a glass of champagne before you start your afternoon tea.[29]

Kataryna pointed to the Mad Hatter Tea at the Sanderson hotel as one of the many thematic teas that have as much to do with ambiance and experience (and costuming) as with food and the drink itself. Mad Hatter–themed teas seem popular in tea shops, such as Sanderson's tea and the American version at Tipple and Rose, mentioned in chapter 3. The controlled chaos of the tea party in *Alice in Wonderland*[30] has made it one of the most well-known tea events in literature, and these themed teas offer equal parts escapism and whimsy.

Kataryna also noted afternoon tea feels like an affordable luxury. "I think there are very interesting parallels to be drawn with the resurgence and searching for national identity during the rejection of European instability and financial collapse," she says. "Afternoon tea is much cheaper than taking your clients for a three-course lunch. It also has a huge 'treat' factor: it is a small yet wonderful luxury for a small group of you and your chosen few to be pampered and treated like a king for a few hours. Besides, it tastes amazing!"[31]

Afternoon tea's continued growth has prompted new lines of products, new shows, and new advertising campaigns to capitalize on the meal. The popularity of *The Great British Bake-Off* and other baking shows[32] is perhaps not surprising, given the public's tastes. And, conversely, a meal often associated with pastry, and particularly with the fancy pastries served in hotel teas, seems likely to flourish in a culture with a renewed interest in gourmet pastry. Even grocery stores are getting in on the trend: The Tesco chain, for example, launched a new range of luxury cakes in 2016 in response to increased demand. Consumers had bought 4.5 million more cakes in 2015 than in the year before, in keeping with nationwide trends in increased gourmet-cake sales over the previous five years. Tesco said it was the rise in afternoon tea's popularity that motivated them to increase the diversity and number of luxury-cake offerings.[33] And the fact that these cakes are being sold through a grocer is also telling: It offers compelling evidence that the meal is not the purview of hotel restaurants and tearooms alone. Instead, luxury cream cakes are being purchased for home use, which makes it clear that afternoon tea is still a part of British private life as well as public.

One relationship between Britons and afternoon tea has remained consistent, even during the meal's decline elsewhere in the world: I'm speaking of the tea interval in cricket. Cricket matches, both in the United Kingdom and in former colonies (like we saw in India), include a tea interval that is as central to cricket as the gameplay itself.[34] Afternoon tea at cricket matches is "completely different" from afternoon tea elsewhere. Kataryna emphasizes that it always starts promptly at 4:00 p.m., "and it's very socially and historically complex with who offers tea and conventions of chivalry and hospitality between sporting gentlemen."[35]

In the interwar period, cricket served as a national symbol as well as a game: it was a marker of English identity and was seen as a reflection of

British qualities.[36] From the most formal matches to amateur matches in villages, decorum was central, and a complex code of etiquette surrounds everything, from the hats worn (and the blazers, for wealthier players) to the food served. One historian of the interwar years remarked that "observance of the tea interval at even the lowest levels of cricket shows how deeply cricket had become pervaded by the sense of proper form and of the need to observe established rituals."[37] That afternoon tea is included as a part of this symbolism shows how deeply it is intertwined with English culture—and how quickly it became so (afternoon tea as a structured meal had only been around about a century as of the interwar period). However, the meal's influence has not always extended to every corner of English society. Whether taken regularly or rarely, tea appears as part of the quintessential English experience, remaining a fixed component of the cricket tradition even as tea has gone in and out of vogue over the years.

John attends cricket matches fairly regularly, where he'll "sometimes work and sometimes go just to watch; if it is an all-day match there is actually a tea interval—it is part of the game and an integral part of the tradition of afternoon tea. . . . At English cricket matches, tea intervals are great as that's usually when an assortment of cakes—like scones, jam and cream, or slices of chocolate cake or Victoria sponge cake—are available. They say that to truly understand English culture one must first truly understand the cricket match, and there is something in that."[38]

In chapter 3 we discussed the lingering influences of the British Empire in the postcolonial world. For some Britons, these influences are of concern and have begun to shape the discourse around global trade and labor practices.[39] In some cases, modern British consumers are conscious of these issues to some extent and want more responsible alternatives—like fair-trade options. According to the World Fair Trade Organization, "Fair Trade is a trading partnership, based on dialogue, transparency and respect, that seeks greater equity in international trade. It contributes to sustainable development by offering better trading conditions to, and securing the rights of, marginalized producers and workers—especially in the [global] South."[40]

Fair trade has an interesting history within Britain. John Ruskin, for example, believed that "strengthening relations between consumer and producer was central to moralizing the market" and that the value of both consumer goods and the human labor that produced them had been undermined by industrialization.[41] "In all buying," Ruskin says, "consider first, what condition of existence you cause in the producers of what you buy; secondly, whether the sum you have paid is just to the producer, and in due proportion, lodged in his hands."[42] Ruskin shows that our very progressive notion to consider the living and working conditions of laborers worldwide was in fact present in British society during the imperial period as well.

Ruskin's contemporaries on the Continent were also sounding the call, condemning Dutch disregard for local populations, for example, which mirrored many of the English colonial practices we have already discussed. Coffee, indigo, and cane sugar were the largest crops for the Dutch, while tea and other exports were grown on a smaller scale.[43] For the English, the largest exports were different, but the economic motivations were the same. Pushback against Dutch and English practices appeared in a range of forms, from publications and speeches to legal cases.[44]

Very gradually, public outcry resulted in changes, although the presence of conservative campaigns like Buy Empire are a reminder that colonial governments were still focused on the bottom line until their eventual demise: At the beginning of the twentieth century, civic-minded consumers pushed for free trade, which would give them the option to purchase items from outside the British Empire without additional financial penalties (like higher import taxes). This is what spurred the Buy Empire campaign, which tried to use pride in Britain as an imperial power, combined with the sentimental tugs found in many advertising campaigns, to elicit loyalty to empire-made goods by the British public.

The fair-trade movement, which had precedents dating back at least from the turn of the twentieth century, really came about in the 1970s. "Fair Trade did not develop *from* the Buy Empire Goods campaign, rather Fair Trade emerged (somewhat belatedly) in *opposition* to this 'conservative imperial consumerism.'"[45] Fair trade encourages consumers to consider where their products come from and how their purchasing behavior impacts others.[46] This concept of a "moral economy" appears repeatedly in the study of British history, albeit for a range of reasons,[47] and is the concept that pressure to be a "good" consumer influences purchasing decisions.[48]

The Church of England has been a great proponent of fair-trade products. In 2002, the Diocese of Chester devised five criteria it wished to meet in order to consider itself a fair-trade diocese (thus setting a precedent for other Anglican dioceses to act similarly). Since that time, many other dioceses have adopted these criteria, and the General Synod has recommended that all Church of England dioceses consider becoming fair trade.

The Diocese of Oxford made its own declaration:

1. Synod passes a resolution
   • to support and promote Fairtrade and further encourage the use and sale of Fairtrade products in the diocese and
   • to serve only Fairtrade coffee and tea at its meetings
2. A range of Fairtrade products is made available and served at Diocesan Church House, and Fairtrade tea and coffee are used at diocesan meetings and diocesan events. Display materials at Diocesan Church House will advertise the fact that Fairtrade products are used and served. The diocese will also encourage and resource other diocesan and C of E establishments within its boundaries.
3. Fairtrade tea, coffee and other products are used and/or sold by more 60% of parishes. There is a target of 80 or 90% within 5 years.
4. Media coverage and popular support is gained for the campaign—to raise awareness of Fair Trade issues within the diocese.
5. A Fairtrade steering group is set up to take responsibility for monitoring that goals continue to be met and are developed over a period of time.[49]

While many resources discussing fair-trade practices focus their attention on coffee, the English dioceses consider tea just as vital a concern. According to the Diocese of Oxford, "Fair dealing in trade is a vital part of our living out the Gospel command that we love our neighbours. As Dewi Hughes says, 'Since Jesus asks us as Christians to love our neighbours as ourselves, and our neighbour is any other human being with whom we come into contact, the demand to love must prevail when we shop.'"[50]

The imperial legacy on English consciences has subtly affected afternoon tea as well. While most other etiquette guidelines do not specify, Debrett's etiquette book tells us that the correct teas to serve at an afternoon tea are both a Chinese and an Indian variety (of course, brewed loose rather than in tea bags). This seemingly unassuming etiquette guideline shows how entrenched English tastes that emerged during the imperial period continue to be. It also speaks to the history of the beverage itself in England, with

Chinese tea being the first tea for which the English developed a taste and the only one they had access to, followed by tea grown by the colonial English in India, which initially was not a success in English markets but was eventually adopted.[51]

While tea and the afternoon tea meal, along with other tea meals and breaks, occupy an important place on the British cultural landscape, they are still subject to the changing social tides, including budget cuts and tightening schedules, as well as restaurant legislation and changing tastes. In 2009, for example, the county of Kent stopped providing its magistrates complimentary tea, coffee, and digestive biscuits as a cost-saving measure, ordered by the Courts Service, which effectively canceled elevenses and teatime. The response was swift, as magistrates complained of hunger, tiredness, and what one journalist called "a blow at a vital element of our traditional way of life."[52]

Elevenses occupies a somewhat different space in British culture than does afternoon tea, but the response in Kent when it was removed recalls the backlash we discussed in chapter 3, when the bank in Kenya canceled the employee afternoon tea. In Britain, as in Kenya, the break for tea—even if just for a cup of tea without a snack—has become an expected part of the day, and this entrenched expectation for a tea break contributes to the meal's continued popularity. People's concerns about the timing and components of afternoon tea or high tea changing in British culture have less to do with hunger between meals or proper etiquette than they may have in the past and more to do with holding on to "tradition," particularly traditions that make one distinctly British.

These ebbing and flowing social tides are evident in how a meal is hosted as a social gathering within the home. Debrett's modern etiquette manual offers advice for hosting an afternoon tea in one's home, hearkening back to the Victorian period when a "tea party" in household and cookery guides described an afternoon tea gathering in the home. Debrett's discusses the home tea as one among many types of entertaining options for a host, focusing more on food than on manners, presuming, perhaps, that the reader is already aware of appropriate behavior. The guidelines for the host of an afternoon tea are few, and there is less guidance still for the guest. In a mere half a page, Debrett's offers that the home afternoon tea is "now a very rare occurrence indeed."[53] It recommends serving tea at 4:30 p.m.—insisting that proper china be used—along with a small amount of food. The rest of the meager advice is focused on the food—suggesting that a simple sweet, like a slice of cake, might be served or a baked good, like a crumpet, or perhaps finger sandwiches.

And this is where we get in to the most detail, about finger sandwiches, and Debrett's admonishes that they "must be made properly."[54] If not, it is tacitly suggested, why serve them at all? The host should use thinly sliced bread spread with butter (never margarine!). Crusts *must* be cut off (yes, original uses italics), and the sandwiches can be filled with traditional fillings like ham, tomato, salmon, egg, and, "best of all, cucumber," which "are still the most popular and delicious." Sticking to tradition with finger sandwiches is critical, we learn, and branching out even into familiar sandwich territory is frowned upon. The brief but stern lecture on afternoon tea closes with a warning to the adventurous cook wishing to break from tradition: "More lurid concoctions such as peanut butter and jelly," Debrett's concludes, "are for children's parties."[55]

Hosting an afternoon tea party may be largely the entertainment of a bygone era, but private afternoon tea in the home is not. This tea might be taken alone, with family members, or perhaps with a friend or two and is more casual than the larger tea party. It also differs in timing. John, who currently lives in England, usually takes his tea around 4:00 p.m. but finds that when he meets friends to take afternoon tea, the time varies significantly and often falls earlier (around 3:00 p.m.) if he is at work with colleagues. Afternoon tea is a regular tradition[56] in John's home, offering him a break and a chance to disconnect briefly from multitasking and from any sort of work activities.

Afternoon tea in the home is often a simple affair, including a tea—John typically reaches for a standard Yorkshire tea, not too strong, with milk and no sugar—and the food—which "depends on many things, but basically if you are at work or not, at home, or on holiday, as well as your demographic. The chief component is tea, as in the drink. Afternoon tea usually involves a pot of tea, as this takes time to both make and consume. A cup of tea, a mug of tea, or teatime (as in the midafternoon event) may not involve the pot and associated rituals."[57] When he's on his own, John usually has a sandwich with a bit of salad on the side and perhaps a cherry Bakewell tart or another small cake—"nothing too heavy, as this is to keep me ticking over until dinnertime." If he's enjoying the meal with someone else, more time is spent preparing and consuming the food, and a wider assortment of options is offered.

Like Kataryna, John says conversation is a critical component of afternoon tea, "usually chitchat and idle gossip, nothing too heavy," which is in keeping with the meal's history, where it's always been a time taken to relax and interact with others. Besides conversation and the presence of tea, the meal can vary considerably in any number of ways—how the tea is made, what is served with it, and so on and so forth. "England is a patchwork quilt of traditions and histories," John points out, "almost too hopelessly complicated to even start to understand. The English also take a quiet pride on being subversively different wherever possible. The traditions in one village—and I speak from exact experience—will be deliberately different from those in a village two miles away. 'Well, those people in Badsey are commoner than us here in Wickhamford; they don't make tea properly there.'"

John says demographics are an important part of who eats and drinks what and when: tourists and English people on holiday will often have an afternoon tea with tea and cakes and sometimes sandwiches in a respectable café. But these have variations, like the Devon cream tea (scones, jam, and cream) and clotted cream tea in Cornwall, and Kataryna agrees, saying that what goes into the meal can be informed by county, local identity, rivalries, and social status (she also points to the Devon and Cornwall rivalry on cream teas, a well-known and oft-referenced disagreement). John goes a step further, reminding us that within each of these traditions are microvariations that might be based on village or even household conventions.

For British expats, tea and tea meals still have a place at the table. Liz was raised in the United States by parents who emigrated from England, and her family's Sunday dinner ritual is an example of household-level variations between English meals. The meal clearly refers to an evening tea meal (which makes sense, as her father is from the northern part of the country where the term *tea* is used) but borrows elements of the afternoon tea meal to form a new hybrid meal: "On Sundays, we had something dad (Northern Industrial) would call 'fruity tea.' It's the evening meal except with teatime-esque foods—bread and jam, maybe cold cuts, sometimes chips, pickles and fruit—basically, whatever they could cheaply fill five kids with. It might be just dad (who is very playful with language in his confusing way), but what 'fruity' means in context is unclear. But it was a distinct kind of meal."[58]

Liz's family had another tea tradition that borrows the social aspect of afternoon tea rather than the foods. What they referred to as "teatime" was distinct from the evening meal of tea or from "all the other tea drinking." They only enjoyed teatime on the weekends, for which Liz's mother would gather the entire family together for tea and to spend time together, rather than taking their cups and going off to do each as they pleased. "Despite [the] lack of tea and presence of beer and fish sticks," they still thought of it as teatime, but in their household the differentiation between tea as a meal versus tea as a quick premeal tea drinking was understood.

This brings up an important point on terminology: throughout the United Kingdom is some amount of disagreement as to what, exactly, one refers to when speaking of *tea* or *teatime*. Afternoon tea seems rather static in meaning across social contexts, however, with the exception of its particular rituals during a cricket match. In late nineteenth- and twentieth-century sources, teatime denoted either the evening meal or a tea break, leaving it up to the researcher to determine which was which based on context.[59]

Contemporary articles on afternoon tea seem to refer to afternoon tea in restaurants rather than the private meal at home, but it is evident in cases like John's that the term is still used to refer to the home meal. Each person I asked about afternoon tea understood what I meant by the term and that it referenced both the private and the public versions of the meal, and this was true no matter what other terms they used for it or other meals.

Hobbs refers to restaurant teas as a "rare teatime treat,"[60] showing the continued variation in the use of these terms: while teatime means dinner time to Liz's family and others, it also refers to an afternoon tea break, which John refers to as "the time to stop and have a communal or solo cup of tea (at any time of the day, including midafternoon when others may be having afternoon tea)." This differentiates the afternoon teatime from afternoon tea and shows that the presence of some sort of food seems to be the determining factor between the types of breaks. Some published sources, particularly news articles, seem to use teatime to refer to the afternoon tea break, whether or not that break includes the accompanying trappings to constitute the afternoon tea meal. However, in conversation with Britons teatime seems to simply refer to the beverage and not the full formality of a meal. As Kataryna says, "Teatime is the desire for a cup of tea and is usually a spoken question when asking another person to make it, like a hint. 'Is it teatime?' really means 'I'd like a cup of tea, will you make one.'"

In other cases, tea denotes the evening meal, just as it does for Paula in Australia and for many in the northern part of England.[61] Using "tea" rather than "dinner," as Kataryna notes, is also related to socioeconomic status as well as geographic location. Tea is usually a working-class term, shortened from the high tea evening meal born of the Industrial Revolution, whereas dinner is the term used in middle- and upper-class households.

In some cases, authors still distinguish between high tea and afternoon tea when discussing the modern-day afternoon and evening meals, as do teahouse and restaurant owners and tea enthusiasts,[62] although in some cases the two terms appear to be used somewhat interchangeably, particularly by those visiting the United Kingdom.[63] This is an interesting point, because, while there seems to be a clear understanding of the difference between the two, some hotels and restaurants intentionally advertise high tea rather than afternoon tea, perhaps to cater to tourists (as one article says, mixing up the two terms is a "dead give-away you're American"[64]), and both terms are still used to refer to afternoon tea in popular literature and even cookbooks of afternoon tea recipes.[65]

Modern British mealtimes also include elevenses, which historian Bruce Richardson speculates appeared in the twentieth century, as there are no references to the meal in earlier literature.[66] This meal is the morning counterpart to the simpler at-home or on-the-go afternoon teatime, which includes taking a snack like a muffin or scone with a cup of coffee or tea. Elevenses may be a recent phenomenon that has caught on quickly, particularly in office settings, where it is considered "a vital part of [the] working day," as Kent learned during its budget-cut fiasco.[67] Outside of the context of workplaces, mentions of elevenses by journalists do not seem especially common, with the exception of articles written for Americans visiting England, explaining British meal customs for foreigners.[68]

This lack of formalized discourse in Britain around elevenses—and its absence from restaurant menus or sources normally offering documentation of accepted mealtimes within a given culture—suggests that either elevenses is not as universally popular as its afternoon counterpart or it refers to a highly informal break without much of the guiding structure of a more formalized meal, save for its specific serving time.

The latter explanation seems more likely, given that when elevenses is mentioned, its importance is clear in office settings, where a late-morning break would not be unreasonable. This also would support Richardson's claim that the meal emerged in the twentieth century as more and more people began working in office settings and their work schedules became more standardized. Just as afternoon tea shifted in response to changing schedules during the Industrial Revolution, it is very possible that elevenses is a response to modern-day rhythms and that it will in time emerge as a meal with a clearer structure and, perhaps, a mention on restaurant menus.

Those restaurant menus do tell us a lot about modern afternoon tea and the persistence of many of the dishes that have been a part of the meal[69] both in Britain and abroad. What menus do not reveal are the modern etiquette expectations surrounding the meal, which are outlined most frequently in articles for Americans and other foreigners looking to take afternoon tea at a restaurant without sticking out like an Ugly Tourist. There is some guidance on mealtime manners in British etiquette books,[70] but most popular resources (like news articles) on etiquette seem squarely focused on tourists dining out in public.

These rules are less stringent than they were in Victorian times, but they still exist. For the most part, afternoon tea etiquette mirrors proper behavior expected in any nice restaurant: put your napkin on your lap, don't make a mess, and so on, and so forth. There are a few tea-specific directives, however, including the age-old edict to add milk to tea, and not tea to milk, to make sure one has the proper ratio.[71] Others include not extending one's pinky out when holding the teacup, not confusing the terms "high tea" and "afternoon tea" at restaurants (where the distinction and overlap is worth noting), and slowly stirring and enjoying one's tea rather than vigorously mixing sugar into the cup (loudly clanking dishes is considered rather rude).[72]

The meal in restaurants often offers a more substantial spread than what one might normally make for a snack, but there are still expectations that a diner not just dive face-first into the food but instead practice some restraint and enjoy the meal slowly.[73] This directive is part etiquette but also part mindset: the meal is ultimately about relaxing, socializing, and taking a break in the day, and tackling it like you would any other to-do-list item with the intent of finishing quickly undermines the meal's purpose. As Kataryna says, "When I was in boarding school we always stopped every day for tea at 4:00, but refreshments and cake at 4:00 are not afternoon tea, and you can't get them mixed up." It seems that while the foods served vary considerably in amount and complexity, afternoon tea's universal tenets as a modern British meal are snack-sized foods rather than entrees and a space to relax and converse rather than to simply have a quick snack break or grab a snack out while on the go.

A relaxed setting is central to afternoon tea, whether at home or out and about. Even though there are plenty of etiquette guidelines offering advice on how to behave during an afternoon tea, even these are rather minimal and not meant to detract from a meal that is all about slowing down and enjoying,[74] even if only briefly. For John, who often takes an afternoon tea break by himself at home, "A core part of afternoon tea is that it isn't a quick thing—i.e., a minute or two—or something that you can do while doing something else—e.g., drinking a mug of tea while typing on social media. It is an activity that takes up a bit of time, and you do it in conjunction with no other activity. I find this good, as my work involves typing and looking at a screen for several hours of the day. True afternoon tea means I take a break from all that, and also a break from thinking about that."[75]

CONCLUSION

It is a challenge to take something as vast and complex as the British Empire and distill even one component of its influence into a single book. Many more aspects of its legacy remain to be explored, and the ever-evolving postcolonial cultures of the former empire will undoubtedly continue to refine and redefine their relationships with cultural vestiges of the imperial age.

It is equally daunting to take a meal that is both a revered tradition and, in some cases, a simple daily comfort and articulate its history and changing role across a wide range of global cultures. As the postcolonial world redefines itself within new identities, some distinct and some homogenous, how will that change afternoon tea? Will it exist as an echo of an earlier era, with similar foods and similar etiquette, but feel distant from modern life? Will it shift into a new meal in some cultures, possibly keeping certain remnants of the old meal—perhaps the timing or the centrality of drinking tea—while transforming into something that better reflects the needs and tastes of that community? Will it change only in some contexts—like morphing into a new manifestation within home life, while remaining static in public eateries? Will it disappear completely?

Bersten[1] argues that afternoon tea is a tea ceremony that can be compared to the Japanese tea ceremony: something akin to a religious ceremony, administered by experts trained in the proper etiquette of performing the meal that makes the experience transcendent. Bersten refers to these meals, and the culture built up around the tea beverage, as ancestor worship: These meals, and the myriad books about both them and the drink, rarely discuss any scientific process for producing a perfect cup of tea. Instead, they focus on the history of the drink, the great scholars and philosophers who waxed poetic about its attributes, or perhaps how different varieties are grown. This emphasis on its history and magic is a way of encoding the tradition of tea, by codifying its social role into a set of historical precedents and semimagical writings. In this way, Bersten argues that afternoon tea is a meal that reinforces tradition[2]: it codifies our relationship with tea as a set of actions that, just like a church service, offer us a key to participating in (or at least encountering) the divine. It is difficult to know whether a meal that reinforces tradition—whether that be of former generations in England or the colonial traditions of another country—will remain an unchanged entity over time.

As of this writing, the United Kingdom has voted to leave the European Union, as permitted under Article 50 of the Treaty on European Union, and Brexit (as it has come to be known) will go into effect on March 29, 2019. As preparations are being made for this massive shift, focus has been trained on an increasingly connected global, or at least regional, culture, where boundaries are thinned and traditions can perhaps be shared across borders more easily.[3]

The same examination would be well focused on the spread of English traditions during the period of British Empire, beginning in the seventeenth century and continuing on through the mid-twentieth. The empire as a unifying force as well as a colonizer exerting control made boundaries between the colonies and the governing country more permeable, through which food traditions spread more freely. And there is certainly an element of coercion to the development of these food traditions: since afternoon tea, as we have seen, was a meal of the powerful, those seeking to engage with and perhaps enjoy some of that power would feel motivated to adopt its traditions in order to be identified as a member of the in-group.[4]

The legacy of colonialism continues worldwide today in a range of ways, and food is one powerful reflection of that legacy's persistence: Food is a central influence in our current models of global trade and labor in developing countries, for example. Laborers picking and processing tea and other commodities are often paid depressed wages that keep the selling prices low in wealthy international markets while impoverishing that same workforce to such a degree that they cannot even afford to purchase the product they labored over.

Colonial legacy is also present in afternoon tea, a quintessentially English meal that has spread from the United Kingdom throughout its empire, where it has become an adopted tradition in many of them. The fact, for example, that afternoon tea is taken in Kenya, a country that was only a part of the empire for perhaps a century, shows the speed with which food traditions may be adopted and also affirms the top-down spread of this particular meal—from the powerful, landed gentry down to the average Briton and into the colonies, across the globe. Surak notes that adoption of cultural trends often comes from the wealthier classes, as more people seek to emulate those with more power, and eventually the trend itself becomes entrenched—as we saw in our conversation of diffusion of innovation earlier on.[5] While in some cases this may be an oversimplification of the transmission of cultural norms, it seems to be so in the case of afternoon tea.[6]

The changing landscape of the postcolonial world serves to remind us that nothing, even something as entrenched as afternoon tea, is immune to change. But it also reminds us that some things do endure: While nothing is guaranteed to withstand cultural change entirely, some traditions are so central that they live on even after the conditions that fostered them no longer exist. As we've seen, afternoon tea has adapted to a changing world and a changing England, and its current popularity suggests that the meal will be around for at least some time to come.

AN AFTERNOON TEA MENU

To close out this book, I wanted to share some favorite adaptations of recipes for foods that you might see on any given afternoon tea table. This starts with a recipe for a proper brew of tea, which is central to successfully hosting an afternoon tea.

Properly Making Tea

Many modern tea drinkers are accustomed to single-serving tea: a mug (or a to-go cup from a shop) with a tea bag. The invention of the tea bag has distanced many people from the art of preparing a proper pot of tea—the water neither too hot nor too cold, the loose leaves fresh and stored properly, and the resulting flavor full of the nuance of those leaves.

Mrs. Beeton's Every-Day Cookery, the compendium of kitchen knowledge that has been a mainstay of cookbook collections across England since it was first published in 1861, offers extensive knowledge on running a Victorian household. This, of course, includes the proper preparation of tea; in fact, the vast majority of its pages are devoted to cooking rather than to household management. The book began as a series of magazine articles, later transitioning to a stand-alone publication,[7] and has remained enormously popular, despite the fact that early versions of the book include quite a few recipes copied from other popular sources, sometimes interspersed with cooking advice that would be anathema today—like boiling pasta for more than an hour.[8]

Mrs. Beeton's instruction for proper tea preparation, and for foods to be served at afternoon tea, appear in early printings on through the twentieth century. The 1907 printing offers the following advice:

> In order to make good tea it is necessary that the water should be quite boiling, but it must on no account be water that has boiled for some time, or been previously boiled, cooled, and then re-boiled.
>
> It is a good plan to empty the kettle and refill it with fresh cold water, and make the tea the moment it reaches the boiling point. Soft water makes the best tea, and boiling softens the water, but after it has boiled some time it again becomes hard. When water is very hard, a tiny pinch of carbonate of soda may be put into the teapot with the tea, but it must be used very sparingly, otherwise it may impart an unpleasant taste to the beverage. Tea is better made in an earthen than a metal pot. One good teaspoonful of tea will be found sufficient for two small cups, if made with boiling water and allowed to stand for 3 to 4 minutes; longer than this it should never be allowed to stand. The delicate flavor of the tea may be preserved, and injurious effects avoided by pouring the tea, after it has stood 3 or 4 minutes, into a clean teapot which has been previously heated.[9]

Afternoon Tea Food

The majority of the foods I offer in the following are common across afternoon teas in former colonies and in the United Kingdom. However, several of the recipes are from former colonies that have incorporated local food traditions into their afternoon tea meals.

Finger Sandwiches

Yield: about 12 sandwiches

Finger sandwiches are one of the mainstays of the afternoon tea meal: simple to prepare and aesthetically pleasing, this type of sandwich is meant to be a small snack rather than a substantial meal on bread. This recipe is my version of the ever-popular cucumber finger sandwich and can be adapted in any number of ways to include other flavorings (like fresh dill), other greens (if watercress is unavailable), or other fillings (like smoked salmon). Since the flavors are so simple, fresh ingredients are critical: Mrs. Beeton, for example, advises readers not to use bread more than one day old. Those using super-market bread loaves may find it difficult to determine freshness, so simply purchasing whatever ingredients look the freshest is sufficient.[10] It is also important to fill the sandwiches first and only then remove the crusts and cut them into triangles, which gives them clean edges.

1 stick butter or 1 container cream cheese, softened
1 English cucumber
1 bunch watercress
1 loaf thinly sliced sandwich bread (white bread is most traditional)
Seasonings (salt and pepper), if desired

1. Spread one side of every slice of bread with a light layer of butter or cream cheese.
2. Thinly slice the cucumber, and arrange the slices on half the slices of prepared bread.
3. Top the cucumber with watercress.
4. Add seasonings to taste.
5. Assemble sandwiches, by placing the remaining prepared slices butter (or cream cheese) side down.
6. Cut the crusts from the sandwiches.
7. Cut the sandwich diagonally, so each is in two triangles.
8. Cut each triangle in half.

Dutch Kockies (Wine Tea Cakes)

Yield: 12–15 small cakes

These cakes are an excellent example of the confluence of multiple colonial traditions within one country. Dutch in origin, these spiced red wine cookies were brought to South Africa, where they became popular during Dutch rule. After the country was taken over as an English colony, the cakes were incorporated into the English afternoon tea meal, where they still regularly appear today. *Tea cakes* may refer to any number of rolled or drop cookies, as well as small frosted cakes.

This recipe is a bit different from modern recipes for soetkoekies, which are a flat, chewy cookie, although many of the ingredients are the same.[11] Dutch kockies are soft and flaky and closer in texture to the tea cakes found in the Southern United States than to flat drop cookies.

This early twentieth-century version of the tea cake is made in a similar manner to biscuit dough: the fat is rubbed in to the flour, to which liquids are added, and the resulting dough is kneaded before being cut into rounds or other shapes. They are somewhat similar to a slightly thick, chewy gingerbread and are often served with citrus preserves: if you want to add preserves to your cakes, just put a small dollop in the center of each before baking.[12]

3 1/3 cups flour
1/2 cup butter (1 stick), softened
1/4 cup lard or shortening
1 1/2 cups brown sugar
3/4 cup almond flour (or almonds ground in a food processor)
1 tbsp ground cloves
1 tsp ground cinnamon
1 tsp baking soda
2 eggs
1/2 cup red wine

1. Preheat the oven to 400 degrees Fahrenheit.
2. Using fingers or a pastry cutter, rub the butter and the lard or shortening into the flour until evenly distributed.
3. Add the sugar, almond flour or almonds, cloves, and cinnamon to the flour mixture.
4. Dissolve the baking soda in 1 tsp warm water, and set aside.
5. Beat the eggs, and add the dissolved soda and the wine.
6. Pour the egg mixture into the flour mixture, and combine well.

7. Knead the dough on a floured surface for several minutes.
8. Roll the dough out into a sheet 1/4-inch thick.
9. Using a biscuit- or cookie-cutter, cut the cakes into shapes, and put them on a greased cookie sheet.
10. Bake for 10–12 minutes or until just lightly golden brown around the edges.
11. Cool and serve.

Lemon Tea Biscuits

Yield: about 12 biscuits

These biscuits are adapted from *A Little Book of Cookery*, published in 1905 by Dora Luck.[13] It was part of the larger "little books" reference series, which were small and concise volumes meant to convey the most regularly used and most important information on a topic. The *Little Book of Cookery* was marketed as a collection of recipes that would most likely be needed by a middle-class homemaker and includes a small selection of recipes for different courses (meats, soups, desserts, etc.), including one for tea biscuits.[14] These biscuits are simple to make and, like the wine cakes above, have a fluffy and flaky texture that comes from rubbing fat into flour before incorporating the wet ingredients.

1 lemon
1/2 cup (1 stick) butter
1 3/4 cups flour
1/2 cup caster (finely ground) sugar
2 eggs
12 blanched almonds

1. Preheat oven to 350 degrees Fahrenheit.
2. Grate the lemon rind; set aside.
3. Using fingers or a pastry cutter, rub the butter thoroughly into the flour. Add the sugar, grated lemon rind, and juice of half a lemon.
4. Whisk the eggs in a bowl, and add to the mixture, beating together for 2–3 minutes.
5. Turn the dough out onto a floured board, and roll into a sheet of about 1/4-inch thickness.
6. Using a biscuit- or cookie-cutter, cut the biscuits into rounds.
7. Place the rounds on a greased cookie sheet.

8. Chop the almonds coarsely, and sprinkle them evenly on top of each biscuit.
9. Bake 10–12 minutes or until lightly golden brown on the edges.
10. Cool and serve.

Scottish Scones

Yield: about 10 scones

The Scots were among the first to be colonized by England and, later, to declare independence, both of which happened more than once over the course of Scottish history. The two countries are next-door neighbors, and so there is some overlap between the cultures, which shows up in the similarities shared between certain shared food preparations and the prevalence of Scottish versions of those foods in English cookbooks. This recipe for scones is an example of both: a Scottish scone from an English cookbook. Scones are a mainstay of afternoon tea in restaurants, often served with jam and clotted cream (although some places outside the United Kingdom substitute whipped cream). This recipe is adapted from *The Country House*, edited in 1867 by Irwin Edward Bainbridge Cox, and was geared toward the middling landowner running a small country estate.[15] This is a very basic scone, and, if desired, you can mix in currants, raisins, nuts, and similar items.[16]

3 1/3 cups flour
1 1/2 tsp baking soda
1 1/2 tsp cream of tartar
1 tsp sea salt
1 3/4 cup buttermilk

1. Preheat oven to 425 degrees Fahrenheit.
2. Sift the flour, baking soda, and cream of tartar together in a bowl.
3. In a separate bowl, add the sea salt to the buttermilk, and whisk to combine.
4. Add the buttermilk mixture to the dry ingredients, and stir to make a stiff dough.
5. Turn the dough out onto a floured surface and knead until it comes together into a ball.
6. Divide dough into 10 equal portions, and place onto a greased baking sheet.
7. Bake for 12–15 minutes or until golden brown.
8. Serve warm or at room temperature.

NOTES

INTRODUCTION

1. Helen Saberi, *Tea: A Global History* (London: Reaktion Books, 2010), 10.

2. Ibid., 10–11.

3. Ibid., 12.

4. Tea harvesting is also done primarily by women and children, which opens the door to plenty of discussions of gender issues, workers' rights, and more that are beyond the scope of this book. For more on women and children in the tea industry, see Saberi, *Tea*.

5. Ibid.

6. According to Saberi, "the word still survives colloquially in the expression 'a cup of char.'" Ibid., 8.

7. See Eric Jay Dolin, *When America First Met China: An Exotic History of Tea, Drugs, and Money in the Age of Sail* (New York: W. W. Norton, 2012), 46.

8. Ibid.

9. Saberi, *Tea*.

10. Dolin, *When America First Met China*.

11. The other necessities were rice, firewood, oil, salt, vinegar, and soy sauce. Ibid., 48.

12. Ibid.

13. Including in ibid., 48; and in Saberi, *Tea*, 7.

14. Quoted in Dolin, *When America First Met China*, 48.

15. Saberi, *Tea*.

16. For an in-depth discussion of the trade between China and Tibet, see Michael Freeman and Selena Ahmed, *Tea Horse Road: China's Ancient Trade Road to Tibet* (London: River Books, 2015).

17. Dolin, *When America First Met China*.

18. For more about tea's early European history, see Dolin, *When America First Met China*, and Saberi, *Tea*.

19. Dolin, *When America First Met China*, 49.

20. Ibid., 49–50.

21. Jane Pettigrew and Bruce Richardson, *A Social History of Tea: Tea's Influence on Commerce, Culture and Commodity*, 2nd ed. (Danville, KY: Benjamin Press, 2014).

22. Chocolate, coffee, and tea were all introduced to England around the same time, although drinking chocolate and (for the most part, at least, save for regional differences) drinking coffee eventually gave way to tea. See, for example, Laura Mason, *Food and Culture in Great Britain* (Wesport, CT: Greenwood Press, 2004), 34.

23. See, for example, Dolin, *When America First Met China*, and also Jane Pettigrew, *A Social History of Tea* (Swindon, England: The National Trust, 2001).

24. Dolin, *When America First Met China*.

25. Ibid.

26. Ibid.

27. See, for example, Pettigrew, *A Social History of Tea*.

28. Dolin, *When America First Met China*, 50.

29. Dolin, *When America First Met China*; and Pettigrew, *A Social History of Tea*.

30. Dolin, *When America First Met China*, 54.

31. James Walvin, *Slavery in Small Things: Slavery and Modern Cultural Habits* (West Sussex, England: John Wiley & Sons, 2017), 27.

32. For example, Mason, *Food and Culture*.

33. Richard B. Sheridan, *Sugar and Slavery: An Economic History of the British West Indies, 1623–1775* (Kingston, Jamaica: Canoe Press, 1994), 28.

34. See, for example, Ralph A. Austen and Woodruff D. Smith, "Private Tooth Decay as Public Economic Virtue: The Slave-Sugar Triangle, Consumerism, and European Industrialization," in *The Atlantic Slave Trade: Effects on Economies, Societies, and Peoples in Africa, the Americas, and Europe*, ed. Joseph E. Inikori and Stanley L. Engerman (Durham, NC: Duke University Press, 1998), 183–204.

35. The same is true of coffee, which other colonial powers (like the Dutch) grew in colonies in Southeast Asia, the Caribbean, and Africa, using the work of enslaved laborers. In the early eighteenth century, the English were importing coffee as well as tea, although the lower price of tea made it more popular in the country.

The coffee, by contrast, was divided up by the East India Company to go to the domestic market or be reexported to other European countries, particularly Holland. See Walvin, *Slavery in Small Things*, 27.

36. For a more in-depth discussion of the legacy of slavery in the modern day, particularly in relation to food, and one person's account of using food as a mechanism for understanding their enslaved ancestors, see Michael Twitty, *The Cooking Gene: A Journey through African American Culinary History in the Old South* (New York: HarperCollins, 2017); see also Michael Twitty's blog, *Afroculinaria*, https://afroculinaria.com/.

37. See, for example, Hugh Thomas, *The Slave Trade: The Story of the Atlantic Slave Trade: 1440–1870* (New York: Simon & Schuster, 1997); and Toby Green, *The Rise of the Trans-Atlantic Slave Trade in Western Africa, 1300–1589* (Cambridge: Cambridge University Press, 2011).

People who were sold into slavery were captured during raids by Europeans as well as during wars between African tribes or through any other number of methods (e.g., a person being sold into slavery to pay a debtor). Green, *Slave Trade in Western Africa*, offers an in-depth discussion of the early slave trade as well as the transatlantic slave trade as it developed.

38. Sheridan, *Sugar and Slavery*, 479.

39. See Pettigrew, *A Social History of Tea*.

40. Sheridan, *Sugar and Slavery*; and Walvin, *Slavery in Small Things*.

41. For example, throughout Adrian Tinniswood, *The Long Weekend: Life in the English Country House, 1918–1939* (New York: Basic Books, 2016). This is also the case in Maggie Black, *Food and Cooking in 19th Century Britain: History and Recipes* (Birmingham: Historic Buildings and Monuments Commission for England, 1985).

42. For example, John Burnett, *Liquid Pleasures: A Social History of Drinks in Modern Britain* (London: Routledge, 1999).

43. For example, Vicky Straker, *Afternoon Tea: A History and Guide to the Great Edwardian Tradition* (Stroud, England: Amberley Publishing, 2015), among many others.

44. For example, Matthew Sterne, "Top 10 High Teas in Cape Town," *Rhino Africa* (blog), April 4, 2013, https://blog.rhinoafrica.com/2013/04/04/high-teas-of-cape-town/.

45. Creating modernized versions of recipes is one of my greatest passions. You can see some other examples in Julia Skinner, *Modernizing Markham: Bringing "The English Housewife" to Today's Readers* (Iowa City: Candle Light Press, 2012). Also check out "What Is Root?" at *Root*, my online food-history community—https://root-kitchens.com/about/.

46. Daniel Holliday, conversation with the author, Atlanta, Georgia, October 3, 2017.

CHAPTER 1

1. A look at a Victorian table setting, for example, is a testament to how particular Victorians were about compartmentalizing their engagement with foods; my favorite examples are pickle and lettuce forks.

2. Austen and Smith, "Private Tooth Decay," 194.

3. When we speak of tea, we refer, of course, to *Camellia sinensis*, which is not to be confused with other infusions—what we today would call "herbal teas," or tisanes, which were common as both beverages and medical treatments.

4. Robert Y. Eng, "Macao (Macau)," in *Colonialism: An International Social, Cultural, and Political Encyclopedia*, vol. 1, ed. Elvin E. Page and Penny M. Sonnenburg (Santa Barbara, CA: ABC-CLIO, 2003), 359; and Dolin, *When America First Met China*, 34.

5. See Geoffrey C. Gunn, *World Trade Systems of the East and West* (Leiden, Neth.: Brill, 2018).

6. Shih-shan Henry Tsai, *Maritime Taiwan: Historical Encounters with the East and West* (London: Routledge, 2009), 64.

7. The Sack of Antwerp was directly precipitated when the Spanish Crown borrowed money from elsewhere in Europe and then defaulted on those loans. The government was unable to pay its soldiers stationed in the Low Countries, who then mutinied, pillaging Antwerp. See Robert W. Kolb, *Sovereign Debt: From Safety to Default* (New York: Wiley, 2011).

8. See Mauricio Drelichman and Hans-Joachim Voth, *Lending to the Borrower from Hell: Debt, Taxes, and Default in the Age of Philip II* (Princeton, NJ: Princeton University Press, 2014).

9. George Daniel Ramsay, *The Queen's Merchants and the Revolt of the Netherlands: The End of the Antwerp Mart*, vol. 2 (Manchester: Manchester University Press, 1986), 121.

10. Jerry Brotton, "England's Forgotten Muslim History," *New York Times*, September 17, 2016, http://www.nytimes.com/2016/09/18/opinion/sunday/englands-forgotten-muslim-history.html. Jerry Brotton, *The Sultan and the Queen: The Untold Story of Elizabeth and Islam* (New York: Viking, 2016).

11. Joel Mokyr, ed., *The Oxford Encyclopedia of Economic History*, vol. 3 (Oxford: Oxford University Press, 2003), 209. David Head, ed., *Encyclopedia of the*

Atlantic World, 1400–1900: Europe, Africa, and the Americas in an Age of Exploration, Trade, and Empires (Santa Barbara, CA: ABC-CLIO, 2018), 341.

12. See Jerry Brotton, "England's Forgotten Muslim History," *New York Times*, September 17, 2016, http://www.nytimes.com/2016/09/18/opinion/sunday/englands-forgotten-muslim-history.html. See also Brotton, *The Sultan and the Queen*, for discussion of the Muscovy Company, founded in 1555 by Queen Mary and King Philip (see page 31), and of the Turkey Company, whose founding in the 1580s during Elizabeth's reign coincided with greater interest in Middle Eastern trading (see, for example, page 113).

13. Brotton, *The Sultan and the Queen*.

14. See M. C. Ricklefs, Bruce Lockhart, Albert Lau, Portia Reyes, and Maitrii Aung-Thwin, *A New History of Southeast Asia* (New York: Palgrave Macmillan, 2010), 133. Another source is Allan Maclean Skinner, *A Geography of the Malay Peninsula and Surrounding Countries: Part I, Malay Peninsula, Borneo* (Singapore: Royal Asiatic Society, 1884). Skinner outlines the history of the British in the Malay Peninsula in greater depth, from trading voyages beginning in the late sixteenth century through the later interactions with the East India Company and the British political and military interventions, which is a particularly interesting study, as he is a British man writing a book about (and published in) Asia during the height of the empire; see, for example, pages 81–86. See also William Harrison Woodward, *A Short History of the Expansion of the British Empire, 1500–1930* (Cambridge: Cambridge University Press, 1952), 64–128.

15. See, for example, Ricklefs et al., *A New History of Southeast Asia*, 133.

16. Robert Southey, *Lives of the British Admirals*, vol. 3 (London: Longman, 1834), 1–3. George Charles Williamson, *George, Third Earl of Cumberland (1558–1605), His Life and Voyages, a Study from Original Documents* (Cambridge: Cambridge University Press, 1920).

17. William H. Ukers, *All About Tea*, vol. 1 (New York: The Tea and Coffee Trade Journal Company, 1935), 67.

The goal of the Company's earliest missions was, in part, colonial expansion and spreading the Christian doctrine and English culture, as well as trade. According to Sir William Monson, "Whereby it should seem that the will of God for our good is (if our weakness could apprehend it) to have us communicate with them in those East Indian treasures, and, by the erection of a lawful traffic, to better our means to advance true religion and his holy service." Southey, *Lives of the British Admirals*, 22.

18. For more on the foundation and structure of the Company, see K. N. Chaudhuri, *The Trading World of Asia and the English East India Company, 1660–1760* (Cambridge: Cambridge University Press, 1978); Southey, *Lives of the British Ad-*

mirals; and Gertrude Z. Thomas, *Richer than Spices: How a Royal Bride's Dowry Introduced Cane, Lacquer, Cottons, Tea, and Porcelain to England, and So Revolutionized Taste, Manners, Craftsmanship, and History in Both England and America* (New York: Alfred A. Knopf, 1965).

19. Thomas, *Richer than Spices*, 17–18.

20. They were also expanding their reach across the Atlantic—for example, to Bermuda. See Alison Games, *The Web of Empire: English Cosmopolitans in an Age of Expansion, 1560–1660* (Oxford: Oxford University Press, 2008).

21. For most of the seventeenth century Britain and the Dutch butted heads commercially and militarily, sometimes resulting in war. Dolin writes, "Ever since the two nations had first ventured to the Far East they had been engaged in a vicious, at times deadly, battle to monopolize as much of the region's trade as possible. Thus the last thing England wanted was to allow their despised competitors to benefit from access to lucrative American markets" (*When America First Met China*, 61).

22. Samuel Purchas, *Purchas His Pilgrimage: or Relations of the World and the Religions Observed in All Ages and Places Discovered, from the Creation unto This Present* (London: William Stansby, 1625), 524.

23. Purchas also had a strong pro-Protestant, anti-Catholic bent, framing the English monarchs and clergy as defenders of truth in the ages-old battle between right and wrong. This ideological framing of the Church of England and the monarchy as intertwining forces for good was central to positioning them and the country's imperial activities in a benevolent light that could be accepted by the masses. For more, see David Armitage, *The Ideological Origins of the British Empire* (Cambridge: Cambridge University Press, 2000), and specifically pages 61–99 for a discussion of Purchas.

24. The Company also dealt in opium, expanding the crop's production in Assam and trading it through a complex network of shipping agents, brokers, and traders into China. See, for example, Dolin, *When America First Met China*.

25. William H. Ukers, *All About Coffee* (New York: The Tea and Coffee Trade Journal Company, 1935), 73.

26. Margot Finn and Kate Smith, *The East India Company at Home, 1757–1857* (London: University College of London Press, 2018), 398.

27. Georgie Wemyss, *The Invisible Empire: White Discourse, Tolerance and Belonging* (London: Routledge, 2009), 57.

28. Ukers, *All About Tea*, 29. John Shaw, *Charters Relating to the East India Company from 1600 to 1761* (Madras: R. Hill, 1887).

29. For a modern take on the diary, Phil Gyford's site, *The Diary of Samuel Pepys*, https://www.pepysdiary.com/, publishes an entry from the diary each day

and allows users to comment on and discuss the work, adding extensive gloss from their own research to the original work.

30. Samuel Pepys, *The Diary of Samuel Pepys: A New and Complete Transcription*, vol. 1, *1660*, ed. Robert Latham and William Matthews (London: HarperCollins, 2000), 25 September 1660.

31. Worden defines the civil war as that between the Crown and parliament from 1642 to 1646, referring to the longer period of political and military conflicts from the 1640s and 1650s as the "civil wars." Blair Worden, *The English Civil Wars, 1640–1660* (London: Orion Books, 2009).

32. Ibid.

33. Charles had fled to safety at the end of the English Civil War, in 1646, at the age of sixteen. Although his father was still alive, it was clear that the Crown was in a precarious position, and so young Charles joined his mother in exile in France. See Don Jordan and Mike Walsh, *The King's Revenge: Charles II and the Greatest Manhunt in British History* (New York: Pegasus Books, 2016), 2–14.

34. Until Queen Catherine came along, "No Englishman at that time considered tea drinking a pleasure. In fact, barely four years before Catherine came to England, tea had been introduced as a medicine. . . . In 1660, Thomas Garway, the first English dealer in tea, hailed it as the panacea for 'preserving a perfect health until extreme Old Age.'" Thomas, *Richer than Spices*, 95–96. The more common drinks in Restoration England were beer, ale, or cider and the occasional sack posset (a custard-like hot drink). Ibid., 98–99.

35. Austen and Smith argue that it is oversimplistic to think of changing trends as a top-down-only activity, however, and note that cultural expectations, financial access, and other factors are also important influencers. Austen and Smith, "Private Tooth Decay," particularly pages 193–94.

36. There is evidence, for example, that Elizabeth Maitland, Duchess of Lauderdale and supporter of Charles II, had a sitting room appointed with a tea chest and other tea service. For more, see chapter 5 of Paul Chrystal, *Tea: A Very British Beverage* (Gloucestershire, England: Amberley Publishing, 2014).

37. Samuel Pepys, *The Diary of Samuel Pepys: A New and Complete Transcription*, vol. 8, *1667*, ed. Robert Latham and William Matthews (London: HarperCollins, 2000), 28 June 1667.

38. For example, Thomas Elyot, *The Castel of Helth Gathered and Made by Syr Thomas Elyot Knyghte, Out of the Chiefe Authors of Physyke, Wherby Euery Manne May Knowe the State of His Owne Body, the Preseruatio[n] of Helthe, and How to Instructe Welle His Physytion in Syckenes that He Be Not Deceyued* (London: Thomas Berteleti, 1539); and Andrew Boorde, *A Compendyous Regyment or a Dyetary of*

Healthe Made in Mountpyllyer, by Andrewe Boorde of Physycke Doctour, Newly Corrected and Imprynted with Dyuers Addycyons Dedycated to the Armypotent Prynce and Valyent Lorde Thomas Duke of Northfolke (London: Wyllyame Powell, 1542).

39. Mason, *Food and Culture*. Skinner, *Modernizing Markham*. Ken Albala, *Eating Right in the Renaissance* (Berkeley: University of California Press, 2002), also discusses cookery books elsewhere in Europe.

40. Robert May "is laden with nostalgia for the golden age the author recalls before the Civil War." These books were often divided into sections that covered medicine, cookery, cosmetics, confectionary, and so on. A good example of this is *The Queen's Closet Opened*, first published in 1655 by "M. W.," and "Printed for Nathaniel Brook at the Angel in Cornhill." Mason, *Food and Culture*, 22.

41. See, for example, Ukers, *All About Coffee*. England and Holland, at war with France, were also pushed out of the Mediterranean at the end of the seventeenth century, which made it difficult to acquire stocks of coffee from the Levant. See Pettigrew, *A Social History of Tea*, 43.

42. Ibid.

43. Ibid., and Ukers, *All About Tea*, 500.

44. British teahouses hit on the idea of creating blends of teas of different origins to meet different tastes and requirements according to the time of day. This is how English tea blends with their various names came into being, the blends themselves varying from one tea shop to another. New blends continued to be added over time—among them, morning tea, brunch tea, and five o'clock tea. Additionally, certain famous blends were created in honor of the British royal family—for example, Queen Victoria or royal morning tea. See L. Gautier, *Tea: Aromas and Flavors around the World* (San Francisco: Chronicle, 2006), 45.

45. See Arnold Palmer, *Movable Feasts: A Reconnaissance of the Origins and Consequences of Fluctuations in Meal-Times with Special Attention to the Introduction of Luncheon and Afternoon Tea* (London: Oxford University Press, 1952), 103.

46. Pettigrew, *A Social History of Tea*, 34–35.

47. Ibid. See also Ukers, *All About Tea*, 494, for a chart mapping the etymology of different terms for tea.

48. Dolin, *When America First Met China*, 53. See also Bruce Richardson, "Recycling Used Tea Leaves in the 18th Century," *The Tea Maestro* (blog), January 6, 2015, http://theteamaestro.blogspot.com/2015/01/recycling-used-tea-leaves-in-17th.html.

49. See Friedrich Christian Accum, *A Treatise on Adulteration of Food, and Culinary Poisons, Exhibiting the Fraudulent Sophistications of Bread, Beer, Wine, Spirituous Liquors, Tea, Oil, Pickles, and Other Articles Employed in Domestic Economy. And Methods of Detecting Them* (Philadelphia: Abraham Small, 1820).

50. Some of the materials used to cut tea were perhaps unpleasant but not unhealthy; however, others (like the logwood used to dye whitethorn leaves to cut into tea) caused gastroenteritis when consumed in quantity. More ominous still was green "tea" that had been boiled and painted with verdigris (copper acetate, which is poisonous). For more about tea adulteration, and the prosecution of growers and sellers in Britain, see Bee Wilson, *Swindled: The Dark History of Food Fraud, from Poisoned Candy to Counterfeit Coffee* (Princeton, NJ: Princeton University Press, 2008).

51. See, for example, an article in the *Times*, cited in Wilson, *Swindled*, 35.

52. Robert Fortune, *A Journey to the Tea Countries of China; Including Sung-Lo and the Bohea Hills; with a Short Notice of the East India Company's Tea Planta-tions in the Himalaya Mountains* (London: J. Murray, 1852). See also Accum, *A Treatise*.

53. For more on this, see Wilson, *Swindled*.

54. See Palmer, *Movable Feasts*.

55. This includes maids, kitchen staff, footmen, gardeners, and a lawyer, among many others.

56. Stead discusses wages in depth as well as commodity prices. For example, "weavers earned only 5d [English pennies] a day, tailors only 6d plus food, farm laborers 7d, day laborers 1/- [1 penny per day], carpenters and masons 1/3. Shop-keepers, tradesmen, and master-craftsmen might get 1 pound a week and could af-ford to eat meat every day. Wages in London were higher but then so were prices." Jennifer Stead, *Food and Cooking in 18th Century Britain: History and Recipes* (London: The Historic Buildings and Monuments Commission for England, 1985), 23.

57. As we will explore later, these figures are hard to pin down exactly, because tea smuggling was a very lucrative, and very common, business—one that caused considerable headaches for the East India Company. For more on tea smuggling, particularly in the Americas, see Dolin, *When America First Met China*.

58. Pettigrew and Richardson, *A Social History of Tea*. Dolin, *When America First Met China*. Pettigrew, *A Social History of Tea*.

59. For the upper classes, tea was not only a status symbol but also established as a part of political navigation, even before prices had dropped considerably. Chalus goes into great detail about some political wrangling by Lady Rockingham, in 1765, on behalf of her husband's interests. The interactions started with feigned interest in purchasing a pair of her political target's horses and ended with a conversation over tea. Dinner followed tea, but the tea was a critical component, as it broke the ice and created a more informal environment where the object of William Pitt's political aspirations might let his guard down. Elaine Chalus, "Elite Women, Social Politics,

and the Political World of Late Eighteenth-Century England," *The Historical Journal* 43, no. 3 (2000): 669–97.

60. Pettigrew and Richardson, *A Social History of Tea*, 25–26.

61. See Kate Colquhoun, *Taste: The Story of Britain through Its Cooking* (London: A&C Black, 2012).

62. Ken Albala, "Superfood or Dangerous Drug? Coffee, Tea, and Chocolate in the Late Seventeenth Century," *EuropeNow*, September 5, 2018, https://www.europenowjournal.org/2018/09/04/superfood-or-dangerous-drug-coffee-tea-and-chocolate-in-the-late-17th-century/.

63. John Ovington, *An Essay upon the Nature and Qualities of Tea* (London: R. Roberts, 1699), 26–27.

64. See Ukers's discussion of Garraway's advertisements in *All About Coffee*, 99.

65. Quoted in Gervas Huxley, *Talking of Tea* (London: Thames and Hudson, 1956), 70.

66. Albala, "Superfood or Dangerous Drug?"

67. Ibid.

68. In 1746, Wesley called a meeting of his London Society of Methodists and asked them to give up tea, which apparently they did. See Pettigrew, *A Social History of Tea*, 74. For more on Wesley and his relationship to tea and other substances, see Luke Tyerman, *The Life and Times of John Wesley, Founder of the Methodists* (London: Hodder, 1870).

69. Pettigrew further notes, "It is ironic that in the next century, tea was to become the symbol and focal point of the temperance movement with John Wesley's Methodists as the leading lights. Perhaps Wesley began to realize tea's benefits as an alternative to the copious quantities of gin and beer being consumed by the poor at the time, for later in life, he took up tea again and even organized tea drinkings for his ministers." Ibid.

70. Albala, "Superfood or Dangerous Drug?"

71. Cited in ibid. This is a particularly interesting point, as the newly imported beverages were Europeans' first exposure to caffeine. Albala notes that such stimulants were not readily available prior to this time.

72. See, for example, Ross W. Jamieson, "The Essence of Commodification: Caffeine Dependencies in the Early Modern World," *Journal of Social History* 35, no. 2 (2001): 269–94.

73. Daniel Duncan, *Wholesome Advice against the Abuse of Hot Liquors, Particularly of Coffee, Chocolate, Tea, Brandy, and Strong-Waters: With Directions to Know What Constitutions They Suit, and When the Use of Them May Be Profitable or Hurtful* (London: H. Rhodes and A. Bell, 1706).

74. His many scathing remarks about English laboring classes' dietary habits include the observation that "the higher ranks use tea as a luxury, while the lower orders make a diet of it." William Buchan, *Observations on the Diet of the Common People, Recommending a Method of Living Less Expensive, and More Conducive to Health, than the Present* (London: A. Strahan, 1797), 397.

75. Cited in Buchan, *Observations*, 409.

76. Since many seventeenth-century farmers relied heavily on temporary labor, this estimate is likely higher than the actual yearly wage of many laborers. These temporary workers would often be paid between three and eight British pennies per day, with higher wages paid to those who brought their own food. However, their status as temporary workers meant that they would not always be given work: they were most in demand from March to November but would have had trouble finding work after harvest season. See Wallace Notestein, *The English People on the Eve of Colonization, 1603–1630* (New York: Harper and Brothers, 1954).

77. See Mason, *Food and Culture*.

78. The duty, which had been two shillings, three pennies, per pound in the 1840s, dropped to six pennies by 1865. See Palmer, *Movable Feasts*, 100.

79. In one account, homemade wine was the standard offering to afternoon visitors in Manchester homes in 1720 but by midcentury had been replaced by tea. See Burnett, *Liquid Pleasures*, 52.

80. Social reformers in England were not necessarily pleased that tea overtook ale as the national beverage. Because its export was established as a monopoly early on by the East India Company, tea faced the disapproval of the Puritans, although its role in later social reform (e.g., the temperance movement) shifted that perception. See Palmer, *Movable Feasts*. Tea was so ubiquitous in British culture that those too poor to afford it would substitute hot water poured over a burned crust of bread to approximate the flavor. Austen and Smith, "Private Tooth Decay."

81. See Ukers, *All About Coffee*, 59.

82. Markman Ellis, *The Coffeehouse: A Cultural History* (London: Orion Publishing Group, 2011).

83. In 2006 U.S. dollars. Gautier, *Tea*.

84. For more about public establishments at this time, see William Biggs Boulton, *The Amusements of Old London*, vol. 1 (London: John C. Nimmo, 1901).

85. It was unclear exactly what made coffeehouse patrons undesirable. Perhaps as the establishments grew in popularity, surrounding streets grew unacceptably congested. Or perhaps a string of particularly rude patrons upset the area residents.

86. Pettigrew and Richardson, *A Social History of Tea*, 12–13.

87. As was the meal of luncheon. Palmer goes on to say that "once again wives and mothers took the situation in hand and found the remedy" (*Movable Feasts*, 97).

Shifting workdays and mealtimes meant tweaks were needed to keep families consistently fed. Palmer's perspective was that women led the charge in these efforts, as they were charged with household management.

88. Writing in 1952, Palmer's ideas about gender and food extend beyond the woman's confinement to the private sphere, to encompass social class. In *Movable Feast* he goes on to question women's dietary choices (or tastes acquired from childhood), suggesting that having a working-class appetite is equivalent to being ill bred:

> Sugar or other forms of sweetening had been popular almost from the first, I think; yet already, by . . . [1730], far-sighted mothers were warning their daughters that a love of sugar, and indeed of cream, would be recognized by watchful bachelors as a sign of ill breeding. It is a curious belief, curious in its origin, its persistence, and its survival, amid a holocaust of class-distinctions, as a mark of a small section of society. Even today the barmaids at railways stations can scarcely be restrained from dropping a lump in the cup; the traveller who likes his tea unsweetened is made to understand that he is one of a very troublesome and cranky minority.

Ibid., 104.

89. For example, Mason, *Food and Culture*.

90. Palmer, writing in *Movable Feasts*, and Mason, in *Food and Culture*, are among the historians arguing the centrality of women to afternoon tea's origins and the Duchess of Bedford to its popularity; in fact, these theories are central to nearly every text on tea in England.

91. Even though women were not able to participate in coffeehouse culture as customers, they did in some cases facilitate it as merchants. Coffeehouse proprietors selling coffee, tea, and alcohol to the greater populace include mentions of a "she-coffee merchant" in 1660 in London *Quaries*, Mary Stringer in 1669, Anne Blunt in 1672, and others. "Women played a not inconspicuous part in establishing businesses for the sale of the coffee drink in England, although the coffeehouses were not for both sexes, as in other European countries." Ukers, *All About Coffee*, 52.

92. For more on this topic, see Martyn J. Powell, "Consumption: Commercial Demand and the Challenges to Regulatory Power in Eighteenth-Century Ireland," in *Mercantilism Reimagined: Political Economy in Early Modern Britain and Its Empire*, ed. Philip J. Stern and Carl Wennerlind (Oxford: Oxford University Press, 2014), 282–303.

93. Ibid., 296.

94. See Powell, "Consumption," and Timothy Breen, *The Marketplace of Revolution: How Consumer Politics Shaped American Independence* (New York: Oxford University Press, 2004), 304.

95. Public gatherings were not long to follow, as teahouses began welcoming unescorted female guests.

96. Although in some cases there seems to be an understanding that the "gossip" being spoken of was not idle chitchat about the weather but conversations of camaraderie and brainstorming meant to bring relief to those facing inequality. For example, "Women still gave up their property upon entering a marriage, and they could neither vote nor serve on juries. This inequality continued into the Victorian age. . . . Often their only relief came at teatime when they met to gossip, a scenario that would be re-created throughout nineteenth-century literature." Pettigrew, *A Social History of Tea*, 105.

97. Ibid., 132.

98. Already throughout eighteenth-century England, "the less fashionable classes who continued to have dinner in the middle of the day had a dish of tea in the afternoon, then had a supper in the evening of cold meats, cold pies, bread and cheese." Stead, *Food and Cooking*, 15.

99. Henry Tattam, *A Memoir of Her Grace the Late Duchess of Bedford* (London: W. M. Watts, 1858).

100. Ibid.

101. For example, Michael J. Coffey, "Is the Duchess of Bedford a Fraud?" *Tea Geek Blogs*, August 31, 2010, http://www.teageek.net/blog/2010/08/is-the -duchess-of-bedford-a-fraud/.

102. These arguments have appeared elsewhere but were borne out in popular discourse on two blogs, one arguing for a reevaluation of Bedford's legacy (ibid.), the other arguing for a nuanced understanding of her role (Peter Davenport, "Understanding Anna," *Leafbox Tea* [formerly *Tea Trade*, blog], September 22, 2010, http://leafboxtea.com/496/understanding-anna/).

103. Afternoon tea precedents are documented prior to 1840. For example, in 1763 in Harrogate, a Yorkshire spa town, there are records of the town's ladies hosting afternoon tea gatherings on a rotating basis, with each one hosting roughly every four to six weeks. See Burnett, *Liquid Pleasures*.

104. "Stylish cities like Bath always included tea drinking after a dance, which Jane Austen wrote about in *Northanger Abbey* (1818). But at home, tea provided a reason to see the neighbors . . . tea was seen as a comforting, refreshing, recuperative beverage. . . . Tea meant rest and pleasure, and its absence would be a severe disappointment." Pettigrew, *A Social History of Tea*, 127.

105. Palmer, *Movable Feasts*, 100–101.

106. There is a good deal of research on this within business and social science, and while these ideas studied sometimes deal with innovation from the perspective of introducing and marketing a new product, the concepts apply to the introduction

of cultural norms as well and show that the difference between the innovation and the existing standard are as important as the innovation's bearing some resemblance to existing practices.

Tidd, for example, says that "the extent to which the innovation fits the existing skills, equipment, procedures and performance criteria of the potential adopter is critical. Few innovations initially fit the user environment into which they are introduced. Significant misalignments between the innovation and the adopting organization will require changes in the innovation or organization or, in the most successful cases of implementation, mutual adaptation of both. Initial compatibility with existing practices may be less important, as it may provide limited opportunity for mutual adaptation to occur." Joseph Tidd, "From Models to the Management of Diffusion," in *Gaining Momentum: Managing the Diffusion of Innovations*, ed. Joseph Tidd (London: Imperial College Press, 2010), 22.

An example I regularly use with non-food historians is the way a Word document renders on a computer: there is no objective reason why the document *needs* to render that way, but the program has been written so that the interface looks like you are typing on a piece of paper. Prior to computers, of course (and even for a while after computers appeared), typewriters were the technology used for producing typewritten pages at home. As computers became more sophisticated and had more complex graphics, they could produce a screen that was evocative of using a typewriter, thus helping people find the familiar in unfamiliar technological waters. To go a bit further afield, this is the same reason why Gutenberg's early movable type press used a typeface that looked like handwriting—so that it would be reminiscent of manuscript pages and thus more familiar. Computers are ubiquitous in modern Western society, but the concept itself would not have been successful had there not been accepted technologies that this new concept could grow from and relate to (e.g., typewriters).

Computers have been around for only a handful of decades but already have become central to many parts of our lives, largely because the right idea was produced at the right time and was shared with people in a way that connected that new idea to ones they were familiar with. Likewise, afternoon tea built on a tradition of afternoon social gatherings that included tea and snacks but were not daily or widespread activities.

107. In Palmer's perspective, but not anywhere else that I've seen, afternoon tea was first adopted to provide "a meal suitable for children and an hour and a half for its digestion. Then, when the serious business of the evening set in, they could 'be packed off (as it is supposed)' to the night nurse" (Palmer, *Movable Feasts*, 101). While nursery tea was a common occurrence in wealthy households, many records

of the time show that the practice originated with adults and was adapted to the nursery as household schedules as a whole shifted.

108. Dinners were moving to 7:30 or 8:00, rather than 6:00 or so. See Pettigrew, *A Social History of Tea*, 130.

109. Dinner was typically a leisurely meal—at least in wealthy households—so after-dinner tea would not have happened until 10:00 p.m. See Pettigrew, *A Social History of Tea*, 130. This practice is mentioned regularly in Regency-era literature—for example, in Jane Austen's *Sense and Sensibility* (1811).

110. Just as with afternoon tea, high tea also moved across socioeconomic classes:

> As the century progressed, the work day was shortened, and since high tea was eaten as soon as the family returned from work, the mealtime came a little earlier. Before the First World War, it was taken at 6 or 6.30; by the 1930s and 1940s, it was more commonly eaten at 5 or 5.30. Although high tea was usually a lower-middle-class and working-class meal, the wealthier classes also served it—especially at weekends for large house parties. "20th c Beetons" meals like these are "governed by time of dinner that preceded them and the kind of supper to be taken afterwards."

Pettigrew, *A Social History of Tea*, 185.

111. For more on diffusion of innovation, see Tidd, "Management of Diffusion."

112. Pettigrew, *A Social History of Tea*, 130–31.

113. Ibid.

114. See Pettigrew, *A Social History of Tea*, 131, and also where Pettigrew's citation of Sitwell continues: "My mother was the first to introduce the custom to Scotland; and this was in consequence of Lord Alexander Russell, who was staying with us at Balmoral, telling her that his mother, the Duchess of Bedford, always had afternoon tea at Woburn." This statement suggests that the tradition moved through aristocratic circles relatively quickly—not surprising, given the other evidence surrounding its adoption. See also Helen Saberi, *Teatimes: A World Tour* (London: Reaktion Books, 2018), http://www.reaktionbooks.co.uk/pdfs/Teatimes_extract_web.pdf, page 21; Lynne Olver, "Afternoon Tea," *The Food Timeline* (website), January 3, 2015, http://www.foodtimeline.org/teatime.html.

115. Pettigrew, *A Social History of Tea*, 131. Kemble in the same letter calls the gathering "private and, I think, rather shamefaced," although she does not elaborate as to why, perhaps because regular meals, as a rule, were taken outside one's own rooms and in the communal dining areas of the home.

116. See ibid., 131–32.

117. See Straker, *Afternoon Tea*.

118. See Pettigrew, *A Social History of Tea*, 131–32. Other popular names for the meal included low tea (because of the low chairs and tables used for the gathering), handed tea (since the host handed the cups around the table rather than having each person serve themselves), and kettledrums (this, Pettigrew thinks, because the tea kettle was a vital part of the experience). Flora Thompson refers to "visitor's tea," which seems to have been a particularly formal version of afternoon tea done for guests rather than just for family and perhaps familiar friends. See Flora Thompson, *Lark Rise to Candleford: A Trilogy* (Boston: David R. Godine, 2009), 298.

119. Clara E. Anderson, *A Character Sketch Entertainment, Entitled Afternoon Tea in Friendly Village, 1862* (Ottawa: J. Hope and Sons, 1912).

120. See, for example, Hildegard Hoeller, "Hunger, Panic, and Refusal: The Gift of Food in Susan Warner's *The Wide, Wide World*," in *Culinary Aesthetics and Practices in Nineteenth-Century American Literature*, ed. Monika Elbert and Mary Drews (New York: Palgrave Macmillan, 2009), 176.

121. Austen and Smith, "Private Tooth Decay," 194.

122. Ibid., 193–95.

123. Cited in Pettigrew, *A Social History of Tea*, 132.

124. Thompson, *Lark*, 190–91.

125. Ibid., 190.

126. See, for example, Pettigrew, *Social History of Tea*, 135.

127. Burnett, *Liquid Pleasures*.

128. See Pettigrew, *A Social History of Tea*.

129. For example, Lucie Heaton Armstrong wrote of informal gatherings as well as formal tea gatherings where the hostess would wear an evening gown rather than a tea gown to greet her guests. See her *Letters to a Bride Including Letters to a Debutante* (London: F. V. White & Company, 1896).

130. See Pettigrew, *A Social History of Tea*, 135. For a discussion of etiquette in America, see also Maureen E. Montgomery, *Displaying Women: Spectacles of Leisure in Edith Wharton's New York* (New York: Routledge, 1998).

131. Mason, *Food and Culture*; Julie Fromer, *A Necessary Luxury: Tea in Victorian England* (Athens: Ohio University Press, 2008).

132. See Ukers, *All About Coffee*. Cold milk or cream was most commonly added to tea in the Victorian era, although occasionally hot milk was used. Variations were regional: for example, the famously rich milk of western England was often used in tea, as it was hefty enough to stand in for the cream that might have been used elsewhere. Other examples of Victorian etiquette that persist today include a prohibition on using one's fork as a toothpick or eating peas off one's knife (which seems like a mechanically improbable feat to accomplish in the first place). For more

examples, see Matthew Sweet, *Inventing the Victorians: What We Think We Know about Them and Why We're Wrong* (New York: St. Martin's Press, 2014).

133. See Pettigrew, *A Social History of Tea*, 142.

134. For more on the history of tea gowns, see Pettigrew, *A Social History of Tea*.

135. See, for example, Armstong, *Letters*, and Isabella Mary Beeton, *Mrs. Beeton's Every-Day Cookery* (London: Ward, Lock & Co., 1907).

136. In Pettigrew, *A Social History of Tea*, 141.

137. The women at these gatherings would likely have been horrified to learn that Britain was importing opium to China, which resulted in a massive epidemic of addiction. The East India Company grew opium in its territories in Northeast India and traded it into China via shipping agents, brokers, and wholesalers (it was illegal but apparently not at all difficult for them to find buyers). A more extensive discussion can be found in Dolin, *When America First Met China*. The moral dilemma is clear: "The tea being drunk in English vicarages, at abolitionist meetings in Boston and in fine manor houses and simple country cottages was nearly all bought with opium." Pettigrew, *A Social History of Tea*, 106.

138. Robert Fulford notes that "the new tea rooms were important for 'respectable' women." He goes on to say that, "in the later part of the century, middle and upper class women were moving more freely in public places, using the more accessible modes of public transport to visit their friends, get to places of study or work, and shop in the new department stores. And yet, there were few acceptable places of refreshment for them." See his *Votes for Women: The Story of a Struggle* (London: Faber and Faber, 1956), 156.

Pettigrew agrees, pointing to tea as a beverage long associated with gentility, and with the increasing popularity of tearooms at the end of the nineteenth century, these became one of the few public spaces where a woman could enjoy refreshments. Pettigrew, *A Social History of Tea*, 157.

139. Fromer, *Necessary Luxury*, 6.

140. Pettigrew, *A Social History of Tea*, 143. Palmer, *Movable Feasts*.

141. High tea dishes might include potato cakes, meat, and haddock poached in milk. See Gautier, *Tea*.

142. Pettigrew notes that fancy afternoon teas might be unrealistic for busy poor families, "but a large pot of strong tea sitting in the middle of the meal table amidst cold meats, pies, fired bacon and potatoes, cheese, home-baked bread or oatmeal cakes was a welcome sight at 5:30 or 6 at the end of a working day. A 'high tea' of filling, hearty foods, also known as 'meat tea' or 'great tea,' was exactly what mine and factory workers needed as soon as they arrived home hungry and thirsty from a 10 hour shift." Pettigrew, *A Social History of Tea*, 137.

143. Thompson, *Lark*, 411.

144. Burnett, *Liquid Pleasures*.

145. See Pettigrew, *A Social History of Tea*.

146. He also gave his workers raises at the same time. See ibid.

147. Black, *Food*.

148. Ibid.

149. Ibid.

150. Mason, *Food and Culture*.

151. Spencer also points to gendered variations on what was served with biscuits, at least for middle- and upper-class consumers: "biscuits and cheese for the gentleman at his club, and sweet biscuits for tea at home for the mistress and her guests." Colin Spencer, *British Food: An Extraordinary Thousand Years of History* (New York: Columbia University Press, 2002), 286.

152. Black, *Food*.

153. Pettigrew, *A Social History of Tea*, 160.

154. See, for example, chapter 4, where John shares his experience with modern afternoon tea breaks in the home.

155. Quoted in Pettigrew, *A Social History of Tea*, 133.

156. See ibid., 133–34. Intimate tea gatherings were still common as well, such as the "drawing room teas" Queen Victoria often held after larger receptions, where a small group of favored ladies were invited to her drawing room to join her for tea—very reminiscent of the early exclusive gatherings held by the Duchess of Bedford.

157. See Beeton, *Every-Day Cookery*; and Pettigrew, *A Social History of Tea*.

158. Lisa Richardson, *The World in Your Teacup: Celebrating Tea Traditions Near and Far* (Eugene, OR: Harvest House Publishers, 2010). See also my interview with Liz in chapter 4, where she discusses her family's traditional weekly "fruity tea."

159. This structure has its roots in medieval meal times, when the midday meal was the largest of the day and the evening meal was smaller. The midday meal shifted to later in the day over time, and by the Victorian period the structure of mealtimes in southern England was much different, with the long gap between meals that facilitated afternoon tea's emergence. For more on medieval mealtimes, see Ken Albala, *Cooking in Europe, 1250–1650* (Westport, CT: Greenwood Press, 2006), 18–19.

160. See, for example, Pettigrew, *A Social History of Tea*.

161. This new tea was not an instant hit: The East India Company had been experimenting with growing tea in India, and Indian tea was auctioned in London for the first time in 1839. However, the public was accustomed to the taste of Chinese tea, and the initial pushes for Indian tea were unsuccessful. Palmer, *Movable Feasts*.

CHAPTER 2

The epigraph is from Shula Marks, "History, the Nation and Empire: Sniping from the Periphery," *History Workshop* 29, no. 1 (1990): 116, in which she quotes Sidney W. Mintz, *Sweetness and Power: The Place of Sugar in Modern History* (London: Penguin Books, 1986), 182.

1. France, Denmark, and Russia, just to name a few.

2. Ashley Jackson, *The British Empire: A Very Short Introduction* (Cambridge: Oxford University Press, 2013), 5.

3. For more on this, see John Rickard, "Eating like a White Man: Nibbling at the Edges of Heart of Darkness," *L'epoque Conradienne* 33 (2007): 49–57.

4. Purchas, *Purchas*.

5. Tea itself is a regular staple in the postcolonial world. Though it was originally brought over by the English for their own comfort, it was also imported for the local populations in the hopes of replacing alcohol consumption. The Luo, for example, recount tales of "being chased with tea," as they put it—a reference to colonial missionaries' attempts to instill concepts of English bourgeois domesticity and sobriety by getting the Luo to substitute tea for beer as a social lubricant.

> The Luo now drink tea only rarely, but Luo *women* consider it the appropriate drink for receiving certain kinds of visitors in the home, and it is usually served with slices of white bread, another alien delicacy that is not otherwise consumed. Tea also requires the purchase of refined sugar (something that the Luo do not use for anything else) and the use of fresh milk (another unique usage, as they generally prefer soured milk). Hence, contrary to the desires of the missionaries, tea has certainly not replaced beer. It is not used in rituals or in male commensality. Nor has it had much impact on Luo domestic habits. What it has done is help to tie women to the national cash economy by creating a periodic need for the purchase of a set of ingredients (tea leaves, sugar, bread) and specialized objects (a teapot and cups) of nonlocal origins.

Michael Dietler, "Culinary Encounters: Food, Identity, and Colonialism," in *The Archaeology of Food and Identity*, occasional paper no. 34, ed. Katheryn C. Twiss (Carbondale: Center for Archaeological Investigations, Southern Illinois University, Carbondale, 2006), 228.

6. Dolin, *When America First Met China*, 67.

7. Joseph Robson Tanner, *Tudor Constitutional Documents, A.D. 1485–1603* (Cambridge: Cambridge University Press, 1922), 41. See this text also for the act's complete text, as well as commentary, and other Tudor constitutional documents.

8. See Philip Jenkins, *A History of Modern Wales, 1536–1990* (New York: Routledge, 2014), for more on the empire's relationship to Wales and for discussion of the Tudors' use of Welsh history to justify English colonialism—for example, by using the history of medieval Prince Madoc, who in legend is said to have discovered America and left a Welsh colony there, as a precedent for colonial exploration.

9. Privateers engaged in state-sanctioned piracy.

10. Johannes Postma, *The Dutch in the Atlantic Slave Trade, 1600–1815* (Cambridge: Cambridge University Press, 1990), 50.

11. Tirthankar, Roy *The East India Company: The World's Most Powerful Corporation* (London: Penguin Books, 2016).

12. Ibid.

13. Ibid.

14. Dolin, *When America First Met China*.

15. Jackson, *British Empire*.

16. As in de Bry's accounts, found in Theodor de Bry, Hans Staden, and Jean de Léry, *Dritte Buch Americae, darinn Brasilia* [America, part 3, therein Brazil] (Frankfurt: Durch Dieterich bry von Lüttich jetzt Burger, 1593).

17. Indentured servitude as a way to bring labor to the New World was also enacted with English subjects and was framed as a way to improve one's lot. In places like Australia, these new colonists were brought from British prisons. Indentured servitude by British subjects began at the tail end of the sixteenth century, with workers brought to plantations in Ireland, and it gradually spread. For discussion of indentured servitude in America, see Karl Frederick Geiser, *Redemptioners and Indentured Servants in the Colony and Commonwealth of Pennsylvania* (New Haven, CT: The Tuttle, Morehouse, & Taylor Co., 1901).

18. The Company's legacy lives on in Powis Castle in Wales, which houses more Mughal artifacts than any museum collection in India. These were plundered by the Company after it conquered Bengal and were moved to Britain to adorn a wealthy country estate. See William Dalrymple, "The East India Company: The Original Corporate Raiders," *The Guardian*, March 4, 2015, https://www.theguardian.com/world/2015/mar/04/east-india-company-original-corporate-raiders.

19. Dolin, *When America First Met China*; and Roy, *The East India Company*.

20. Kenneth Pomeranz, *The Great Divergence: China, Europe, and the Making of the Modern World Economy* (Princeton, NJ: Princeton University Press, 2000), 161, 267.

21. See, for example, Troy Bickham, "Eating the Empire: Intersections of Food, Cookery and Imperialism in Eighteenth Century Britain," *Past & Present* 198, no. 1 (2008): 71–109.

22. Mary Lou Heiss and Robert J. Heiss, *The Story of Tea: A Cultural History and Drinking Guide* (New York: Ten Speed Press, 2007), 25.

23. The British Empire was ruthless in its movement of flora and fauna throughout the colonial world, taking the rubber plant to Ceylon and Malaya, coconuts to the Bahamas, and more. It also brought disease and pest animals (like rabbits to Australia) as well as livestock (like sheep to New Zealand) that are still a part of the postcolonial fabric. In addition to altering flora and fauna on a global scale, the empire moved laborers (both willing migrant laborers and indentured and enslaved ones), thus changing the face of the global population. L. C. B. Seaman, *Victorian England: Aspects of English and Imperial History, 1837–1901* (London: Routledge, 2002), 413.

24. You can still visit some of these tea plantations, which are discussed in greater detail in chapter 3. See also Fortune, *Journey*.

25. Dietler, "Culinary Encounters," 224, and then 218.

26. Ibid., 224. See also Mary Douglas, "Standard Social Uses of Food: Introduction," in *Food in the Social Order: Studies of Food and Festivities in Three American Communities*, ed. Mary Douglas (New York: Russell Sage Foundation, 1984), 28.

27. To read some of the debate, see Sylvanus Urban, review of *Remarks on the Present Distresses of the Poor*, 3rd ed., by G. H. Law, Lord Bishop of Bath and Canterbury, in *The Gentleman's Magazine* (April 1836): 385–93.

28. Gladstone also halved duties on other consumer goods, such as soap, at this time.

29. Seaman, *Victorian England*, 182–83.

30. Yates points to one example in a footnote of his record of Gladstone's second administration: "As Sir. M. Hicks-Beach has denied that he suggested additional taxation on tea, we give an extract from his speech in the House of Commons against the Childers' Budget of June 9th. 'It was evident from the returns that the consumption of tea was largely increasing in the country, and that by imposing a comparatively small addition to the duty on tea the Chancellor of the Exchequer would have obtained from that article as large a revenue as the most sanguine estimates of the right hon. Gentleman anticipated from the increased duties on spirits and beer.'" Arthur C. Yates, *1880–1885: A Record of Mr. Gladstone's Second Administration* (Manchester, England: Abel Heywood & Son, 1885), 18.

31. His proper title was Robert Arthur Talbot Gascoyne-Cecil, Third Marquess of Salisbury.

32. Seaman, *Victorian England*, 282.

33. See Yates, *1880–1885*.

34. See Pierre Saunier, "Food Production: Industrial Processing Begins to Gain Ground," in *A Cultural History of Food in the Age of Empire*, vol. 5, ed. Martin Bruegel (London: Berg, 2012), 27–48.

35. Dolin, *When America First Met China*.

36. America also imported less Chinese tea as preferences shifted to Japanese and Dutch East Indies green tea and to black teas from India and Ceylon. See Pettigrew, *A Social History of Tea*, 173.

37. Anna Davin, "Family and Domesticity: Food in Poor Households," in *A Cultural History of Food in the Age of Empire*, vol. 5, ed. Martin Bruegel (London: Berg, 2012), 141–64.

38. Davin, "Family and Domesticity," 143.

39. Tea constituted a considerable amount of the diet of poor women and children, often to the outcry (coupled with inaction) of public-health officials. In "Family and Domesticity," Davin writes,

> In the poorer working-class family only the father would have any regular amount of meat or fish. Maud Pember Reeves commented that, with a budget for food of ten shillings at most, "only one kind of diet is possible, and that is the man's diet. The children have what is left over." (Mothers had even less.)
>
> James Kerr, London school medical officer in the 1900s, noted that children from poor households never had enough vegetables or fresh milk, and they lived on tea, bread, and sugar, and were unlikely to get protein except for possibly during Sunday dinner. . . .
>
> Most of the basic components of the working-class diet were regarded as unsuitable for children. . . . The advice-givers thought that underfed children must come from the families whose domestic practices were all wrong. If children were hungry, parents were probably neglectful and perhaps drunken; if they were undernourished it was not shortage of food that was responsible, but the fact that it was the wrong food, eaten at the wrong time in the wrong place. ("Family and Domesticity," 149, 159)

40. Pettigrew, *A Social History of Tea*, 187. For more on tea from Ceylon becoming more popular on the global market, see Angela McCarthy and T. M. Devine, *Tea and Empire: James Taylor in Victorian Ceylon* (Manchester: Manchester University Press, 2017).

41. Agnes Bertha Marshall, *Mrs. A. B. Marshall's Larger Cookery Book of Extra Recipes* (London: Marshall's School of Cookery, 1902), 477.

42. See, for example, Lesley Lewis, *The Private Life of a Country House* (Stroud: Alan Sutton Publishing Ltd., 1997).

43. Teasmades are still a popular consumer item. Early teasmade models used a pilot light, which remained lit continuously, but these were replaced by electric models in the 1930s. See "Heritage" at the Teasmade website, https://teasmade .com/pages/heritage.

44. See Tinniswood, *Long Weekend.*

45. See Peter Scholliers, "Eating Out," in *A Cultural History of Food in the Age of Empire*, vol. 5, ed. Martin Bruegel (London: Berg, 2012), 107–22.

46. See Saunier, "Food Production," 43–44.

47. Pettigrew, *A Social History of Tea*, 191.

48. Niall Ferguson, *Empire: The Rise and Demise of the British World Order and the Lessons for Global Power* (New York: Basic Books, 2002).

49. Ibid.

50. Ronald Hyam, *Understanding the British Empire* (Cambridge: Cambridge University Press, 2010), 56.

51. Bickham, "Eating the Empire," 72.

52. Amy B. Trubek, "Professional Cooking, Kitchens, and Service Work," in *A Cultural History of Food in the Age of Empire*, vol. 5, ed. Martin Bruegel (London: Berg, 2012), 127.

53. Davin, "Family and Domesticity," 143.

54. For example, one hotel in Singapore is still touted by visitors as "the epitome of the once great British Empire's life of luxury in Asia. [T]his is a living legacy to that time in history." See Dale G's review of Raffles Hotel Singapore at *TripAdvisor*, June 18, 2014, https://www.tripadvisor.com/ShowUserReviews-g294265 -d301583-r212538612-Raffles_Hotel_Singapore-Singapore.html.

Hong Kong, a recent departure from English rule, also still shows strong English influences, and many hotels continue to hold very traditional afternoon teas. Blogger Melissa Stevens, for example, lists several that offer tea alongside tiered trays of petits fours and finger sandwiches, nearly all of which primarily show English influences rather than culinary influences of Hong Kong or its more immediate neighbors: see "Your Hong Kong High Tea Bucket List" in *Expat Living*, April 12, 2017, https://expatliving.hk/high-tea-hong-kong/.

55. See Pettigrew, *A Social History of Tea*, and Dolin, *When America First Met China*. It's worth noting that the East India Company had been first formed half a century earlier to combat the Portuguese monopoly on trade with Asia, which shows how much alliances and the needs and desires of colonizing countries can shift over a relatively short period.

56. John Clark Marshman, *History of India from the Earliest Period to the Close of the East India Company's Government* (Cambridge: Cambridge University Press, 2010), 470–90.

57. Even so, British and other colonial powers increasingly encroached on Chinese land, both during the wars and after: a treaty in 1842, for example, forced China to surrender Hong Kong to Britain and open its ports to foreign commerce. See Fabio Parasecoli, "World Food: The Age of Empire c. 1800–1920," in *A Cultural History of Food in the Age of Empire*, vol. 5, ed. Martin Bruegel (London: Berg, 2012), 199–208.

58. Ibid.

59. Mason, *Food and Culture*.

60. According to one report, "The prevalence of anemia among tea-garden coolies and agricultural labourers is partly due to hookworm infection. Add to this malaria and chronic undernourishment, and you have a picture of the state of health of our labouring class." From N. Gangulee, *Health and Nutrition in India* (London: Faber and Faber Ltd., 1939), 124. While anemia had been known for centuries, about fifty years prior to the report's 1939 publication it had been discovered that its prevalence could be mitigated by addressing pollution in the soil—an expenditure the report argues the British government was unwilling to make.

61. Ibid., 229.

62. Ibid., 225.

63. Ibid., 196.

64. Ibid., 276.

65. See, for example, Pettigrew, *A Social History of Tea*. In one instance, workers on a Guiana plantation went on strike in 1904 to protest the sexual harassment and abuse of female laborers. For exploration of abuse around the empire, see Richard Gott, *Britain's Empire: Resistance, Repression, and Revolt* (London: Verso, 2011).

66. Gangulee, *Health and Nutrition*, 191. This is interesting and in opposition to Western perspectives framing tea as a healthful, antioxidant-rich beverage.

67. See, for example, Parasecoli, "World Food," and Saunier, "Food Production."

68. For a complete discussion of European missionaries in India from an Indiocentric perspective—rather than a Eurocentric view only showing exchange from colonizer to colonized—see Robert Eric Frykenberg and Alaine M. Low, *Christians and Missionaries in India: Cross-cultural Communication since 1500* (Grand Rapids, MI: William B. Eerdmans Publishing Company, 2003).

69. Roy, *The East India Company*.

70. Ramrishna Mukherjee, *The Rise and Fall of the East India Company* (New York: Monthly Review Press, 2009).

71. This was originally a Portuguese colony, whose inhabitants were closer with the Mughal court and more established in the area due to the work of Jesuit diplomats years before. See ibid.

72. Ibid.

73. Ibid.

74. See Pettigrew, *A Social History of Tea*, 92.

75. See ibid.

76. See ibid.

77. Closer to home, Americans also used language about their fears of being enslaved under British rule. Many of course owned slaves themselves—and did not take issue with the existence of the institution—but most likely were afraid of being treated the way they treated others. Material circulated in America immediately prior to the Revolution places this conversation directly in relation to tea:

> "A Mechanic," writing in a broadside dated December 4, 1773, warned his fellow citizens of the extreme dangers of continuing to buy and drink British tea: "The East India Company, if once they get footing in this (once) happy country, will leave no stone unturned to become your masters. They are an opulent body, and money or credit is not wanting amongst them. They have a designing, depraved and despotic ministry to assist and support them. They themselves are well versed in TYRRANNY, PLUNDER, OPPRESSION, and BLOODSHED. Whole provinces laboring under the distresses of oppression, slavery, famine, and the sword, are familiar to them. Thus they have enriched themselves—thus they are become the most powerful trading Company in the universe."

Quoted in Dolin, *When America First Met China*, 69.

78. Ibid., 57.

79. Tea became so popular in America that visitors from England remarked upon it. Joseph Bennett, visiting in 1740, noted that "The ladies here visit, drink tea, and indulge every little piece of gentility to the height of the mode, and neglect the affairs of their families with as good a grace as the finest ladies in London." Quoted in ibid.

80. Given the long-standing tension between the Dutch and English for control of American markets, and the fact that some American residents still had Dutch connections, this legislation was not surprising and is one of many examples of British legislation bolstering the East India Company's business endeavors.

81. Hardly any American colonists had been to China, save for perhaps a handful of sailors, and there are no known American writings relaying these experiences. However, colonists could look to European accounts of China, which usually painted a very favorable picture. It appears that many Americans knew little to nothing about Chinese culture, although they were avid consumers of Chinese goods.

82. According to Dolin, "Many of them set forth with the encouragement—or at least the complicity—of colonial governors, appointed by the Crown. In return the

governors often received payment in the form of Far Eastern booty." Dolin, *When America First Met China*, 60.

83. Margarette Lincoln, *British Pirates and Society, 1680–1730* (New York: Routledge, 2014).

84. Parson Woodforde's account of March 29, 1777, shows how much cheaper smuggled tea was than the legally imported tea: "Andrews the Smuggler brought me this night about 11 o'clock a bagg of Hyson Tea 6 Pd weight. He frightened us a little by whistling under the Parlour Window just as we were going to bed. I gave him some Geneva and paid him for the tea at 10/6 per pound." Quoted in Stead, *Food and Cooking*, 22.

Parson Woodforde was willing to put up with the late-night visitor because of the exorbitant cost of legally imported tea, which was roughly six times more expensive than the smuggled tea he purchased. See Janet Clarkson, *Food History Almanac: Over 1,300 Years of World Culinary History, Culture, and Social Influence*, vol. 1 (Lanham, MD: Rowman & Littlefield, 2013), 297.

85. See Dolin, *When America First Met China*.

86. Quoted in ibid., 65.

87. Including plunging stock, decreasing revenues from India, and economic depression. See ibid., 67–68.

88. Ibid., 68–69.

89. Robert J. Allison, *American Revolution: A Concise History* (Oxford: Oxford University Press, 2011), 16–18.

90. Benjamin L. Carp, "Did Dutch Smugglers Provoke the Boston Tea Party?" *Early American Studies: An Interdisciplinary Journal* 10, no. 2 (2012): 335–59; Alfred P. Young, *The Shoemaker and the Tea Party: Memory and the American Revolution* (Boston: Beacon Press, 1999).

91. Its universal appreciation by colonists facilitated a shared experience of outrage and anger when new taxes and other restrictions arose, and this shared experience could be translated into collective action. Breen, *Marketplace of Revolution*.

92. See Dolin, *When America First Met China*, 58.

93. Lisa L. Petrovich, "More than the Boston Tea Party: Tea in American Culture, 1760s–1840s," MA thesis, University of Colorado–Boulder, 2013, https://scholar.colorado.edu/cgi/viewcontent.cgi?article=1017&context=hist_gradetds, 59. One striking example of the centrality of tea to revolutionary fervor comes from a letter John Adams sent his wife, Abigail, on July 6, 1774:

When I first came to this House it was late in the Afternoon, and I had ridden 35 miles at least. "Madam" said I to Mrs. Huston, "is it lawfull for a weary Traveller to refresh himself with a Dish of Tea provided it has been honestly smuggled, or paid no Duties?" "No sir, said she, we have renounced all Tea in this Place. I cant make Tea, but I'le make you Coffee." Accordingly I have drank Coffee every Afternoon since, and have borne it very well. Tea must be universally renounced. I must be weaned, and the sooner, the better.

John Adams to Abigail Adams, July 6, 1774, in *Founding Families: Digital Editions of the Papers of the Winthrops and the Adamses*, ed. C. James Taylor (Boston: Massachusetts Historical Society, 2018), http://www.masshist.org/publications/ adams-papers/index.php/view/ADMS-04-01-02-0087#sn=0.

94. *Boston Gazette*, 1768, quoted in Pettigrew, *A Social History of Tea*, 85. This infusion, brewed from *Ceanothus americanus*, was also shipped to England and the rest of Europe as one of America's earliest exports. *Ceanothus* is more commonly known as New Jersey tea—or Walpole tea, Indian tea, or redroot—and while this particular resource notes that it grows in Maine, it was largely grown in New Jersey—hence the name.

95. Abigail Adams to John Adams, July 15, 1778, in *Adams Family Papers: An Electronic Archive*, ed. Massachusetts Historical Society, http://www.masshist.org/ digitaladams/archive/doc?id=L17780715aa&bc=%2Fdigitaladams%2Farchive%2 Fbrowse%2Fletters_1778_1779.php.

96. Young, *The Shoemaker*, xvii.

97. Ukers, for example, says that the "tea tax is undoubtedly responsible for our becoming a nation of coffee drinkers instead of tea drinkers, like the English." Ukers, *All About Coffee*, 102.

98. Ibid.

99. Dolin, *When America First Met China*, 91.

100. Daniel J. Toll, *A Narrative Embracing the History of Two or Three of the First Settlers and Their Families of Schenectady* (Schenectady, NY: Daniel J. Toll, 1847).

101. Ibid.

102. For example, how much are the Townshend Acts alone to blame for the discontent that led to revolution? How big a factor was the East India Company? And so on.

103. "The American. Providence: Friday, January 28, 1831," published on page 2 of the *Rhode Island American and Gazette* 2, no. 57, January 28, 1831, and found in the Gale Digital Collections "19th Century U.S. Newspapers" database. As quoted in Petrovich, "More than the Boston Tea Party."

104. Stefan Goodwin, *African Legacies of Urbanization: Unfolding Saga of a Continent* (Lanham, MD: Lexington Books, 2006), 314.

105. Robert M. Maxon and Thomas P. Ofcansky, *Historical Dictionary of Kenya* (Lanham, MD: Scarecrow Press, 2000).

106. Ibid.

107. See Saunier, "Food Production."

108. Maxon and Ofcansky, *Kenya*.

109. Mistreatment of Africans continued among the settlers. For example, the *kipande*, an identification card and passbook introduced after World War I, was required for African workers. If a settler did not like the worker's work or behavior, it was not uncommon for them to tear up the *kipande* and, in so doing, leave the African worker unable to get another job.

110. Lee Jolliffe, ed., *Tea and Tourism: Tourists, Traditions and Transformations* (Buffalo, NY: Channel View Publications, 2007).

111. Among those in the first transport, Susie Khamis identifies only one gardener, one fisherperson, two brickmakers and two bricklayers, and one mason as likely having relevant skills for building a new colony. See "A Taste for Tea: How Tea Travelled to (and Through) Australian Culture," *ACH: The Journal of the History of Culture in Australia* 24 (2006): 57–79.

112. See Khamis, "A Taste for Tea."

113. "Letter from a Female Convict," Historical Records of New South Wales, vol. 2, pp. 746–47, as referenced in Alan Birch and David S. Macmillan, eds., *The Sydney Scene 1788–1960* (Sydney: Hale and Iremonger, 1982), 34. And for a deeper discussion of women in early Australian colonial society, see Portia Robinson, *The Women of Botany Bay: A Reinterpretation of the Role of Women in the Origins of Australian Society* (Victoria, Australia: Penguin Books, 1993).

114. Khamis, "A Taste for Tea."

115. Ibid.

116. For a more complete discussion of this, see Khamis, "A Taste for Tea."

117. Colonizers can also introduce less benign practices, like displacement, genocide, forced or undercompensated labor, and so on, all of which, of course, also contribute significantly to how a native community changes.

118. See Ian Southwell and Robert Lowe, eds., *Tea Tree: The Genus Melaleuca* (Amsterdam: Harwood Academic Publishers, 1999).

119. Anne Brewster, *Reading Aboriginal Women's Life Stories* (Sydney: Sydney University Press, 2015), 4.

120. Sally Morgan, *My Place* (Freemantle, Australia: Freemantle Press, 1987).

121. Brewster, *Reading*, 4.

122. See Brewster, *Reading*, and Morgan, *My Place*.

123. Uwe Jens Rudolf and Warren G. Berg, *Historical Dictionary of Malta*, 2nd ed. (Lanham, MD: Scarecrow Press, 2010).

124. In 2013, Malta had a mere half million residents. See *Visit Malta*, "History," accessed December 15, 2017, http://www.visitmalta.com/en/history.

125. Winifred Stuart, *Chronicles of Service Life in Malta* (London: Edward Arnold, 1908).

126. Robert Lugg, "Tea and History: Revel in Marvellous Malta's Sunshine, Beauty and English Heritage," *Daily Mail* (London), December 22, 2013, https://www.dailymail.co.uk/travel/article-2429930/Holidays-Malta-Revel-islands -sunshine-beauty-English-heritage.html.

127. Margaret Dexter, *Malta Remembered: Then and Now; A Love Story* (Bloomington, IN: iUniverse, 2013).

128. For example, see "Afternoon Tea" at Corinthia Hotel St. Georges Bay, Malta, https://www.corinthia.com/en/hotels/malta-stgeorgesbay/dining/bars/ le-cafe/afternoon-tea.

129. Jodie Matthews and Daniel Travers, eds., *Islands and Britishness: A Global Perspective* (Newcastle upon Tyne, England: Cambridge Scholars Publishing, 2012).

130. Leonard Thompson, *A History of South Africa* (New Haven, CT: Yale Nota Bene, 2001).

131. Ibid.

132. Ibid.

133. Ibid.

134. Ibid.

135. Ibid. Apartheid—literally meaning "separateness" in Afrikaans—was a system of institutionalized racial segregation that was the law of the land in South Africa for the better part of the second half of the twentieth century.

136. Ibid.

137. Akira Takada, *Narratives on San Enthnicity: The Cultural and Ecological Foundations of Lifeworld among the !Xun of North-Central Namibia* (Kyoto, Japan: Kyoto University Press, 2015), 55.

138. Dudley Kidd, *Echoes from the Battlefields of South Africa* (London: Marshall Brothers, 1900).

139. P. T. Ross, *A Yeoman's Letters from the Boer War* (London: Simpkin, Marshall, Hamilton, Kent, & Co. Ltd., 1901), 128.

140. For more on this subject, see, for example, Andrew Porter, ed., *The Oxford History of the British Empire*, vol. 3, *The Nineteenth Century* (New York: Oxford University Press, 1999).

141. See Judith M. Brown and William Roger Louis, eds., *The Oxford History of the British Empire*, vol. 4, *The Twentieth Century* (Oxford: Oxford University Press, 1998). Food rationing from World War II did not end until 1954, and the quality of the tea was poor, which may be part of the reason why taking tea declined in popularity in the postwar period. See Mason, *Food and Culture*.

142. For more on this subject, see, for example, Trevor Owen Lloyd, *The British Empire, 1558–1995* (Oxford: Oxford University Press, 1996).

143. BBC, "Charles' Diary Lays Thoughts Bare," News, last modified February 22, 2006, http://news.bbc.co.uk/2/hi/uk_news/4740684.stm. Brown and Louis, *Oxford History*.

CHAPTER 3

Ashley Jackson, *The British Empire: A Very Short Introduction* (Cambridge: Oxford University Press, 2013), 3.

1. It was once common practice in hotels and catering establishments to use the same serving and storage vessels for tea and coffee, often resulting in subpar, coffee-flavored tea. Ken Albala, e-mail message to author, July 11, 2018.

2. Cape Grace Hotel, "Afternoon Tea," accessed December 4, 2017, https://www.capegrace.com/culinary-delights/afternoon-tea.

3. Although today's grand tea services are prepared by hired staff, early British tea tradition was for the host to make and serve the meal.

4. One hotel says its afternoon tea adds a "dash of vintage glamour" to one's stay. Inn at Perry Cabin by Belmond, "Dining," accessed January 12, 2018, https://www.belmond.com/hotels/north-america/usa/md/st-michaels/inn-at-perry-cabin/dining.

5. Ibid.

6. Although tea in modern-day Britain, like any meal anywhere, is not universal in its consumption or its component parts—types of snacks served, starting time, etc.

7. For more on the intricacies of British-imposed systems and their relationships to laborers and to the Indian caste system, see Usha Jha, *Land, Labour, and Power: Agrarian Crisis and the State in Bihar (1937–52)* (Delhi: Aakar Books, 2003), and Pramod Kumar Agrawal, *Land Reforms in India: Constitutional and Legal Approach* (New Dehli: MD Publications Pvt. Ltd., 1993).

8. For more information on this period of Indian history, see National Portal of the Government of the Republic of India, "Indian Freedom Struggle (1857–1947),"

India.gov.in Archive, October 10, 2011, https://archive.india.gov.in/knowindia/culture_heritage.php?id=4.

9. In 2001, the spelling of the city was changed to "Kolkata" to match Bengali pronunciation.

10. The 1909 Morley-Minto reforms were meant to modestly increase Indian participation in government. But many Indians felt the act was actually divisive for Hindus and Muslims and failed to further the goal of representative government in India.

11. Gandhi maintained his pacifist stance even though the British regularly employed violent tactics to suppress protest, such as in the Jallianwala Bagh massacre of 1919.

12. Paula Maiorano, a former resident of India, shared her recollections of bed tea in an e-mail interview with author, August 29, 2016. Throughout this work, transcriptions of e-mail interviews may be lightly edited for clarity.

13. Certain expectations are suspended, of course, for informal pickup matches among neighbors.

14. Rodney P. Carlisle, ed., *Encyclopedia of Play in Today's Society* (Los Angeles: Sage, 2009), 156.

15. Colleen Taylor Sen, "India," in *At the Table: Food and Family around the World*, ed. Ken Albala (Santa Barbara, CA: Greenwood, 2016), 126–27.

16. The local merges with the colonial past elsewhere in the world as well: one afternoon tea in Singapore, for example, served curry puffs. Vir Sanghvi, "The Indian Tea Party," *Hindustan Times*, updated April 16, 2011, https://www.hindustantimes.com/india/the-indian-tea-party/story-y2sUjGzFw8ZsvHq36WOJrJ.html.

17. Ibid.

18. Kathryn La Barre, e-mail interview with the author, January 28, 2018.

19. Vir Sanghvi, "The Indian Tea Party," *Hindustan Times*, updated April 16, 2011, https://www.hindustantimes.com/india/the-indian-tea-party/story-y2sUjGzFw8ZsvHq36WOJrJ.html.

20. The cities were still officially called Bombay and Poona in the 1960s but were changed to Mumbai and Pune in 1995 and 1978, respectively.

21. Vir Sanghvi, "The Indian Tea Party," *Hindustan Times*, updated April 16, 2011, https://www.hindustantimes.com/india/the-indian-tea-party/story-y2sUjGzFw8ZsvHq36WOJrJ.html.

22. Ibid.

23. Jolliffe, *Tea and Tourism*, 11.

24. Early coffeehouses in the American colonies were taverns, dispensing alcoholic beverages as well as tea and coffee; as a result, the coffee they served was not

as popular as the liquor and was slower to catch on. While coffee became popular in England in the late seventeenth and early eighteenth centuries, it would take until the Revolutionary War for Americans to begin the switch (and even then many still enjoyed drinking tea). Coffee did have its adherents, however: William Penn introduced the drink to the Quaker colony of Philadelphia, and records show that he was sending orders to New York for coffee in 1683. For more about coffee's history in the United States, see Pettigrew, *A Social History of Tea*, 21–25.

25. America also bought tea from Japan. For more on this, see Dolin, *When America First Met China*.

26. Sarah Rose, *For All the Tea in China: How England Stole the World's Favorite Drink and Changed History* (New York: Viking, 2010). And for more on Fortune and tea, see Pettigrew, *A Social History of Tea*.

27. Businessman Thomas Lipton is one of the more famous figures in the history of tea, whose influence is felt in America today, even though he was Scottish. Lipton arrived in the United States from Glasgow just before the end of the Civil War, and for the next five years he worked a number of odd jobs before moving back to Scotland, where he opened his first shop. His approach was to offer a well-stocked and attractive store and win sales based on excellent selection and ambiance rather than trying to pass off every product as first-rate. At that time, Scotland's shops were often poorly lit and had little on the shelves, so his model was a huge success. Most important, in an era when many merchants would repackage used tea and sell it as new to save money, Lipton recognized the need for reliably good tea in the United Kingdom. His emphasis on reliable goods, selection, and affordable prices influenced the tea-drinking market at home and abroad. He was quite the showman, and in one of his more storied exploits, he imported the world's largest cheese from New York in 1881 and had it cut up and sold in his Glasgow shop before a throng of cheering onlookers; it sold out in two hours, and he went on to repeat the feat annually each Christmas season. Michael D'Antonio, *A Full Cup: Sir Thomas Lipton's Extraordinary Life and His Quest for the America's Cup* (New York: Riverhead Books, 2010).

28. Pettigrew, *A Social History of Tea*. Pettigrew and Richardson, *A Social History of Tea*.

29. It is relatively uncommon for Americans without some ties to Britain or to other former colonies to partake of the meal regularly in their homes, although it was more common at the turn of the twentieth century.

30. For example, Catharine Esther Beecher, *Miss Beecher's Domestic Receipt Book* (New York: Harper & Brothers, 1846).

31. For more on the restaurant, called the Chinese Umbrella, see Jan Whitaker, "Americans in Paris: The Chinese Umbrella," *Restaurant-ing through History*

(blog), October 8, 2017, https://restaurant-ingthroughhistory.com/2017/10/08/americans-in-paris-the-chinese-umbrella/.

32. Jan Whitaker, "Taste of a Decade: Restaurants, 1900–1910," *Restaurant-ing through History* (blog), January 28, 2010, https://restaurant-ingthroughhistory.com/2010/01/28/taste-of-a-decade-restaurants-1900-1910/.

33. Christine Terhune Herrick, *Consolidated Library of Modern Cooking and Household Recipes* (New York: R. J. Bodmer, 1904), 53.

34. For example, in Lucy G. Allen, *Table Service* (Boston: Little, Brown, and Company, 1927).

35. See Beecher, *Miss Beecher's Domestic Receipt Book*, for example; each setting has a plate, knife, napkin, and small cup-plate.

36. Christine Terhune Herrick, *A-B-C of Housekeeping* (New York: Harper & Brothers, 1915), 107.

37. For a more comprehensive look at the history of women, cocktail parties, and alcohol consumption, including a discussion of drinking in the home as a contributing factor to the failure of Prohibition, see Catherine Gilbert Murdock, *Domesticating Drink: Women, Men, and Alcohol in America, 1870–1940* (Baltimore: Johns Hopkins University Press, 1998).

38. Linda Most, e-mail interview with the author, August 30, 2016.

39. James Beard refers to the cultural divide: "In England, teatime is the time for relaxation and good talk. We in America take for granted that it is the cocktail hour, but I strongly recommend a revival of this civilized custom. If we could only resurrect the pleasure of the tea hour and then move on to cocktails later, we'd be much better fortified and prepared for the evening." In *Beard on Food* (New York: Alfred A. Knopf, 1974), 192–93.

40. To see the complete Schrafft's menu, visit Jan Whitaker, "An Annotated Menu," *Restaurant-ing through History* (blog), November 14, 2012, https://restaurant-ingthroughhistory.com/2012/11/14/an-annotated-menu/.

41. Jan Whitaker, *Tea at the Blue Lantern Inn: A Social History of the Tea Room Craze in America* (New York: St. Martin's Press, 2015).

42. An ideology of maintaining separate public and private spheres was much discussed during the Industrial Revolution and held that men, through biology and even, in some cases, divine will, were better adapted to handle the public sphere, which included business and politics, while women were better equipped to operate in the domestic sphere and care for home and family. For more on this concept, see Christopher Wells, "Separate Spheres," in *Encyclopedia of Feminist Literary Theory*, ed. Elizabeth Kowaleski-Wallace (New York: Routledge, 2009), 519.

43. Pettigrew, *A Social History of Tea*, 194.

44. Whitaker, *Tea at the Blue Lantern Inn.*

45. Pettigrew, *A Social History of Tea.*

46. Mary Catharine Lewis, *Pouring Tea for Profit: The Tea Room Institute of the Lewis Training Schools* (Washington, DC: Lewis Hotel Training Schools, 1925).

47. Jan Whitaker, "African-American Tea Rooms," *Restauranting through History* (blog), February 13, 2011, https://restaurant-ingthroughhistory .com/2011/02/13/african-american-tea-rooms/.

48. Pettigrew, *A Social History of Tea.*

49. Ibid.

50. Ibid.

51. James Norwood Pratt, *The Tea Lover's Treasury* (San Francisco: 101 Productions, 1982).

52. *New York Times*, "Opinion: Tea Snobs and Coffee Bigots," November 30, 1983, http://www.nytimes.com/1983/11/30/opinion/tea-snobs-and-coffee-bigots .html.

53. I have included a recipe for tea cakes in the conclusion of this book.

54. On antebellum plantations, slaves would have only perhaps tasted a tea cake during Christmas celebrations. See Andrew Smith, *The Oxford Encyclopedia of Food and Drink in America*, vol. 2 (New York: Oxford University Press, 2013), 696.

55. Beard, *Beard on Food.*

56. Dr. Bombay's Underwater Tea Party, "Menu," accessed January 3, 2018, http://www.drbombays.com/menu/.

57. British establishments tend to more strictly adhere to the traditional time-table for afternoon tea than do American teahouses. See my interview with Kataryna in chapter 4.

58. In *A Social History of Tea*, 127, Pettigrew discusses a passage from *Alice in Wonderland* to point out the different perceptions American and British readers may have of proper mealtime etiquette: American readers, she explains, might miss the complexities of the "Mad Tea-Party" chapter because it plays on ingrained British teatime rituals and expected behavior:

> Thus Lewis Carroll's masterful scene is interpreted differently on the two sides of the Atlantic. For Americans, a tea party is often viewed as a special event where dressed-up children and stuffed animals preside over the table. The tea party in *Alice in Wonderland* conforms to American expectations—it's an occasion that relies on the power of the child's imagination to function. Yet in Great Britain, tea is an everyday ceremony with certain boundaries. British readers have expectations of how Alice's tea party should proceed; there is a precedent which is obviously not being followed here. What

is normal, if whimsical, to an American reader is highly abnormal and upsetting to a British one.

Alice's attempts to instill order and discipline at the table seem natural if one considers the child Alice as the hostess. Yet she is only a guest, and her efforts to control other characters are therefore rude. The ritual of the tea party is violated, a subtlety Britons are quick to grasp. Alice believes that the tea ritual will provide her with everything missing since her tumble into Wonderland, a place that feels like home, with all of its connotations of moral, spiritual, and physical comfort. In short, Alice wishes to feel welcomed, but does not. Thus she attempts to control the situation as a hostess or disciplinarian, which the other participants dislike. But what some may see as a clever retort from the Mad Hatter—"'Really, now you ask me,' said Alice, very much confused, 'I don't think—' 'Then you shouldn't talk,' said the Hatter"—British readers (and Alice herself) view as an unforgivable violation of essential teatime manners. The tea party violently breaks all expectations of decorum and respect for teatime rituals, and it is this lack of correctness, more than anything, that makes the tea party truly mad.

Fromer echoes this analysis: "The tea party . . . represents everything a tea party is *not* meant to be—it is, of course, a nonsensical tea party. Carroll thus plays on the idea of expectations; he assumes that we as readers, like Alice, have certain expectations of what a tea party offers, and he continually frustrates those expectations." Fromer, *Necessary Luxury*, 169.

Pettigrew's analysis above is a useful reminder of how norms and expectations can shift rather quickly in a postcolonial country, particularly in one not steeped in the imported ritual. The owners of Tipple and Rose, however, are very aware of the afternoon tea tradition and its history and have deliberately chosen to create a range of traditional and nontraditional offerings for their guests. See Tipple and Rose Tea Parlor and Apothecary, scrolling down to "Traditional High Tea Menu," accessed January 4, 2018, https://www.tippleandrose.com/.

For additional perspective on etiquette and tea in children's literature, see Amy Webster, "Tea, Table Manners and . . . a Tiger! An Exploration of How Children's Literature Transforms the Traditional English Tea Time," article 12, *Feast: Consuming Children* 1, http://feastjournal.co.uk/article/tea-table-manners-and-a -tiger-an-exploration-of-how-childrens-literature-transforms-the-traditional -english-tea-time/.

59. John Kirriemuir, e-mail interview with the author, August 31, 2016.

60. This began the Mau Mau movement, and the subsequent rebellion as well; the British responded by imprisoning or hanging the freedom fighters and attempting to maintain control by putting the colony under a prolonged state of emergency from 1952 to 1959, during which time thousands of Kenyans were incarcerated in detention camps.

61. Embassy of the Republic of Kenya in Japan, "A Brief History on Kenya," accessed February 12, 2018, http://www.kenyarep-jp.com/kenya/history_e.html.

62. Jolliffe, *Tea and Tourism*.

63. Joliffe's *Tea and Tourism* matter-of-factly points to the English planter as the source of the town's name (p. 154). Kenyan Hotels Ltd., however, is a bit more poetic: "The name Kericho has a legendary connection to a certain popular and powerful herbalist who lived in the district at the turn of the century. The herbalist's name is said to have been Kerich, who had his base of operation in the present-day Kericho and Bomet districts. It is in his honor that Kericho town was named." Kenyan Hotels Ltd., "Kericho Tea Hotel," Lets Travel Kenya, accessed January 12, 2018, http://www.kenyahotelsltd.com/place/kericho-tea-hotel/.

64. Catherine Quinn, "High Tea," *The Guardian* (London), October 31, 2006, https://www.theguardian.com/travel/2006/oct/31/travelfoodanddrink .foodanddrink.kenya.

65. In one piece on Kericho, a travel writer fairly languidly references Kenya's past living under British rule: "African colour and colonial grandeur are a well-balanced blend in a community where it's always teatime." Catherine Quinn, "High Tea," *The Guardian* (London), October 31, 2006, https://www.theguardian.com/ travel/2006/oct/31/travelfoodanddrink.foodanddrink.kenya.

66. The World Bank, "Kenya," accessed December 27, 2017, https://data .worldbank.org/country/Kenya.

67. Kenyan Hotels Ltd., "Kericho Tea Hotel," Lets Travel Kenya, accessed January 12, 2018, http://www.kenyahotelsltd.com/place/kericho-tea-hotel/.

68. Catherine Quinn, "High Tea," *The Guardian* (London), October 31, 2006, https://www.theguardian.com/travel/2006/oct/31/travelfoodanddrink .foodanddrink.kenya. The author goes on to rather languidly reference Kenya's past under British rule: "African colour and colonial grandeur are a well-balanced blend in a community where it's always teatime."

69. Kiambethu Farm at Limuru, "Tours," *Kiambethu* (website), accessed January 12, 2018, http://www.kiambethufarm.com/tours/.

70. Jolliffe, *Tea and Tourism*.

71. Richardson, *World in Your Teacup*.

72. Zen Garden Nairobi, *Fashion High Tea* (website), accessed 2018, http:// fashionhightea.com/.

73. *Business Today*, "No More Afternoon Tea at Family Bank," August 22, 2017, https://businesstoday.co.ke/no-afternoon-tea-family-bank-tightens-belt/. See also Fred Obura, "New Directive Comes at a Time When Industry Is Experiencing Challenges Related to Interest Capping Law," *Standard Digital*, August 22,

2017, https://www.standardmedia.co.ke/business/article/2001252230/family-bank-suspends-staff-tea-in-cost-cutting-measure.

74. Evelyne Musambi, "Family Bank Learns How Not to Suspend Afternoon Staff Tea (The Hard Way)," *Nairobi News*, August 22, 2017, http://nairobinews.nation.co.ke/news/family-bank-learns-how-not-to-suspend-afternoon-staff-tea-the-hard-way/.

75. Francis Gordon Clarke, *The History of Australia* (Westport, CT: Greenwood Press, 2002), 1.

76. Australia is also one of the most culturally diverse countries, and women make up more than 50 percent of the population. Clarke notes that this makes obsolete older media descriptions of a country composed of white males, although newer representations have yet to reflect the reality of diverse, urban-dwelling Australian communities. See ibid., 3.

77. Australian Legal Information Institute, "Australia Act 1986" [archived from original], accessed February 23, 2018, https://www.webcitation.org/659ddyVZ4?url=http://www.austlii.edu.au/au/legis/cth/consol_act/aa1986114/index.html.

78. Ken Albala, ed., *Food Cultures of the World Encyclopedia*, vol. 2, *The Americas* (Santa Barbara, CA: Greenwood, 2011), 24.

79. Paula Maiorano, e-mail interview with author, August 29, 2016.

80. For example, in 1994 *Mason v. Tritton* held that the Aboriginal defendant had violated laws surrounding limits on oyster harvesting and that he had not offered sufficient proof for why his harvesting practices were appropriate within the limits of Australian law. Moore argues that this is an example of the difficulties Aboriginal communities face when trying to consolidate traditional food practices within modern Australian legal and social structures. Anthony Moore, "Aboriginal Land Rights in South Australia," in *Indigenous Australians and the Law*, ed. Elliot Johnston, Martin Hinton, and Daryle Rigney (Sydney: Cavendish Publishing, 1997), 133–48.

81. NAIDOC stands for National Aborigines and Islanders Day Observance Committee. See Aboriginal Health Centre, "Afternoon Tea," accessed January 4, 2018, http://aboriginalhealthcentre.com/event/afternoon-tea/. See also Deborah Stokes, "15076 NAIDOC Week Afternoon Tea," remarks addressed to the National Aborigines and Islanders Day Observance Committee, Port Moresby, Papua New Guinea, July 6, 2015, http://png.embassy.gov.au/pmsb/502.html.

82. Rozelle Public School, "Aboriginal Education," accessed February 15, 2018, https://www.rozellepublicschool.com.au/aboriginal-education.html; Carla Capalbo, "Yaama Dhiyaan," *Slow Food* (website), June 30, 2011, https://www.slowfood.com/yaama-dhiyaan/.

83. Hilton Malta, "Vista Lobby Lounge Menu," accessed January 20, 2018, http://www3.hilton.com/resources/media/hi/MLAHITW/en_US/pdf/en_MLAHITW_VISTALOUNGE-TERRACEMENU_Jan18.pdf.

84. Elaine, "Afternoon Tea at the Hilton Malta," *Some of My Favourite Things* (blog), April 19, 2016, http://someofmyfavouritethings.com/food/afternoon-tea-hilton-malta/.

85. Elia Café, "Elia Café," accessed November 3, 2017, http://www.elia.com.mt/caffe-elia.

86. Marlene Zammit, "Sinizza," *A Maltese Mouthful* (blog), September 13, 2015, http://www.amaltesemouthful.com/sinizza/. See also Marlene Zammit, "Maltese Christmas Honey/Treacle Rings (Qaghaq ta' L-Ghasel)," *A Maltese Mouthful* (blog), December 19, 2015, http://www.amaltesemouthful.com/maltese-christmas-honeytreacle-rings-qaghaq-tal-ghasel/.

87. Robert Lugg, "Tea and History: Revel in Marvellous Malta's Sunshine, Beauty and English Heritage," *Daily Mail* (London), December 22, 2013, https://www.dailymail.co.uk/travel/article-2429930/Holidays-Malta-Revel-islands-sunshine-beauty-English-heritage.html.

88. *Malta Independent*, "The Malta Historical Society Afternoon Tea," October 11, 2009, http://www.independent.com.mt/articles/2009-10-11/local-news/The-Malta-Historical-Society-Afternoon-Tea-264506.

89. Arts Council Malta, "At the Crossroads? Cultural Leadership in the 21st Century," program for the seventh World Summit on Arts and Culture, October 18–21, 2016, Valetta, Malta, International Federation of Arts Councils and Culture Agencies (website), retrieved February 4, 2017, https://ifacca.org/media/filer_public/65/4b/654bcd77-48dd-4db5-a791-91dad1558e60/7th_world_summit_on_arts_and_culture_programme.pdf.

90. Thompson, *History*.

91. Vestiges of the British tea break are still found in university tearooms, where staff regularly break to deliberate issues in their disciplines or the world at large over a cup of tea. See, for example, Gustav Visser, Ronnie Donaldson, and Cecil Seethal, eds., *The Origin and Growth of Geography as a Discipline at South African Universities* (Cape Town: Sun Press, 2016), 21 and 284.

92. Other elements of British culture assumed by many South Africans include rugby and cricket. See David Ross Black and John Nauright, *Rugby in the South African Nation: Sport, Cultures, Politics, and Power in the Old and New South Africas* (New York: Manchester University Press, 1998).

93. Cape Grace Hotel, "Afternoon Tea," accessed December 4, 2017, https://www.capegrace.com/culinary-delights/afternoon-tea.

94. Jodi-Anne Williams-Rogers, "Afternoon Tea Under the African Sun," in *Tea Reader: Living Life One Cup at a Time*, ed. Katrina Avila Munichiello (Clarendon, VT: Tuttle Publishing, 2012), 50–52.

95. The black South African elite is small but growing, which in coming decades may change the face of afternoon tea in upscale dining. See, for example, *The Economist*, "South Africa's Inequality Is No Longer about Race," Middle East and Africa, May 20, 2017, https://www.economist.com/news/middle-east-and-africa/21722155-democracy-has-brought-wealth-only-few. See also Jason Cowley, "Mandela's Stoicism, Tea with Ian Smith, and South Africa's Civil War that Never Was," *New Statesman*, December 17, 2013, https://www.newstatesman.com/politics/2013/12/mandela%E2%80%99s-stoicism-tea-ian-smith-and-south-africas-civil-war-never-was, which points to the many ways the black majority of the country continues to be underserved.

96. Belmond Mount Nelson Hotel, "Lounge Tea Menu," accessed January 24, 2018, http://belmondcdn.azureedge.net/pdfs/ocap_menu_afternoon_tea.pdf.

97. Red Carnation Hotel Collection, "Chesterfield Palm Beach," accessed December 5, 2017, https://www.chesterfieldpb.com/; Red Carnation Hotel Collection, "The RCH Story," accessed December 5, 2017, https://www.redcarnationhotels.com/about/the-rch-story; and Red Carnation Hotel Collection, "The Twelve Apostles," accessed December 5, 2017, https://www.12apostleshotel.com/.

98. See Belmond Hotel das Cataratas, "Dining," accessed January 12, 2018, https://www.belmond.com/hotels/south-america/brazil/iguassu-falls/belmond-hotel-das-cataratas/dining; Belmond Hotel Group, "About," accessed January 23, 2018, https://www.belmond.com/about; Belmond Manoir aux Quat'Saisons, "Dining," accessed January 15, 2018, https://www.belmond.com/hotels/europe/uk/oxfordshire/belmond-le-manoir-aux-quat-saisons/dining; Belmond Mount Nelson Hotel, "Lounge Tea Menu," accessed January 24, 2018, http://belmondcdn.azureedge.net/pdfs/ocap_menu_afternoon_tea.pdf; and Inn at Perry Cabin by Belmond, "Dining," accessed January 12, 2018, https://www.belmond.com/hotels/north-america/usa/md/st-michaels/inn-at-perry-cabin/dining.

99. Kim Maxwell, "Tea Is Served, Ma'am," *Food and Home*, January 7, 2009, https://www.foodandhome.co.za/entertaining/tea-is-served-maam.

100. Although Belmond does nod to the colonial history of many of the countries its hotels inhabit, such as the "colonial-inspired" Bar Taroba in its Iguazu Falls, Brazil, location.

101. Grant Michalski, e-mail interview with the author, August 30, 2016.

102. Lerato Umah-Shaylor, "Wild Africa on the Seafront," Billetto UK, posted 2016, accessed January 15, 2018, https://billetto.co.uk/e/wild-africa-on

-the-seafront-tickets-164018. See also Ben Norum, "An African Afternoon Tea Is Coming to London," *Evening Standard* (London), August 15, 2016, https://www.standard.co.uk/go/london/restaurants/an-african-afternoon-tea-is-coming-to-london-a3320356.html.

103. England and its former colonies do not have a monopoly on tea meals: in Chile, for example, *onces* are meals with tea or coffee and a snack, served in the afternoon or evening to tide one over until dinner. See Sally Baho, "Chile," in *At the Table: Food and Family around the World*, ed. Ken Albala (Santa Barbara, CA: Greenwood Press, 2016), 56.

104. Annie Levy, "Great Britain: Wales," in *At the Table: Food and Family around the World*, ed. Ken Albala (Santa Barbara, CA: Greenwood, 2016), 103–8.

105. Deconstructing the effects of colonialism has been a decades-long process. "The Empire is also controversial because something as large defies easy summary, and perspectives on it vary wildly. . . . As the headlong decolonization of the European empires gathered pace in the 1960s, Jean-Paul Sartre wrote that, 'We in Europe too are being decolonized . . . The settler which is in every one of us is being savagely rooted out. . . . It was nothing but an ideology of lies, a perfect justification for pillage; its honeyed words, its affectation of sensibility were only alibis for our aggressions.'" Jackson, *The British Empire*, 4.

106. For one example of one group looking at the origins of the goods they purchase, see Diocese of Oxford, "Just Our Cup of Tea: Fairtrade in the Diocese of Oxford," accessed September 3, 2017, http://www.oxford.anglican.org/mission-ministry/faith-in-action/fair-trade/just-our-cup-of-tea-fairtrade-in-the-diocese-of-oxford/.

107. The history of the distribution of tea beverage, of course, is a different story, and there are many publications that talk about the tea trade and its relationship to the British Empire at length.

108. Sotheby's, "Sotheby's Indian Afternoon Tea Service," October 3, 2014, http://www.sothebys.com/en/news-video/blogs/all-blogs/on-india/2014/10/indian-afternoon-tea-service.html (link no longer available).

109. See, for example, Jackson, *The British Empire*. The discussion of colonizer and colonized occurs outside of academic discourse too, such as in the Diocese of Oxford's discussion of its decision to serve fair-trade products, as discussed above.

110. Vir Sanghvi, "The Indian Tea Party," *Hindustan Times*, updated April 16, 2011, https://www.hindustantimes.com/india/the-indian-tea-party/story-y2sUjGzFw8ZsvHq36WOJrJ.html.

111. While a meal or a product itself may not be inherently exploitative, often its past is, and one critical thing we in the modern world have done to address this is to

reconsider the food or food tradition in a way that divorces it from its exploitative context—for example, by purchasing ethically sourced tea and coffee rather than coffee produced by laborers making below-living wages. While buying fair-trade tea is one step toward the good (and to say that it solves problems on a large scale without creating new ones is a dramatic oversimplification), it is a simple step that feels accessible to many people, and taking that first step helps them shift their thinking to the sourcing of their food and (increasingly, it seems) to the colonial history behind that food. See, for example, the Diocese of Oxford's fair-trade site (above) or Matthew Anderson, *A History of Fair Trade in Contemporary Britain: From Civil Society Campaigns to Corporate Compliance* (New York: Palgrave Macmillan, 2015).

112. Kate Black, "Our Top 10 High Tea Hideaways," *High Tea with Elephants* (website), December 16, 2015, http://www.highteawithelephants.com/destinations/top-10-high-tea-hideaways/.

113. W. Sutcliffe, "Kenyan Safari: Beast, Blanket, Babylon," *The Independent*, October 22, 2005, retrieved July 2006, http://travel.independent.co.uk/africa/article32129 7.ece, as cited in Mónica Cejas, "Tourism 'Back in Time': Performing 'the Essence of Safari' in Africa," *Intercultural Communication Studies* 16, no. 3 (2007): 121–34, https://web.uri.edu/iaics/files/10-M¨®nica-Cejas.pdf.

114. Although in some areas, as we have seen, there are more casual afternoon tea traditions that are taken in the home. However, it was hard for me to determine in many former colonies whether this tradition existed as a more universal phenomenon, often because there is little documentation of home tea breaks, afternoon tea, high tea, and so on.

115. Kenya is one such country; see the World Bank, "Kenya," accessed December 27, 2017, https://data.worldbank.org/country/Kenya.

116. Undoubtedly, sometimes the signaled elitism is unintentional, but the implications of the term are present nonetheless, which becomes even more fraught when the elitism is very much intended. For example, the Red Carnation hotel group was formed by a South African couple who emigrated to England, and their hotels worldwide offer "afternoon tea." This is done to show that their teas are more traditionally British, with less of the fanfare of some high teas offering a range of eclectic foods and beverage, choosing instead to focus on high-end service that sticks to the basics (finger sandwiches, pastries, etc.).

117. Kate Black, "Our Top 10 High Tea Hideaways," *High Tea with Elephants* (website), December 16, 2015, http://www.highteawithelephants.com/destinations/top-10-high-tea-hideaways/. The tea recommendations from High Tea with Elephants come with an additional nod to the safari industry's colonial roots: almost every image on their webpage shows either beautiful scenery or a table laden with food, but never with any people present. There are a few exceptions: One is

an image of a white woman, lounging and sipping tea, and in the foreground a table of petits fours, teacups, and freshly cut flowers. This image would be perfectly at home on the website for a hotel restaurant in the United Kingdom, but as the first human being pictured on a website about traveling in Africa, the choice is both jarring and significant.

Farther down the page is an image of a black woman—one of a surprisingly small number of black Africans depicted on the site. This picture is perhaps more troubling than the first: The woman, wearing an apron, head wrap, and button-down uniform, stacks sweets on a large, tiered tray, with a mess of mismatched teacups before her. She is flanked by two white children, who are so close to her that it seems a wonder that she has the space to do her work. The two children are standing on chairs on either side of her—looming over her as she sets up for service— laser-focused on the sweets in front of them. Here the African woman is almost part of the backdrop: she is there simply to serve food and drink, and the viewer's gaze is directed to the real subject of the picture: the two children, placed as the most important part of the narrative being woven about this particular safari lodge. The company embraces colonial imagery to promote afternoon tea, a choice presumably tailored to its clientele's expectations and values.

118. Modern interpretations of high tea and afternoon tea do not always reflect the historical past accurately but, in some cases, combine the English colonial past with modern tourism. In one example, an onshore excursion for the Royal Caribbean cruise line serves passengers in Jamaica a "1700s High Tea" at a former Jamaican plantation. See Royal Caribbean, "Shore Excursions: 1700's High Tea at Good Hope Estate," accessed January 15, 2018, http://www.royalcaribbean .com/shoreExcursions/product/detail/view.do?sourcePage=shorexByPort&Produ ctCode=FYA5&DestinationCode=. Besides the fact that afternoon tea would not have been taken on a 1700s Jamaican plantation, this particular cruise excursion interplays with the country's slaveholding past. The event location is at Good Hope Estate, a former sugar estate owned by John Tharp, the largest slave owner (and landowner) in the colony. See Visit Jamaica, "Jamaica: Good Hope," accessed January 14, 2018, http://www.visitjamaica.com/good-hope.

119. Heritage North East Pvt. Ltd., "About Us," accessed January 4, 2018, http://www.heritagetourismindia.com/.

120. Ibid.

121. WildFilmsIndia, "India Tea Garden Workers Pluck Leaves—Assam," You-Tube video, 2:18, posted November 3, 2015, https://youtu.be/UFOc_ZmG18g.

122. Heritage North East is a particularly interesting example, as it is run by longtime residents of the region rather than by white expats (or the descendants of

white expats). Their properties do not mention whether afternoon tea is served or anything about the meals available, beyond that they focus on Indian and Chinese cuisines in one instance, have a fine-dining restaurant in another, and have round-the-clock room service.

123. Mason, *Food and Culture*.

124. Publisher's Circular, *The Publishers' Circular and Booksellers' Record of British and Foreign Literature*, vol. 59, *July–December 1893* (London: Sampson Low, Marston & Company, Ltd., 1893), https://babel.hathitrust.org/cgi/pt?id=njp .32101079672133;view=1up;seq=9, page 219.

125. Other agricultural properties besides tea plantations offer tourist experiences. For example, the Watagala Estate offers stays near plantation grounds and is situated on a mahogany plantation. See TripAdvisor, "Leaf Leisure: Watagala Estate," accessed January 29, 2018, https://www.tripadvisor.com/Hotel_ Review-g3814834-d10317232-Reviews-Leaf_Leisure-Avissawella_Western_ Province.html. See also AirBnB, "The Chalet, Kosgama," accessed February 10, 2018, https://www.airbnb.com/rooms/6354342?location=Ruwanwella%2C%20 Sri%20Lanka&s=qjGJYnmC.

126. See, for example, Vince Bamford, "More Tea, Tesco? Revival in British Tradition Prompts Cakes Range Launch," *BakeryandSnacks* (website), last modified May 10, 2016, https://www.bakeryandsnacks.com/Article/2016/05/10/More -tea-Tesco-Revival-in-British-tradition-prompts-cakes-launch. See also Pettigrew, *A Social History of Tea*.

127. See Pettigrew, *A Social History of Tea*.

128. See Mary-Jane Daffy, "Flight of Fancy: Traditional High Tea Enjoying a Revival," *Herald Sun* (Victoria, Australia), June 22, 2015, http://www.heraldsun .com.au/news/victoria/flight-of-fancy-traditional-high-tea-enjoying-a-revival/ news-story/c64eec3e6fe402658925174e5ead5e0f.

CHAPTER 4

1. Priscilla Boniface, *Tasting Tourism: Traveling for Food and Drink* (Aldershot, England: Ashgate, 2003), 116.

2. John Kirriemuir, e-mail interview with the author, August 31, 2016.

3. Colin Spencer also seems to consider only the expensive restaurant version of the meal, saying that in Britain both afternoon tea and high tea have "almost vanished entirely, except as part of a day's trip out." Spencer, *British Food*, 309.

4. See, for example, John's interview, later in this chapter.

5. See, for example, Beverley Nichols, *Down the Kitchen Sink: A Memoir* (Portland, OR: Timber Press, 2006), and Laura Trevelyan, *A Very British Family: The Trevelyans and Their World* (London: I. B. Tauris, 2006).

6. Among many other examples, famous and obscure, see J. M. Barrie, *Peter Pan*, 100th anniversary edition (New York: Henry Holt & Company, 2003); see also Thompson, *Lark Rise to Candleford*. *A Houseful of Girls* by Mrs. George de Horne Vaizey, for example, has a scene with afternoon tea as well as a smattering of mentions of the meal (first published in 1901; illustrated edition reprinted Gloucester, England: Dodo Press, 2007).

7. See, for example, *Daily Mail*, "Afternoon Tea More Popular than Ever as Hotels Get Huge Boost in Business Thanks to the Brew," last updated April 11, 2011, http://www.dailymail.co.uk/femail/article-1373944/Afternoon-tea-popular -hotels-huge-boost-business-thanks-brew.html.

8. Guy Hobbs, "The Cost of Afternoon Tea: High Tea or Highway Robbery?" *Which? Conversation*, April 9, 2012, https://conversation.which.co.uk/food-drink/ afternoon-tea-high-cost-london-hotels/.

9. Ibid.

10. *Daily Mail*, "Afternoon Tea More Popular than Ever as Hotels Get Huge Boost in Business Thanks to the Brew," last updated April 11, 2011, http://www .dailymail.co.uk/femail/article-1373944/Afternoon-tea-popular-hotels-huge-boost -business-thanks-brew.html. This is also found in hotel afternoon tea menus from the Bedford and Red Carnation chains.

11. Guy Hobbs, "The Cost of Afternoon Tea: High Tea or Highway Robbery?" *Which? Conversation*, April 9, 2012, https://conversation.which.co.uk/food-drink/ afternoon-tea-high-cost-london-hotels/. See also *Daily Mail*, "Afternoon Tea More Popular than Ever as Hotels Get Huge Boost in Business Thanks to the Brew," last updated April 11, 2011, http://www.dailymail.co.uk/femail/article-1373944/ Afternoon-tea-popular-hotels-huge-boost-business-thanks-brew.html.

12. Pettigrew, *A Social History of Tea*, 138.

13. Kataryna Leach, e-mail interview with the author, August 30, 2016.

14. Ibid.

15. Like John Kirriemuir, e-mail interview with the author, August 31, 2016.

16. Pettigrew, *A Social History of Tea*.

17. Ibid., 169.

18. While the meal was becoming less popular by this time, it continued to be served in places like the Edinburgh University Tea Club, which is interesting, as it was a men's group. Between 1920 and 1945, the club often hosted afternoon teas in addition to other gatherings.

Ingrid Jeacle says afternoon tea is overlooked by many researchers because it is considered a feminine activity and because casual activities like having tea and conversation are sometimes viewed as inconsequential and ignored in favor of discussing broader social trends or broader disciplinary concerns. While this idea was not explicitly noted in research elsewhere, Jeacle's perception at least is that the ritual of having afternoon tea continued to be, at least through the 1940s, largely an activity engaged in by women. However, Jeacle's research shows that the reality is much more nuanced, and while there may be a perception that women are the only ones partaking in social tea gatherings, many men did as well, informally as well as formally. Ingrid Jeacle, "Accounting and the Annual General Meeting: The Case of the Edinburgh University Tea Club, 1920–1945," *Accounting History* 13, no. 4 (2008): 451–78.

19. John Burnett, *Plenty and Want: A Social History of Food in England from 1815 to the Present Day*, 3rd ed. (New York: Routledge, 1989).

20. For example, "In January 1955, Allied Bakeries made a successful bid for the Aerated Bread Company (ABC) shops and restaurants, which then gradually disappeared from London's high streets." Pettigrew, *A Social History of Tea*, 206.

21. Ibid.

22. Ibid.

23. At least when they were playing tourist and visiting these sites. The wider availability of, and interest in, the meal would not come until later.

24. See, for example, Pettigrew, *A Social History of Tea*.

25. See, for example, Shana Zhang and J. T. Hunter, *The Wild Truth of Tea: Unraveling the Complex Tea Business, Keys to Health and Chinese Culture* (Kunming, China: Wild Tea Qi and International Tea Academy Publishing, 2015).

26. See, for example, Pettigrew, *A Social History of Tea*.

27. Ibid., 167.

28. Ibid.

29. Kataryna Leach, e-mail interview with the author, August 30, 2016.

30. Lewis Carroll, *Alice's Adventures in Wonderland* (Boston: International Pocket Library, 1941).

31. Kataryna Leach, e-mail interview with the author, August 30, 2016. See also Andrea Doyle, "High Tea at Meetings," Meetings Strategies, *Successful Meetings*, December 1, 2015, http://www.successfulmeetings.com/Strategy/Meeting-Strategies/Afternoon-Tea-Meetings-Networking/.

32. Vince Bamford, "More Tea, Tesco? Revival in British Tradition Prompts Cakes Range Launch," *BakeryandSnacks* (website), last modified May 10, 2016, https://www.bakeryandsnacks.com/Article/2016/05/10/More-tea-Tesco-Revival-in-British-tradition-prompts-cakes-launch.

33. Ibid.

34. Both Kataryna and John agree.

35. Kataryna Leach, e-mail interview with the author, August 30, 2016.

36. See Peter Davies and Robert Light, *Cricket and Community in England: 1800 to the Present Day* (Manchester: Manchester University Press, 2012), 92–97. See also Jack Williams, *Cricket and England: A Cultural and Social History of the Inter-war Years* (London: Frank Cass, 1999).

37. Williams, *Cricket*, 15.

38. John Kirriemuir, e-mail interview with the author, August 31, 2016.

39. For some Britons, though, the desire to connect to the imperial past is still a driver. The East India Company (or at least its namesake, as the original company itself was dissolved in the Victorian period) lives on as a retail outlet for imported goods. Its website proudly touts the imperial legacy of the company name and the goods sold, explicitly connecting these to consumers in a way that evokes an almost Jungian perspective on the Company's impact on the modern world:

> When you hear our name you will probably already have a sense of who we are. Deep within the world's sub-consciousness is an awareness of The East India Company, powerful pictures of who we are. You'll feel something for us; you'll have a connection to us, even if you don't know us.
>
> The East India Company made a wide range of elusive, exclusive and exotic ingredients familiar, affordable and available to the world; ingredients which today form part of our daily and national cuisines. Today we continue to develop and market unique and innovative products that breathe life into the history of The Company. We trade foods crafted by artisans and specialists from around the world, with carefully sourced ingredients, unique recipes and distinguished provenances.

The East India Company, "The Company Today," accessed February 10, 2018, https://www.theeastindiacompany.com/fine-foods/the-company/the-east-india -company-today/.

40. World Fair Trade Organization, "Definition of Fair Trade," accessed January 21, 2018, https://wfto.com/fair-trade/definition-fair-trade. It goes on to say that "Fair Trade organisations have a clear commitment to Fair Trade as the principal core of their mission." These organizations must meet a number of criteria that show the centrality of fair-trade principles to their mission, including advocating for the interests of producers.

41. Anderson, *History of Fair Trade*, 8–9.

42. In *Unto This Last* (1862), quoted in ibid. Anderson adds, "The challenge for Fair Trade was how to integrate these simple sounding lessons into the commercial practices of international business." Anderson extensively quotes and

builds upon Frank Trentmann's perspectives on the origins of fair trade. See Frank Trentmann, *Free Trade Nation: Commerce, Consumption, and Civil Society in Modern Britain* (Oxford: Oxford University Press, 2009), and also Frank Trentmann, "Before 'Fair Trade': Empire, Free Trade, and the Moral Economics of Food in the Modern World," *Environment and Planning D: Society and Space* 25, no. 5 (2007): 1079–1102.

43. Cornelius Fasseur, *The Politics of Colonial Exploitation: Java, the Dutch, and the Cultivation System*, trans. R. E. Elson and Ary Kraal (Ithaca, NY: Cornell University Southeast Asia Program, 1992).

44. For a range of examples, see Fasseur, *Politics*, and Anderson, *History of Fair Trade*.

45. Anderson, *History of Fair Trade*, 8.

46. Just as the fair-trade movement is affecting purchasing habits, concerns about health trends may as well. As there has been elsewhere in the former colonies (like the United States), there is a major public-health crisis in England related to rising obesity levels (Mason, *Food and Culture*). It will be interesting to see whether this situation results in a shift in the types of foods eaten during afternoon tea, although so far it seems to have not.

47. See Anderson, *History of Fair Trade*, particularly page 8, for examples.

48. The concept of a moral economy has appeared elsewhere in this book as well, such as Americans shifting from drinking tea to drinking "Liberty teas," although in that case they were protesting not the living and working conditions of impoverished or enslaved laborers, but rather their own economic and political situation.

49. Diocese of Oxford, "Just Our Cup of Tea: Fairtrade in the Diocese of Oxford," accessed September 3, 2017, http://www.oxford.anglican.org/mission-ministry/faith-in-action/fair-trade/just-our-cup-of-tea-fairtrade-in-the-diocese-of-oxford/.

50. Ibid.

51. Imperial pride wound itself into twentieth-century commercialism, too, which attempted to connect feelings of pride in the empire with certain food products. "Stretched across each ocean and time zone," according to Jackson,

the proud claim that "the sun never set on the British Empire" was actually true (some said that this was because the British could not be trusted in the dark). Until the 1950s the hackneyed sun-never-set phrase was a commonplace of boys' adventure comics and advertisements for products as diverse as Bird's custard powder and Craven tobacco, illustrating the manner in which themes relating to empire and the non-European world, and Britain's exulted place within it, penetrated British culture and contributed to the formation of an inchoate but powerful imperial mind-set and a sense of British superiority and fitness to rule other peoples.

Jackson, *British Empire*, 5.

52. Michael Leapman, "Elevenses: A Vital Part of Our Working Day," *The Telegraph* (London), March 25, 2009, http://www.telegraph.co.uk/news/uknews/5044403/Elevenses-a-vital-part-of-our-working-day.html.

53. John Morgan, *Debrett's New Guide to Etiquette and Modern Manners: The Indispensible Handbook* (New York: St. Martin's Press, 1996), 255. It goes on to lament this fact, given that tea parties are a great way to entertain easily and economically, echoing the virtues of afternoon tea gatherings in older household manuals.

54. Ibid.

55. Ibid. Debrett's then moves into the section on planning children's parties, which sound like terrifying affairs, described as "not for the faint-hearted" and requiring "the precision and courage of a military campaign."

56. Although as John notes, "*tradition* is a loaded word to many English people, and there's probably a massively distracting debate about what is a tradition, a ritual, and a habit and what the differences [between them] are. As well as what afternoon tea is." John Kirriemuir, e-mail interview with the author, August 31, 2016.

57. John notes that an added benefit to afternoon tea is that it is caffeinated but not overly so, which doesn't interfere with sleep: "This is why I struggle a bit in Sweden, where the equivalent [break]—*fika*—involves drinking coffee with your friends or colleagues at the same time as you'd be drinking tea in England." Ibid.

58. Liz Holdsworth, e-mail interview with the author, November 11, 2016.

59. See Burnett, *Plenty and Want*.

60. Guy Hobbs, "The Cost of Afternoon Tea: High Tea or Highway Robbery?" *Which? Conversation*, April 9, 2012, https://conversation.which.co.uk/food-drink/afternoon-tea-high-cost-london-hotels/.

61. This came to light in my interviews with John, Kataryna, and Liz.

62. For example, Angie Brown, "High Tea vs. Afternoon Tea," *Tea Time Magazine* (website), August 14, 2017, https://www.teatimemagazine.com/high-tea-vs-afternoon-tea/. See also Kristin Tice Studeman, "How to Drink Tea like a Royal: Dos and Don'ts from the Queen's Favorite Hotel," *Vogue*, July 23, 2017, https://www.vogue.com/article/english-teatime-etiquette-how-to.

63. And in many cases, as mentioned elsewhere, high tea has come to describe the higher-end restaurant version of the meal—at least outside of England.

64. Nadia Whitehead, "High Tea, Afternoon Tea, Elevenses: English Tea Times for Dummies," *The Salt* (blog), June 30, 2015, https://www.npr.org/sections/thesalt/2015/06/30/418660351/high-tea-afternoon-tea-elevenses-english-tea-times-for-dummies.

65. For example, Dolores Snyder's *Tea Time Entertaining: A Collection of Tea Themes and Recipes* (Memphis: Wimmer, 2004) is an American-published book offer-

ing advice on traditional teas, including etiquette. And Douglas Adams's *Long Dark Tea-Time of the Soul* (New York: Simon & Schuster, 2014), for example, describes the afternoon tea break in his title, which readers would understand references the typical light, relaxing midday break, a humorous juxtaposition with the heavy, dramatic title.

66. As interviewed in Nadia Whitehead, "High Tea, Afternoon Tea, Elevenses: English Tea Times for Dummies," *The Salt* (blog), June 30, 2015, https://www.npr.org/sections/thesalt/2015/06/30/418660351/high-tea-afternoon-tea-elevenses-english-tea-times-for-dummies.

67. Michael Leapman, "Elevenses: A Vital Part of Our Working Day," *The Telegraph* (London), March 25, 2009, http://www.telegraph.co.uk/news/uknews/5044403/Elevenses-a-vital-part-of-our-working-day.html.

68. As in the NPR article referenced in notes 64 and 66. Elevenses are also mentioned occasionally in fictional literature, perhaps most famously as one of the seven daily meals of hobbits in J. R. R. Tolkien's *Lord of the Rings*.

69. For example, scones and finger sandwiches have long been standard afternoon tea fare.

70. For example, as in Morgan, *Debrett's*, the information in etiquette books deals more with the food being served than proper manners at the meal.

71. For example, Kristin Tice Studeman, "How to Drink Tea like a Royal: Dos and Don'ts from the Queen's Favorite Hotel," *Vogue*, July 23, 2017, https://www.vogue.com/article/english-teatime-etiquette-how-to.

72. Nadia Whitehead, "High Tea, Afternoon Tea, Elevenses: English Tea Times For Dummies," *The Salt* (blog), June 30, 2015, https://www.npr.org/sections/thesalt/2015/06/30/418660351/high-tea-afternoon-tea-elevenses-english-tea-times-for-dummies. See also Kristin Tice Studeman, "How to Drink Tea like a Royal: Dos and Don'ts from the Queen's Favorite Hotel," *Vogue*, July 23, 2017, https://www.vogue.com/article/english-teatime-etiquette-how-to.

73. For example, Studeman, "How to Drink Tea like a Royal."

74. For example, tea historian Bruce Richardson, coauthor of *A Social History of Tea*, advises that one not "get too hung up on proper behavior and not making a fool of yourself. British teatime is meant to be relaxing." He goes on to say that "if you pay attention to your manners, put the napkin in your lap, and keep your feet off the table, you'll probably be OK." Cited in Nadia Whitehead, "High Tea, Afternoon Tea, Elevenses: English Tea Times for Dummies," *The Salt* (blog), June 30, 2015, https://www.npr.org/sections/thesalt/2015/06/30/418660351/high-tea-afternoon-tea-elevenses-english-tea-times-for-dummies. See also Bruce Richardson and Jane Pettigrew, *A Social History of Tea: Tea's Influence on Commerce, Culture and Community* (Danville, KY: Benjamin Press, 2015).

75. John Kirriemuir, e-mail interview with the author, August 31, 2016.

CONCLUSION

1. Ian Bersten, *Tea: How Tradition Stood in the Way of the Perfect Cup* (Fremantle, Australia: Vivid Publishing, 2009).

2. In his words, "The role of religion is to support tradition." Bersten, *Tea*, 82.

3. Scotland, for example, has recently been murmuring about whether to hold another referendum to leave Great Britain. What this means for British nationalism and politics is still unclear. And what implications a potential break would have for British food culture are also uncertain. Were Scotland to leave, for example, would its food traditions become increasingly divorced from its neighbor to the south, or would their shared border mean that both will always (to some extent) have a shared cuisine?

For more on Brexit, see HM Government, "Brexit," GOV.UK, accessed October 22, 2018, https://www.gov.uk/government/Brexit.

4. Albert B. Cleage, *Black Christian Nationalism: New Directions for the Black Church* (New York: William Morrow and Company, 1972), for example, frames colonialism and a white-dominated society as institutions that required black people to adopt every aspect of white society and to reject all other cultural practices. For an additional discussion of Cleage's background and perspective, see Carole Counihan and Penny Van Esterik, *Food and Culture: A Reader*, 3rd ed. (New York: Routledge, 2013). For examples of this kind of adoption in language, see Bill Ashcroft, Gareth Griffiths, and Helen Tiffin, *The Empire Writes Back: Theory and Practice in Postcolonial Literatures*, 2nd ed. (New York: Routledge, 1989).

5. Tangentially related to our discussions in this book, Surak also talks about different depths of inclusion within a community or culture, and this is important to an understanding of afternoon tea because it speaks to the interplay between colonial and indigenous cultures. While Surak doesn't hazard to guess as to the exact extent to which a colonial culture divorces people from their indigenous culture, her work offers a valuable framework for understanding the extent to which one may participate in a cultural practice depending on their perceived role within that culture while also raising questions about whether colonial culture has created a completely new hybrid culture or whether (or perhaps how) that colonial culture will be expunged or changed as time goes on. Based on the existing literature, Surak offers several ways to break down our understanding of the different aspects of culture:

> While intensities of religious faith are captured by the term *religiosity* and qualifications of gender attributes may be expressed by *femininity* or *masculinity*, there are no equivalent English terms such as *ethninity* or *nationalosity* to convey relative degrees

of membership in ethnic or national categories. Although observable, these differentiations have received little sustained study.

Consideration of nation-work, however, suggests that these may be captured by noting three possible operations it can involve. The first is simply *distinction*—that is, the identification of traits that distinguish the nation from other nations, as in the classic we-they contrasts studied by Barth. The second is *specification*. Membership in a given social category is not always direct, but may be mediated by other categories, as a substantial literature on the way intersecting axes of social categorization, such as gender, race/ethnicitiy, and class can construct one another, has shown. Historically, as is well known, nation formation conditioned the relationship between the individual and the state by gender: men could serve the state as soldiers, and therewith in many cases enjoyed the right to vote, from which women, who could serve the state as mothers, were excluded.

Nation-work, however, may also involve a third kind of categorization—*differentiation*. Who "we" are may be established not only vis-à-vis "them" but also other members of "us." A person may be a particularly good or bad member, a typical or strange member, an exemplary or phony member, of the national community. Here the contrast is with neither an external other nor even an internal other. Indeed, there is no "other" in such cases—the comparison is with fellows precisely as fellows, for it is shared membership that enables the differentiation. Often such evaluations are crafted against a standard ideal—patriotism measured by the gauge of a war hero who has risked or sacrificed his life for the country—a *real* American showing up those who are, in a pointed adjective, *un*-American. But if in some cases what makes a good compatriot is clear enough, conflict over judgments of this kind may also occur.

Kristin Surak, *Making Tea, Making Japan: Cultural Nationalism in Practice* (Stanford: Stanford University Press, 2013), 7–8.

6. Surak argues that practices from the working classes may also be widely adopted, provided that their origins are obscured enough to facilitate adoption by the wealthy. She offers the Cuban rumba and Argentinean tango as examples of bottom-up cultural transmission. Surak, *Making Tea*.

7. Isabella Beeton's serial installments were published from 1859 to 1861, at which time they were collected into her book of household management. Mason, *Food and Culture*.

8. The concept of intellectual property in the Victorian era was different from today's: violations were not regularly enforced then, and modern standards were still being codified (modern patent law, for example, was not introduced until 1852). As a result, in many books even in this period it would not be uncommon to find material directly lifted from elsewhere. See, for example, the National Archives, "History of the Intellectual Property Office," Intellectual Property Office, accessed

January 12, 2018, http://webarchive.nationalarchives.gov.uk/20140603101018/
http://www.ipo.gov.uk/about/history/history-office.htm.

9. Beeton, *Every-Day Cookery*, 667.

10. Traditionally women wore gloves during afternoon tea gatherings, and for this reason the outside of many finger sandwiches are left unadorned (even today, when gloves are not in vogue). Mrs. Beeton encourages leaving sandwiches without adornment unless they are to be eaten with a fork, in which case "some pretty effects may be produced by decorating them with variously-coloured chaud-froid sauces. Or they may be decorated with cold aspic jelly and garnished with lobster coral, Krona pepper, parsley, egg, etc." See Beeton, *Every-Day Cookery*, 92.

11. *A Cookie for Every Country*, "South Africa: Soetkoekies (Spicy Wine Cookies)," January 25, 2008, http://globalcookies.blogspot.com/2008/01/south-africa-soetkoekies-spicy-wine.html.

12. This recipe is adapted from Mrs. Beeton's (ibid., 341) and has been updated with cooking times and temperatures that reflect modern appliances. The red wine used is claret, which historically (in the Middle Ages to the early modern period) referred to a rose-colored red wine but gradually in popular discourse has come to refer to any red wine from Bordeaux. I simply put "red wine" in the recipe for simplicity's sake, but if you can find claret for this recipe, it will taste even more authentic. The original recipe calls for sheep-tail fat, which, if you can find it, would be the ideal choice. I have substituted lard or shortening here, which change the flavor a bit but are much easier ingredients for the modern cook to source.

13. Dora Luck, *A Little Book of Cookery* (London: Sands and Company, 1905).

14. For a review of the book, see Publishers' Circular, *The Publishers' Circular and Booksellers' Record*, vol. 87, *July–December 1907* (London: Office of "The Publishers' Circular" Limited, 1907), https://babel.hathitrust.org/cgi/pt?id=njp.32 101079672372;view=1up;seq=14, page 745.

15. Irwin Edward Bainbridge Cox, ed., *The Country House: A Collection of Useful Information and Recipes: Adapted to the Country Gentleman and His Household, and of the Greatest Utility to the Housekeeper Generally* (London: Horace Cox, 1867). This book is reminiscent of earlier texts on the subject by Gervase Markham, who wrote in the seventeenth century. Markham's works geared toward the country gentleman advised on livestock or planting, but *The English Housewife*—arguably his most famous work—aimed to provide a complete overview of a woman's tasks in a country home with an eye toward thrift (this included medical care, cookery, and brewing, among other subjects). For more on Markham, see Michael R. Best, ed., *Gervase Markham's "The English Housewife"* (Montreal: McGill-Queen's University Press, 1994), and Skinner, *Modernizing Markham*.

16. In some parts of the country, clotted cream is served with scones during afternoon tea. Clotted cream has been a regular visitor to English tables for centuries and is sometimes called Devonshire cream or Cornish cream because of its popularity in these counties (located in Southwest England). It appears, for example, in Markham's 1615 publication, *The English Housewife*, albeit as an ingredient in a separate dish called a fool, as well as in Mavor's travel guide through Britain, published in 1798. See William Fordyce Mavor, *The British Tourists, or, Traveller's Pocket Companion: Through England, Wales, Scotland, and Ireland; Comprehending the Most Celebrated Tours in the British islands* (London: E. Newberry, 1798).

Some local sources point to clotted cream and bread being served in Tavistock Abbey in Devon as far back as the eleventh century, well before tea was introduced, claiming this is the origin of the popular "cream tea" still served in the region. See, for example, Bedford Hotel, "Cream Tea in Devon," accessed December 3, 2016, https://www.bedford-hotel.co.uk/eat-at-the-bedford/cream-tea-in-devon/; or BBC, "Were Cream Teas 'Invented' in Tavistock?" *BBC Devon* (website), January 17, 2004, http://www.bbc.co.uk/devon/news_features/2004/tavistock_cream_tea .shtml.

Our current conceptions of clotted cream range from the traditional version (where the fat of the cream separates from the whey through low and slow cooking) to quick-serve versions that try to emulate the real deal through, for example, mixing sour cream with whipped cream. The dish is usually a slightly buttery color with a rich but fluffy consistency, although some versions incorporate fruit juice or other colorings. For example, Elizabeth Raffald, in *The Experienced English Housekeeper: For the Use and Ease of Ladies, Housekeepers, Cooks, &c. Written Purely from Practice . . . Consisting of Several Hundred Original Receipts, Most of Which Never Appeared in Print* (London: R. Baldwin, 1782), suggests adding raspberry juice to produce a light pink color.

Many older recipes call for rennet to separate the curds and whey. Occasionally others—like the clotted cream recipe in *The Family Cookery Book*—take a longer time to make but do not require rennet: "Set two gallons of milk from the cow, in a broad earthen or tin pan, till the next day; then move it very gently, and set it on a stove that is not too hot; let it stand half an hour, till it is nearly hot; then remove it back again till quite cold; then skim it." Anon. [An Experienced Housekeeper], *The Family Cookery Book; or, Improved System of Domestic Economy; Containing above Eight Hundred Valuable Receipts, Many of Which Are Entirely Original; the Whole Forming a Most Useful Economical Companion* (Coventry, England: Merridew and Son, 1812), 293.

If you decide to try your hand at clotted cream, make sure to use cream that is not ultra-pasteurized for best results.

BIBLIOGRAPHY

Accum, Friedrich Christian. *A Treatise on Adulteration of Food, and Culinary Poisons, Exhibiting the Fraudulent Sophistications of Bread, Beer, Wine, Spirituous Liquors, Tea, Oil, Pickles, and Other Articles Employed in Domestic Economy. And Methods of Detecting Them.* Philadelphia: Abraham Small, 1820.

Acton, Eliza. *Modern Cookery, in All Its Branches.* London: Longman, Brown, Green, and Longmans, 1845.

Adams, Abigail. Abigail Adams to John Adams, July 15, 1778. In *Adams Family Papers: An Electronic Archive*, edited by the Massachusetts Historical Society. http://www.masshist.org/digitaladams/archive/doc?id=L17780715aa&bc=%2F digitaladams%2Farchive%2Fbrowse%2Fletters_1778_1779.php.

Adams, Douglas. *The Long Dark Tea-Time of the Soul.* New York: Simon & Schuster, 2014.

Adams, John. John Adams to Abigail Adams, July 6, 1774. In *Founding Families: Digital Editions of the Papers of the Winthrops and the Adamses*, edited by C. James Taylor. Boston: Massachusetts Historical Society, 2018. http://www.masshist.org/publications/adams-papers/index.php/view/ADMS-04-01 -02-0087#sn=0.

Agrawal, Pramod Kumar. *Land Reforms in India: Constitutional and Legal Approach.* New Dehli: MD Publications Pvt. Ltd., 1993.

Albala, Ken. *Cooking in Europe, 1250–1650.* Westport, CT: Greenwood Press, 2006.

———. *Eating Right in the Renaissance.* Berkeley: University of California Press, 2002.

———, ed. *Food Cultures of the World Encyclopedia.* Vol. 2, *The Americas.* Santa Barbara: Greenwood, 2011.

——. *The Food History Reader: Primary Sources*. London: Bloomsbury, 2014.

——. "Superfood or Dangerous Drug? Coffee, Tea, and Chocolate in the Late Seventeenth Century." *EuropeNow*, September 5, 2018. https://www .europenowjournal.org/2018/09/04/superfood-or-dangerous-drug-coffee -tea-and-chocolate-in-the-late-17th-century/.

Allen, Lucy G. *Table Service*. Boston: Little, Brown, and Company, 1927.

Allison, Robert J. *American Revolution: A Concise History*. Oxford: Oxford University Press, 2011.

Anderson, Clara E. *A Character Sketch Entertainment, Entitled Afternoon Tea in Friendly Village, 1862*. Ottawa: J. Hope and Sons, 1912.

Anderson, David. *Histories of the Hanged: War in Kenya and the End of Empire*. New York: W. W. Norton, 2005.

Anderson, Matthew. *A History of Fair Trade in Contemporary Britain: From Civil Society Campaigns to Corporate Compliance*. New York: Palgrave Macmillan, 2015.

Anon. [An Experienced Housekeeper]. *The Family Cookery Book; or, Improved System of Domestic Economy; Containing above Eight Hundred Valuable Receipts, Many of Which Are Entirely Original; the Whole Forming a Most Useful Economical Companion*. Coventry, England: Merridew and Son, 1812.

Armitage, David. *The Ideological Origins of the British Empire*. Cambridge: Cambridge University Press, 2000.

Armstrong, Lucie Heaton. *Letters to a Bride Including Letters to a Debutante*. London: F. V. White & Company, 1896.

Ashcroft, Bill, Gareth Griffiths, and Helen Tiffin. *The Empire Writes Back: Theory and Practice in Post-colonial Literatures*. 2nd ed. New York: Routledge, 1989.

Austen, Ralph A., and Woodruff D. Smith. "Private Tooth Decay as Public Economic Virtue: The Slave-Sugar Triangle, Consumerism, and European Industrialization." In *The Atlantic Slave Trade: Effects on Economies, Societies, and Peoples in Africa, the Americas, and Europe*, edited by Joseph E. Inikori and Stanley L. Engerman, 183–204. Durham, NC: Duke University Press, 1998.

Baho, Sally. "Chile." In *At the Table: Food and Family around the World*, edited by Ken Albala, 55–62. Santa Barbara, CA: Greenwood Press, 2016.

Barrie, J. M. *Peter Pan*. 100th anniversary edition. New York: Henry Holt & Company, 2003.

Beard, James. *Beard on Food*. New York: Alfred A. Knopf, 1974.

Beecher, Catharine Esther. *Miss Beecher's Domestic Receipt Book*. New York: Harper & Brothers, 1846.

Beeton, Isabella Mary. *Mrs. Beeton's Every-Day Cookery*. London: Ward, Lock & Co., 1907.

Bersten, Ian. *Tea: How Tradition Stood in the Way of the Perfect Cup*. Fremantle, Australia: Vivid Publishing, 2009.

Best, Michael R., ed. *Gervase Markham's "The English Housewife."* Montreal: McGill-Queen's University Press, 1994.

Bickham, Troy. "Eating the Empire: Intersections of Food, Cookery and Imperialism in Eighteenth Century Britain." *Past & Present* 198, no. 1 (2008): 71–109.

Birch, Alan, and David S. Macmillan, eds. *The Sydney Scene 1788–1960*. Sydney: Hale and Iremonger, 1982.

Black, David Ross, and John Nauright. *Rugby in the South African Nation: Sport, Cultures, Politics, and Power in the Old and New South Africas*. New York: Manchester University Press, 1998.

Black, Maggie. *Food and Cooking in 19th Century Britain: History and Recipes*. Birmingham: Historic Buildings and Monuments Commission for England, 1985.

Boniface, Priscilla. *Tasting Tourism: Traveling for Food and Drink*. Aldershot, England: Ashgate, 2003.

Boorde, Andrew. *A Compendyous Regyment or a Dyetary of Healthe Made in Mountpyllyer, by Andrewe Boorde of Physycke Doctour, Newly Corrected and Imprynted with Dyuers Addycyons Dedycated to the Armypotent Prynce and Valyent Lorde Thomas Duke of Northfolke*. London: Wyllyame Powell, 1542.

Boulton, William Biggs. *The Amusements of Old London*, vol. 1. London: John C. Nimmo, 1901.

Breen, Timothy. *The Marketplace of Revolution: How Consumer Politics Shaped American Independence*. New York: Oxford University Press, 2004.

Brewster, Anne. *Reading Aboriginal Women's Life Stories*. Sydney: Sydney University Press, 2015.

Brotton, Jerry. *The Sultan and the Queen: The Untold Story of Elizabeth and Islam*. New York: Viking, 2016.

Brown, Judith M., and William Roger Louis, eds. *The Oxford History of the British Empire*. Vol. 4, *The Twentieth Century*. Oxford: Oxford University Press, 1998.

Bruegel, Martin, ed. *A Cultural History of Food in the Age of Empire*, vol. 5. London: Berg, 2012.

Buchan, William. *Observations on the Diet of the Common People, Recommending a Method of Living Less Expensive, and More Conducive to Health, than the Present*. London: A. Strahan, 1797.

Burnett, John. *Liquid Pleasures: A Social History of Drinks in Modern Britain*. London: Routledge, 1999.

———. *Plenty and Want: A Social History of Food in England from 1815 to the Present Day*. 3rd ed. New York: Routledge, 1989.

Carlisle, Rodney P., ed. *Encyclopedia of Play in Today's Society*. Los Angeles: Sage, 2009.

Carp, Benjamin L. "Did Dutch Smugglers Provoke the Boston Tea Party?" *Early American Studies: An Interdisciplinary Journal* 10, no. 2 (2012): 335–59.

Carroll, Lewis. *Alice's Adventures in Wonderland*. Boston: International Pocket Library, 1941.

Cejas, Mónica. "Tourism 'Back in Time': Performing 'the Essence of Safari' in Africa." *Intercultural Communication Studies* 16, no. 3 (2007): 121–34. https://web.uri.edu/iaics/files/10-M¨®nica-Cejas.pdf.

Chalus, Elaine. "Elite Women, Social Politics, and the Political World of Late Eighteenth-Century England." *The Historical Journal* 43, no. 3 (2000): 669–97.

Chaudhuri, K. N. *The Trading World of Asia and the English East India Company: 1660–1760*. Cambridge: Cambridge University Press, 1978.

Chrystal, Paul. *Tea: A Very British Beverage*. Gloucestershire, England: Amberley Publishing, 2014.

Clarke, Francis Gordon. *The History of Australia*. Westport, CT: Greenwood Press, 2002.

Clarkson, Janet. *Food History Almanac: Over 1,300 Years of World Culinary History, Culture, and Social Influence*, vol. 1. Lanham, MD: Rowman & Littlefield, 2013.

Cleage, Albert B. *Black Christian Nationalism: New Directions for the Black Church*. New York: William Morrow and Company, 1972.

Colquhoun, Kate. *Taste: The Story of Britain through Its Cooking*. London: A&C Black, 2012.

Counihan, Carole, and Penny Van Esterik. *Food and Culture: A Reader*. 3rd ed. New York: Routledge, 2013.

Cox, Irwin Edward Bainbridge, ed. *The Country House: A Collection of Useful Information and Recipes: Adapted to the Country Gentleman and His Household, and of the Greatest Utility to the Housekeeper Generally*. London: Horace Cox, 1867.

D'Antonio, Michael. *A Full Cup: Sir Thomas Lipton's Extraordinary Life and His Quest for the America's Cup*. New York: Riverhead Books, 2010.

Davies, Peter, and Robert Light. *Cricket and Community in England: 1800 to the Present Day*. Manchester: Manchester University Press, 2012.

Davin, Anna. "Family and Domesticity: Food in Poor Households." In *A Cultural History of Food in the Age of Empire*, vol. 5, edited by Martin Bruegel, 141–64. London: Berg, 2012.

de Bry, Theodor, Hans Staden, and Jean de Léry. *Dritte Buch Americae, darinn Brasilia* [America, part 3, therein Brazil]. Frankfurt: Durch Dieterich bry von Lüttich jetzt Burger, 1593.

De Horne Vaizey, Mrs. George. *A Houseful of Girls*. Illustrated edition. Gloucester, England: Dodo Press, 2007.

Dexter, Margaret. *Malta Remembered: Then and Now; A Love Story*. Bloomington, IN: iUniverse, 2013.

Dietler, Michael. "Culinary Encounters: Food, Identity, and Colonialism." In *The Archaeology of Food and Identity*, occasional paper no. 34, edited by Katheryn C. Twiss, 218–42. Carbondale: Center for Archaeological Investigations, Southern Illinois University, Carbondale, 2006.

Dolin, Eric Jay. *When America First Met China: An Exotic History of Tea, Drugs, and Money in the Age of Sail*. New York: W. W. Norton, 2012.

Douglas, Mary. "Standard Social Uses of Food: Introduction." In *Food in the Social Order: Studies of Food and Festivities in Three American Communities*, edited by Mary Douglas, 1–39. New York: Russell Sage Foundation, 1984.

Doyle, Andrea. "High Tea at Meetings." Meetings Strategies. *Successful Meetings*, December 1, 2015. http://www.successfulmeetings.com/Strategy/Meeting-Strategies/Afternoon-Tea-Meetings-Networking/.

Drelichman, Mauricio, and Hans-Joachim Voth. *Lending to the Borrower from Hell: Debt, Taxes, and Default in the Age of Philip II*. Princeton, NJ: Princeton University Press, 2014.

Duncan, Daniel. *Wholesome Advice against the Abuse of Hot Liquors, Particularly of Coffee, Chocolate, Tea, Brandy, and Strong-Waters: With Directions to Know What Constitutions They Suit, and When the Use of Them May Be Profitable or Hurtful*. London: H. Rhodes and A. Bell, 1706.

Ellis, Markman. *The Coffeehouse: A Cultural History*. London: Orion Publishing Group, 2011.

——, gen. ed. *Tea and the Tea-Table in Eighteenth-Century England*. 4 vols. London: Pickering & Chatto, 2010.

Elyot, Thomas. *The Castel of Helth Gathered and Made by Syr Thomas Elyot Knyghte, Out of the Chiefe Authors of Physyke, Wherby Euery Manne May Knowe the State of His Owne Body, the Preseruatio[n] of Helthe, and How to Instructe Welle His Physytion in Syckenes that He Be Not Deceyued*. London: Thomas Berteleti, 1539.

Eng, Robert Y. "Macao (Macau)." In *Colonialism: An International Social, Cultural, and Political Encyclopedia*, vol. 1, edited by Elvin E. Page and Penny M. Sonnenburg, 359. Santa Barbara, CA: ABC-CLIO, 2003.

Fasseur, Cornelius. *The Politics of Colonial Exploitation: Java, the Dutch, and the Cultivation System*. Translated by R. E. Elson and Ary Kraal. Ithaca, NY: Cornell University Southeast Asia Program, 1992.

Ferguson, Niall. *Empire: The Rise and Demise of the British World Order and the Lessons for Global Power*. New York: Basic Books, 2002.

Finn, Margot, and Kate Smith. *The East India Company at Home, 1757–1857*. London: University College of London Press, 2018.

Fortune, Robert. *A Journey to the Tea Countries of China; Including Sung-Lo and the Bohea Hills; with a Short Notice of the East India Company's Tea Plantations in the Himalaya Mountains*. London: J. Murray, 1852.

Freeman, Michael, and Selena Ahmed. *Tea Horse Road: China's Ancient Trade Road to Tibet*. London: River Books, 2015.

Fromer, Julie. *A Necessary Luxury: Tea in Victorian England*. Athens: Ohio University Press, 2008.

Frykenberg, Robert Eric, and Alaine M. Low. *Christians and Missionaries in India: Cross-cultural Communication since 1500*. Grand Rapids, MI: William B. Eerdmans Publishing Company, 2003.

Fulford, Robert. *Votes for Women: The Story of a Struggle*. London: Faber and Faber, 1956.

Games, Alison. *The Web of Empire: English Cosmopolitans in an Age of Expansion, 1560–1660*. Oxford: Oxford University Press, 2008.

Gangulee, N. *Health and Nutrition in India*. London: Faber and Faber Ltd., 1939.

Gascoigne, John. *Science in the Service of Empire: Joseph Banks, the British State and the Uses of Science in the Age of Revolution*. Cambridge: Cambridge University Press, 1998.

Gascoyne, Kevin. *Tea: History, Terroirs, Varities*. Ontario: Firefly Books, 2011.

Gautier, L. *Tea: Aromas and Flavors around the World*. San Francisco: Chronicle, 2006.

Geiser, Karl Frederick. *Redemptioners and Indentured Servants in the Colony and Commonwealth of Pennsylvania*. New Haven, CT: The Tuttle, Morehouse, & Taylor Co., 1901.

Goodwin, Stefan. *African Legacies of Urbanization: Unfolding Saga of a Continent*. Lanham, MD: Lexington Books, 2006.

Gott, Richard. *Britain's Empire: Resistance, Repression, and Revolt*. London: Verso, 2011.

Green, Toby. *The Rise of the Trans-Atlantic Slave Trade in Western Africa, 1300–1589*. Cambridge: Cambridge University Press, 2011.

Gunn, Geoffrey C. *World Trade Systems of the East and West*. Leiden, Neth.: Brill, 2018.

Hainsworth, D. R., ed. *Builders and Adventurers: The Traders and the Emergence of the Colony, 1788–1821*. Sydney, AU: Cassell Australia, 1968.

Head, David, ed. *Encyclopedia of the Atlantic World, 1400–1900: Europe, Africa, and the Americas in an Age of Exploration, Trade, and Empires.* Santa Barbara, CA: ABC-CLIO, 2018.

Heilbron, J. L. "Benjamin Franklin in Europe: Electrician, Academician, Politician." *Notes and Records of the Royal Society* 61 (2007): 353–73.

Heiss, Mary Lou, and Robert J. Heiss. *The Story of Tea: A Cultural History and Drinking Guide.* New York: Ten Speed Press, 2007.

Herrick, Christine Terhune. *A-B-C of Housekeeping.* New York: Harper & Brothers, 1915.

———. *Consolidated Library of Modern Cooking and Household Recipes.* New York: R. J. Bodmer, 1904.

Hoeller, Hildegard. "Hunger, Panic, and Refusal: The Gift of Food in Susan Warner's *The Wide, Wide World.*" In *Culinary Aesthetics and Practices in Nineteenth-Century American Literature,* edited by Monika Elbert and Mary Drews, 173–88. New York: Palgrave Macmillan, 2009.

Huxley, Gervas. *Talking of Tea.* London: Thames and Hudson, 1956.

Hyam, Ronald. *Understanding the British Empire.* Cambridge: Cambridge University Press, 2010.

Jackson, Ashley. *The British Empire: A Very Short Introduction.* Cambridge: Oxford University Press, 2013.

Jamieson, Ross W. "The Essence of Commodification: Caffeine Dependencies in the Early Modern World." *Journal of Social History* 35, no. 2 (2001): 269–94.

Jeacle, Ingrid. "Accounting and the Annual General Meeting: The Case of the Edinburgh University Tea Club, 1920–1945." *Accounting History* 13, no. 4 (2008): 451–78.

Jenkins, Philip. *A History of Modern Wales, 1536–1990.* New York: Routledge, 2014.

Jha, Usha. *Land, Labour, and Power: Agrarian Crisis and the State in Bihar (1937–52).* Dehli: Aakar Books, 2003.

Jolliffe, Lee, ed. *Tea and Tourism: Tourists, Traditions and Transformations.* Buffalo, NY: Channel View Publications, 2007.

Jordan, Don, and Mike Walsh. *The King's Revenge: Charles II and the Greatest Manhunt in British History.* New York: Pegasus Books, 2016.

Khamis, Susie. "A Taste for Tea: How Tea Travelled to (and Through) Australian Culture." *ACH: The Journal of the History of Culture in Australia* 24 (2006): 57–79.

Kidd, Dudley. *Echoes from the Battlefields of South Africa.* London: Marshall Brothers, 1900.

Kolb, Robert W. *Sovereign Debt: From Safety to Default*. New York: Wiley, 2011.

Levy, Annie. "Great Britain: Wales." In *At the Table: Food and Family around the World*, edited by Ken Albala, 103–8. Santa Barbara, CA: Greenwood, 2016.

Lewis, Lesley. *The Private Life of a Country House*. Stroud: Alan Sutton Publishing Ltd., 1997.

Lewis, Mary Catharine. *Pouring Tea for Profit: The Tea Room Institute of the Lewis Training Schools*. Washington, DC: Lewis Hotel Training Schools, 1925.

Lincoln, Margarette. *British Pirates and Society, 1680–1730*. New York: Routledge, 2014.

Lloyd, Trevor Owen. *The British Empire, 1558–1995*. Oxford: Oxford University Press, 1996.

Luck, Dora. *A Little Book of Cookery*. London: Sands and Company, 1905.

Macfarlane, Alan, and Iris Macfarlane. *The Empire of Tea: The Remarkable History of the Plant that Took Over the World*. New York: Overlook Press, 2004.

MacGregor, David Roy. *The Tea Clippers: Their History and Development, 1833–1875*. 2nd ed. London: Conway Maritime Press, 1983.

Marks, Shula. "History, the Nation and Empire: Sniping from the Periphery." *History Workshop* 29, no. 1 (1990): 111–19.

Marshall, Agnes Bertha. *Mrs. A. B. Marshall's Larger Cookery Book of Extra Recipes*. London: Marshall's School of Cookery, 1902.

Marshman, John Clark. *History of India from the Earliest Period to the Close of the East India Company's Government*. Cambridge: Cambridge University Press, 2010.

Martin, Laura C. *Tea: The Drink That Changed the World*. New Clarendon, VT: Tuttle Publishing, 2007.

Mason, Laura. *Food and Culture in Great Britain*. Wesport, CT: Greenwood Press, 2004.

Matthews, Jodie, and Daniel Travers, eds. *Islands and Britishness: A Global Perspective*. Newcastle upon Tyne, England: Cambridge Scholars Publishing, 2012.

Mavor, William Fordyce. *The British Tourists, or, Traveller's Pocket Companion: Through England, Wales, Scotland, and Ireland; Comprehending the Most Celebrated Tours in the British islands*. London: E. Newberry, 1798.

Maxon, Robert M., and Thomas P. Ofcansky. *Historical Dictionary of Kenya*. Lanham, MD: Scarecrow Press, 2000.

Maxwell, Kim. "Tea Is Served, Ma'am." *Food and Home*, January 7, 2009. https://www.foodandhome.co.za/entertaining/tea-is-served-maam.

McCarthy, Angela, and T. M. Devine. *Tea and Empire: James Taylor in Victorian Ceylon*. Manchester: Manchester University Press, 2017.

McGee, Harold. *On Food and Cooking: The Science and Lore of the Kitchen.* New York: Scribner, 2004.

Mokyr, Joel, ed. *The Oxford Encyclopedia of Economic History,* vol. 3. Oxford: Oxford University Press, 2003.

Montgomery, Maureen E. *Displaying Women: Spectacles of Leisure in Edith Wharton's New York.* New York: Routledge, 1998.

Moore, Anthony. "Aboriginal Land Rights in South Australia." In *Indigenous Australians and the Law,* edited by Elliot Johnston, Martin Hinton, and Daryle Rigney, 133–48. Sydney: Cavendish Publishing, 1997.

Morgan, John. *Debrett's New Guide to Etiquette and Modern Manners: The Indispensible Handbook.* New York: St. Martin's Press, 1996.

Morgan, Sally. *My Place.* Freemantle, Australia: Freemantle Press, 1987.

Mukherjee, Ramrishna. *The Rise and Fall of the East India Company.* New York: Monthly Review Press, 2009.

Murdock, Catherine Gilbert. *Domesticating Drink: Women, Men, and Alcohol in America, 1870–1940.* Baltimore: Johns Hopkins University Press, 1998.

M. W. *The Queen's Closet Opened.* S.L.: Printed for Nathaniel Brook at the Angel in Cornhill, 1655.

Nichols, Beverley. *Down the Kitchen Sink: A Memoir.* Portland, OR: Timber Press, 2006.

Notestein, Wallace. *The English People on the Eve of Colonization, 1603–1630.* New York: Harper and Brothers, 1954.

Ovington, John. *An Essay upon the Nature and Qualities of Tea.* London: R. Roberts, 1699.

Palmer, Arnold. *Movable Feasts: A Reconnaissance of the Origins and Consequences of Fluctuations in Meal-Times with Special Attention to the Introduction of Luncheon and Afternoon Tea.* London: Oxford University Press, 1952.

Parasecoli, Fabio. "World Food: The Age of Empire c. 1800–1920." In *A Cultural History of Food in the Age of Empire,* vol. 5, edited by Martin Bruegel, 199–208. London: Berg, 2012.

Pepys, Samuel. *The Diary of Samuel Pepys: A New and Complete Transcription.* Vol. 1, *1660.* Edited by Robert Latham and William Matthews. London: HarperCollins, 2000.

——. *The Diary of Samuel Pepys: A New and Complete Transcription.* Vol. 8, *1667.* Edited by Robert Latham and William Matthews. London: HarperCollins, 2000.

Petrovich, Lisa L. "More than the Boston Tea Party: Tea in American Culture, 1760s–1840s." MA thesis, University of Colorado–Boulder, 2013. https://scholar.colorado.edu/cgi/viewcontent.cgi?article=1017&context=hist_gradetds.

Pettigrew, Jane. *A Social History of Tea*. Swindon, England: The National Trust, 2001.

Pettigrew, Jane, and Bruce Richardson. *A Social History of Tea: Tea's Influence on Commerce, Culture and Commodity*. 2nd ed. Danville, KY: Benjamin Press, 2014.

Pomeranz, Kenneth. *The Great Divergence: China, Europe, and the Making of the Modern World Economy*. Princeton, NJ: Princeton University Press, 2000.

Porter, Andrew, ed. *The Oxford History of the British Empire*. Vol. 3, *The Nineteenth Century*. New York: Oxford University Press, 1999.

Postma, Johannes. *The Dutch in the Atlantic Slave Trade, 1600–1815*. Cambridge: Cambridge University Press, 1990.

Powell, Martyn J. "Consumption: Commercial Demand and the Challenges to Regulatory Power in Eighteenth-Century Ireland." In *Mercantilism Reimagined: Political Economy in Early Modern Britain and Its Empire*, edited by Philip J. Stern and Carl Wennerlind, 282–303. Oxford: Oxford University Press, 2014.

Pratt, James Norwood. *The Tea Lover's Treasury*. San Francisco: 101 Productions, 1982.

Publishers' Circular. *The Publishers' Circular and Booksellers' Record*. Vol. 87, *July–December 1907*. London: Office of "The Publishers' Circular" Limited, 1907. https://babel.hathitrust.org/cgi/pt?id=njp.32101079672372;view=1up; seq=14.

———. *The Publishers' Circular and Booksellers' Record of British and Foreign Literature*. Vol. 59, *July–December 1893*. London: Sampson Low, Marston & Company, Ltd., 1893. https://babel.hathitrust.org/cgi/pt?id=njp.32101079672 133;view=1up;seq=9.

Purchas, Samuel. *Purchas His Pilgrimage: or Relations of the World and the Religions Observed in All Ages and Places Discovered, from the Creation unto This Present*. London: William Stansby, 1625.

Raffald, Elizabeth. *The Experienced English Housekeeper: For the Use and Ease of Ladies, Housekeepers, Cooks, &c. Written Purely from Practice . . . Consisting of Several Hundred Original Receipts, Most of Which Never Appeared in Print*. London: R. Baldwin, 1782.

Ramsay, George Daniel. *The Queen's Merchants and the Revolt of the Netherlands: The End of the Antwerp Mart*, vol. 2. Manchester: Manchester University Press, 1986.

Richardson, Bruce, and Jane Pettigrew. *A Social History of Tea: Tea's Influence on Commerce, Culture and Community*. Danville, KY: Benjamin Press, 2015.

Richardson, Lisa. *The World in Your Teacup: Celebrating Tea Traditions Near and Far*. Eugene, OR: Harvest House Publishers, 2010.

Rickard, John. "Eating like a White Man: Nibbling at the Edges of Heart of Darkness." *L'epoque Conradienne* 33 (2007): 49–57.

Ricklefs, M. C., Bruce Lockhart, Albert Lau, Portia Reyes, and Maitrii Aung-Thwin. *A New History of Southeast Asia*. New York: Palgrave Macmillan, 2010.

Robinson, Portia. *The Women of Botany Bay: A Reinterpretation of the Role of Women in the Origins of Australian Society*. Victoria, Australia: Penguin Books, 1993.

Rose, Sarah. *For All the Tea in China: How England Stole the World's Favorite Drink and Changed History*. New York: Viking, 2010.

Ross, P. T. *A Yeoman's Letters from the Boer War*. London: Simpkin, Marshall, Hamilton, Kent, & Co. Ltd., 1901.

Roy, Tirthankar. *The East India Company: The World's Most Powerful Corporation*. London: Penguin Books, 2016.

Rudolf, Uwe Jens, and Warren G. Berg. *Historical Dictionary of Malta*. 2nd ed. Lanham, MD: Scarecrow Press, 2010.

Saberi, Helen. *Tea: A Global History*. London: Reaktion Books, 2010. http://www.reaktionbooks.co.uk/pdfs/Teatimes_extract_web.pdf.

———. *Teatimes: A World Tour*. London: Reaktion Books, 2018. http://www.reaktionbooks.co.uk/pdfs/Teatimes_extract_web.pdf.

Saunier, Pierre. "Food Production: Industrial Processing Begins to Gain Ground." In *A Cultural History of Food in the Age of Empire*, vol. 5, edited by Martin Bruegel, 27–48. London: Berg, 2012.

Scholliers, Peter. "Eating Out." In *A Cultural History of Food in the Age of Empire*, vol. 5, edited by Martin Bruegel, 107–22. London: Berg, 2012.

Seaman, L. C. B. *Victorian England: Aspects of English and Imperial History, 1837–1901*. London: Routledge, 2002.

Sen, Colleen Taylor. "India." In *At the Table: Food and Family around the World*, edited by Ken Albala, 125–32. Santa Barbara, CA: Greenwood, 2016.

Shaw, John. *Charters Relating to the East India Company from 1600 to 1761*. Madras: R. Hill, 1887.

Sheridan, Richard B. *Sugar and Slavery: An Economic History of the British West Indies, 1623–1775*. Kingston, Jamaica: Canoe Press, 1994.

Skinner, Allan Maclean. *A Geography of the Malay Peninsula and Surrounding Countries: Part I, Malay Peninsula, Borneo*. Singapore: Royal Asiatic Society, 1884.

Skinner, Julia. *Modernizing Markham: Bringing "The English Housewife" to Today's Readers*. Iowa City: Candle Light Press, 2012.

Smith, Andrew. *The Oxford Encyclopedia of Food and Drink in America*, vol. 2. New York: Oxford University Press, 2013.

Snyder, Dolores. *Tea Time Entertaining: A Collection of Tea Themes and Recipes.* Memphis: Wimmer, 2004.

Southey, Robert. *Lives of the British Admirals*, vol. 3. London: Longman, 1834.

Southwell, Ian, and Robert Lowe, eds. *Tea Tree: The Genus Melaleuca.* Amsterdam: Harwood Academic Publishers, 1999.

Spencer, Colin. *British Food: An Extraordinary Thousand Years of History.* New York: Columbia University Press, 2002.

Stead, Jennifer. *Food and Cooking in 18th Century Britain: History and Recipes.* London: The Historic Buildings and Monuments Commission for England, 1985.

Stevens, Becca. *The Way of Tea and Justice.* Nashville: FaithWords, 2014.

Straker, Vicky. *Afternoon Tea: A History and Guide to the Great Edwardian Tradition.* Stroud, England: Amberley Publishing, 2015.

Stuart, Winifred. *Chronicles of Service Life in Malta.* London: Edward Arnold, 1908.

Studeman, Kristin Tice. "How to Drink Tea like a Royal: Dos and Don'ts from the Queen's Favorite Hotel." *Vogue*, July 23, 2017. https://www.vogue.com/article/english-teatime-etiquette-how-to.

Surak, Kristin. *Making Tea, Making Japan: Cultural Nationalism in Practice.* Stanford: Stanford University Press, 2013.

Sweet, Matthew. *Inventing the Victorians: What We Think We Know about Them and Why We're Wrong.* New York: St. Martin's Press, 2014.

Takada, Akira. *Narratives on San Enthnicity: The Cultural and Ecological Foundations of Lifeworld among the !Xun of North-Central Namibia.* Kyoto, Japan: Kyoto University Press, 2015.

Tanner, Joseph Robson. *Tudor Constitutional Documents, A.D. 1485–1603.* Cambridge: Cambridge University Press, 1922.

Tattam, Henry. *A Memoir of Her Grace the Late Duchess of Bedford.* London: W. M. Watts, 1858.

Thomas, Gertrude Z. *Richer than Spices: How a Royal Bride's Dowry Introduced Cane, Lacquer, Cottons, Tea, and Porcelain to England, and So Revolutionized Taste, Manners, Craftsmanship, and History in Both England and America.* New York: Alfred A. Knopf, 1965.

Thomas, Hugh. *The Slave Trade: The Story of the Atlantic Slave Trade: 1440–1870.* New York: Simon & Schuster, 1997.

Thompson, Flora. *Lark Rise to Candleford: A Trilogy.* Boston: David R. Godine, 2009.

Thompson, Leonard. *A History of South Africa.* New Haven, CT: Yale Nota Bene, 2001.

Tidd, Joseph. "From Models to the Management of Diffusion." In *Gaining Momentum: Managing the Diffusion of Innovations*, edited by Joseph Tidd, 3–46. London: Imperial College Press, 2010.

Tinniswood, Adrian. *The Long Weekend: Life in the English Country House, 1918–1939*. New York: Basic Books, 2016.

Toll, Daniel J. *A Narrative Embracing the History of Two or Three of the First Settlers and Their Families of Schenectady*. Schenectady, NY: Daniel J. Toll, 1847.

Trentmann, Frank. "Before 'Fair Trade': Empire, Free Trade, and the Moral Economics of Food in the Modern World." *Environment and Planning D: Society and Space* 25, no. 5 (2007): 1079–1102.

——. *Free Trade Nation: Commerce, Consumption, and Civil Society in Modern Britain*. Oxford: Oxford University Press, 2009.

Trevelyan, Laura. *A Very British Family: The Trevelyans and Their World*. London: I. B. Tauris, 2006.

Trubek, Amy B. "Professional Cooking, Kitchens, and Service Work." In *A Cultural History of Food in the Age of Empire*, vol. 5, edited by Martin Bruegel, 123–40. London: Berg, 2012.

Tsai, Shih-shan Henry. *Maritime Taiwan: Historical Encounters with the East and West*. London: Routledge, 2009.

Twitty, Michael. *The Cooking Gene: A Journey through African American Culinary History in the Old South*. New York: HarperCollins, 2017.

Tyerman, Luke. *The Life and Times of John Wesley, Founder of the Methodists*. London: Hodder, 1870.

Ukers, William H. *All About Coffee*. New York: The Tea and Coffee Trade Journal Company, 1935.

——. *All About Tea*, vol. 1. New York: The Tea and Coffee Trade Journal Company, 1935.

Urban, Sylvanus. Review of *Remarks on the Present Distresses of the Poor*, 3rd ed., by G. H. Law, Lord Bishop of Bath and Canterbury. In *The Gentleman's Magazine* (April 1836): 385–93.

Visser, Gustav, Ronnie Donaldson, and Cecil Seethal, eds. *The Origin and Growth of Geography as a Discipline at South African Universities*. Cape Town: Sun Press, 2016.

Walvin, James. *Slavery in Small Things: Slavery and Modern Cultural Habits*. West Sussex, England: John Wiley & Sons, 2017.

Webster, Amy. "Tea, Table Manners and . . . a Tiger! An Exploration of How Children's Literature Transforms the Traditional English Tea Time," article 12. *Feast: Consuming Children* 1. http://feastjournal.co.uk/article/tea-table

-manners-and-a-tiger-an-exploration-of-how-childrens-literature-transforms
-the-traditional-english-tea-time/.

Wells, Christopher. "Separate Spheres." In *Encyclopedia of Feminist Literary Theory*, edited by Elizabeth Kowaleski-Wallace, 519. New York: Routledge, 2009.

Wemyss, Georgie. *The Invisible Empire: White Discourse, Tolerance and Belonging*. London: Routledge, 2009.

Whitaker, Jan. *Tea at the Blue Lantern Inn: A Social History of the Tea Room Craze in America*. New York: St. Martin's Press, 2015.

Williams, Jack. *Cricket and England: A Cultural and Social History of the Inter-war Years*. London: Frank Cass, 1999.

Williamson, George Charles. *George, Third Earl of Cumberland (1558–1605), His Life and Voyages, a Study from Original Documents*. Cambridge: Cambridge University Press, 1920.

Williams-Rogers, Jodi-Anne. "Afternoon Tea Under the African Sun." In *Tea Reader: Living Life One Cup at a Time*, edited by Katrina Avila Munichiello, 50–52. Clarendon, VT: Tuttle Publishing, 2012.

Wilson, Bee. *Swindled: The Dark History of Food Fraud, from Poisoned Candy to Counterfeit Coffee*. Princeton, NJ: Princeton University Press, 2008.

Woodward, William Harrison. *A Short History of the Expansion of the British Empire, 1500–1930*. Cambridge: Cambridge University Press, 1952.

Worden, Blair. *The English Civil Wars, 1640–1660*. London: Orion Books, 2009.

Yates, Arthur C. *1880–1885: A Record of Mr. Gladstone's Second Administration*. Manchester, England: Abel Heywood & Son, 1885.

Young, Alfred P. *The Shoemaker and the Tea Party: Memory and the American Revolution*. Boston: Beacon Press, 1999.

Zhang, Shana, and J. T. Hunter. *The Wild Truth of Tea: Unraveling the Complex Tea Business, Keys to Health and Chinese Culture*. Kunming, China: Wild Tea Qi and International Tea Academy Publishing, 2015.

INDEX

aboriginal cultures, Australian, 77–79, 105–6, 183n80

Accum, Friedrich Christian, 21

Adams, Abigail, 69, 172n93

Adams, John, 69, 172n93

advertising, tea and, 23–24, 27, 88–89, 111, 120, 127, 129, 135

Africa, 7–9, 48, 55, 58, 73–75, 79, 81–84, 98, 101, 107–10, 113, 117, 118, 149n36–37, 174n109, 175n135, 182n65, 185n95, 187nn114–17. *See also* Kenya

African Americans, 98

afternoon tea: and colonialism, 1, 8, 9, 44, 47, 57, 61–62, 70–80, 83, 84, 87–88, 91–93, 102–3, 105–9, 112–20, 130, 139–41, 144, 146, 177n16, 182n65, 187n116–17, 188n118, 196n5; and English history, xi, 1, 8, 11, 31–36, 39, 40, 42–44, 52, 72–73, 75, 77–79, 80, 83, 88, 115–16, 120, 121, 122, 124–26, 128, 130, 134, 140, 141, 159nn98–104, 160n107, 161n114, 164nn155–59, 199n16; etiquette, 6, 8, 36–38, 43, 78, 80, 88, 95, 101, 108, 111–12, 114, 120, 124, 130–33, 136–37, 180n58, 195n74, 198n10; foods served, 37–40, 42, 54–55, 73, 78, 83, 88, 91–93, 95, 98–101, 103–6, 109–16, 118, 122, 124, 126–27, 131–34, 137, 141–46, 193n46, 198n10, 198n12–15, 199n16; meal, 1, 8, 11, 29, 32–33, 35–36, 43, 73, 77, 81, 91–95, 96, 98, 100–101, 108, 120, 125–26, 128, 132–33, 139–40, 141–46, 160n107, 161nn110–14, 187n114; in modern United Kingdom, 38–39, 44, 88–89, 98–99, 101, 103, 109, 111–12, 114–15, 120, 121–28, 131–37, 139–40; and social class, 11, 31–34, 37–39, 42, 44, 61, 78–79, 88–89, 92–93, 95–96, 103, 106, 108, 110–12, 118–19, 121–23, 127, 131, 140–41, 160n107, 161nn109–10, 189n3; Russell and, 11, 31–34, 39; timing of, xi, 29, 33, 35, 38,

ABOUT THE AUTHOR

Dr. Julia Skinner is the owner of Root, a company that uses food history and fermentation to educate people and build community connections. She is also a chef and uses her background in fermentation and food history to help restaurants rethink their food programs. She has published multiple books and articles within food studies and within her other field of study, library science. When not writing, cooking, or teaching, she is tending to her wild plant garden, playing outside, or going on some sort of an adventure. She lives in Atlanta, Georgia.

Living Our Soul's Wisdom:

Beyond Separation in the Presence of Divine Love

by Mary Linda Landauer

Living Our Souls Wisdom

Mary Linda Landauer

Ohio, USA

Marylinda1111@gmail.com

Ordering Information:

Special discounts are available on quantity purchases by corporations, associations, educational institutions, and others. For details, contact Mary Linda Landauer above.

Printed in the United States of America

First Edition

Softcover ISBN 978-1-5136-9755-0

eBook ISBN 978-1-5136-9754-3

Publisher

Winsome Entertainment Group LLC

Cover Image by Brian Luke Seaward

This book is dedicated in deepest gratitude to Annie Ames for believing in me and making this book possible through her generous contribution. I love you dear friend!

Acknowledgments

This book has been a labor of Divine Love mostly transmitted through to me so my thanks must begin with acknowledging my own beautiful soul, Beloved Mystery and the always, small persona MaryLinda, challenged to her final surrender.

Thanks to my neighbor, Jamie Wells, who began the first editing process. Then to Kristy Boyd Johnson who lovingly edited and weaved the poetics and writing in a most unified way. Thanks to Jared Rosen, with Dream Sculpt Books and Media who helped develop the book for final publishing and the video giving a beautiful visual of the books soul poetic Divine Love. Also a shout out to Juliet Clark for the final book cover and design and final publishing. All of you and so many more making this book possible.

Thanks to my family! Children-Keith Biedenharn and his wife Jennifer, Rebecca Cressy and her husband David, and Denny English and his wife Jen. To my amazing and loving six grandchildren- Micah Cressy Trist and husband Nick, Henry Biedenharn, Alex Biedenharn, David H. Cressy, Tyler English and Addie English. All of you are my light in my darkest moments. Brother Thompy and wife Mary Palmer, and Aron Biedenharn Coates like my own family.

Thanks to so many friends…if I've left anyone out please forgive me. Brian Luke Seaward, your friendship can never be measured in words but my gratitude forever for a most beautiful forward and photo for the book cover. All my ya ya girlfriends. Sue Schneier, Kathy Bedell, Chrystal Elliott, Pam Liebert, Annie Ames-making this book possible- Barbara Newell and Dana Lisle. Virginia Landry, Laura and David Cressy, Libby, Raina and all the goof ball friends- you know who you are! Brian K and David H, Brigid Brown, Bernie Fitterer, Richard Brendan, Anna and Perry Brown, Jochen Becker, Nomali Perera, Lisa Evert, Bonnie Vallette, Barbara LeMeur. To Ken Wilber, Corey W. DeVos, Diane Hamilton, Jeff Salzman and, gone but never forgotten, Terry Patten, and all my Beloved Integral friends. To the many friends on Facebook and Instagram, too numerous, but your loving support forever appreciated. Last, but never least, to my loving Real Estate family friends; so many clients over 32 years. All of you are my life support and without you my life would lack so much meaning! I love you!

Table of Contents

Foreword

"You may say I'm a dreamer,
but I'm not the only one.
I hope someday you'll join us
And the world will be as one."

-

John Lennon

I have to admit, when I first heard the song *Imagine* by John Lennon, I didn't quite get it. I understood, even yearned for the concept of oneness, but I didn't grasp all the nuances conveyed in the lyrics. I was 15 years old and at an age when I was trying to make sense of a very confused world: the Vietnam war, civil unrest, high school teen angst, alcoholic parents, and Watergate looming in the not too distant future. What I understood even then, was that the standard worldview of division and separation wasn't working. John Lennon's song offered a beacon of light in the darkness of an ego-based world in chaos.

Shift ahead 50 or more years and it is abundantly clear that the ruling perspective of division and separation is not only NOT working, it is destroying the planet: political strife, religious wars, racial disparity, economic tensions, and environmental destruction top the list. What Lennon's song illustrated is a way of being called unity consciousness. It's a state of awareness where we see ourselves in a most incredible, dynamic, and loving relationship with all aspects of life – oneness. What may seem like an unreachable utopian dream is very much within our grasp. This great shift in consciousness,

1

however, takes some effort. It is not going to happen all by itself.

In college I began a simple meditation practice. Several months later, with one or two mystical experiences, a veil was lifted. One such experience, during a profound meditation, brought me first through a dark tunnel, then through a wall of flames and finally into what I can best describe as an immense area of loving light. In this place/state I was connected through light and thought to everyone and everything. The feeling was sublime, divine, and unforgettable.

Through meditation, and then throughout the course of each day, I found that I could walk each step with a lighter heart, a smile on my face, and a song in my heart. Today, my meditation practice is both grounding and liberating. I practice the Golden Rule daily. I have more moments of amazing synchronicities, profound gratitude, and awe. The web of life is not only good, it is astounding.

To understand the concept of oneness or unity consciousness, it helps to examine our standard state of awareness that's often called duality (or polarity) consciousness. Duality consciousness focuses on noticing, then judging differences between ourselves and others. After we notice differences, our thought processes begin to slight or diminish those who are different. This creates a fear-based, hierarchical structure, one that promotes ignorance, alienation, selfishness, discrimination, and hatred.

One school of thought suggests that Planet Earth is a type of educational academy where souls come to learn about duality consciousness and divisions: male/female, right/wrong, good/bad, gay/straight, ego/soul, fear/love, and so on. Duality consciousness is considered a lower level of consciousness, particularly because in the process of examining the

2

pieces, we fail to recognize the whole. Ageless wisdom reminds us that the whole is always greater than the sum of the parts. Ageless wisdom also reminds us that there is help along the way.

Mary Linda is no stranger to the concept of oneness and our sacred connection to the divine. I have known her for well over 25 years and I have always known her to be in communion with divine oneness, whether it her daily meditation practice, her love of nature, or her talent with poetry, a talent she gladly credits to the divine source. Mary Linda, through her words, extends a hand to help you along your way.

What you are about to read in these pages is perhaps nothing new. Rather it is a reminder of what you already know, yet inherent wisdom so often forgotten in the day to day struggles of Earth School. How can we best shift/evolve our consciousness to a higher level, as in John Lennon's song, *Imagine*? How can we imagine a better world? How can we develop our minds so we can experience oneness? While the answers may be simple, the execution is a bit more challenging. Luckily you have an expert guide to walk you through the steps, and through her wisdoms and insights, guide you through the next passage on this journey we call life.

Brian Luke Seaward, Ph.D.
Author, *Stand Like Mountain, Flow Like Water; Reflections on Stress and Human Spirituality*

Let's begin with Sorrow!
Your dog dies. A searing pain
enters into your whole being.
Thoughts run through remembering the first day
your brought him home.
Grief now comes to keep you company.
Sorrow and Grief partner in all our many losses!

What about Joy?
Joy often the antidote to much Sorrow and Suffering.
We find a new dog at the animal shelter.
Our heart beats a different vibrancy and frequency.
Stress lessens and our entire being lights up with gratitude.

Then there is Humor!
We share funny stories about our dog.
Hearing another laugh awareness says...
this is
Lightness of Being

Living Our Soul's Wisdom
life whispers We live through both Sorrow and Joy
Balanced and Harmonized
In
Lightness of Being
By
Becoming aware to Let Go
when Sorrow/Grief needs to fade away
Finding our Joy
Always, forever snuggled within Divine Love!

Prologue

Anne Baring, *The Dream of the Cosmos: A Quest for the Soul*, says, "For thousands of years we have been influenced by two primary stories: the Christian one of a transcendent Creator-God and a fallen creation, and the more recent scientific one which says that we exist in an inanimate universe which is without consciousness, meaning or purpose."

Thomas Berry, *The Dream of The Earth*, says, "It's all a question of story. We are in trouble just now because we do not have a good story. We are in between stories. The old story, the account of how we fit into it, is no longer effective. Yet we have not learned the new story."

Bill Plotkin, *The Journey of Soul Initiation: A Field Guide for Visionaries, Evolutionaries, and Revolutionaries* says, "The initiatory practices we need now for cultural renaissance and human evolution are in vital ways unprecedented, something never-before-seen— different in structure and destination as well as in methods."

Are We Today Witnessing a Turning-of-the-wheel of Stories?

A story, eons ago, was taught and embedded within our human mind that we are separate from anyone or anything and that science has no meaning. Today, many of us are being directly confronted within to the always, forever true story now arising. An inclusive story where we all fit in; a story of our sacred unity that lives within each of our unique, sacred souls of loving wisdom. This revelation is our soul's presence, her essence, and her always-missing-link in the old story of separation. Yet, she is within us all as embodied Divine Love. With her return, through her inner creative fire of love, she will unify with the separate mind to dissolve all the old programmed stories, long

5

lived in separation and division. Her creative light today is revealing our dark human dilemma of this believed and taught separation from each other, our Mystery Source, and Earth.

Beauty and the Beast

This story has long captivated me. Through the years in my growing and development, it became clear these archetypal characters are within me. Within all women and men. How our mind can become beastly with its long-held shadows and beliefs so programmed into us from early in our life, always showing up to fill us with judgments and memories of each's beastly traumatized past.

Then when meeting up with my beauty—my beautiful wise, sensual soul presence within my heart—she began helping me confront my beast so in need of love and guidance from her. My him, of the beastly mind ego self, finally to enjoin in a long-awaited love story with her, my sensual soul heart wisdom.

She fires the cauldron of our heart, releasing its pure creative light energies. She seduces our mind with her creative love to dance the waltz of inclusion. Together, we love our Earth, and we remain in loving relationships to tend the Earth. We know Divine Love is our way—a creative, sacred loving presence as old as time.

Early in my life, a loving presence emerged, guiding me on how to live in the in-between space—not here, not there. Always on the edge of what is visible and invisible. It was hard. My soul's loving presence will be shared throughout this book. Her musings came through in writings, unusual and unexpected experiences, then slowly, it occurred to me to begin writing these in my journal or through poems. My creative fire of love and light was emerging. Every morning, upon waking the sacred doors of my heart, opened me to enter me into her quiet temple, where my mind let go of its noise and my body softened to just surrender all its pains and emotions stored.

But it was to be the discovery of a small lump in my breast, diagnosed as cancer, that became the darkest night taking me to total surrender. This story will be shared in later chapters.

Our surface world lived in today, mostly within the five senses, without our soul's presence of multi-sensory gifts, gets harder to understand. Our sensual soul is sensitive; she is innocent to the polarized cruelty she sees being played out upon life's stage. Our sacred souls live in a more subtle cosmic-inclusive energy, where her protection comes from being within a greater Beloved Mystery presence, a firing of creative sacred Divine Love. Our Beloved Presence—my name for our creative mystery—is our one causal energy, our creative light of sacred Divine Love of all the Earth world and beyond, and all beings living upon any surface. Cosmic and infinite! Words here challenge me to describe the indescribable.

Our sacred soul presence teaches our persona smallness, governed by the five senses. We must now come into greater awareness and realization that without our higher creative light of creative guidance, through each's awakened soul, and one with our Beloved, that what is now being created by the smallness of **egos** is slowly becoming more destructive and polarized. The old story of separation is reaching its apex, as stress within the human mind and stress upon the Earth both need a higher source to help manage today. This timeless source is our own soul presence of wisdom. Let me introduce our soul's presence in an inclusive story, too long missing. One morning, journaling to Beloved, a powerful transmission came through.

Dear Soul,

I come through now using words that can be understood. Earth is now my court room; a great trial is being held and everything and everyone is in my court of Light and being exposed. Those who have used their dark minds of corruption now must come before my Light. These dark minds of a small will have used my teachings, that came through many great souls for eons of time and across many places, for their selfish purposes to control Earth and all its gifts so given.

Their dark means to have power over the Earth and humanity are now on trial. They've falsely believed they could use a means, they named as sin, to do their dark deeds, then in the end, just say "forgive me." Forgiveness must be of humble and authentic means. Yet, they do their sins daily, then carry a book or sit in a building saying "forgive me" only to return to their dark corruption day in and day out, over eons of time. This must end. These dark minds have never taken responsibility for their actions that have created weapons of mass destruction, killing so many, and their means of controlling others through their control of money, land and all upon the beautiful Earth.

They believe they own the women, children, and all the inhabitants to do as they please. This must end. There is no Divine Love within these dark corrupt minds other than their love of power to control and their love of money used to control my meek and humble, who have long understood the power of my love resides within my kingdom, given within them, to open and live their lives from my Divine Love. The fallen, from my kingdom within, now must face my radiating Light coming in many ways now to expose them.

Those living within my kingdom of Divine Love, within your heart/soul, do not fear, as your love and service to my depth of Divine Love releases you now to go back upon the Earth to gather together, living my Timeless Presence of Divine Love, to restore the lands, the peace and harmony upon the Earth, and my love forever within you. I love you for your never wavering from living my Power of Love within you over any other external power for small selfish reasons. Yes, you have strayed many times, but always you come back home within in gratitude and authentic grace and go back with a higher responsibility to become more of my Divine Love. This is how souls grow and develop into higher integration and how evolution of

8

Earth and consciousness was meant to be by doing the great work of becoming my beautiful souls of Divine Love.

But these small dark minds who have lost their depth of inner kingdom so to elevate themselves as superior and supremacy over Earth and humanity have become atrophied in their soul growth and higher Divine Love development. From those who have fallen, my Light will remove all darkness, but only after each serve time, in many ways, so to finally gain understanding and come back within yourself to my Divine Love.

My Power of Divine Love and its radiating Light must become understood as the only means and purpose to come to Earth, as souls, within these forms for the glorious experience to have the higher sensual joys of loving each other with the responsibility to serve my Divine Love as caretakers and great leaders of Earth for all who come after inheriting my gifts and these extraordinary experiences to become aware souls living within human like forms.

We Change the Old Narrative of Separation
Into a Story of Sacred Unity
Living Our Soul's Wisdom
Within Presence of Divine Love

We are taught to place all our problems in the hands of God! Have you seen God or his hands? I ask because maybe God always had another plan! Did Jesus and others appear to remind us We must save ourselves…did they remind us the kingdom is within each to do this? What is this kingdom? Perhaps it is time to find out! How do we do this if We don't take that journey within ourselves?

What awaits within? For me cancer was found, shadows like ghosts everywhere! What? Then it happened! Deep beneath all these rotten pieces of me, from my mind separated from my soul's wisdom, and where all these taught crazy stories had lived me—a more truer sweet, subtle soul message came— Listen; surrender these old stories! Healing begins!

We have no secrets; each human form born out of the earth elements to embody our unique, subtle souls who come to live through each's diverse form upon the earth of diversity. How beautiful, joyous to be given these times together to explore, to discover and grow and develop our understanding of how we use the miraculous mind and senses to see, hear, touch, intuit, smell and create together new ideas, innovations for our earth to continually evolve what Divine Love originally gave and intended for us to come and visit.

When a small mind will was given it became misunderstood thus it exploited its small power. We must become aware today so to realize how this wrong small mind, in its mis-understanding, today has reached an apex of danger. We are operating and living out of a wrong power chosen by the small mind, often referred to as an ego. This ego has lost its soul connection and is unable to quench its animal like appetite of domination and control of all life.

We must now use our higher senses of intuition that are directly informed by our higher information, our own unique soul. Thus we travel back into our inner roots where our depth of Love, our Divine Power, awaits us to correct and re-align with our higher guidance. It is our light like movement that activates our divine codes of truth, and what is our real purpose and our goodness of true meaning attuned to beauty so we begin again where We now Listen to the Wisdom of Our Soul then We Live Our Souls Wisdom together within Divine Love!

Our daily practice begins and ends with being soul aware; we each live our soul's essence by being in Presence of Divine Love so we become grounded within Divine Love. We live through loving grace, restoration and forgiveness, understanding our karma is individual, collective and ancestral and all seen as past traumas.

When we connect to our soul's light movement, through each of us, we attune back within our original Divine Love thus aligning each soul with all our creator's gifts, so bestowed within, for entering into the earth field. This leads to each unique soul's purpose 'to being of service' while upon the earth.

We are given boundaries, yet, today are we being asked to walk right through? The other side may be the way to understanding how We meet in the middle of our now dangerous tensions. When We can hold true to our Divine Love, within each's depth, this love now flows upwards to the surface for higher integration.

My hand reaches for your hand, my heart opens to your heart. I see you in your pain as you see me in mine and, perhaps, together if we dare to hold enough of our divine love we can now drop our tug of war ropes that bind us to these eons of tension/traumas and keep our small minds separated from each other to never cross any and all boundary lines. Yet we must! We must meet Divine Love within each of us if we are to ever live in peace among our unique differences so given to each of us for living life experiences in divine loving relationships with each other!

Simplicity says to bear witness to your life's experiences, just as they happened, without being victim to them. Integrity says if these had been different we would be different. So we face our trauma in truth—other wise we become our past living in our present, as these traumas, over and over. Compassion says we can't change what happened in our past traumatic experiences. We can only become aware and bear witness to them today in this present moment. Our Soul's wisdom now becomes the internal, intimate and intuitive voice we listen too. Her whisper says Living our Soul's Wisdom will require great change.

Change says We can ask what could we be like if we say no more? What if we choose today to stand at this now crossroad of our life, earth's life—past/present, and all living out of these old energies taught and programmed into each's small mind—what if we each dare to be brave to walk the path unknown to us? A path, perhaps, always beckoning us! We can only try!

Our Soul whispers
this may make all the difference!
I am here within—musing you forward!

Chapter 1

Our Sacred Unity Beginnings!

Our story of sacred unity, embedded within our sacred Divine Love, began when a small planet called Earth had its earliest evidence 13.9 billion years ago. Some say longer. In this book, the timeline is to help us understand that something extraordinary happened. We also know everything on the planet was in perfect aligned unity to begin creating the very conditions to give and support life. From fossils to single cells to multi-cell organisms, this unity and Divine Love would seek the means to create life and dissolve what wasn't needed as a means to continue evolution into ever higher realization for living. And, here we are today, with over eight billion people, yet, most of our creation has been to develop outwardly while inwardly our core sacred Divine Love is all but depleted. The conveyor belt of evolution has been halted by a small mind without its soul wisdom.

Sadly, our great sacred love story is slowly losing its creative inner power to an outer power where love is of material things. We might say humans also fell into this category of something to be owned. How did this happen? This book will help us understand how we went off the core sacred unity Divine Love story, resulting in beliefs of disconnection and separation we all live today and, most important, how we must reconnect with our soul's sacred loving presence and each other. We and our planet need this reconnection to survive.

It's quite amazing how everything falls into an orderly place except our lives. We wake to the sun and fall asleep to the moon and stars. The planets, universes, and galaxies all seem to follow some innate instruction with little disruptions occurring. Yet, today, we can be healthy with great boundless energy only to wake up with severe headaches and often succumb to a diagnosis our life soon will end. There is no stabilizing orbit we follow as we live our lives in stories dividing and separating everyone into what they believe, where they live, what color their skin is, and how they gender appear. We even separate our inner body parts with little understanding they too are created in a healing orbit within us to follow innate instructions on how to heal.

We must ask the big questions today to better understand. If the original intention was always to become inwardly activated by our spark of light from our presence of soul love and beloved, thus creating together a more inclusive, beautiful world for all to come and share to live in a peaceful loving means, but instead we became thwarted, then what happened? Many powerful transmissions have come through me and many others asking our new story be shared within these pages to help us understand so we restart the evolutionary conveyor belt. And, most important, how we must do this together. May we all deeply listen for the sacred resonance resounding from these mostly transmitted words.

Are we and our planet being confronted with big questions, asking, what is awakening or awareness? But to now witness ourselves and our Earth being so polarized from our blindness of what we have created through a wrong separation story lived, and—the only way out—is to become soul realized within these minds of thoughts and bodies of cells, today it is now time to take responsibility to live our soul's presence and become the change for our new story!

We bring forth greater understanding that our physical forms of humanness and Earth are simply the instruments by which our sacred unity is to become understood through our sacred Divine Love, deeply felt as our soul presence. This becomes Earth's means to evolve into its true meaning and its true purpose. Our sacred love, out of our sacred unity, is the fire of creative light itself moving evolution.

Each sacred soul begins living within her sacred love as an invisible presence within all forms. When our small surface ego love can no longer sustain through separate destructive means, then our form becomes activated, wired in its cells and DNA, for our soul presence to help partner in its higher growth and awakening, thus beginning the process of our higher soul's emergence.

That moment when surrendering into my own vulnerability, a higher power was found secluded within every cell of my being. Why wasn't this known? Our world is constructed within structures of many beliefs, so if we show our vulnerability by becoming transparent, we believe this will render us powerless. Yet, just the opposite is true. Let's go deeper into some vulnerabilities. We can't be loved unless we become what our taught mind believes makes us lovable. For me, beliefs of people-pleasing and being body-perfect fit into this old structure that love comes from another or something external; money and power often companions here too.

Surrendering our old mind concepts empowers us to become naked in our vulnerability and transparency, and we begin to recognize how we've lost our true self, our empowered sacred soul presence, buried deep within and just beneath all the many learned and taught mind beliefs since our original birth. It is our surrender of this old story of separation taught that can begin our awakening into our soul awareness and our new birth of our beautiful soul presence.

This new birth emerges out of becoming once more childlike in curiosity and playfulness, yet, possessing all our adult awareness of how to use our given gifts of each's senses in a more loving and sensual way. We become energy sensors, able to transmit our vulnerability and transparency to others aware with open receptors to recognize each's power within us, as soul-loving free spirits, to dance with them in life.

Together, we become the way out of messy chaos and into a more balanced, harmonious, transparent loving soul consciousness, away from small self-centered ego consciousness. We become sacred Divine Love to act out of this sacred love in our vulnerability and authentic transparency. Fear can no longer hold us captive as we're able now to surrender the fearful taught beliefs that we are separate from each other, our soul, and beloved presence.

The Fall into Our Separation Story!

Sadly, us humans, long ago in our early appearance upon the Earth, created a story of separation out of fear. We were less evolved, as was the Earth, so our small minds saw everything as outside ourselves, and our ego surface love became our means to survive. We saw our God as some force who punished and judged, and this began a false worship, out of our false self, of a separate God much like ourselves. We humans, at these earlier stages, had within us only our fearful mind that evolved this fear living in our story of separation.

Thus, we evolved ourselves as sole superpower and supremacy. Men were taught to rule over the woman, child, Earth, and all species upon the Earth. Today, this brutality of our beastly mind must meet the loving wisdom of our sacred soul. We lost our sacred memory!

Traveling within myself has required patience. May we all find this patience as we are entering into a new territory with a new language and no map to where we are being led. We must surrender to trust with faith our own soul presence guiding; she is our loving innate wisdom, ever so subtle in our beginnings, guiding us with courage and patience. Yet, like me, we all may come up against a dark shadowy terrain too. Both becoming our teachers for remembering!

My shadows came from places long forgotten, a ghost town where fragment like bones scattered everywhere with eyes sunken deep. My dark nights spent within kept me leaving my inner terrain only to return over and over. It became clear to get into my heart, where my soul presence patiently waited. My journey through the dark deserted places of myself must be met and understood so to release these dark false mind energy stories. Trauma today in our world is both personal and collective. We have a long history of abuse to be healed and released from our fallen separation story.

My release became my freedom to meet up with my soul, who would journey with me, within myself, to finally come home to her soul, loving presence—her wisdom. Today, this inner journey is ongoing, but the beast of my mind illusions are finally being met with "who I am," the beauty of my sacred heart/soul wisdom. We have learned there is no separation. There are only inclusive relationships to be lived within and with each other upon the Earth. We are in joy to finally have this realization and awareness. Yet, my work requires each day to surrender my resistance, so to meet up with what shows up; sadness and joy in a forever dance. These are my edges. Then cancer showed up to be my biggest edge. More to come!

Having now true understanding around my purpose and its meaning for coming to the Earth is helping me to heal my story and also be in service to help heal our collective story. I do believe this is all our true purpose and meaning; we are here to help heal the false story that we are separate from our own sacred soul, loving presence, Mystery Source Presence, and each other. What is amazing is everything has been given, within each of us, so we can awaken to realize this gift, given to all, and then live it upon the Earth.

17

We're also now being awakened to realize the Earth is only one of many true heavenly homes where our true self, as souls, come to journey within a mind/body spacesuit so to have divine physical experiences in and through our gift given of physical senses. Now these senses can become elevated to become truly sensual in a pure core sacred love of our inclusive relationships. Beloved and soul can now dance together through the physical forms.

Today, we each must become responsible for our waking up, so to grow up, then we open up our heart to finally show up as soul-loving presence within our forms, with our Beloved of Mystery Presence. When it's time to leave Earth, we simply take off the human space suit where it decomposes back into the Earth and star dust elements, then we travel beyond in our light subtle bodies to have new adventures with other souls and our Beloved Mystery, who has many cosmic addresses.

It's also interesting timing that the new Webb Telescope just released amazing visuals of cosmic space with countless universes and galaxies. We are part of this cosmic home moving us in this cosmic field where we must let go of our limiting stories from such limited small mind egos. It's time to wake up!

Wow! Amazing how our Divine Mystery of creative fire pulsates core sacred love to bring first the Earth into its existence to have it all in working order before bringing forth us human mind/body's with an ability to become conscious of ourselves through thousands of years of evolution then—finally—us human mind/body's begin to be awakened through our sacred soul's presence into our true realization within our greater awareness that it's time to tame our beastly mind of wrong programs and stories, back into the enjoining of our sacred unity—our sacred souls love story. Beauty and the Beast within integrate to become one with our greater mystery core love to go live our inclusive story upon Earth.

Yet, we must understand and remember how time-space works; it was only seconds ago in cosmic time that Earth was created, then life abundance created, then us humans. And only seconds ago, many of us began our awakening to remember. Big Yawn!! May we start loving and living together our sacred love within our inclusive partnerships, our divine trinity of soul, mind/body, and Beloved Mystery. We must also remember we are wired into our higher grid— called by many our kingdom within—for our activation and now awakening. Our wiring—an embedded Divine Love spark within us—gets us alchemically fired to be a creator as our Divine Source, and what better spark than the spark of our soul presence as sacred love within sacred unity. Let's explore further our fall into separation. But first a poetic writing transmitted through me.

Dear Soul,

Awareness grows stronger upon earth—I Am that awareness. This will become the guiding principle to help humanity free themselves from their caged personas. Remember, time is a construct upon earth and is considered slow—there is no time in Infinite, eternal Divine Love. Keep breathing in Divine Love to cleanse and resurrect your Soul's Presence of Wisdom, then live my Divine Love!

We don't need to hold onto anything. Let it go. We've already been shaped by what matters. Divine Love came into the world with us, and Divine Love we take back when we leave. Find this Love now…live this Love now. This is all you will ever need because this Love will bring forth what you need. Divine Love is the flowing waters, the soaring mountains, and the forest of trees. It's the soil for all that brings forth food and beauty you will ever need. It's all there for surviving each body form.

What Divine Love asks today is to bring forth its nutrition for our soul's survival within us all in these forms. This is kindness, compassion, it's caring for the earth, and its caring for all life upon the earth. Our Divine Love will survive all life breaths and only asks us to use our senses given to smell it, taste it, listen to it, touch it, and see it everywhere in its beauty, truth, and goodness given.

Divine Love is our innate wisdom abiding within us all as our own soul always, already present if we simply let go of everything no longer serving our Divine Love. Then it arises, like our breathing, free of toxic pollution, and shines on us like the sun, radiating our light to live as souls of Divine Love upon earth in pure awareness. Our bodies are the gift of experiences to know 'who we are' to live as beautiful wise souls of Divine Love.

How Did We Form These Personal Identities?

Our identity is often determined by political, religious, and country of origin ideology. We can add skin color and gender too. We have a visa to further determine these identities, and then we even go further, asking how much our financial worth is. In our fall into our separation story, these, sadly, have come to determine our values and who we are. We live these surface-brutal lives, and often they can end brutally too. Our focus has become on our outer achievements, missing our direct soul inner experiences that give us Divine Love.

Our small surface separation story guiding most of humanity today is the fallacy taught from many religions that the woman ate a forbidden apple, thus the fall out of sacred unity. Then this fall continued its darkness, giving the man supremacy over the Earth, woman, child, and all species. This dark story of separation began the wars erupting within and without for thousands of years. Our false judgments trapping us all in this story of separation. Of course, kindness must be a higher judgment than meanness. Sacred love is always higher than hate, and peace is superior to war, which is why we must develop into higher and higher understandings and development of who we are and why we are here upon the Earth.

Today, are we witness to our development, like a moving evolutionary conveyor belt that is arrested, and has—frighteningly—been stopped for the many thousands of years? We might even say we are moving backwards in time seeing these dark corrupt minds change our constitutional laws to maintain their dark power of control. Until we each take responsibility to start our own conveyor belt of growth and development moving again, by becoming more aware and realized, we all may be facing humanity's extinction and possibly our most beautiful Earth planet given to all species.

We ask how many today still hold the belief that our Beloved Source of Mystery is a man image somewhere in a heaven looking upon the Earth judging one color of skin better, one religion better, one politics better, one country/culture better, then off to battle we fight and kill each other by destroying the lands from these toxic beliefs of our mystery image we humans have created. This story we've created has long separated us from our souls and infinite mystery, giving us this belief that we fell from our grace into separation from each other, the Earth, and our inner Mystery Source. This false story is slowly destroying us. We've never fallen from Grace or Divine Love! This fallacy story so embedded within us is creating chaos.

This fall into our separation story has played out for thousands of years, keeping people stuck in minds of the devil—also created by man—and minds who also judge the devil made us do it. This story has created us as sinners, forever needing the control of these dark man-made lies. We've fallen from our direct inner Divine Love within each's kingdom of this inner Divine Love into a small mind who uses our Beloved God as means to keep us caged in these lies.

Thus, the concepts of blame, shame, and guilt creating wounds and traumas that get projected over and over again. This keeps the man/woman/mind always trapped in their devilishly held duality of beliefs. All this programmed into a sweet innocent child's mind since coming into this world. How did or do any of us survive this horrific fallen separation story?

In one country, a woman is covered from head to toe; she is taught her unworthiness compared and judged by men. Actually, if we are deeply truthful, we can see this through the historical times as most cultures still today live by this system known as patriarchy, where the man stands in judgment and rules as supreme power, and this power becomes the means to control as he uses his belief and image of God he's created as his justification to reign superior and control over anyone and everything. In this year, 2022, look no further than our Supreme Court. This toxic belief system today shows itself in a pandemic of diseases, climate change everywhere threatening all of us, and, even more heartbreaking, sacred Divine Love—our most valuable resource—is all but depleted.

Surviving in most places is impossible, and even the few at the elite top are miserable in their fear of losing this fallacy of corrupt power and judgment over the lands and people. Earth is not a loving place to live today. A war has erupted by a man named Putin, the dictator of Russia, giving rise to this patriarchal story of separation as he now brutally takes his warheads into a country, Ukraine, to take control and domination for himself over their freedoms. Yet, the people, both Russian and Ukrainian, are beginning to question— knowing this is wrong. Is our Beloved Mystery of creative fire sending out its message of Light everywhere, exposing this now-dark corruption?

Corruption is becoming so dark that we all cringe thinking about what is to happen. Yet, the many beautiful men and women who journey within, and are taking up their courage cross to develop themselves into their higher soul consciousness and understanding, are standing strong together to help us take down this system of long-held patriarchal of power over the Earth and people, and entering us today into a higher power, and this power comes from within; one with our higher soul and beloved presence, guiding us all within through our creative fires of sacred Divine Love.

These insidious beliefs, held for so long in our history, have become the judgment fallacy of separation from our God Mystery Source, the Earth, and each other, and gives those still trying to hold on to this false power of lies and darkness a now confrontation by the sacred light and love, held in the depths of our soul's presence that we must end this wrong story to begin our true inclusive story. That Beloved Mystery lives within us in a most beautiful sacred loving soul presence, and the time is now for entering back into our sacred Divine Love.

Death of Separation...Return of Our Soul's Presence!

Is it time, we must ask, to come up to the surface from the long-lived separation to see our one incredible creation that we were all born into but today is becoming destroyed by us humans over the thousands of years? By becoming aware, we can save us with what lies beneath this false separation story. No one has ever seen what we call Beloved God Mystery or by other names used. Yet, many have seen the signs of so many miracles, and we've felt the undeniably direct presence of our sacred love within us that takes us to our humble knees in gratitude and grace. Many of us have witnessed the miracle of healings, the moments when the raging storm passes to be lifted by the sun and all its light of calm.

We have these gifts of something greater, something felt so much bigger and loving than our smallness to know we aren't alone. Many, like me, have also had the experience of an out-of-body or near-death experience, where we directly touched our own soul and to never feel truly mortal or separated again. We realize only our bodies die while we, as souls of Divine Love, live on as immortal beings within a presence that is infinite consciousness itself. A higher field of a living creative fire dissolving all separation. We have greater awareness of our own felt sacred soul presence emerging out of this creative fire, pulsating life both visible and invisible. Why cancer and death don't scare me but only make me surrender deeper to live its teachings!

Father Richard Rohr says:

"The only way evil can succeed is to disguise itself as good. And one of the best disguises for evil is religion. Just pretend to love God, go to church every Sunday, recite the creed, and say all the right things. Someone can be racist, be against the poor, hate immigrants, and be totally concerned about making money and being a materialist, but still go to church each Sunday and be "justified" in the eyes of religion."

Is the role of the prophet to bring a higher understanding to the outdated religious teachings? After all we learned our world is round not flat! We learned all beings have an inner direct guidance to become souls of wisdom! Yet our religions and our prophets still keep themselves separated!

Separation is the earth's biggest challenge creating, since our beginnings, on going wars of chaos and crisis? Why? Perhaps it's how the few control the many! Perhaps it's how the love of money became more important than the Love of equality! We shift and change by becoming more God like in our realized soul essence. We see each other as pure Divine Love in resonance with our great miraculous, mystery, and greater than all material means that will eventually disappear but our Souls always remaining to continue our Divine Love!

Perhaps We must begin to contemplate as our beloved prophets taught so We save ourselves and our earth planet and we begin to finally end this war of separation! We become soul prophets together where our religions, politics and businesses co-enjoin to bring forth the greatest Love upon earth in our capacity to honor both capitalism and socialism. What a beautiful world we can evolve for all us soul beings!

Just like at death, what we are all faced with is our moral face. What does this face look like? What does this inner character look like? You see, at death, this is the only thing of real value. What we acquired in material form isn't taken with us. What we acquired within ourselves, as direct realization that we are Soul Presence of Divine Love, is always taken into our next adventure. Today, we must die before our death. We must look closely to ask, how much did I love my neighbor—regardless of their skin color, gender, ethnicity, politics, religion, or any difference? We must die to our separation story!

We have created a war of capitalism versus socialism when both are so badly needed for any balance and harmony to ever exist again. So many great teachers came to help us see the need for this ability to weave our dualities and difference into a higher soul consciousness of understanding. Jesus taught socialization in healing and tending to the poor and sick, trying to teach the capitalist politicians and priests by upturning their temples of corruption. Buddha left all his wealth when confronted with mass suffering, vowing to find a more loving and just way for all. Now our sensual sacred soul, loving presence returns to confront the ego, taking the mind/body into her tenderness and her wisdom how sacred love must be how we live together, co-creating our sacred love story where we both capitalize and socialize our world in loving balanced partnerships to create harmony. We tend to all the Earth and all sentient beings.

Capitalism is a beautiful gift given to humanity to become great entrepreneurs, teachers, creators of needs like cars, trucks, farm equipment, banks, and stores, and we can name so much that capitalism has given to help us grow and develop. We've created a shared democracy to give opportunity and equality to all. But when it swings the pendulum to just capital and more capital, without care of its social partner to tend the social needs, then we become out of balance, and disharmony and chaos erupt. We need our soul presence. She gives wisdom to unify the alone separate mind.

We need each other now on this cliff, holding hands so we all don't fall off into this darkness now swirling in its chaos, division, and its separation story, potential of all our destruction. We hold tight to the only truth we all know—that sacred love within a shared sacred unity is our way and that this is a felt presence of direct experience guiding with both soul wisdom and mind reason and comes from each's unique divine creative fire of sacred love. Awakening into soul awareness we, and all physical movements, are powered by the same energies of power that manifest form, then dissolve form back into dust. All with the exception of our subtle energy soul body self. Yet, this is rarely talked about or explored to wonder how these subtle energies do inhabit the form, guiding the form and mind, much like the guiding of the Earth orbit, sun, and moon. This exploration is our sacred science giving us meaning and purpose.

Our minds can be filled with information, an ongoing data plus the stories filled with beliefs. Does our mind live us or is there a gap where an alive soul awareness begins living us? And, we must ask, who is aware and what is missing? Is deep beneath all the surface stories and data something more sensual, light-filled, and often surging within our body's, even mind, a pure love unlike the surface love usually felt? This must get our attention to awaken us, shake us, and rattle our very bones. Is time ready for us to dive deep within this more subtle aware space. Do we want to know this Divine Love?

Now, we think so.

We're waking up from these old patterns and beliefs that are always keeping us from our deeper sensual sacred love. Who and what is this deeper love…she came to me in a deep trance to share she is my very sensual soul love…she is me. She is the creative fire to live me.

How do I know now?

Because one night, she floated out of me, turned to smile at me, then floated through the room. What happened? It's very clear something happened and she now takes my small data mind with body senses to dance with her in every moment alive. She wants to dance us all.

We're dissolving, merging, integrating, morphing, like a small caterpillar from its mind cocoon, and waking up to see ourselves as a beautiful sensual soul love presence, come to partner with our small mind. We now see the world and everyone so much clearer.

Did we wake up…maybe?

This is for all of us to take our inner journey to experience. Many today, like me, are living a much more aware life. Call it anything we like…but it's about all our transformation from mere separate small mind selves into being a part and whole of everything. It's about inclusion, not separation. For me, and hopefully you too, it's about living now each moment as an awakened sensual soul presence, within this gift of a human form, elevating all our senses to being sacred Divine Love and taking creative actions to service this love within our sacred unity with each other and our world.

Poems From My Soul to End This Chapter

The Wisdom of Patience

She teaches me to sit by the stream,
listening to the gentle bubbling
water as it runs over the rocks slowing
its movement.

She teaches silence when the voices
all around me fight with their 'my way
retort,' getting louder and louder.
Uncertainty frightens everyone.

She teaches within me my breath, and
my heart pulsates to rhythms set in motion
from the beginning of time by a most loving,
greater cosmic mystery.

She teaches trust and faith in this pulsating
rhythm. She teaches that which creates
is within me...teaching me...she says

Listen!

She teaches great change unfolds when one
way no longer serves to sustain life, thus new
life and ways must be embodied, and this requires
great patience.

*She teaches the old story lived for eons is now
slowly morphing into its new story. This will
require great patience with faith. It heralds in
our great new soul's love story...long-awaited
upon the Earth.*

*She teaches this new story will be told through
those of us who remain patient and true to love.
Love pulsates the heart and the breath...Be Patient!*

*Our Soul is likened to a great sculptor
aware the human form, a beautiful abode
for its own becoming.*

*Slowly through its inner sculpting away the dark
outer experiences over eons
of time/space, the Light eternal begins to reveal
itself in all its beauty, truth, and authentic
goodness.*

*The dark masks, one by one,
are taken off, then the soul is revealed to walk the earthly
way in its finished body form where it meets
its many sisters and brothers too now revealed.*

*Life upon Earth now under the
Light of authenticity slowly begins a more unified living
together as each soul unique in its
meaning and purpose begin sculpting the Earth for its now
transformation back into the garden*

*home for all to come and experience through
out time for these very sensual experiences
through the gifts of bringing Divine Love to everyone and everything.*

*Divine Love is both God/Goddess
revealed from its inner kingdom within each form as
Souls of Divine Love and can be understood in
whatever gender it is called to be,
whatever color is its purpose to experience, and
whatever place it is now to live upon Earth for greater
understanding of its meaning in this time
it has chosen to be upon the Earth. All are the
unique gifts given to each soul to be upon the Earth garden
home for its short stay.*

*The great prerequisite
is surrendering the false truth to living the only truth, and that truth
is by being loving to ourselves, we always are loving each other!
Being kind to ourselves, we are always being kind to others.*

*We finally see ourselves
through a clean, clear lens, giving us clarity within ourselves, there
is only our soul presence as us…this is our great awareness!*

*One pulsating Love
from the beginning of time, seeking to express itself through our
heart, breathing all the many life stories to finally realize love is our
way to peace and the celebration of this gift called living in human
forms upon the Earth form. We make and live love with each other,
thereby planting love seeds to sustain Earth always!*

Remember this:
There is a barrier we create! A wall we falsely believe protects our
heart! This was created from being, sadly, abused earlier in our
lives. Only each of us can remove that wall away from our sweet,
sensual, and sensitive heart. This emerges our soul's presence.

This takes courage!
This takes an inner guidance of sacred love we often must seek
and is not always easy! Yet, to continue to live within our closed
and walled-off heart slowly depletes us of our true life energy,
paradoxically, which is the creative fire of our sacred love! Seek and
ye shall find...the door of each heart awaits us all, and many await
us to take our hand to help walk us back home to sacred love within
our sacred unity!

This land of our sacred unity
is where Beloved Mystery wants to live within and through each
awake and realized heart/soul! We slowly dissolve our fear that
has kept us all so separated from each other, and from our Beloved
Mystery, to begin living a more transparent and authentic life with
each other! Our trust slowly being restored! Our inner light shines
more brightly.

I live in many worlds!
How is that possible
you ask?

Living from inner to outer
my senses have seen from
many worlds helping me to
see what is important when
looking into this outer world.

I hear symphonies from long
ago and my touch knows your
skin before even touching as
you know mine.

My smell whiffs of some aroma
long lived in some far away place.
I intuitively know something long
before it happens.

Intuition is our soul's gift to each
of us. This is our true voice. The
ego mind voice is on default We
must switch to our intuitive voice.

This is my soul living within me
who has lived many lives in many
ways in many worlds. Opening to
her whispers she guides me in how
to best live.

I listen to her before listening to the news or some other voice. This keeps me in peace and keeps me loving all things knowing the outer darkness is simply needing my soul's light and her Divine Love!

When enough ego voices switch to their inner intuitive soul voice We will begin to shift the now darkness back into a more loving, light filled planet where our guidance will come from each's soul aligned with our greater, divine source of all creation so we co-create our earth anew!

We must make this switch to our always inner Soul voice-encoded within us-becoming aware begins our activation to become realized.

Chapter 2

My Story: A Love Affair with My Soul's Presence

In March of 2022, after having forty-year-old implants break and capsulate, they were removed. One month later, a lump appeared in my right breast. An ultrasound biopsy was done to reveal it was cancerous. Shock took me into disbelief as it also devastated my family and friends. After all, my deep work of surrender, since a child, along with out-of-body experiences and already many dark nights of my soul, wasn't I surrendered enough? Not even close!

Yet, this was to be my greatest experience and teaching of Divine Love and where cancer became a radiating Light, revealed in its dark mass, as so much more. I'm still upon this journey, living each breath and moment in direct surrender of not knowing anything except what each of these breaths and moments unfold right in front of me. Surprise is my most frequent guest in my now unfolding.

The decision to have chemo, along with other integrative treatments like acupuncture and energy massages, became my new way of life. My doctors, oncologist and breast specialist/surgeon, began to align with my inner deep spiritual practices, enjoined and unified together but only after many confrontations.I deeply listened to my soul's presence voice to empower my often-small persona voice. This unification was to become greater than the cancer, as this dark mass became filled with light to catalyze how science meets and enjoins with Spirit and how my outer body with cancer met and enjoined with inner Divine Loving Presence, free of any cancer. Wow!

After four months, today, the dark tumor is almost dissolved, and everyone on my team listens. It became clear my body was too fragile to do chemo treatment every week. My blood levels were depleted, and the side effects of extreme fatigue and nerve issues in my legs and feet made it difficult to walk in nature; it's my lifelong love to be in direct contact with invisible presence through all the natural elements. I finally made the decision to only do chemo every other week or sometimes every three weeks to give my body the rest it needed. This allowed me to have the more alternative treatments in between. This gave me back my walking and vital energies of presence—my soul Divine Love. My listening deep!

Slowly, the small self-voice totally surrendered to the fact she may die in form, but she also became held in so much Divine Love, living through her, that she slowly dissolved any and all separation, much like the tumor was dissolving. Our integration as one entity, Soul Me, became understood that we aren't separate but One Divine Soul Love living, within an outer form, to delight in the gifts of senses to be sensual in physical manifestations and become in greater service to teach others the Power of Divine Love by an active participation, as who we are. Family and friends felt this Love and began themselves to taste this Divine Love. Transparency and transformation, within the vulnerability of death, living me, gave to me authentic living with everyone and life.

Our thoughts can become their own body of water. We must be careful to not drown in them. Today, may we all let go of our stories created by these thoughts that we may become someone not ever known before. Our more truer soul self ready to make her appearance.

Today, Spirit asks, shall we follow the old familiar mind road or the open heart unknown path? My soul, ever so subtle, winks at my silly old mind with all its old-held distortions to let them go. We now choose the open road of adventure, holding hands where she lovingly guides us both. She whispers *Just be*, then guides us with wisdom along our path of forever love where flowers bloom, the sun brightly shines, the animals greet us, and our laughter and curiosity bring forth any and all to ever be experienced. Wait…someone is ahead on the path…they seem to be waiting for me to catch up. A smile comes as my walk speeds up…finally we meet…finally true love comes. Divine Love waits just ahead to greet us.

It's clear much of my life has been lived by these thoughts given to me from a culture, a family and its beliefs, and it's all mostly just words…just data…my emotions and feelings derived from what these ongoing mind/data stories speak. This has created so much of my suffering by me making decisions in my life to be what someone else wanted me to be and not becoming the "someone ever before known." Life finds many ways and sources to teach and help us. These many ways and sources that come are not enemies. I'm learning to embrace my cancer and live each day how life is precious. Some lose a limb, some lose a loved one or job, but regardless of what is lost, we must also embrace what is given.

My Soul's Subtle Voice

Well, truth is, something began saving me quite early. A voice deep within my unconscious, or perhaps not even within me but me within this higher love. An intuitive voice that found its way into my heart to begin to change my story, quite the opposite of my mere data mind persona. Whispers came each morning, then the big whisper spoke, impossible for me to ignore.

Whispers in the morning came softly to say *You have the courage, the faith, and trust to know it's time now to end what's not true so to begin—wisdom of truth—from your soul presence in all its felt moments*

37

within a sacred unity. Today, let us all take the unknown path. Many you will meet, and you will recognize each other from each's sacred soul, loving presence, as all will be living within sacred unity too.

A creative fire of light seeks to open all our hearts with our soul's presence of her wisdom to begin spreading this sacred love through each's gifts of artistic innovations. Each artist knows that fire, in its heat, in its beginnings, can shape all possibilities and all potential. This fire is our creative flame to give us our faith because we have within us all the greatest power, which is the energy of sacred love, out of our one sacred unity, which is forever pulsating this sacred love to move the stars, planets, sun, and moon. Would we ever believe that this sacred love, within sacred unity, would not move us too? So we take this unknown path, leaving what is known behind. We have our courage, remember? All endings create new beginnings, and now we have our soul's wisdom on our new path.

My soul voice intuits there is no separation from Divine Love, the Earth, or each other. Our bodies are made of earth elements, mystery of all is Divine Love, and our soul's presence is one with this love. This love is wired into all DNA through our soul's presence, buried deep within our hearts, waiting for the mind persona to become aware and realized enough to hear her whispers. It's time to wake up from these stories of separation.

My path is within me and is to become my own yellow brick road into my soul's presence, wanting to emerge that she is the someone not known, but must now become known. She is me! My courage to come out has not been easy. Yet, it's so clear the mind/data is derailing everyone and leading us into a drop off the cliff, a dark abyss, to our possible death. What is trying to die?

My heart has broken into a million pieces. Sadness is holding me, witnessing fragments of my old resemblance dissolve, and is very challenging. Her whispers guide to trust, as this emptying process will leave me uncertain of life. It's like death has opened its door too; dying but still breathing. Cancer is close, saying listen. Surrender is my true way now onto this unknown path with no clear direction except moment-to-moment unfolding, requiring attentive awareness. Even love asks to have a deeper understanding; it has long been limited how it's experienced. Surface love must dive deep within me into the only true love—Divine Love!

Clarity to follow this path guides to only take my most vulnerable and fragile self, along with my soul presence too. Maybe along the path, our souls will meet up. How will we recognize each other? Perhaps we will just sense a deeper knowing—our sacred souls emerging out of wonder and mystery, guiding us with sacred Divine Love. Sometimes, we tell our story to a friend who only hears a sad life. Then there is that one friend who listens to hear our courage, our sacred love, and we hold each other through heartbreak. It is this friend who will draw a strength from another's pain, then together, both emerge deep compassion to become each's nectar to drink courage to face whatever is challenging both. We hold hands!

We need to all become someone not ever known before. A higher soul species who can shift the mind back into her wisdom of love, inclusive soul partnerships, and where the whole becomes holy in pursuit of unity and harmony upon the Earth. Responsibility, through responsible actions, is the means to put ourselves back on a track of compassion for us all. This will lead us to our higher meaning and purpose of why we are here upon the Earth. We have intuition, our subtle voice, and all guiding us to know we are here to make the Earth a place for all future souls to visit, within forms, so we can experience each other through our higher elevated senses. The presence of god, as sacred Divine Love within us all, will be our creative source, firing our soul's presence of wisdom into the persona, all in sacred partnerships. How beautiful is this?

Earth is the soul of her gifts for us to be here in a form. Our form body is made of its same elements so to give the body the gravity to remain on Earth for a short visit. Yet, it's the lightness of our soul, her wisdom, one with an infinite higher presence of love, that uses the mind/senses to harvest and cultivate the gardens of Earth for all to live, to be creative, and to share in all our unique diversity offered to accomplish this. Then, when it's time to leave, the body becomes Earth again, and us souls, of a subtle light body, move out to return to another cosmic address. Our dense body ends, but not our subtle soul body. Our souls are immortal and have only beginnings. They love adventure.

So it's time for us all to come out of the closet of our mind programs of separation and division, so we all become someone never before known, but ready now to proclaim the big truth to the big lie. No division and separation, only our goodness and our beauty out of our inclusive Divine Love. We have for too long given all our attention to the mind/body that lives only a short time in its illusion of separation while giving very little attention to our higher, subtle soul voice that is immortal. We all long and yearn for this inner intimacy.

Sadly, we were taught to look for it in others and material possessions, and we look for it in a God that is somewhere else in a place called heaven, and we are all born sinners—sorry, just the way it is. So this sets up from our beginnings, upon the Earth, a war-like behavior to get what you can while you can, as it's me against you. Then off we go, ready to fight, hate, and have war against everyone not believing how we believe. These are primitive structures, long needing to be transcended, yet, we always include and embody our higher truth learned to take into our new story.

40

Learning to free myself from this dark separation story back into an inclusive core Divine Love story required me to meet this story and my own shadows through many dark nights of my soul so she could begin to arise and emerge her creative fire of wisdom to burn away these old energies of false beliefs of a false story. Cancer of Love came to be my tipping point. Thank you, although not at all pleasant in many ways. Yet, the final deep dive into surrender and into the power of Divine Love, I'll do over and over to come home. But remember, this is my soul's way, but each soul is unique in how to get each's persona form back into alignment with the true story of Divine Love and each's soul wisdom.

My soul's loving voice of wisdom met up with all these mind distortions to slowly melt them, freeing me to her unconditional Divine Love within me, and also freeing great Beloved Mystery's unconditional love through me. All in direct oneness with Divine Love, the felt direct experience shifting everything. Our one intimacy mutating everything within not congruent with our Divine Love's eternal presence.

All this is challenging to put into human language and why so much came through as transmissions of poetic writing.

My Revelation Continues Today!

In this breath is a fine moment to live and to die. Looking into the mirror for the first time, it was truly me looking back—seeing my beauty, truth, and goodness smiling back at me. The years, like a river stream, have worn away most of my surface lived to reveal my true beauty. Every wrinkle in time a memory of living through it all.

Bearing witness to my vulnerability, cancer revealed truth of death and life living in partnership moment to moment, becoming my transparency to live this now-truth in every action taken—even when so many others see me differently. Looking closer now into my eyes reveals a light that has been with me since my arrival upon the Earth. This light grows brighter to reveal how my soul's presence deeply loves me. Her wisdom speaks into my shadows of a false belief carried most of my life, believing myself unworthy of this love. Abandoned by those loving me falsely taught me love will always abandon me. Yet, truth is, it was me abandoning love, believing this would protect me and make me safe.

My small self believed hiding my vulnerability and transparency from the world and others would keep me from ever being hurt and abused again. Yet, this only added more layers of pain and suffering. My breath rises and falls today in this now-truth. So today, in this moment, and in this breath, is a fine moment to live or die. Love is revealing itself always within me, and my soul's presence of her wisdom and light is always shining our way home. Home is Divine Love! We all are Divine Love!

The many separation stories taught to me from childhood said to only love those like me or who believed like me. Thus, many who were different, a sadness came, because my heart sensed they were fun and kind and we liked each other. Then this teaching extended to only like my country or my color until one day a great insight occurred to me while in nature. Being in nature, my sanctuary, gave to me so much wisdom and understanding. I saw how the trees, animals, and birds all so different. Even the bushes, flowers, and fish in the pond. They all got along great. So why couldn't we humans?

Then, when reading the Bible much later, it also had so much intolerance until reading closely about this man named Jesus. Wow, he taught in nature, he loved everyone, and he taught this inclusive, unconditional love. He was poor of the material but rich of spirit!

He tended the sick, poor of spirit, and poor of means to live. His anger only showed towards those of a hypocrisy—the deemed preachers and politicians who taught to love their wealth, only their kind who obeyed how they believed, and thus they kept war, hate, and an ongoing separation story, thus giving them more power and more control over the mass of people. Jesus fought this autocracy!

He walked with everyone, and he loved everyone. Yet, many years after his death, they turned his teachings into the way they needed, once more, so to control and dominate. Today, the righteous still talk their love of Jesus while also, behind their doors, many hate their neighbors and any and all who do not worship and believe as they do. The politicians will use God to get votes, then use people's money to fill their pockets. The big lie supports separation stories!

We can also look how this man Buddha gave up all his wealth when he discovered behind his safe walls people lived who were starving and being slaughtered, and so he left his wealth to walk among the people to learn and understand their suffering. He vowed to open his heart, thus giving this unconditional Divine Love like Jesus did. History shows how many beautiful souls came through time trying to teach us all. Sadly, we didn't listen or learn.

Today, the Earth is crying, humanity is crying and, perhaps it's time to now open our hearts to bring forth our higher soul self to heal us and our planet. Soon, it may be too late. So very sad. We must understand our humanity and our Earth are today in a state of crises and chaos because we do not follow the depth of our soul's loving divine presence within our heart. Our soul's wisdom is so needed to fill our distorted minds and sick bodies with her unconditional pure Divine Love.

My soul presence reveals we each must become someone unknown to us in our minds, but deeply known in the depth and

43

stillness of our heart. We become our own unique soul self, and this returns our teaching within. We each now live this sacred Divine Love, and we each now take responsibility to help save our humanity and the Earth given to all. Divine Love becomes our way home.

Before beginning my story, this poem transmitted through to share, giving us greater understanding how we all must come back home!

Moments come softly
to give knowing. Words
can't describe this depth
of knowing, only it's felt
grace.

What is grace? For me,
Divine Love enters into
my being unlike any love,
and even calling it love
limits this presence of me.

Yes, it is me. Words again
too limited to name me, but
she is my immortal self who
I call soul me.

She guides and comes in
strange and unusual ways
so this small mind/body is
frozen with her presence.

*I again say she, but there
is no gender, no color, no
age or cancer. She flies me
free of gravity or density as
her lightness takes us into any
universes or galaxies chosen.
This mind/body is mostly now
quiet within our Divine Loving
Presence as she now lives us
more stable within this form to
use the gifts of our form senses
to have earthly experiences.*

*When she travels outside the
Form, all feels lost, and the form
feels lost too. But she isn't away
too long before Divine Love enters,
vibrating us back into our loving
One Presence.*

*She teaches Divine Love is the
higher frequency entering this
planet to shift all from being off
course, living from only a small
will form, believing itself always
separate from its higher divine
loving soul will.*

*Sadly, this small alone mind has
created much destruction versus*

partnership with its soul Divine
Love for ongoing creation where
its soul light travels to be in forms
in many places for having its loving
sensual experiences.

Divine Love on Earth becomes
activated through surrender of
one's small will. Each human
form is already programmed
within for this shift to occur.

Many are aware, and this higher
awareness is the key to opening
the heart for Divine Love to flow
through forms to enter into each's
higher frequency of light flowing
Divine Love through into Earth and
all us awake souls.

My Story's Beginnings! My Intimate Voice Grows Stronger!

My months in the womb were both safe and filled with fear of what's to come; a felt pain of my sweet mama and his angry voice. A father who would abandon me at a young age. For days before my birth, my small will didn't want to live or come into the pain. My soul's higher will pushed me forward. My soul me knew the pain and journey ahead would give to small me the lessons of humanness.

Yet, our intimate bond would be forever through her whispers of intuitive guidance, throughout all the experiences coming forth in my human form. She was always a step ahead with courage for me to follow her guidance. Experiences that would be needed for full freedom, belongingness, and pure realization of final aware awakening and integration into our wholeness. Today, I believe this is for all humanity, certainly not just me. Yet, sharing my experiences, hopefully, will open your soul's awareness too.

I was born in New Orleans, Louisiana. My mother rushed to Charity Hospital because I lay half in her womb and half outside. The facility at Charity Hospital had doctors and the means to assist my mother as we both lay in critical condition. This condition—half in and half out—has been, metaphorically, how much of my life has been lived. Finally, the doctors agreed to take me by force; time was of the essence. The day after my birth, weighing in at less than six pounds and bruised all over with a cone head, my father and uncle declared me the ugliest baby in the ward—maybe even the ugliest baby ever to be born. But being ugly was not to become my conditional teaching. Quite the opposite.

My childhood was spent mostly in nature, where it became a haven for me to escape pain and abuse from my grandparents and uncles. Paradoxically, grace in the woods became a place of magic and imagination, while within my home, lessons of how to live came from a church that preached hell and brimstone. The old story of separation was preached from the pulpit, and my home taught a story of how me, a small child, was born a sinner, and only through Jesus was my salvation to go far away to a place called heaven, where a God-like man sat in judgment of me. Now, this is also paradoxical as the beautiful man named Jesus would eventually show me my soul's way of sacred Divine Love through intimate moments of experiencing his grace through a more loving story of inclusion of nature and humanity. But I'm jumping ahead here.

47

Spending time in nature taught me a more subtle teaching of love and forgiveness and that within me was the power to do anything if my faith was strong enough. This is what came through to me and not the preachings on Sunday morning of a literal, fundamentalist teaching. After much pleading with my mother—who I loved and adored, as she did me—she finally allowed me to stop going to the fundamentalist church.

My father had started drinking and gambling. He would become abusive to my mother when he came home drunk. She asked my grandparents if we could live with them until she found a means to support us. My father burst in one day to announce he was leaving for Alaska. He wanted a divorce. Back in the 1950s, this was frowned upon. My grandmother refused her request, saying she had raised eight children, three still at home, and my mother needed to figure it out.

Mother went to speak with the minister at the Methodist church I began attending. The minister suggested she put me and my brother in the Methodist children's home until she found a means to support us. It would be in the Methodist children's home, where a powerful intimate moment would begin to change me. The voice came sweetly. A sensual sweetness, a loving presence entered into my soul essence an inner direct Divine Love that would be within me for the rest of my life. Many learned conditions would test me whether to follow my inner inspiring, guiding voice, always coming through this bigger presence, or follow the external conditional words so programmed into my unconscious, or even my peers, where being accepted and fitting in felt so important.

Interestingly, my mom transitioned on Friday, May 13, 2016. Some may say this not a great day to transition. For me, it was perfect. My unconventional and, what many may deem heretic inner knowings, proved a beautiful time for her last breath. Even more special, several days before her passing, my heart took me on a walk only to find myself standing in front of the Methodist church, the only church where, as a child, connections with beloved felt more aligned.

Upon opening the door, the minister came to greet me, taking my hand and sharing how he knew my mom and stepdad. We talked briefly about my mom's imminent transition. When entering the chapel, almost immediately, this loving presence filled me with blissful love and light. Sitting in one of the pews, tears flowed in a steady stream down my face. The intimacy of the moment gave to me, again, that same intimacy when feeling so alone in the Methodist children's orphanage. Always within me, my soul presence, and in all the intimate walks in nature with Beloved, these intimacies became my greatest companion.

My partnership with my sensual soul, loving presence and Beloved, even in the womb and prior, was awakening me to realize that my greater meaning and purpose was to live these partnerships, in every moment, before my own death. Cancer being so close today, I'm living my inner divine loving partnerships more important than ever. Deep within me, a world exists very different from the world outside of me, but it's taken a journey of many years, where my choices and conditioning have kept me locked in a self-contained prison of fear. Now, surrender of all these beliefs is my only choice to release myself from this caged bondage. It has been said that which keeps you in bondage will also set you free. It was my yearning to go home, this grace so powerful, and when a fourth marriage failed, my soul presence whispered *it's time*.

It's time to wake up living in separation from everything and everyone, then grow up my small will self by cleaning up all my ghosts and shadows long living me. Only then will it be possible to enter back into the womb of my core Divine Love to live my remaining moments in sacred partnerships within and without. The time was now to meet and embrace all my buried-away shadows, so long hidden, just beneath the surface of my life lived. My work of surrender lovingly opened the back of my heart, where it became a gateway for my subtle soul, in her transparency, to move into the infinite dimension, one with our Mystery Source. This gateway was also open in the front of my heart into the finite physical world.

My heart-opening became the means for my soul to move in and out to help my small persona ego begin dissolving and clearing old wounds to integrate with her and Beloved. This mutation began transfiguring my body form, allowing my transformation to slowly occur. Then cancer came as final surrender. This will also be how, when final death comes, she will depart the body.

Our old narrative, so long the conditioning of collective minds, has been passed down from generation to generation. Much of our individual and collected human trauma can be witnessed today in our political polarization and wars being fought. Racial and gender divides so painful. Our greatest hope will be the process of entering into a greater unity awareness, helping us to see into how all the horrific wars fought, disparity, and how our one-sided beliefs always competing for power have kept us tightly bound in these separate belief systems, creating hate and fear that was, and is, our small separate ego's fuel for destruction and individual power and greed.

Integrating my internal relationship of ego, sensual soul, and divine presence began dissolving this separation. It is this belief of separation that is the most destructive and causing the most suffering. It is this separation that has broken our inner moral compass, thus stagnating our moral character. We will go deeper into this in later writings and chapters.

Living on my grandparents' farm taught me the beauty of nature. I felt alive and intimate with the trees, plants, animals, and the small pond where the insects, frogs, and turtles became my friends. Maybe it was the quiet stillness when only the wind was felt ushering in its sounds of the small creatures hiding away. Nature's intimacy also opened me to my outer aloneness and the need for a greater inner intimacy.

Moments of Direct Intimacy

Not enough of them for me…how about you? Why is real intimacy so hard? Yes, we can have sex, but how often after sex do you feel so empty…something is missing?

Perhaps intimacy first begins within each of us! Are we able to be intimate with our own thoughts? Our own shadows? Where is our own soul?

Is she our missing self who brings us inner intimacy to meet our own unconscious needs, becoming witness to our small mind kept living out of its separation story!

When our soul wisdom and mind/ body can meet to have intimacy within us, then when meeting up in the external world with you, our intimacy becomes my first response to you: whether friend, lover, spouse, or family. Direct intimacy becomes the way of inclusiveness in our relationships.

There was no intimacy, only the loud voices inside my grandparents' house screaming, accusing, and frightening me. Learning to read their energy languages of everything and everyone kept me safe. Trust wasn't easy, yet, a tiny drop of rain on a small leaf could give me comfort and closeness. A rainbow would appear, calling me to leave my own body and join in its beauty with the higher horizon. Where did it come from and where could it take me? Anywhere would be more peaceful than the meanness so felt within my own family.

The Dark Backdrop to My Soul!

My mother was my only means of safety, but often, she too, so sick and betrayed, found distraction in her mind escapes. The conditional behaviors and beliefs surrounding me were primitive and foreign to everything intimate going on within me. Yet, to share my inner world would have punished me more, so learning to keep my inner world private kept me living two worlds. Again, there was the metaphor half in and half out, two worlds always edging up against the other, one my haven and the other a hell. One my beauty and the other my beast.

Around ten years of age, sickness, out-of-body experiences, and waking unable to breathe sent me to the hospital many times.

Once, sitting in the back of my mom's car, thunder and lightning struck an electrical pole, and bolts of lightning ran through me. My remembrance is faint, but many thought me dead. This resulted in the start of many powerful energetic movements that would course through my body most of my life. The creative fire of my soul, love presence was beginning.

Always accompanying these electrical-like movements through my body was an even more powerful energy—my subtle light soul.

My soul became so close and intimate that death felt like the only means to being in these intimate embraces. I wanted more. Death was touched many times; thus, fear of dying no longer held me captive. Even today, having cancer, death doesn't frighten me, only gives to me the precious realization to live authentically where both inner and outer realties enjoin together, guiding me to give as much Divine Love to others and into the world in every moment, whatever time remains.

Death taught me there are only beginnings. The presence of sacred Divine Love accompanied each beginning where my heart slowly opened to trusting the inner movement, out of one reality no longer serving meaning and purpose, into a higher reality where divine intimacy resided.

A lucid dream came one night where stairs ascended into the sky.

At the top was a doorway, but a large beastly animal blocked its entrance. These dreams frightened me as my small mind didn't understand at the time. After many years of these dark night passages, a revelation came to enter through the doorway to confront this beast; this beast—my unconscious hidden shadows.

My dying to one reality would then open me to enter into a higher, greater awareness, and became a way of living life differently. I became a pilgrim walking out of one developmental process into higher developments as my consciousness, soul, love presence continued to expand and grow. This process also grew me into greater and greater unity awareness.

Because no one could find a physical cause to my unusual illness, my mom decided to take me to a large children's hospital in Houston, Texas, where an uncle was a pediatrician. Every test imaginable was run, but nothing ever found. After much debate, it was decided my illness was a result of mental issues. The next process was to bring a team of psychologists and specialists to begin tests.

The night before these tests were to begin, one of my most powerful experiences of intimate messaging occurred. Feeling so alone in the dark, a strange blinking of an outside light put me into a trance-like state. These states happened quite frequently and gave me the feeling of traveling out of my body. The light began traveling inside my room, beaming bright illumination and then blinking on a Bible lying next to the bed. Words began floating through my mind, another beautiful experience that now happens moment to moment within my loving intimate partnership with beloved presence and soul me. These messages always soft and childlike, much like me, only ten years old.

The message was filled with so much love, very similar when in the children's orphanage. "I am here. You're not alone. Go to sleep and all will be okay." These messages still come having cancer. The next morning, when the nurses came into my room, they gasped as all over me were, what they described, the worst case of red measles ever seen. A diagnosis was quickly made to send me home. Case dismissed. Our medical institutions are taught to diagnose through objective evidence, and they now had their evidence.

The fact is that since much of my unusual behavior could not be found in textbooks, they were simply dismissed. It was the measles causing all this unusual behavior. This taught me to hide my powerful mystical experiences from most of the world and also set up most of my dark shadows living in my unconscious and subconscious. The beast, in my lucid dream, always guarding the door. My unusual experiences, however, have continued right up to the present time today.

Having cancer in my body, not my soul essence, is now being surrendered to trust with faith more than ever these powerful transmissions coming through. My small self has become vulnerable to live in pure authentic Divine Love, whatever is to happen. We are all in peaceful joy to just experience Divine Love in every precious breath. It's also changing many around me: family, friends, even the science/medical doctors. My many out-of-body travels, electrical-like charges running through my being, lucid-like dreams, and near-death experiences all resulting in the most beautiful intimate moments with Beloved, soul me, and sweet MaryLinda prepared cancer to come with my ultimate surrender. Today, we are a sacred unified partnership always and forever.

The ugly duckling born that day in Charity Hospital turned into a beautiful young girl and woman. In high school, the physics scholarship earned was not awarded; instead, the principal said the scholarship would be given to a boy who needed it. "After all," the principal said, "you are so beautiful. You will go and find a husband to take care of you." Hmm...and that I did. I married four times trying to live out of the conditions imposed upon me.

Each man saw me as an object to behold and fed me material goods as their way to control and have ownership while they, three of them, had many other women they consorted with on the side. Trying to hide my pain to become what others wanted me to be led to much sickness and despair, and eventually forced me to always leave. It took four marriages for me to finally understand a relationship lived through a different lens of reality, where one seeks to control the other, can never work. Small ego love wasn't fulfilling as my deeper soul presence, so buried, kept me longing for her release, so to experience real core sacred love with Beloved.

All these relationships lived out of the separation story, thus, no one saw each other in our inner soul essence. How could we? All my marriages were grounded in the old narrative of separation and that men were superior and women and children inferior. An insidious, subtle undercurrent flowing through from the thousands of years of collective consciousness, much like racism and power to control the lands and the institutions, still today. These four men became my greatest teachers. In many ways, we deceived and betrayed each other. So there is no blame, only pain and suffering for us all.

Growing up in the '60s, '70s, and '80s, intimacy, through transparency and mutual support within relationships, was rare. Being true to each other's higher selves while simultaneously both being committed to help bring greater awareness and consciousness to the planet were only just emerging. Today, in 2022, more of these relationships are showing up as their souls are emerging.

Yet, we are also witness to this old story fighting to hold its control. Our Supreme Court, mostly men, have overturned Roe v. Wade, once again taking away the rights of women to their own bodies. It's as though our world, like me, has a disease of cancer. It's living big lies that now are meeting up with big truths. We all must seek our courage to take off our shadow masks and live in our authentic truth. This requires us all to become vulnerable to take responsibility for being Divine Love in our actions so to be free.

Beloved and my sensual soul, one with eternal love essence, was hidden for a while. Yet, those four men played their beautiful part in the world of conditional love, showing me in many ways the opposite of what my inner inspired, intimate world was trying to teach me. My inner teacher, Beloved Spirit, one with my soul's presence, continued to show this real love within me. My only search today is to mirror my Beloved/soul, loving presence, which is always already within me, so to find this same love within another.

The challenge then, and still is today, is that most love is conditional love based on the old separation story. Our souls are still buried, and few have made their inner journey into the territory of the beloved and sacred soul. A great gift with these four men is we've remained friends. My experiences with each of them helped me gain clarity and trust and slowly brought me out of hiding, knowing what my soul presence wanted was sensual soul loving partnerships.

Beautiful writings came through one morning after being in three Sundays of conversation with others and David Whyte, poet and author. Tears flowed as he spoke and read poems that touched my own souls' intimacy. One poem he shared, along with his story, was one on his self-portrait. The story was taking off his false self to reveal his true authentic self. I share with you now my self-portrait taken from within by my soul. Perhaps you may want to take some quiet time to listen to your soul reveal you...

My True Portrait...

My soul holds the camera now to snap my true portrait. I'm frightened of what she may reveal. All my fragments lived; each one believed true me. Yet, they're only my scars of a life half lived in its dark shadows, too afraid for you to see me. I don't believe in your proclaimed God...one so cruel and judging me all the time. I don't believe in your laws and principles that were written for only those of white color. I am white too, but always seeing my shades of mixed color from the sun shining in diversity. Always trying to enhance my true beauty buried just beneath. What is it about the color of skin that creates so much pain—even war?

I don't believe money and material possessions will make me happy—I tried so hard but they didn't. I don't believe anyone loved me. How could they when they didn't know or see me except in only a few fragments of myself? My pretty face, my nice lean body, my fake happiness for you while pain within myself was in great despair trying to be all you wanted me to be. Always trying to fit into a belief system and conditions imposed upon me. Believing it was the only way to be loved. Becoming a people pleaser—bypassing my pain to portray a false self externally. Yet, the truth is, this bypassing only set up more shadows as internally my authenticity, as an emerging soul presence, was wanting to emerge in her true realization. Please, it's not your fault. It's no one's fault because none of us feel, or perhaps have ever felt, the courage to have the camera take our true portrait from within.

Fatigue has settled into my body. Surrender knocks on my heart that it's time to open into the gateway of my soul, forever patient, waiting for me to allow my real light to illuminate my true self. So, here, sitting with you dear soul, please take the inner camera and now take my picture, so real soul me can finally be seen...as you see me. I also feel this picture now being revealed to me will also now be revealed to others, but only a few may recognize me or be willing to accept me. I will take some time now to die to everything known so what time remains will be true to my service of sacred love. Love always my core, deepest need to be seen and loved for this truth and depth as a non-believer in the story that was taught so long ago of division and separation. My truth, perhaps, is part of a greater truth that is also being revealed today through many souls here, like me, telling our true story, still needing to be heard and understood as our own great mystics and heretics taught through the thousands of years.

A story always seeking to be revealed from the soul of the world and our higher sensual soul love presence, so long denied for an outer power and dominion of all. Jesus and the Mary's, the inner healers called heretics, spoke so long ago into my heart as a child. Yet, my fear to listen drove me to live two worlds. One that would often punish me for my revolutionary ways, and the other always keeping me safe in my inner sanctuary, within myself, waiting for me to be ready. Today, I sit for my portrait...I am ready to come out to be free to be true me...a beautiful, sensual, sacred, soul, loving presence... One with my beloved sacred presence always forever within me. I am safe within here...as I am safe within Mother Nature. My true portrait finally is being revealed.

If you are thirsty
sip water from the tree of life
that resides within you.

If you are hungry
eat the the ripen fruit from your
heart that never spoils.

If you feel lonely
go sit in the window between your
soul and divine love.

If you are tired
rest upon the pillow of grass atop
the mountain listening to
the nightingale's song.

If you feel radiant joy
go share it with all beings.

If you feel Divine Love
be grateful; you are home!

Chapter 3

My Intimate Personal Story Continues to Evolve!

After my last relationship ended, despair took me into isolation. I picked up Ken Wilbur's book *Grace and Grit* and reread it for a second time. My pain began to ease while reading of the deep personal loss of his soul partner, his beloved. My grief was over never having experienced this beloved soul love, and his grief was the loss of his beloved soul love. But he knew each's soul in partnership with deeper beloved, each had shared, never would be lost. My tears shifted from me to them, finally realizing this was my pain. I wanted to know and experience the love between beloveds, just like Jesus and Mary Magdalene. Yes, my heart believes the relationship between them was possible.

Today in this year, 2022, this intimacy is found directly within me.

When enough of us find this love and intimacy within in divine partnership with our soul, ego-mind, and body in oneness with greater Beloved Mystery, then we will mirror this into the external world to find these partnerships with each other. This is our higher new story we must now create together. Our soul's presence story: her love's creative wisdom unifies our human separation.

This powerful writing emerged, coming to a greater understanding around my true beauty...

Being good-looking
with a hot body gets us attention. Our soul
goes into hiding...what is she/he doing?

Yet, that
pretty face and sizzling body
rarely gets us love. Just a lot of never-ending work.
Right?

Today, my
body and my mind are enjoined with my soul.
Yea...she's returned.
Her wisdom teaches my body about good health
and my mind about good healthy beliefs.

My body
likes walking in the woods, exercise, and eats light
healthy food...lots of water too.
My mind suffers the most...it has had to
surrender everything it once believed as truth.

Stripping away
old held truths now turns on my inner soul wisdom.
This is a higher, loving truth
that my love is within and doesn't look at my body
or my mind. It simply emerges forth
One truth...that truth is I Am Love. We are Love!

Today, a powerful
presence of love sustains me and is always there
if my mind or body gets off course
or confused...they often can.

But I

always drop deeper...right into my heart,
then soul me smiles and my
beloved presence fills my entire being with a
most beautiful energy of Divine Love. Ahh...

Every night when going to sleep, joy is on my left and sorrow on my right. When waking, it's unknown which one will be with me through the day. Yet, over the years, my respect has grown for them both. They've taught me much about my life and the lives of others. Neither will stay too long before one peeks through my being and the other fades away for a while. One is never favored over the other as sleeping and spending time with each gives me great teaching, and without each one, something would feel lost. Joy, you have made me laugh, appreciate, and feel so much love. Sorrow, you have made me understand compassion, empathy, and the sheer pain of loss. Each says to live my life fully. So my heart holds deep gratitude, knowing my life would be incomplete without you both. This is my unity awareness.

Another Intimate Moment with Beloved Says to Me,

"I travel the road of your heart to infinity. We ride together to the beat and rhythm of your pulsating love. We stop along the way to pick flowers and swim in the creeks and ponds. We feed the birds and ducks. We pick up lonely people along the infinity road of your loving and compassionate heart and give them a ride to the city of joy and laughter. We share our love with children and they share their open wonder and curiosity. We become their co-creative partners in their playful dance of life with us on our forever soul journey together. We never leave the open road of your heart as we travel up the mountains

and through valleys, stopping to gaze at sunrises and sunsets. We never stop gazing into each other's soulful eyes where we drink in each's kindness and innate knowing that we will never be alone for dinner. I love riding with you along the open road of your infinite heart, dear Soul. I love you."

This is how sensual soul friends and sensual soul partnerships with beloved grace live in a reality created from bonds of intimacy with each other. This is a story of inclusion, where everyone and everything is enjoined in soul loving intimacy. Does this speak to your soul? Does your heart melt within knowing this is how we are all meant to live on this planet together? I cry writing this now.

Soul Relationships Showing Up!

Eight years ago, I met a man at the Integral Living Room in Boulder, Colorado. It is a beautiful gathering of like-minded souls, beating to unconventional rhythms, wanting to create, innovate, and bring forth higher consciousness through our souls from Beloved.

He walked up to me and looked deep into my eyes and said, "I see you." My sensual soul recognized his sensual soul at once. At first, my small personality began bringing forth old patterns, which he witnessed and brought to my attention. It was clear to him our relationship with each other was to be soul friend to soul friend. Yet, our sensual intimacy as friends gave authentic relating to open our hearts to each other.

We were to be part of the emerging new love story wanting to birth a different way of relating to each other as part of a new reality in a new paradigm. We both spent hours gazing into our souls and surrendering and releasing anything and everything that did not serve our soul's mission and purpose. We both held each other when one needed support and unconditional love, knowing our love traveled the world of infinity and forever we would be there for each other. We shared our deepest, darkest secrets, knowing forgiveness and compassion would help each of us to let those karmic patterns and energies go. It has been the most beautiful and sometimes challenging relationship. It is a relationship that is possible between two awakened souls in beloved partnership and relationship with the divine and greater God intelligence. It is the relationship my whole life has waited patiently for, knowing in my heart that these sensual soul loving relationships can exist. Our level of trust, patience, kindness, and compassion was nothing short of extraordinary and miraculous. But it is also the way all relationships and partnerships should be. We are a very new species of emerging souls slowly awakening and being birthed through our heart womb. Today, my friend Jochen and I live in different countries, but we remain still best soul friends. We talk regularly, but our inclusive friendship is felt daily for us both.

Another sensual soul friend gave me a very powerful experience of both light and dark in our growing and experiencing together. We met through powerful synchronized events. I was ending my last marriage, having finished my holistic master's degree, and taking a break from my career as a realtor into becoming a counselor/coach. He was doing a workshop at a wellness conference where a work scholarship was given for me to attend. His teaching was an all-day event and would cost extra money, but when standing outside the large conference room, reading the large sign about him and his work, my soul whispered *We must attend*. The actress and country star Naomi Judd was also there and had become friends with him. She had been diagnosed with Hepatitis and was eager to attend his day-long presentation on how stress often is a disconnect from our Soul/Spirit. He had done his doctorate on stress management, writing a book still used today in its tenth revision in colleges and nurses training all over the globe. His book is called *Managing Stress: A Creative Journal*, and his name is Brian Luke Seaward, Ph.D. To me, he is my soul-friend Luke.

Being graced to attend at the end of the conference and standing in line with the more than two hundred, my heart pulsated. A deep-felt sense of knowing this man's very loving, deep wisdom vibrated my being. When facing him, he too felt our souls. He gave me his phone number and suggested calling in about six months, as he was traveling and finishing up a book to be released later in the year. That friendship has taken us both on a journey spanning today over twenty-five years. We grew together in our friendship through both light and dark experiences. We parted for about six years, giving us both a means to deeply understand our soul friendship, especially me. Yet, we found our way back as souls of the heart always do.

Today, our soul friendship flourishes in presence of beloved love, knowing the time of the Earth turning on its axis is about our new story of sacred love within sacred unity. The healing of old wounds to be dissolved of mere egos, so our soul species may arise from the ashes of the surrendered ego attachment to all its learned, separate self conditions. Today, our soul friendship continues to hold sacred space for each to do this great work. Today, he has found his sensual soul partner, his wife, a most soul loving partnership.

But it was the discovery of an author, Ken Wilber, and his books and teachings of an Integral perspective that finally lead me on the path to home. Everything began to fall into place. His Integral map of both an inner and outer reality had me in joy. Attending most of his Integral seminars, when he spoke, the joy of his inspired words coming through him had so long been intimately arising within me.

Beloved grace was showing up in so many people through the Integral community, and we all shared our gratitude. Coming together was likened to experiencing a frequency of light and love that mirrored the teachings of so many great earlier revolutionaries who had pioneered the way for Integral to finally emerge. Meeting Ken was through a grace encounter. My dear friend Luke, mentioned above, was having a seminar in Estes Park, where I flew into Colorado to attend. The strangest moment happened when we were driving from the airport and words came asking him, "How do I meet Ken Wilber?" He laughed and said, "Well he is a recluse in the mountains so the odds of this happening very slim."

At his workshop in Estes Park, we worked on a reflection of our lives. The work was to write down five things we wanted to manifest, kind of like our bucket list. I had been working on a manuscript at the time, so one of my five was to have my book published. The next was to meet and talk with Ken Wilber.

That evening after the workshop, my friend asked me to share my five things. He smiled, knowing my list was a tall order.

The next day, upon waking and with great urgency, I told him we must go to the Boulder book store. He laughed and suggested we eat first. All through our brunch, a restlessness moved through me, so finally he agreed to go. We were within walking distance, with my friend walking a bit ahead, when he looked into the window of the bookstore, then stopped dead in his tracks, turning to say, "Oh my!"

Looking in the window, a large sign read, "Come and meet Ken Wilber."

This was to be the launching of Integral and the first time Ken would address an audience. It was to take place in the Methodist Church—again, how symbolic is this?—and it was taking place in three weeks. My friend looked at me, and it was clear to both of us finding the means to return and attend important. Arriving back to Colorado to be in the presence of the man who helped me begin my journey home and begin bridging both my worlds of inner soul presence and outer conditions had me hyperventilating.

We arrived several hours early and stood in line so we could sit in the front pew. After standing in line for a while, my inner voice inspired me to go next door to the Buddhist temple to meditate. The Buddhist temple was across the street from the large Methodist church, which was chosen for Ken due to its ability to hold over a thousand people, which they expected. Hmm...East meets West and inner meets outer. My soul guides!

Returning, my friend was a bit frustrated, having taken so long because Ken had just arrived and my hand could have literally reached out and touched him. Yet, a somewhat altered state was clearly vibrating my soul and beloved presence powerfully through me with so much Divine Love. Here was the most amazing opportunity to be up close to Ken and directly feel his own loving, graceful light.

We were able to be seated in the first pew, steps away from the podium where a chair sat waiting for Ken. My friend whispered he was going to the bathroom, having waited in line for so long. This next part is still unclear for me. Ken came out and sat down, then all of a sudden, this powerful vibrating energy within, greater than anything directly experienced before and more powerful than many altered like experiences most of my life, moved and guided me up on the stage where, bending down next to Ken, we talked. I don't know what was said, nor do I remember walking up or back to my seat.

My friend was an ashen color. He just looked at me and said, "What happened?" My voice simply said, "I don't know." Several weeks later, Integral Institute was launched, and the first was to be an Integral Leadership Seminar. To attend, one had to fill out a long resume, along with a picture. Only forty people would be chosen to attend, and I was able to attend the second one. Ken is known to have a photogenic memory. I believe on that stage weeks earlier, whatever was said, he remembered and he remembered my face.

Elation and joy to be chosen to be part of the second leadership seminar kept me altered for weeks leading up to the conference. Meeting Ken along with Tami Simon of Sounds True, Terry Patten, Jeff Salzman and so many, some still today, my life-loving soul friends. It was a life-changing experience. This was the beginning of my entering into the Integral Community, where so many friends remain today. I found my soul community. It also took me deeper into my transformation from a world of conditioned personality to my true home of beloved, as an awakened, sensual soul presence and where gratitude would become my mantra and my soul's way of Divine Love my teaching. My book was also finished, *When Water Runs Uphill*, self-published in 2007. It was written as a fictional story of one woman's transformation—that woman is me.

Writing it in novel form gave me liberties to take the story deeper with more understanding of the powerful means of surrender to my divine essence and my soul presence. The publishing also came about through another synchronized meeting. Several years after meeting Ken, Deepak Chopra was hosting a retreat in Sedona. Feeling much sadness at having learned that Ken was very ill, my soul guided for us to attend. On a group hike in the mountains, in a brief talk with Deepak about Ken, he shared how Ken was a great influence in his life, and he had tried to call Ken but was unable to reach him. Deepak too was concerned.

The next day, Deepak told a story of a man traveling with him who did Vedic Astrology. Deepak shared that many years ago, someone had done a Vedic chart for him, giving information about his mother—impossible for the man to know. It gave validation to Deepak that we are much more connected to our cosmic world through our inner self and how it all has great significance on our birthday, year, and time. This fascinated me, but also brought some skepticism. After our afternoon session, my curiosity took me to meet with Brent, the man traveling with Deepak and who created Vedic Astrology charts, to talk about having my chart done. He was booked for the next six months but took all my information and said he would be in touch.

Three weeks after arriving home from Sedona, Brent called to say he took a peek at my chart and discovered some powerful energies working through me, which caused him to drop everything and focus on finishing my chart. Brent knew nothing about me or my life. But right there in the planets, on my birth and charted through my life, was everything aligned for my inner realization of my soul, higher self emerging. Everything Brent stated has been my life experience. He then asked if my writing had been published. What? How did he know a manuscript lay in a box under my bed? I trembled in my answer. He suggested taking the manuscript out and getting it published. He also said my writing would continue for years to come. Wow!!

I wrote *When Water Runs Uphill* as a fictional story because, at that time, fear still clutched my heart. Coming out in the open to stand in my truth—so long denied and buried—was scary. My long-lived fear of being abandoned and unworthy plagued me. I'm a revolutionary and my family follows a more traditional, almost fundamentalist, approach to religion. I wasn't going to be burned at the stake, but what if the people I love the most rejected me? What if, like that little girl growing up in the deep South, who was rejected by her father and many relatives, experienced again this fear of not being loved by the conditions in the external world? Writing that book gave to me a deeper understanding of my journey and also helped me release more of my long-held shadows.

Here is a passage from that book to share:

"As I look across at the mountains, a quiet, subtle voice whispers to me: surrender to your faith, trust in your destiny by paying close attention to life's signals; remain present to how the energy inside your body elevates to become a messenger of truth. My inner voice whispers, "thank you" and I close my eyes. When I am fully aware and present, my soul voice continues to teach me gratitude."

Sometimes, it feels my life is coming to an end, and other times, it feels it's just beginning! A small child so traumatized becoming an adult feeling so unworthy. Making so many errors while also being opened into greater realized awareness how to make higher, more loving choices. Now all of us are traveling lighter; only Divine Love, peace, kindness, and gratitude are accompanying us within this inner, more subtle energy to make our journey home together. Our destiny is still unknown, but we aren't alone anymore. We have each other, and we have our Beloved Mystery of sacred Divine Love shining light for us into this unknown. We move into our home of sacred unity.

Our field of consciousness holds all life, visible and invisible. The greater our awareness and attention within this field, the greater becomes our realization we dance within our fire of creativity, within this field, to emerge forth, with each other, innovation, higher ideas, and a more effective means to care for the Earth herself. My direct experience of Spirit opened me to directly intuit my soul's presence taking me deeper, and the depth began revealing everything is this direct movement of Spirit. Spirit is everywhere and in everything. From the highest mountain to the deepest forest to the smallest creature within the soils. My soul wisdom says we can read the words becoming an experience, but our spirit is not the book. We can experience the energy within the structure, but it's not the building.

71

This is why mystics often are called hieratic's, because they don't follow the traditional path. They follow a direct path within themselves leading to direct intimate knowing. They can no longer give themselves over to a church authority or spiritual movement because their authority and movement are within them. The mystic also becomes very vulnerable, as outsiders, especially their loved ones, often reject them because they walk this mystical path.

I've had many dark nights of my soul trying to fit in, to please others, and then finally surrendering to my soul courage as my inner angsts became too much to bear. One day, we all shall walk the mystical path...our true realization we all are mystics.

Two Mystical Writings Through My Soul's Divine Loving Presence!

In the stillness, my heart opens to vast oceans of travels where it's destination unknown. Can I do this? My life jacket sits beside me, yet, it's feels unnecessary now that this boat of myself knows drowning into my depths must happen.

There is a Presence here within me. Oh, how my eyes want to see you, my hands want to touch you, my ears want to hear your sweet voice assuring me all will be okay. Our sensual love. My emotions, like ocean waves, begin to swell where my sadness flows into my unstable boat. But you are here, Beloved...soul me too. We are all here!

Trust and faith now my oars, like wings, to just surrender to this awaiting shore somewhere in time. The dark depths lure me to jump overboard into an unknown territory. Promise you will jump with me...somehow your hand will appear guiding us back into the light of your Presence of Love.

My mind is the shadow, my Soul it's eternal light. Working to release my shadows turns on my light. My Soul Love Presence finally to awaken. My mind now integrates to become an embodiment of true partnerships. Soul wisdom, in unity awareness with mind intellect, body feelings, and all serving our greatest partnership; to be Love in the world in oneness with our Divine Spirit in action through us all.

There are two channels of power. One seeks power over the Earth and people, and the other power is our inner power seeking to unite with our Earth and all humanity. One creates fear and separation, and the other creates sacred Divine Love from our soul's presence and beloved. When our sacred Divine Love is released, it seeks to manifest itself through acts of beauty, truth, and goodness. It seeks our sacred unity.

Have We Been Looking for and Living Love in All the Wrong Places?

How long have we been living in our old stories, shadow energies of shame, blame or guilt? I ask, why? Why relive over and over what keeps us caged like a bird of prey? These toxic energies create our toxic pain!

Let us together strap on wings, then hold hands to jump out of this toxic cage, letting the wind take us, like our breath, to a new story of adventure!

The shadow of us can now become the power of us, where beneath these old stories, wrongly taught and lived, our pain lights up our soul, long awaiting to teach us our new story!

What is this new story, you ask? Well, let's fly deep enough, wide enough, and be open enough to find out…let's not fear us anymore or fear our deeper calling! Let's taste a new flavor of love…one that is the true flavor of us all!

Are we really alone? One small earth planet in the cosmic cluster of universes and galaxies? And, we must ask…Who or what is driving this cosmic orbit?

Let's call it Divine Love, and let's let it take us all to a place where we've never been before and to each meet someone we've never before known! Don't you want to meet yourself…you, as a beautiful aware soul? What an adventure!

And Divine Love whispers, *once my love is tasted no other love will be satisfying.* So come, dear ones, let us surrender to this Divine taste of Love to take us all beneath these old pains of blame and shame, causing so much of our disturbance and toxic weather within our mind and body. Our inner toxic weather we've projected, sadly, for eons of time upon this beautiful earth planet, also needing to come home to Divine Love too!

Our Divine Love will free each of us to live each moment alive within our soul awareness with a now greater realization. We all must take responsibility to clean up our internal and external falsely taught messy stories! It's impossible to begin living a new story as long as we keep living an old story!

We will finally come to know we are home in the only Love that can set us all free. A Divine Love we all came into the Earth to live and the only Love we take with us when we each depart Earth. Why not live it for our short stay upon the Earth?

We were taught a wrong story of separation from each other, our Divine Love and our Earth to live our Divine Love. For eons of time, we've lived these small surface loves of trying to find love in external and material ways, only to be denied over and over. A surface small love keeps us caged, trying to be and become what we've been taught, in all the ideologies and by these controlling small ego personas needing to keep the masses separated by living in fear and pain their toxic stories and lives over and over.

We, each of us, can change this story! Come, let us, dear ones, enjoin together to now fly free within our Divine Love given to all. Divine Love within us all, now realized, will transform planet Earth back into its true and its right orbit, always originally intended!

Having cancer has opened my heart, flooding me with so much Divine Love from so many people—family, friends, and even strangers reflecting Divine Love. I feel it vibrating my entire being and what is being reflected is the entire cosmic Divine Love within us all.

We become the cosmic Divine Love—we become the butterfly effect—how extraordinary!

"Too often we underestimate the power of a touch, a smile, a kind word, a listening ear, an honest compliment, or the smallest act of caring, all of which have the potential to turn a life around."
~Leo Buscaglia

Chapter 4

The Tragedy of Soulless Love

*"Only those who will risk going too far can possibly
find out how far one can go."*
~T.S. Elliot

Let us begin with a poetic Love Story…

Patty met up with Peter, then both jumped down the hole. Their eyes met, then each remembered they couldn't make it alone. Not just for having babies, not just for their wild, passionate sex, although both did happen.

They met up because neither could find their way in this 'hole of a world' without the other. Sadly, each had been taught a story of being separate in this world. I'm here…you are over there…I'm here…God is over there. I'm here…the Earth is over there. I'm here…the universe is out there. On and on this story of separation with me here and you and everyone and everything, as other, over there.

Peter had a great mind, and Patty had a wise, sensual soul heart. Together, perhaps, they could weave the hole back into holy, but even better, back to whole. Patty believed she was a part separate, and Peter believed he a part separate, yet, if each could remember their sacred unity—each's sensual heart/soul partnered with each's mind/body and within them both—maybe, just maybe, their parts could be become whole again. Truth is, Peter is inside of Patty and Patty is inside of

Peter. Their sensual soul and sacred unity within them both. They, and everyone and everything, are in truth, inclusive…not separate. At first, it may feel a little like madness to all of us Peters and Pattys, until we realize it's the separation that's madness. We may all become a bit strange to many in our awakening process, and this can bring a certain felt isolation.

Richard Rohr says, "When we've gotten too comfortable with our separate self and we call it Life, we will get trapped at that level and we will hold onto it for dear life—because that's the only dear life we think we have. Unless someone tells us about the Bigger Life or we've had a conscious connection with the deepest ground of our being, we will continue to live as though we are separate from God. Your True Self is Life and Being and Love. Love is what you were made for and love is who you are. When you live outside of Love, you are not living from your true Being or with full consciousness. The Song of Songs says that "Love is stronger than death. . . . The flash of love is a flash of fire, a flame of YHWH" (Song of Songs 8:6, Jerusalem Bible). Your True Self is a tiny flame of this Universal Reality that is Life itself, Consciousness itself, Being itself, Love itself, God's very self."

So, for me, my feet must keep walking this unknown path, my hands keep writing the many words coming from this place within that many question, and many secretly thinking me mad. But my heart is flung wide open where there is no separation from you, and my door into this loving sacred space invites anyone to visit. My soul smiles to bring us inner touches, inner hands always holding me, and the inner kisses keep my face moist with wet like tears that I'm never alone…just often living in solitude. Hey…want to come in? Love can be our fire to keep us forever warm and only requires us to keep our hearts open to fan its Divine Love. We can be mad hatters together!

What if our immortal souls are emerging now within us to help all of us Pattys and Peters to remember our true story? We are the sacred, creative fire to flame forth to melt any and all not of our loving inclusion. Our human forms, made of the same elements as Earth, take residence within our true light, subtle soul bodies, guiding us to awaken to our rightful realization that the big universe also is inside of us. Everything forever is divinely connected!

How is this possible? We ask. Our consciousness is original creation, and everything is within this mystery of creation. We are evolving today into our much-needed next leap within this field of aware consciousness. We are becoming ever expanded, emerging our higher self souls, who we are, that we may become more aware of our great realization and revelation …yes…yes! The sun gives light to all to live and all moves within a beautiful creative energy of sensual, sacred Divine Love. Well it must be Divine Love, right? How else could the sun, moon and planets, including Earth, never grow tired of giving of its resources and abundance to us all? This is our sacred unified love story becoming aware and conscious of itself.

How else could us Pattys and Peters—all of us alive beings— be drawn together if not out of Love for Love? This is our true inclusive, soul sensual love story, one with unique meaning and purpose for each of us and why we are all here to proclaim; we are this creative fire here to express with greater innovation and higher novelty to restore the Earth and all upon the Earth. Us Pattys and Peters smile, holding each other close. We are ready to now live our authentic story together as beautiful, sensual, sacred souls of Divine Love. We are in the beginnings of how we are to accomplish this great higher leap; we begin with much-needed inquiries into our souls.

The Big Inquiry!

What is the real meaning of sex? We must have this inquiry into the ecstasy of orgasm, often not talked about. Tender, sensual, and in those seconds, a moment we never want to end. Yet, what leads up to this moment is, perhaps, the most important. Touch, heart open, deep-felt feelings of sacred Divine Love for the one you hold, to look and gaze into their sensual soul Divine Love. An inclusive intimacy of that kundalini moment of release. Now if this isn't the experience and you're hurting someone to achieve a selfish act, this is ego-driven and a surface love—this is the rampant and rage going on in the ego day in and day out. This is separation believing it can do whatever to another person.

True love and real intimacy becomes two sensual, sacred souls loving each's divine light within them both, then when that final moment of release is felt, this ecstasy becomes their sacred unity of each's sensual soul, persona, and Beloved Presence to forever go back out into the world and create this, our sacred unity, with everything. This begins awakened sensual, sacred soul loving partnerships. This is sacred inclusion. This is Divine Love.

Sex becomes a sacred soul Divine Love between two enjoined souls who've both taken their own inner journeys to unite each's mind persona with each's soul loving wisdom and both unified with Beloved Mystery Source of pure creative fire. This sparks each one to seek each other in the outer world to bring forth through the sensual sacred of him, entering into the sensual sacred of her, so to feel their ecstasy of pure sacred love, thus, further awakening each's creativity. This not only gives support to each other's unique gift and purpose, but also to help bring higher service and creativity of this higher sacred Divine Love to others and the world.

Our story of separation we've lived for so long is a soulless tragedy.

This tragedy shows itself in many ways both within us and without upon the Earth. Let's together hold hands as we look at how this division and separation is showing up everywhere, but mostly how it got programmed within us before we even had a chance to do anything about it. We all fell down this rabbit hole of separation when entering into the world.

The result is that today we live in a world where lies, corruption, and terrorism rule the world. This is not beloved sacred love or our sensual soul, but a small separate self-personality, lost in the world and who believes everyone not like him/her is the enemy. Sit with this big inquiry! We are living out of the wrong story. The mind of reason and below reason, our small him ego persona, within both men and women, is incomplete without our her, our sensual, sacred soul wisdom. We are born, enjoined at birth, within sacred unity with our beloved source and our soul Divine Love, but this is slowly forgotten as the old story of separation gets taught and programmed into our alone minds. We became lost in the world, believing it's all about conquer, ownership, and control of each other and the Earth. Let's be clear from the onset: no matter the gender, we've all been living out of a more mind ego separation from our sensual soul love of inclusion. Our mind of data information rules and runs each's life.

Our heart can open to feel and intuit in moments of inspiration, grief, and deep suffering, but it isn't stable within. Stability, true transformation, occurs from our deeper soul intuitive awareness that guides we're living falsely out of a wrong identity of who we are. It is the return of our sacred soul, loving presence, within whatever gender, that begins the shift of our consciousness from the story of separation back to the original intended story of our sacred unity. Each of us began our life out of the womb of inclusion into the world of separation. Yet, in the beginning of time, our creative fire of sacred love consciousness began out of Our Sacred Unity. The orbit of Earth within a sun and moon gives both light and dark. We sleep in the night, then wake into the day. All this is taken for granted. All this orbit brings abundance into the Earth for life. Again, we take this for granted living out of our very early programmed beliefs and we forget.

There is a sadness, a deep grief permeating us all. We need to listen!

Grief is a thread among many threads weaving our life together. Grief, like all threads, becomes a teacher taking us to places, if we quietly listen, why it's making us aware of its presence. So we listen closely to this guest—why it hurts, why it cries its tears, and why it wants our attention. Sometimes it's obvious, but often it is subtle and has been brooding for a long time. Something we, perhaps, have ignored or neglected to listen to and take action. We are this guest.

Grief, like all our feelings, becomes an emotion of a great intelligence guiding us in life. Yet, not attended too, often will become a more serious physical pain…one that can enter into the body's structure, causing our hearts, lungs, or other body parts to break down. Having cancer became the powerful catalyst to my final surrender to deeply listen. So we listen to the intelligence of all our great emotional threads as each weaves for us our web of life we live. How amazing this gift of a body form, downloaded from our birth, with all its sacred intelligences to help our sacred soul one day emerge to then further guide our body/minds with all its beautiful gifts to be used in a more divine and loving means for humanity's and Earth's greater evolution.

What a grand plan our creative mystery began billions of years ago. Now, as we begin to awaken as sacred souls of Divine Love, we, with Beloved Mystery, can co-create together this great beautiful plan to even higher and more beautiful means to live together. We use our small will, given to surrender, so to take responsibility, enjoining with our higher soul self, already enjoined with mystery of pure creative fire of sacred love, to becoming a trinity of divine purpose and meaning how we live together, tending each other and Earth. We ask, is it time, in this moment, to shift back within to our sacred unity?

Today, hate and fear are out of control, leading humanity off the cliff of life. It's now a pandemic within and without. Our soulless tragedy has all of us Peters and Pattys caged down this rabbit hole, living out of this wrong separation story. This old story needs to die. Our sacred Divine Love is our creative fire always evolving us into each's greater awareness of our higher ability to express itself to help dissolve our separation.

A cut bleeding will repair, as will bruised joints, when we stop to aid their healing. All of this given. Our breath continues through day and night, keeping us supplied with the right amounts of needed carbon and oxygen to be exchanged if we take care of our body and the Earth body. Remember? Our sacred unity of inner and outer movement, the divine rising of the sun, setting the moon and us too.

Releasing our Shadows to Birth our Souls!

Our minds can forget, to become lost in their selfish ways. Thus, we never grow up from our childish want of more and more. We play with a toy for an hour to discard and want another. More and more, we consume for wants and not needs until the land dries up, its rich ingredients destroyed from abuse. Our airways become polluted with too much carbon, as do our soils. We begin to breathe toxins, and our bodies can no longer respond with their healing system, nor the lands and airways. We become disconnected and separated from our sacred unity.

We slowly became programmed with propaganda to no longer see each other as all sparks and sacred souls of Spirit. We separate and we divide up the lands, people, and even the foul and animals.

We use surface ego love as another means to have another pretty face or another means to give us what we want, like bigger houses or fancy lifestyles. We see the homeless as someone who did their circumstances to themselves, so we disdain them as we do refugees forced to leave because of wars and economic loss. We find ways through each's origins of untruth, and we use that untruth to get what we want. We all have done this, sadly, and our shadows live us.

Our soulless tragedy belongs to all of us and is all our responsibility to wake up from this dream of separation. We use politics and religion to incite violence and hate when they are against our deemed way we say right. The worst soulless tragedy is we use God as a means to make our way right. We all have done this from a false story and a false self. Our shadows living us all. But are we being called in this hour to look out upon this beautiful planet to see our results? Do we feel good about this? Is all the money worth this? Is all the loss of life worth this? Is any one political party or religion worth this? Our shadow self is another mirror we must look into.

Is it time to fall to our knees and kiss the ground and turn to look into the eyes of each other? Is it time to reach out our hands to each other and say no more? Is it time to gather now at the rivers, mountain summits, across the plains, and in our hearts to say, *Please, Beloved God, help us. Please guide our sacred soul's emergence to assist our selfish minds and its fallen ways back into sacred loving souls. Please help us return back within our sacred unity. Please help us remember and may this remembrance activate our always within Divine Love!*

"The Shadow is the place where everything we have forgotten, denied, rejected, or not yet discovered goes to live."
~Richard Rohr

84

This shadow place resides within each of us as these old programs taught early in our development. Some will open this shadow door. Most keep it closed, yet, these dark hidden places creep out to project by creating judgments, an intolerable ideology or anger and hate at differences. We all have a shadow...we all have trauma and pain.

Today, these shadows are like a dark cloud above the Earth, meeting other clouds creating violent storms, and the Earth herself shakes.

Be still and know...Be aware and listen. May we become a brave humanity to take the most important journey we will ever take—a journey within to now open each's door of our long-held shadows to meet them, greet them, and just be ever present with them. This may not only change your life, but may just begin to dissipate the collective trauma clouds upon the Earth.

When we open this shadow door, the only thing needed is our sacred soul love presence because these shadow parts of us need to be held and loved from our sacred Divine Love that has always been deep within as our own sacred soul. The release of our sacred Divine Love, like a fire, will begin to burn and melt away everything that keeps our presence of soul and God from flaming this sacred Divine Love in us and in the world.

My new insight gives to me an appreciation of how life unfolds and enfolds. If something appears to break my heart, then by allowing my heart to feel my intensity of pain, my soul love comes to aid. By breathing in to relax, this further helps me to let it go. If an event follows with an experience of fun and delight, then the pain of intensity can be released to dance in the new experience. Feelings and emotions need freedom to be seen, felt, and heard so they can move on through. There is the night for my soul travels, where my body/mind gets to rest and be transfigured from the day's travels, then when waking the next morning in my "home of sacred presence of love," my sacred soul and body/mind, we're all ready for the days' new adventures to be experienced. This is how our higher new species of sensual, sacred soul self gets to become realized within her new home. Our sacred unity kingdom within holds our presence of sacred Divine Love. This begins our sacred unity story.

Curiosity has become a favorite companion today. Why do so many people walk past, some briefly making our acquaintance, while a few come and our soul lights up with a powerful recognition of knowing them? Our heart beats open to hold them again within our space. Have we, perhaps, traveled once again through time and space to meet up, however briefly, or we stay with great joy knowing we're found again? Yes, my curious soul now, without having any expectations, wants us to just allow again this sacred meeting up to once again embrace.

Christopher Bamford wrote, "There is a path of love and knowledge to which the West is heir. Once on this path, the pilgrim is no longer alone, but in a visionary company of 'friends of God'... This prophetic religion of Sophia, forever moved by love and beauty, is a living transmission and a perpetual renaissance; it has no formal church or earthly institution but is revealed only in the hearts and minds of human beings. Of the spirit, it is present whenever two or three are gathered together in the service of the ensouling of the world — of the return of the soul to God by way of the soul's return to her true self."

Again we ask, doesn't it make sense to partner with our beloved grace and our beautiful sensual souls to create a beautiful Earth garden home? Without a direct intimate partnership and relationship with our higher Beloved internal God and our soul, we miss the mark. And thousands of years of this living without intimate partnership gives to us a big fact truth check that it is impossible.

As William James said many years ago, "The fruit is in the experience. We look at our world today and we can see the big mess of experiences, getting messier by the minute."

Either we wake up, grow up, open up, clean up and start showing up in these partnerships, with our sensual sacred souls, our divine grace presence, and other awakened souls, or our Earth might just need to take some drastic measures. We are already experiencing some of these events. Global warming, extinctions, economic failures, a few thriving while most barely surviving, wars flaring everywhere, new strains of disease, and humans becoming refugees, being forced in many cultures to leave their homes. Politics, religion, and science are also being challenged with so much division and separation between them, pushing our hearts more towards hate and fear instead of sacred Divine Love.

You will find reading these pages sacred Divine Love, sensual soul, divine presence, Beloved Source, and sacred unity used time and again. This is done intentionally to begin helping our ego to lessen—to let go—so our souls may integrate this small ego self into our greater sensual, sacred soul love. If we look at the world, we see how divided into multiple cultures we have become. It is like mini realities lived on one planet. We can witness disagreements and war-like behaviors among ourselves everywhere on this small planet.

From an integral, developmental perspective, there exists on this planet very primitive forms of realities as well as more advanced forms, some having an ability to take higher and more advanced perspectives. Many today are seeing through a lens of perception into a greater, more aware and loving consciousness that is inclusive of all perspectives, yet, each lives from their more higher developmental self, through each's greater unique gifts to share.

The Art of Hypocrisy

My anger gets fueled when those who profess their God permits them to preach from their pulpits that hell and damnation are coming for those who don't follow their literal teachings, whether Christian, Buddhist, Islam, or any proclaimed religion, or even dictator government that controls people and Earth with authority the way, for so long, they've done. Then they go forth into the lands to dominate others through their greed, slavery, and any means to have power over people and things. War has long been the way our old story of separation perpetuates itself. Hate and fear its biggest weapon, needing to design guns and nuclear power to have control.

Politics and religions, sadly, have joined together in this insidious hypocrisy. Religions have used their high and mighty to take money from the rich and poor to build their million-dollar temples, then they live lifestyles of the rich and famous while using their Bibles to put into people fear and the belief that if their followers don't abide, then they will suffer greatly from the judgment of God somewhere separate. Yet, it's us humans who create judgments, and then we all suffer trying to live from those judgments.

This is the highest art of hypocrisy that has gone on for thousands of years. A false story told of our beloved mystical teachers were turned into heretics to be punished. These autocratic humans have taken the power of sacred Divine Love that our Jesus taught in the hills and valleys and where he sought to empower the hearts and souls of all people, and instead used their power over the people for their need to have control of the people. Beloved Jesus taught that the unity kingdom and real temple is within each of us, and by doing the great work of core sacred love and kindness, with great faith, then we will do and be even greater than he, and this message is still the only truth today that will save us. We must save ourselves through our internal sacred presence of soul love, embodied within each of us, needing today to guide us out of this false story of our separation from God, ourselves, and our own soul. We must become our trinity embodiment.

This is our responsibility to wake up from this insidious dream of a human-created separation story. We do this through transparency and vulnerability by opening and exposing our inner hearts to help one another and our planet. Yes, the art of hypocrisy is another disease, along with so many diseases that are taking over our lives and inducing deadly amounts of toxic fear into the minds and bodies.

This old separation story today is leading to an apocalypse. Beloved Mystery, like many of us, is recoiling through showing up in how the Earth is also recoiling with climate storms and pandemics. This wrong story must come to its end. It must be revealed and unveiled. And we now must come to understand the real meaning and purpose of an apocalypse—to unveil the false story of separation created by us humans to the true authentic original story of an Earth as an inclusive sacred Divine Love of all. Our Sacred Unity Story!

This becomes heaven upon the Earth, where us sacred souls come often to be in form to create and playfully live among the beautiful mountains, oceans, and streams with alive trees, flowers, birds, animals, and crawly insects within the rich abundant soils. And we do so within a sacred Divine Love and with sacred soul loving partnerships. Core sacred Divine Love is and always must be the highest energy to be harnessed and given and received. Pattys and Peters must emerge from their long dark hole of separation into each's light of their wholeness. Why, we must ask, would we ever leave the development and creation of this small blue planet to a small ego or to self-inflated human personalities? Well sadly, today, we know why— our world suffers in its soulless tragedy everywhere.

Bede Griffiths states, "Each man must discover this Centre in himself, this Ground of his being, this Law of his life. It is hidden in the depths of every soul, waiting to be discovered. It is the treasure hidden in a field, the pearl of great price. It is the one thing which is necessary, which can satisfy all our desires and answer all our needs. But it is hidden now under deep layers of habit and convention. The world builds up a great protective barrier around it."

Our mystery called life has both cosmic and Earth roots. Our bodies emerge like the flowers to live life experiences only to return to its Earth roots one day, but our sacred soul, a more subtle essence, shall return once more to her cosmic roots with our great mystery.

Just as a great banquet table has many dishes where many flavors are blended to give our taste buds an experience of something never before tasted, with only just one flavor. We can arise our higher sacred soul way of being into the world, with other unique soul flavors in our diversity, weaving together more creative harmony and balance in the many different ideas and artistic innovations.

What a wonderful world we can live together. Where does any new novelty arise from if not from this stillness…our grounded center of being in the arms of our Beloved loving Source?

Our awareness begins to help us see all the choices now on the banquet table, within our now expanded consciousness, and how now in our relative life, we can make the right choices. Just recently, one morning after meditation, tears flowed from feeling so filled with the relative world's divides and all its suffering. I had an inner dialogue with Beloved; here it is in words to share with all of you.

SoulMe...Are you there, Beloved?

Beloved...I'm here.

*SoulMe...Why are there days I feel so me...pain is lessened,
but other days everything floats up and pain is
unbearable...I can't stop crying...not just my pain
but a pain like tapping into all pain. My heart is
like an open container of suffering. This is hard.*

*Beloved...I feel this too with you. I am holding you now
in my Love that no pain or suffering can escape
its power to transform that pain. The power of
my love will wash this pain through, then you
will return back into a lightness of your being.*

*SoulMe...Is a part of my being on the Earth planet to
help with the dark suffering?*

*Beloved...Yes...through you and other souls, I bring forth
my greater Love for healing and awakening
the many souls now to join us with this Light
radiating through the Earth and through this
darkness that has long reigned for a higher
understanding of these polarities.*

*SoulMe... Are you always here...never to leave me? I often
feel lonely walking the Earth path...nature helps.*

*Beloved...I Am always, forever here within you. I find many
ways to show this to you...the hawk flying in your
path to almost touch you...and remember all the
hummingbirds and the one you held in your hand?
Remember all those moments, the perfect aligned
meetings of so many people showing up to bring
you closer to me? I can go on with more if you like?*

SoulMe... I remember, Beloved, and so many more too. You are

91

always helping us find our new home. That
moment in the orphanage when you first came...
and never left again. I remember. I love you!
Beloved...I love you too!

Intimate Divine Partnerships

These intimate moments can bring us all closer into a shared field of our consciousness space within a higher felt oneness with all things and, most importantly, with each other. We need each other. It is only together in our shared sensual, sacred souls and beloved partnerships that visions, creative innovations, and new novelty come through from the Divine to empower a collective new story. We are given rise to a new species—divine loving sacred souls.

Shakespeare wrote, *"The fault is not in our stars, but in ourselves."*

Meditation and contemplative prayer have opened a vast expanded territory within me to discover portals leading into many dimensions within this raw, undiscovered inner world of consciousness that some call the kingdom within, or my soul says our sacred unity. This sacred Divine Love, unlike any human ego surface love, continues to call me into her chamber of intimacy, where soul me continues to love and partner with my Beloved Source. Together, we are a team, co-partnered to help also now partner with the small human personality at birth.

Through this trinity of Beloved, sacred soul, and human personality, my human form, in its higher awareness, becomes an open instrument to play divine music of love and light through all the sensual experiences. My temple form becomes the vessel to hold our great sacred trinity, vibrating out my soul resonance of love in both human and Divine experiences. This is the beautiful part we can look forward to. Imagine having spiritual intimate partnerships, soul to soul in friendships, or one that takes the friendship into a more romantic soul partnership.

These Divine relationships, partnering with our beloved, can bring children into a world that remains stable in their original grace presence. These trinity partnerships with personality, soul, and Beloved Source seek to be in service of light and sacred love to others and the world for sacred unity and sacred peace. The problem is we are not hooked up to our powerful internal source of guidance and direction.

Our within system is wired within us all. It's time to plug into this higher operating system of sacred loving guidance. Our true authentic love story. Our responsibility, once we have surrendered small self to become integrated with sacred soul self, is to plug into our higher sacred mystery network within the invisible field, where portals of guidance await. Both men and women carry within a masculine reason and a pearl of feminine soul wisdom. Both wisdom and reason are now seeking to be unified within humanity.

The world of form is rich and alive in all its colorful diversity. We are all so uniquely gifted with an ability to grow and to expand our awareness of this diversity, thereby, we choose what best honors, compliments, and merges our sacred soul uniqueness. The poets, artists, mystics, and misfits became frowned upon, and often their writings, paintings, and sculptures became buried or burned. Today, many of us are feeling our sacred soul of wisdom calling in her many ways telling us it's time. We must have the courage to do this work of releasing the old story to include our soul of wisdom, thereby also releasing our long-held shadows to be healed.

Today, perhaps our chaos is simply to gain a greater light of clarity to witness the lopsided way we have structured our systems like politics, religions, businesses, and sadly, the harshest, our relationships with each other. We have operated out of a separate polarized existence. What we need in this day and time is a great inclusive leadership, the mind of reason integrated with the soul of wisdom and both informed within by our higher guidance of Divine Presence of sacred Love...greater mystery! This leads to great leadership inwardly and outwardly in the world.

Qualities of Great Soul Leadership

When we want someone to lead our country, it becomes important to look for his/her leadership qualities. Does he/she have a wide lens of perception whereby they can see into the many diverse and unique people they will be leading? Do they have an expanded, aware experience of empathy, caring, and a greater vision of how to have great leaders surround them in areas they may be weaker? Do they have clarity; how leading a country and people is through empowering others to come together in their local and state to bring new ideas and innovations and that the whole of a country is the sum of its parts working in harmony for the greater good, truth, and beauty of everyone? This is an inclusive story of empowering sacred love.

Do they have an even greater vision that they are also one country among many countries and becoming a great ally to their fellow leaders of other countries bringing support for the whole of the nation?

Is their leadership a love of peace and goodwill? Do they lead with both their rational mind and wise soul heart? Can they cry with the pain of their people, knowing it's their pain too? Does their leadership have moral character? We must look, when choosing a leader, for these deep qualities and choose wisely because our leaders can bring us to the top of the mountain or they can throw us all off the mountain to our demise. Today, we are experiencing this demise in great chaos.

Our life force is the same, but how each unique soul is here to express and experience our higher loving presence is very different. Out of our One Mystery is birthed the many sacred, unique souls.

Thus how diversity came to be within the natural world of nature and each human ego mind/body's inner nature. It's all quite beautiful and miraculous how our one divine creative fire, within all living things, and the Earth soils herself, provide all the abundance ever needed so all could experience and have one day our sacred soul love realization.

Believing we are separate from each other, our creative fire within and without, and the Earth herself began our wounds and trauma. We became consumer addicts, wanting the Earth for selfish means to consume, and we used God, each other, and even all the natural species as our trophy's and to have even more consumption. Many cry "my God is better and only loves my way and supports my way." How childish and immature. Yet, even sadder is this abundance is enjoyed by only about fifteen percent of the population, where the rest have become a wasteland of refugees and servants for the very top, who own all the material abundance.

Real soulful leadership sees and knows the Earth needs to be replenished with right means, as does all its species, including the human alone species, that can only survive now by evolving into its higher species, a sacred soul Divine Love self. We wake up our soul, loving presence through growing up the immature ego of small mind, then we begin taking action to clean up all our shadow messes from the last several thousand years so we can finally all show

95

up together, taking each other and the Earth into its next highest realization, our sacred unity, within Beloved Mystery Source, awaiting us with open, loving, living arms to embrace us back home to live authentic Divine Love.

Chapter 5

Gratitude Partners with Grace

*"There cannot ever be an enlightened person;
there is just the realization that there is no separation."*
Halina Pytlasinska

My Prayer of Gratitude
*May each morning my awareness take me right into my heart home
of gratitude, and may gratitude help me give and give of my love and
my caring to everything and everyone.*

*This is my prayer…I am Divine Love…I am grateful…and may
I surrender to being and living within this gift of awareness of
abundance within and without. May my gratitude of creativity create
more love and more gratitude.*

*Thank you, Beloved great Presence, for your fire of creativity and
how you express through my sacred soul/mind to live this always-
radiating life with its beauty, goodness, and Love…*

*Sacred Divine Love is our greatest flame of creativity and our being
grateful to know you, to know this Love, be this Love and be in service
with you for this Love is to be humble to live within our form upon the
Earth and to know you are within us, guiding us in our awareness.*

When we become engaged in a daily practice of meditation, prayer, and walks in the natural world, we open to becoming more grateful, compassionate, kind, and empathic to our loving brothers and sisters living all over this planet. We begin taking responsible actions to use our internal guidance for helping others to wake up from their separation story. Grace becomes our intimate partner with our gratitude to become the actions needed for great change.

> *"My experience is what I agree to attend to.*
> *Only those items which I notice shape my mind."*
> ~William James

Our Choices Become Our Changes

There is a smorgasbord of beliefs, opinions, and just plain made-up stories on the banquet table of our life to choose from. What will we choose? Why will we choose? How will we come to our decision to choose? Where will these choices take us, those we love, and the Earth we now live upon? Today, these are our most profound questions we each must confront in our life. Are we motivated by moral character or money and external power, or maybe just a need to be right for the want of a fight with another who has a different perception/perspective?

Today, on this banquet table of choices, what we decide to choose most likely will come from where we each live within our own aware, developed higher consciousness. It's either a mythical story coming from the past, the present where the capitalist story is in an ongoing war with the socialist story, or tomorrow's future story, still unknown, because the decisions that we make today are going to determine our tomorrow/future story. The stories we live today are mostly stories of separation—divide and conquer. Here is why we all are being called today to mutate this eons-old separation story.

Living from two selves is getting harder, and more dangerous too.

There is our inner soul of each of us, our true guiding intuitive voice, and then the outer ego voice of learned beliefs of always feeling we are separated from each other and becoming more and more fearful of each other with little trust and faith. This is the now tension upon the Earth and within humanity. Stress is becoming a danger, reaching levels we've never experienced. Death coming for too many and much too soon. Everywhere, these outer alone ego selves are fighting through medias, politics, and religions. These egos demanding more power and more control. Their hands close to the nuclear war heads.

Relationships of men and women also are being challenged due to intimacy and tenderness lost to this false alone selfish self. We need our true, loving, wise, sacred soul for returning us all back to our wisdom of her guidance and sacred Divine Love. Surrendering to our higher sacred loving soul voice will seem at first challenging because we must face the outer false voice with all its dark shadows, long locked away like our ghosts of the past.

Many are taking this challenge today as the old story of separation, long taught, is reaching its apex. Our soul voice is becoming clearer with her now loving presence. It is time…the hour draws near. She whispers the ego, alone voice, is within all humans, no matter gender, color, or culture, and no longer can it sustain or live in separation, nor can the Earth now provide with this false love lived from a false self and all vying for power and control through war, divide and conquer.

So we each must ask the question: are enough of us willing to take this inner journey back home into our heart of true authenticity, where our soul, higher true self, wants to emerge to partner with our small ego self so to create inner sacred partnerships with and through our sacred Divine Love? Really contemplate this for yourself. These sacred inner partnerships will then morph, like butterflies, into outer sacred loving partnerships. A beautiful new Earth arises from her dark cocoon to be lovingly experienced.

May we attend and choose from our wise heart/soul aligned with a grown up, mature mind. And may both align with our higher creative mystery to be in service for the highest good, truth, and beauty for all of us beings and the Earth. P.S. Here is a hint: the capitalist story of entrepreneurships and ideals is at its most beautiful when it can have partnership with its socialist story through responsible action to care the sick, poor, fallen, and elders.

Sacred Loving Partnerships Within Become Outermost Leaders

Listen and rest into what this may feel like living within our more inclusive, balanced, and harmonious existence. Can we gain deep understanding and clarity about how the Earth and all living things upon the Earth are in a relationship? Can we begin to have realization that we can't survive when these relationships believe we are all in separation from each other, our soul, and God? How this has created dis-harmony and imbalance with everything; the now chaos we live. We can't keep being in ongoing wars we create.

Once our internal relationships are back in sacred unity, they move externally to bring all relationships back into integration. How powerful is this creative flame of sacred Divine Love? This is the now inclusion story being felt within our awakened hearts, through our sensual souls, musing us all back into our remembrance. The story of the butterfly effect is the concept that small causes can have large effects. It is a great metaphor for all of us in accepting that a small change within us triggers a change within another. When enough of us are living our great new story of us as emerging divine souls, one with our Beloved Mystery creator, then butterfly souls begin to appear all over the planet. The alone ego mind surrenders to serve the wise soul and, both integrated, serve all beings and the Earth. A true leadership of the people!

We begin to become co-creator partnerships to bring forth a higher leadership for the people as the people become the leaders. We tap into our larger field of consciousness within our greater awareness to receive higher information and wisdom on how to take care of each other and our planet. The journey within is our way to navigate into our new soul's love story. Remember, we wake each day to a new mysterious beginning. Just as the sun wakes us, so do our souls.

"No words can explain how inspired words spring out of silence."
~Rumi

My story has its changing twists and turns. So who am I in all these stories—a young and beautiful face/body morphed into an aging face/body while my soul remains forever the same. My mind of being smart wasn't acknowledged. It grew in its self-doubt as being beautiful brought more attention, especially from men. Did they see me, a shy, timid, dreamy, visionary who saw much more than being wife, mother, writer, or counselor? Or was this hidden in the shadow closet, too afraid my inner world was not real enough? Being now much older, my true self, soul wisdom, teaches me not to define myself by another or an ideology or a religion but to see deeply hidden within my heart, my always yearning for freedom and to be understood. Freedom can never be understood or experienced so long as fear and resistance control our minds through our learned conditions. The small ego-mind must let go into its integration with the divine heart-mind. A true loving soul partnership is co-created.

One morning, a walk in the woods emerged insight; this place of me, you, us…do you wonder? One day, we walk freely, only the next day to stumble and be no more! What is this flow we call love? Do you feel if another doesn't give it to you that it doesn't exist? Is it possible to stand alone in a woods with only the wind, earth floor, infinite sky above, sun blazing through the trees, and an occasional furry animal, and feel this love? I wonder a lot anymore. Waking in the night, there is this sensual loving presence waking me. What is it and where does it emerge from? My love feels as old as time and as new as a newborn sliding out of the womb. My Divine Love seeks me. My Divine Love wants to hold me tenderly, yet, when wrestling to be in her arms, like a subtle breeze, she dances all around me.

My sensual, sacred Divine Love asks nothing, yet gives everything. Slowly, she expands my heart, squeezing out anything not of its sacred presence. When leaving the woods, my heart smiles knowing now my sensual soul love is who I am and all she asks of me is to give and share my Divine Love…she will always find her way back to snuggle me, her presence forever within…me…you…us. We can just share it together! Yes, I am coming back home, directly within me, to my finally opened heart. Sacred Divine Love is my creative fire flaming my soul alive.

My sensual soul tenderly holds my human mind/body to dissolve its long-held belief that it could ever be separated from our sacred unity presence. She smiles away his long mind battle to warrior, control, or dominate by waking his sensual mind now longing to merge with her subtle wisdom soul, loving presence. They were always meant to be in an inner inclusive, loving relationship together. A beautiful intimacy of shared guidance with each other—leaders together.

Together, we sit to watch the sunset or sunrise to be taken into its creative miracle. Oh, my sensual soul love, how was it ever possible to not know you are here, within my grail heart, where together we are taken to experience this subtle sensual love in every moment and every breath, enjoined always, forever as One. My sensual soul love now becomes the alchemical fire and the ego it's flame for dissolving any separation, uniting us both in our blaze of creativity and loving partnership to go forth together saving the Earth and bringing forth our gifts of higher ideals to emerge higher novelty.

Our body/mind gets triggered through something said or done, bringing forth sadness or anger. Our soul expanded awareness of the mind witnesses this emotion and quickly discerns the cause. Our sensual soul now comes forth with loving compassion and kindness to work with our ego to enter into this emotion to help dissolve the held trauma, thus freeing our body, mind, and emotion so that it can return to our more sustainable higher soul Divine Love. This begins the emergence of our unity awareness and how both mind/body and soul can be witnessed within our expanded consciousness in partnership. Our responsibility is to stay attentive within ourselves moment to moment so to remain aware within our consciousness. This is how we do our daily work of dissolution and dismantling all learned conditioning and behaviors when they arise, trying to block our flow of who we are as beautiful sacred loving souls.

"Realization is not acquisition of anything new nor is it a new faculty.
It is only removal of all camouflage."
~Ramana Maharishi

Listening to Our Separation Stories Arises Our Unity Awareness!

So here we are gathered around a campfire. Big decisions rest in our hearts. The rational mind, our ego, believing itself supreme power, is now being confronted with its loss of soul, its caring, nurturing, and loving wise goodness. It's being shown how its raw appetite for money, ownership of objects, and control over people have long led humans into a world filled with corruption and the destruction of nature. We egos all listen how the long separation story, spanning over the many thousands of years, has created a division between God, us as humanity, our soul, and Earth nature. We hear what has been lost is our ability to listen. We have been self-absorbed, choosing our tribe based upon whom we agree with, and we go after those who dare to disagree. We only listen to each's story. So today, we are all gathered together to listen to all stories.

Let us come into this circle to sit with each other and each share what is our sameness with each other. There is much to be celebrated in what gives each of us joy and love. Perhaps it is our children, our love of nature or the arts, or maybe fishing, sports, or crossword puzzles. We may each find a common interest. It could be our work, love of travel, or love of gardening or woodwork. Let's close our eyes and imagine sitting around this fire with a group of people from all walks of life. Let's hold a vision of laughing together, crying together as we share our stories. We begin to see and feel into how sitting within this circle together, outside of differences, we enter into just one heart space of our sacred freedoms. Our hearts flow with surges of our together Divine Love, then our Divine Love begins to flow outward.

We begin to entrain and experience this sacred love, understanding that if a disaster happens tomorrow, we will stop our differences immediately to help each other survive the disaster. It has been shown that this is true many times in our history. Today, this is happening in the country of Ukraine, where its democracy is being threatened by an autocratic government. Countries everywhere are coming together to embrace the people to help them fight for their freedom. All genders, religions, and democracies give support.

Our listening opens us to know our differences and opposites upon this world banquet table, where we all come to the feast, we cannot possibly fill our own life plate with all experiences offered. But looking at so many plates, filled with so much different than mine, can open me and you to smile with our own curiosity and wonder to give us all a greater understanding. When our presence of sacred Divine Love, as forever abiding within each of us, begins emerging, she comes softly and sweetly, yet her power of love now shifts our entire inner understanding of how our love changes everything within and without. How, you might ask? Let us also now sit to begin listening to our children.

We are all born through a womb into the Earth. We are born into different cultures, races, genders, and some are poor and some rich. Whatever the religion, politics, or norms in the family, these become, for the most part, conditioned into the children. Even love! A child will be rewarded or will be punished to follow the dictates of his/her conditions. Love, as a surface small love, is also given or withheld.

The child enters into its environment with their felt divine loving presence in the first seven years, and it becomes important to not separate this away from the child but have this presence of love be his/her guiding inner primal, life force, their original creative fire, they came into the world with. Yet, sadly, it gets hidden as they instead are programmed with the conditions they are born into.

The child in those first years sees through imaginal realms; they have this loving divine presence vibrating their being. They love

105

freely and openly, and they can't see differences, nor do they care about all the conditional ways to live that soon they will be taught. Yet, this soon ends for the child as the bullies begin to appear on the playground and in the home, who are starting to judge, like they've been judged in their home and community. This is how the Earth human over the globe, for thousands of years, lived upon the Earth. Perhaps some rare exceptions of souls coming into Earth to teach. What if we listened to the children versus programming them? What if we listened to the mystical teachers versus changing their stories over time or killing them for their inclusive stories?

When our soul presence of sacred Divine Love becomes the only felt experience, and this experience is shared with all life, both in nature and human nature, our soul's presence becomes one's means to see this loving sacredness in all regardless of where born, to whom born, and what conditions of rich or poor born into. We listen! Our senses can become elevated by our soul's presence to see and hear in a more loving and inclusive way. Our emotions, from this depth of loving presence, only want to serve our sacred Divine Love, knowing we will receive back this love through partnerships with others, all living from this sameness of Divine Love, albeit, expressed in its varieties of experiences.

We must remember our soul's presence of sacred love, within a sacred unity, is what brought together the first living forms upon Earth, and through this higher Divine Love, single cells to the now multi-cells, grew and became greater and greater within this creative fire of Divine Love. It is our sacred souls to flame this love to all beings. Once born, this sacred love seeks itself through some way to be in relationship with itself in another, through its given sensual experiences. Today, many are beginning to awaken back to this remembrance.

106

We must, because the old model of separation and its programs taught that we are separate from our soul's presence of love, called by many names across the globe, also believe we are separate from each other and the Earth. The taught program is that one culture, one race, or one gender can be more superior than another, thus, our sacred love has been deeply forgotten to be replaced by egos of self-love. We are witness to this false love everywhere in its need to have power over the Earth and people. Our sacred unity has become fragmented into parts dividing and separating Earth and humanity. We must stop…We must listen!

"Feelings come and go like clouds in a windy sky.
Conscious breathing is my anchor."
~Thich Nhat Hanh

This great teacher, who recently transitioned, lived mindfulness; his awareness focused in the present moment. If children are taught this early and not programmed with past data, then their future can be more a reflection of their mindfulness moments. Their original nature of sacred love remains while their persona of egos can grow and mature in the senses/emotions to better understand that variety of differences and diversity is beautiful. Yet, for those of us programmed since early childhood, this becomes harder. We must enter into these learned shadow-like programs to deactivate them, thus releasing and surrendering them. Only then, like Thich Nhat Hanh, are we able to begin living each moment in greater awareness of what is here right before us.

When enough of us come together in higher relationships, living these aware mindful moments, to partner in all systems, religion, spiritual service, business, and our politics, we gain a greater understanding of how our divisions have separated us and so we strive in all endeavors and higher innovations how best to all become greater leaders together. We work for the higher and greater meaning and purpose to make our Earth and all beings upon the Earth a home for beloved presence to also live within each of us, thus thriving and sustaining the world externally. Many powerful teachers of soul presence came to help demonstrate how this is done through their examples and experiences and how we all must bring forth our higher soul presence.

Today, we each face disaster, causing, possibly, our very own democracy and our own planet's survival herself. A virus has spread globally. Our beautiful Statue of Liberty can remind us all that we are all immigrants born into this Earth planet. We need each other in our own space, and we need our allies in all the other spaces. We need our smiles more than our smears and our hugs more than our fists. We need to share our bread more than stealing another's. And most importantly, we need our sacred love. Without this inner nectar of love, we turn to hate...hate becomes the rope... that ongoing tug of war.

My dearest friend Terry Patten, who just recently transitioned, says in his book *A New Republic Of The Heart: An Ethos For Revolutionaries*, "Subtle soul work is necessary—and it cannot be fruitful unless it is informed by transcendental non-dual wholeness."

Slowing Down the Pace We Move Brings Mindfulness!

Our feet walk along a path, moving at a pace to feel the wind blowing through our hair, touching our skin. We can also notice how it gives movement to the leaves and water while simultaneously flying the fowl above. We notice! We are aware. We ride a bike, taking us a bit faster, yet we still feel everything through our senses. We remain aware. We must pay attention. We are pedaling, and we are directly sensing through our intuitive soul's musing.

We ride inside a car, train, plane, or bus. Now the pace is becoming much faster, and we are also enclosed, unable to feel the natural elements. Everything goes by so quickly that it is all a bit blurry. Our awareness feels the differences inside and outside—we don't hold much close. It all becomes separate—something is missing.

We ride inside our body, where our mind becomes the means to move us faster and faster. We miss most of what is happening outside in the natural world. We catch the news but not the rainbow. We catch the mind of another's thinking, to spend now hours within our mind in disagreements, putting more division between us. We miss hours of what just happened in real time.

If only we had just been aware of just being more present-minded.

And…we begin to miss seeing our sameness and our uniqueness, lost so much now in our differences. We forget to respect each other, not realizing that all of these differences could teach us to come closer versus dividing us and keeping us so separate. We don't listen to each other, just to our mind's fast pace of conspiracy caught on the news or through friends. We go so fast our soul is left far behind our driven ego mind. Yet, her love and wisdom trying to slow us down.

May Divine Love be given to you today, and every day, that you then may love it forward to those you meet, that you may listen for whispers from your soul, asking you to join in a slower pace. This slower pace to feel again, see again, hear again, and touch again the stillness of life where love blooms the flower, the wind blows the leaf, birds sing their song, and the touch of an animal or a child brings back love and its lightness of being, by simply slowing down the pace. Come walk with me…we will hold hands…we will experience life in all its fullness and freedom…today…tomorrow. Our soul love will sustain us all, becoming the momentous shift of change we all are here to co-create together and experience. How beautiful is this? All the work of surrender will be worth every moment to become "Who We Are."

Today, watching the snowfall gently and snuggled under a warm blanket, there is peace within my inner world with my loving soul and my Beloved Mystery. Yet, my awareness also grows, knowing this old story of division and separation, where war and destruction of the Earth have reigned for thousands of years, will not go gently but fight to its ends. It will not willingly give up its control and attachment to its ownership of people, places, and things.

Alone ego's often fight to grow into maturity. The fire of our soul love opens us into guiding our maturity. We begin to feel deeply in our bodies how we've lived for thousands of years this old narrative.

We are all carriers of this disease, and the only antidote to cure it is to bring forth a healthy moral character within each of us, developed from core sacred love; our higher soul presence we each came into the world to be, as a spark and flame of our Divine Love. But we also feel the tension mounting; these two realities now in conflict. My soul whispers *Be at peace*. Love will prevail, and people, places, and things will come to be understood, not as ownership, but as the gift for all to simply enjoy, share, and experience for the short time each is here on the planet. Slowing down our pace helps us to be more in tune with our own inner soul whispers, and the natural world opens us to our soul.

We must all begin the work of maturing our personalities so our true unique souls can emerge and become free to fully inhabit with Divine, beloved presence. We must bring this greater mystery of Divine intelligence called wisdom into the instrument body so that its loving movement can become the power to mutate, transfigure, and transform the lower personality identity. We are not egos.

110

*"We may not be responsible for the world that created our minds,
but we can take responsibility for the mind with which
we create our world."*
~Dr. Gabor Maté

A great start to my morning is this small prayer. When eyes first open become still. Take a few moments to center into your heart. Teach the mind to say *I Am grateful...I am Loving...I surrender to being in service today in gratitude and love.* We begin with a slower pace becoming more mindful.

Every Morning...Be grateful unto yourself
Be kind unto yourself...Be love unto yourself
Be compassionate unto yourself
Be joy...Be sorrow...Be true unto yourself
Be laughter...Be tears...unto yourself
Be all you can Be unto yourself
Now go do all of this unto the world into All Beings!

A powerful poetic transmission emerged after witnessing Hurricane Ida devastate the state of Louisiana, where I was born.

Our world changes
to reflect our stories. Our stories
must be true,
authentic, and with meaning and purpose for all.

Each heart shining
its light of Grace. Each heart, like a river, flowing

kindness and compassion for each other,
and each heart filled
with a desire to live and know peace for
supporting and having each other's highest best.

Our story must
become the story of 'Who We All Are'...
Souls of Love born from and out of a higher Love of Grace
...our Beloved Source.

If our world is
now burning or drowning from the old stories,
Let us Let Go
to rise out of these ashes and toxic waters
into the Phoenix of our Souls.
Let's begin our rebirth so to recreate
and redesign our beautiful Earth planet out of this higher Love.

We now live from
our inner kingdom where our Soul Love flows
from God Love!
We now feel and know Love is our Saving Grace!

Today, we are all witness to our world in an extreme out-of-balance state. Mother Nature is crying; we kill off the topsoils, we cut down too many trees, and we fracture the land, taking and taking, while not giving enough back. Can you see how this separation of opposites, living out of only one side, is creating our separation from each other, nature, and God? Just like we live out of one side, our personality ego while our soul wisdom side is mostly arrested. We need both to live in sacred unity.

Our democracy is created with different branches of government to keep everything in balance and harmony, but if some authoritarian government tries to dismantle this democracy, then chaos and disharmony arise. We witness all suffer under a ruler wanting to control all the people and all the governments. This takes away all the checks and balances. This takes away all our freedoms. Authoritarian leadership is without moral and ethical compass within itself, acting out of bullying and chronic ego pathological behaviors. This is narcissism where the individual ego acts alone without partnership with his/her soul/wisdom. We live an I/me versus us/we. Living from this small one-sided way takes and takes with little giving, and no one is listening.

Where we are in this moment in time in our world is our greatest wake-up call. We have lost the soul of the natural world and our soul of ourselves. It's like all the rivers being blocked off from moving into the larger seas and oceans. Everything gets dammed and blocked, creating a backlog and backlash of a civilization that can no longer operate and live from its old narratives. So what is this old narrative? Again let me repeat: it is the old belief that we are separate. This separation from each other also teaches that we are separate from our invisible world from whence we all came. This must be deeply felt and experienced. Yet, we do not pay attention. We aren't listening. This is so important to hear, so my soul repeats!

Understanding Our Duality and Diversity Brings Novelty!

Where does any artist draw inspiration? Where does technology get its ideas? Where do the saints or mystics receive their deep ecology of sacred love? How do people get up every day with a reason to explore and adventure? We can go on and on about how all of us are, and always will be, influenced by this invisible world of vision, hope, and creative fire. This is called awareness and intuitive knowing to the vision. We are inseparable from the

113

invisible and visible. This is our new inclusive soul love story! How can we be separate from that which created everything? We are part and whole of this creation. We must now embrace this big question to come to our realization that we must dissolve our old story of division and separation and its narratives into our together creative fires of sacred unity living from sacred love. Please read this paragraph again!

There is one web of life, and this web contains within us living threads that must be in harmony and balance with every other thread so that the whole web may be sustainable. We are not separate but interdependent and intra-dependent with everything. We are energy threads weaving in and out, touching, seeing, hearing, tasting, and intuiting each other and our world. What one part does to the whole is felt by all parts. We take this extraordinary miracle for granted, falling into a false narrative and story of separation.

Duality is not separation; it is the many diverse ways to come to know wholeness through experiment and experience. Our non-dual greater loving consciousness, the container of all, holds the dual parts where we learn to weave through our responses, our highest and best choices, to keep balance and harmony moving towards ever greater wholes. This emerges all great novelty. In essence, we develop into higher and greater perspectives, whereby we can hold multiple perspectives. Again…we listen…we learn…we grow…we mature… we emerge our higher self soul.

My neighbor is republican while my political choice is democratic. We have dinner together where our conversation becomes riddled with differences. We both are highly conscious and aware. We agree to find the third side, working from our higher unity awareness. This third side takes the best of his position and the best of my position, weaving them into a newer, higher position.

We find the way through always, which requires thinking outside each other's perspective and opinion.

Our higher soul in partnership with our mind of reason knows there is always novelty that can emerge. But if two small ego minds grudgingly tug each end of the rope war, then anger will surely send the neighbor home, and the differences will declare them enemies. They will be unable to live and solve from their sameness. Dualities and opposites don't go away, but how we respond from a higher altitude and attitude, within a higher loving consciousness, changes the story. This great teaching expands our consciousness where it is large enough to hold all within our great sacred unity, our web of life. We're able now to choose each moment how best to use these dualities towards the greater good. We can become witnesses to everything arising within and without, empowering us to make these higher decisions. This witness is our unity awareness within this field of loving consciousness. We operate from our awakened soul, and our breath becomes our anchor and meditative focus in each moment.

We become skilled in how to use our dual emotions, and we come to realize the gift of duality and differences. Both can offer greater vision when brought into collaboration with each other. We can no longer operate from just a small immature ego-mind for me and just a few who obey me. This small mind is selfish and acts out in selfish actions. Yet, it can mature so that it opens back its heart where its soul wisdom, it's partner, so long dammed away, can emerge to enjoin back with the mind to bring back wholeness and holiness. This is what will bring us and our world back into balance and harmony. This will be repeated over and over so the small ego wakes up!

This is how we emerge a more beautiful civilization with its narrative of a non-dual, non-separation through its realization that sacred unity is simply the balance and harmony of all the opposites and differences brought together by seeing through the lens of wholeness.

Pierre Teilhard de Chardin speaks to creative fire and love: "Someday, after mastering the winds, the waves, the tides, and gravity, we shall harness for God the energies of love, and then, for a second time in the history of the world, man will have discovered fire." "Love is the affinity which links and draws together the elements of the world...Love, in fact, is the agent of universal synthesis."

Jesus says, "You must bring forth what is within you, and if you do not, what is within you will destroy you." It's taken my entire life to understand what he meant. Jesus walked with the feminine—the Marys. This wisdom of the feminine is our soul, the rose blooming out of our thorns, our resurrection, our beloved presence in Divine union with our soul. God/Soul is within both man/woman, shining light through onto Earth, into our hearts, awakening us to remember this revelation and great realization. This is the new discovery of creative fire, Love, as our means to dissolve human separation.

Perhaps we now come to fully embody our unknown mystery. We can put down the study of God to live godly principles fully and holy until God lives in us. We let go of all that keeps us from living our Divine inclusive experiences. We become elevated in our sensual moments within taking us back to see the world differently, and we listen more deeply to our soul voice aligning us with these higher abilities to use our senses. Our relationship with what is visible, conceptual, rational, and sensual is made intimate with that which is invisible, Soul/God bringing forth our imaginal powers of imagination, innovation, and the means of soul and God to create together through human existence. We need this loving relationship, I do believe, brought forth so we become these relationships.

When humanity couldn't take responsibility for their actions, Satan was created, thus, blame came into existence. When humanity could not own their behaviors, doing the work to transform their behaviors, they were told a savior would do it for them, allowing them to continue these behaviors. Yet, the beautiful teacher/mystic Jesus came to teach and show us how we save ourselves. The politicians and preachers instead just put this responsibility on him to save us after his death. This began the lived separation story and its teachings. Jesus was an inclusive teacher, teaching how we save ourselves through loving our neighbor as ourself.

Until we, as a collective people, become aware to realize that our thousands of years history of divide and conquer and its history of long separation is our today's collective trauma and is taking us all to the edge of this cliff hanger, then we all may fall off. We stand at this place in our history where instead we must leap in our awareness. We must rise above into a greater, higher, and wider understanding; we have all been living out of one side of the whole. We have divided our whole into you versus me versus, understanding it's always, forever about We—both sides that are now needed. We can never be separated; the power of sacred love is the creative fire of existence itself. Our Sacred Unity!

We are all standing on this bridge today with great opportunity and potential to make the most profound and powerful changes to save our planet and each other. We each must take responsibility, and we each must make sacrifices to create together our new story. We do this for all generations to come. We do this for each other. And, very important, we become humble. Humility meets me daily to bring me down...down...down. The power of sacred love must do this else the human ego rides itself like an inflated balloon. I do believe in timeless love. Perhaps we are soul time travelers! Love finds itself through me, you, the blooms that give sweet nectar and to life itself, breathing the air within to know this love. You come softly, opening my heart with your smile, warmth of touch, and eyes that see into my soul. A remembrance from a time ever immortal itself.

Our Erotic Souls Who Know...

My soul longs for you now. I've tasted many loves
always looking for you. Now
it feels you also search
for me. How will we know it's us...what is that known
recognition that we've finally
found each other?
Do our eyes know, our beating hearts,
or a first touch or kiss? Come
seek me, Beloved...I'm ready but it's you who must say to me...
you are my soul love we've both
long awaited and searched and now I'm here to embrace you
in my open arms. Love keeps me pulsating
from within until somewhere in time
we meet up once more. Our souls time travel,
anticipating our touch, our gaze, our smiles...we always forever
remember. We kiss softly.

We've danced upon subtle floors for eons of time. Occasionally, we've put on a surface skin so to bask in our sensual senses of each's soul again. I love how we remember...now once more we are both here...a larger meaning and purpose as our souls are ready to become aware, awake with other souls to bring about our timeless soul awareness so to take the Earth higher in her knowing, realization and, yet, we get to experience each other bodily as sensual souls too.

Your fingerprint upon my face, your lips slightly open succulent with juicy-like nectar…I tremble in your arms with jubilant anticipation that our souls finally get to explore the sacred love so alive within us both. A love as old as time itself finally coming to be realized through us both. Beloved Source smiles…our souls smile. Our joy is sensually expressed and experienced together.

Wild Again…Beguiled Again…Enough world…I take myself to the woods. Beneath that big old tree, I sit. Now smiling, my friends come to dance me wild again. The sun shines through the tree tops into my heart…the hummingbird flutters all around me, teasing *try to catch me if you can*, while the butterfly lands on my head.

Now they all come to climb into my lap, playfully edging me up to dance along the stream where only love whispers into my heart. One day, the world will awaken to the soundtrack of nature's music, and all shall come together to divinely dance. I return back now to my suffering world to join with our coming together to dance wild love becoming beguiled by our inner soul presence of love.

Chapter 6

Remembering Our Wholeness

"A single event can awaken within us a stranger totally unknown to us.
To live is to be slowly born."
~Antoine de Saint-Exupery

One morning upon waking, a lucid dream hovered, leaving me in tears of its powerful experience. It was a quiet, still morning moving slowly on a boat out upon the sea. I didn't see it coming, then it was there. This giant tsunami moving fast towards us—the boat and my heart both began to shake—no time. When it hovered over us, I felt a moment of stillness, allowing me to see through to some strange otherworld. I knew to let go—I did. Then, with great force, we rode this giant, moving wave onto the shore.

Blinking my eyes, a beautiful sight came into view of a lush green forest, people smiling everywhere while birds flew above many animals, and all were at peace. How did this happen? Did it happen? Could it be this is the miracle of life? We ride out the storms to wake up along a more peaceful shore if we can just let go and trust with a bit of faith. Darkness can't survive for too long, just isn't the way our Beloved invisible presence loves us all. In the beginning was light... then lots and lots of Divine Love to bring everything together on this shore of Earth for all of us to come into existence to keep it all moving towards more love.

We must remember now, we must come back together on this Earth shore to bring back our vibrant light and sacred Divine Love—we have lots of help—remember? Listen, come closer, our souls are whispering!

Come Closer

Humanity has written
many books
and said
God wrote through them.

Yet if We all
are honest, We will come to
see that
God wrote only One book.

This book given
to all of humanity to study,
come to
understand and within this
book was
all the instructions how to live,
ways to live, many
places to live and all means
to live with everyone.

This book is called: Earth!

My grandson said to me, "Mimi, did you know Jesus was a socialist? He fought for the oppressed, fed the poor, healed the sick, spoke only Love, and tore down the temple, where he was witness to priests and politicians controlling the people with propaganda, fear, and control. So would you rather have an authoritarianism, dictatorship, or a democracy of socialism/capitalism?" Hmm! I've been contemplating this a lot.

I want a democracy where we follow the rule of law for the people and by the people and that we also follow the Divine Love and actions of many advanced souls like Jesus and Buddha. Most of the poems and writings throughout this book came from my deep inquiry.

Living with cancer today, a tumor slowly shrinking like my own shadows, my life is being lived stripped and surrendered of everything except Divine Love. This Divine Love has brought awareness that I'm a most beautiful soul now to be lived within this persona of humanness as Divine Love. What a most beautiful revelation! What humble teachings life and death, such close companions, and both to be lived wide awake the gifts of living.

How do we promote anti-corruption principles without shining light on corrupt people? How do we take a stand against hate and separation for what's right, even when risking death, so not to be pulled into corrupt behaviors? These questions are now heavy within my soul. When people march and die for color and gender equality, is this right? And many who hid Jews from the Hitler dictatorship and stood up and against his propaganda that only white lives matter, did they take this higher stand for right and truth from a place deep within them because they knew in their souls that these lies being dictated were wrong? Today, in this year 2022, are we being faced and tested again to remember our truth, our beauty given to us, and our goodness as a means to take down this dark corrupt greed everywhere, trying to take away our soul freedoms?

I sit with these questions today in my heart. Perhaps many of you do too. My sensual soul muses to me, when freedom is taken away from the many, so to give privileges to the few, we need to listen. Writing this, my hands tremble. When our laws were written into our constitution by our early founding fathers, were they listening to a greater, wiser source of fire pulsating through them? We have witnessed people in power over the years where so many leaders have taken away the constitutional powers through their lies, corrupt behaviors, and even when brought forth with proven evidence of their corruption, those in power dismissed these malicious acts so to keep their power. These are both dark and light moments in our history where we are witnessing people stand up to this dark power, risking their lives.

Our Sacred Unity Meets Up with Lost Dark Corrupt Minds

So today, we witness history again being changed. Some are happy believing it means that power over others will give them more money, more control, and a greater means to continue doing whatever they want—to rape the land, rape the people, and own all the wealth. Some are stunned. They question justice and question that our world is sacred anymore. Already they struggle to even survive, and many will give up hope.

But we, the majority, will know this is only the beginning of an end to a long dark civilization and its way of living to use its power over the people to control and abuse for the pursuit of its domination over slaves, the women, and the land itself. It's been a long-held supremacy power that has for eons of time lived to separate everyone and everything by those using their small mind of ego, long separated from their wise, loving soul. The sacred, sensual soul love of this dark civilization has been, for thousands of years, long-buried, deeply within its own closed-off heart. It has long believed its God also separate, and, like them, a dictated power that judges over.

Their believed God is seen also as a punishing and racist God. Their God was imagined and created in their image to be like them to justify all their wars and horrific abuse of others, deemed to be different, for all these thousands of years. Thus, slavery was deemed okay as was the abuse of the Native Americans. Today, this hatred and this dictator way threaten our very Earth and each other. Today, we see the arsenal of nuclear weapons, both external and internal, in their now-reigning power of control over everything.

These insatiable appetites of patriarchy and control, on their banquet table of divide and conquer beliefs, are filled to capacity and dangerous. We must hold with faith and hope this dark today is meeting up with our now-awakened soul-awareness majority of love and light who are willing to stand up to dissolve this dark energy cabal. Yet, we fight with a very different kind of weapon—no weapon! We open our heart portal to fuel our mind/body with its creative fire of our inner essence of sacred Divine soul love, enjoined with Beloved Mystery Presence.

The means of taking on this very dark disease is through the now return of our sacred, wise soul love, within our sacred unity with God. These higher partnerships will bring us all into a higher self species where the small ego persona isn't making the decisions alone but with each's sensual divine soul and enjoined with other higher sensual divine souls. Our power comes from an invisible presence within, sourced by our great mystery, that has created all existence with the many diverse connections and all collaborating within our roots of infinite core Divine Love. We now begin to enter into our miracle of life given to co-create with each other within our sacred unity.

Much of life on Earth depends on the extraordinary dynamics's hidden within the Earth soils in her incredibly complex interrelationships of plant roots, bacteria, fungi, insects, and minerals that make our continued existence above ground possible. This is also true that we depend on the extraordinary dynamics of life hidden within our bodies and minds. These are also complex relationships of atoms, molecules, bacteria, minerals, organs, brain, blood, and so much more making and giving us life. Our heart is our most precious as home of our sensual soul love. It is also true that we depend upon what's above the Earth. The sun, moon, and stars giving light for both Earth and humanity to grow and survive. The clouds to bring forth rain, the air we breathe, and who knows what is still to be discovered in all the galactic dimensions.

Duality's Gift—Our Ability to Choose Sacred Divine Love

Now we ask, what is there to fight about? Isn't it time we give up our immature way the mind uses duality? Duality is quite the gift. We can choose. There are certainly enough religions and spiritual movements available so everyone can choose, then go and be grateful with sacred grace in our heart. Why fight one is better than another. Politics get tricky too and so immature how we can't wait to spend all our time in front of the news channels to become enraged because someone has a different opinion or view. We can make tons of money, but if we feel we need to share or give any away, that becomes the focus and not our gratitude to have money sitting in the bank. Crazy making! Madness! Right?

And then there is the individual who will also use his/her mind in rage someone will take away their rights. Don't you dare say wear a mask or get a vaccination. Don't you dare take any of my millions to pay taxes. Don't you dare say anything about me owning high caliber guns or my right to use them to kill someone disagreeing. We forget rights come with mature, aware responsibility. What would happen if we didn't have a democracy of rules, regulations, and laws? Well, for starters, we women still couldn't vote, people of color would still be slaves, and if you feel it's your right to go out and kill, then too bad—that's your right. This could become quite scary. This is how a few could become the dictators of the many.

Maybe let's contemplate this a bit. Yes, life can be messy, but it's also beautiful. Go back up and read the miracle of us being here by all the deep connections within Earth, us, and above Earth. Doesn't it feel good when you give love? Or when you receive love? We need a good intercessor to help our mind/body always in its separation stories or fight and flight armor. Who is this intercessor but our own loving, wise, sensual soul love to calm our mind. She becomes his partner to not take an "either/side" but to find a third side—the best of each side becomes our way forward.

Where is our sacred soul Divine Love? Is she waiting patiently for us to open our heart to reveal her presence? It is said our small mind ego, once grown up and matured, stops being our enemy to become our loving, sensual soul's ally to experience within form. This ends our separation to begin our partnerships for bringing a more inclusive harmony and balance to our much-divided world. How beautiful! Our internal healing system to these diseases of viruses and wars, separating us all and permeating across the planet, is our sensual, sacred soul wisdom within, and one with our invisible mystery presence. Together, with our mind/bodies, a light is flamed to activate within us to spread into all the lands, and all arising souls for living our sacred unity upon Earth.

Oh, how the mind loves to go into the Disney parks to fantasize with all the characters, yet is afraid to go within our imaginal truth realm for creativity. A place where our soul comes forth to take us out of the park of our immaturity, to grow up the small self-ego and fly us into the imaginal consciousness of our invisible beloved presence, a pure creativity, where all great ideas spring forth to write the book, invent the computer, or introduce us to our higher self soul, who we are.

And remember, our greatest, truest, and most wise authentic self in any story is our own soul, within our sacred Divine Love, to help us live our sacred unity together upon this most beautiful planet given to all us beautiful souls.

So let's go now together into our greater awareness to meet up with our loving source of all creativity that we all emerged from and where we all shall return. Hold my hand, sweet one, and off we go into the imaginal field to plant our seeds of sacred Divine Love. The Earth needs us. When our mind of reason enjoins with our heart of soul wisdom out of our higher field of an invisible presence, our realm of creativity and pure imagination, it frees also the soul of the world and the soul of its people who all now will bring forth our creative fire, beaming from each's heart resonance of vibrating love with our minds of justice and truth that has never been known or felt before.

It's the cosmic Divine Love of all creation. This darkness today, with its disease of hate and control, will not be able to withstand our higher, more inclusive, connecting power of loving truth blazing forth our creative fire of our higher minds in partnership with our loving wise souls.

Only a shift now into our higher vibration of sacred Divine Love will save us. Our sacred partnerships begin our story of sacred unity out of our story of separation. Our sacred Divine Love becomes the fire dissolving the now beliefs and alone minds old stories of divide and conquer. Our inner, invisible presence of love with its illuminating light will restore the lands so loved, our humanity so loved, and our creatures everywhere so loved.

We come to understand our breath of all living breathes from the airways of time immemorial. Our breath inhalation also holds the record of life from its beginnings, and what is breathed back out gets recorded into these airways. The airways of breath must be cleansed and dissolved of all our now darkness so that light can be brought into our innermost being, giving all us sentient beings the needed goodness, truth, and beauty to restore all that is now living and breathing from and into our airways of life. If you hear this and feel this deep within your soul, you are part of the majority to now act in the service of enjoining together with all awakening souls on our Earth planet to heal, restore, and return our world and ourselves into a more sustainable Earth.

Understanding Power Through Internal Sacred Unity

Our democracy was established to become a balance of principles and ideals for both social and capitalist needs. This gives the power to the people to choose their higher representatives for what is needed. Yet, as earlier stated, we need good sacred leaders who don't want to use their power for a few or themselves. We need them as humble servants for the true needs of the country and people. Who has the right to become so powerful that no right of law can stop them? I shudder in my fear, remembering the riots for black and women's freedoms when I was growing up. Are we being asked to stand up for something greater, truer, and more endearing than just a political party today? What's at stake here?

These divisions fighting now are dividing our country, our own families, and like a wildfire, they spread across the oceans to other countries. It's like a virus with no means to stop or control its toxic fears and hate. Even our Earth suffers from these divisions, crying her tears too. Yet, who are to hear these cries but us. Are "We the Ones" now, the majority, to listen, see, and be witness to our climate dangers, hate, and divisive rhetoric on the media, in the many religions, and governments? Small businesses being ousted by large corporations monopolizing the money and becoming greedier. Are we ready to step in like the firefighters to serve and respond?

The Power of our Internal Labor can Transform Humanity/Earth!

We endure labor for something to be born. We study for an exam to become a teacher, nurse or realtor. We endure chemo to cure cancer, or see a therapist to understand our addictions for escaping pain. We build a road through the forest or path up the mountain or we labor through childbirth.

Everything requires some form of labor to manifest some form of new creation. Yet, mostly we do this for an outward creation.

What if We come to understand all the suffering within us also requires some form of labor to be with the suffering and pain we feel. What can our internal suffering teach us if we are willing to be in labor with it? Endure its pain like a childbirth? What if we can become aware and attentive enough to sit with this internal suffering, even ask a close friend to help mid-wife?

Perhaps beneath our suffering there is within us all guidance we never knew there! How do we ever find this loving guidance if we aren't willing to go through the labor for this miraculous birth of who we are?

Divine Love is the creative fire of all ever born and this fire of Love is the only real Love to save us all. One taste and We are forever it's carriers to everything we encounter. We birth and emerge our very own unique soul, higher self. This is who we all are but requires going through the tough labor of surrender of our small self ego, the carrier of suffering.

The alone mind then can enjoin with its inner soul wisdom to come home. This will become the greatest birth ever to be experienced and will be the greatest transformation upon the earth.

We, as a humanity, over millions of years, have become conscious and aware of ourself. Many now are witness to their own minds in dialogue with all its learned beliefs and behaviors. This is another great inner gift we've been encoded with directly within. We've also developed ourself to have greater understanding of our nature/Earth. It's just miraculous how our great loving Mystery Source Presence understood our evolution would reach these tipping points to move us into higher developments, thus emerging our intuitive wise souls to help us enjoin with our minds to further aid their maturity and surrender to a higher sacred unity within sacred partnerships.

When this happens, we don't look to be saved by someone but understand this saving grace is within us, as our great earlier teachers came to teach. It's now our responsibility to go within to begin our higher development, where we confront these dark frozen, repressed, and isolated fears, bringing them into the light for greater truth. By freeing our inner world of half-truths and learned distortion, we then experience us becoming filled with our core sacred origins of who we are. We begin recognizing our beautiful, sensual souls wanting to emerge to restore balance to the distorted alone minds. We don't ascend or transcend these fears, we surrender to them, trusting the healing sacred Divine Love we came from, then we face them one by one to release them. This is done in our depths of our being.

We are now coming home into our unity with Spirit and our soul. We are meeting up to have these loving embodied experiences where Beloved Spirit and our own soul, both now realized in the human awareness, that this is...Who We Are...beautiful souls being guided by our Beloved Spirit and all revealed within the human form. We become a higher species upon the Earth planet, in sacred unity with each other, the Earth, and the cosmic intelligence to guide us all in the Earth's higher realization. This is the planet where us souls, with Beloved Spirit, come to have experiences in the space suit forms to have touch, sight, taste, smell, and an inner realization that always, forever, we are divine beings of our great cosmic life force. What a revelation!

The HeartMath Institute has proven that the more we resonate with loving, kind, and harmonious thoughts and behaviors, the more our mind operates with more connections to our heart/soul, and then our bodies respond with healthy blood pressure, a healthy heart, and internal organs. In other words, everything within is connected with everything without, and once in a more loving, coherent resonance, both inner and outer become more harmonious.

Our sensual soul's love story becomes exciting, knowing through connections and collaborations, with all great leaders, we can share ideas, innovation, and use the gifts of all unique souls for greater creativity. We gain wisdom that helping the Earth in these changing times and helping all of humanity is our way into a more sacred unity. We no longer see anyone or anything as separate because we realize we are all beautifully woven threads in the web of life, each thread needed and loved for its unique contribution.

Our awareness helps wake us each morning to begin acknowledging our invisible presence of sacred love pulsating within us. Our greatest moments can be spent in loving embrace of the gifts given to us while on the Earth for our short stay. Rich moments to experience the sun shining and the moon beaming or a walk among the forest of trees with many scurrying animals. The gift of arms hugging us through family, friends, or a sweet lover. Our awareness to know our greatest Divine Love is within us always, forever.

Mahatma Gandhi says, "Power is of two kinds. One is obtained by the fear of punishment and the other by acts of love. Power based on love is a thousand times more effective and permanent than the one derived from fear of punishment."

In this book, you will be reading the words Divine Love over and over. You will read how our presence of sacred Divine Love is to be experienced directly within then without, once you have courage and faith to open your heart and allow yourself to become vulnerable and transparent to directly feel everything. You see, once we've all tasted and felt our soul essence, who we are, souls of sacred Divine Love, never will we have an appetite for anything less. So repetition is to help keep us all in awareness within our heartfelt space. Sacred Divine Love then becomes our highest vibration, encoded within us and the Earth. It's time to sing our soul song; it has the activating power to wake us all.

There is a song
in my soul.
No one is listening. There is a tear in my eye.
No one sees its sadness.
There is a loneliness
in my heart. No one feels it anymore.
Yet, my
soul, my tear, my sadness, my loneliness are
within you too.

We all share this. When my song
is enjoined with your song, we create a choir, when
my tear is enjoined with your tear, we create
an ocean to adventure,

and when our loneliness is shared, we create a larger
circle to bring forth friendship and dance.
We need each other.
Amazing, isn't it, our waves of energy pulsating through us.
Never are we separated...ever!
We are the creative fire of soul, loving presence.

A loving meditation and visualization daily for me is to close my eyes, then to visualize my heart wide open. There is a stairway leading out for me to take a few steps each morning to sit upon and just be present within this all-knowing and all-powerful and all-embodying, invisible presence of sacred love that has created this all-encompassing reality. From invisible to visible...from energy to matter...from the smallest single cell to multi-celled organisms like us. How can this be? I am so humble this creative One lives through me.

Returning into the other side of my open heart, there is this always now light shining, Divine Love flowing, and ongoing inspiration helping me write, serve others through my work, family, and to serve with my greater unity awareness, gained from sitting on that stairway into the infinite expansion of my own beloved/soul loving consciousness to forever live each moment and experience within this invisible presence, source of all. I bow in humble awe. Fear is replaced with original pure, core, sacred Divine Love. Imagine our inclusive Earth as a large island that's emerged in the middle of the cosmic ocean.

Only those who
have given up their minds
lived in separation
can come to live.

Only those with love
in their hearts, kindness in
their actions, and
smiles on their faces will
be able to survive in
the peaceful airs and soils.

Come with a
backpack filled with your
compassion as your
admittance and you will be greeted in Divine Love.

This is the island called Unity of Sacred Earth!

Understanding How Stress Awareness Invites Spirit Awareness

On our Earth today, we blame everything and everyone for the world's problems without ever looking within ourselves. We are so controlled by our learned behaviors and beliefs that to bear the pain of our deeper yearning for our soul's return, we numb this pain through the use of many addictions to distract. Today, not only is fear the mechanism that keeps the conditioned personality controlled, but these addictions are another power that fuels and controls the personality. So we must Be patient…Be resilient…Be aware that we become empowered with right choice!

The great Indian Saint Kabir warned that if we can't love while here in our bodies, do we believe we will die and find this love elsewhere? He says, "If you don't break your ropes while you're alive, do you think ghosts will do it after?" Bodies and ego personas die, but it's our souls, often unrealized in their Divine Love while in the body, that travels in great sadness. Kabir says, "Listen, my friend. He who loves understands."

Stress emits into the body a low-grade fear that produces the energy cortisol. This low-grade energy over time wears the body down, and eventually, the disease shows up as a result. What can get us through is living from a place of loving surrender! Dr. Marc Schoen, psychologist and faculty member at UCLA's Geffen School of Medicine, has written a book, *Your Survival Instinct is Killing You*. What does he mean? He says, "My book is all about fear." He goes on to explain how many do not realize and recognize, or simply are unaware, that "the stress response really emanates from a fear response." Today, Dr. Schoen states that many of us live in chronic stress, causing panic attacks, anxiety disorders, depression, headaches, and probably the most frightening of all, deadly addictive behaviors. These addictive behaviors cause us to reach for a drug of choice to give us a few hours of experiencing something other than fear.

More deaths happen as a result of overdoses from these drugs because it takes more and more of the drug to give them the high of something bigger than their fear. We are living out of our survival limbic brain structure. This structure is only there to give us what is needed to survive under such circumstances as burning houses, car accidents, or tornadoes. These are true survival conditions, not conditions that are mere feelings of discomfort from what he calls agitance, a chronic state of misalignment. We aren't able to relax because we are multitasking watching television, texting, answering emails, and living a big part of our lives on social media. We cannot relax. He says we've become agitance junkies. We demand perfection—a black and white world. But what is touched and felt in the drug world is a taste of feeling something very familiar. We just aren't aware enough to understand that this is our deeper home of grace, of sacred love without all the conditions that create the fear and chronic stress in the first place.

Jesus healed through inviting each's sacred love and grace to emerge within him and the other. This greater power witnessed often messages the body's own self-healing system. Our bodies are coded to self-heal, given the right energies pulsating through it.

This is our natural drug, present already within each of us. No, not everyone heals, yet, that mystery can offer many reasons why healing is not just body healing but the trinity of body, mind, and energy emotions flowing through the body and the soul, our soul often denied. Let's explore this further.

My academic background is in counseling. I didn't follow a traditional counseling path, deciding instead to follow a more holistic path. Intuitively, I felt leaving out a spiritual component, along with the mind/body component, was incomplete. I worked out of my home, trusting my services would find their way to the right people, and that is exactly what happened. Let me share two stories of how miraculous healing works in different ways.

A man was referred to me who was forty-one years old. He had been diagnosed with a deadly lung cancer and given three to six months to live. He was told to have chemotherapy, along with a few other treatments to help hopefully slow down his cancer, giving him a few more months to live. He came to see me so to learn meditation and visualization to help with the stress he and his family felt.

That first day, he and his wife sat in my home and shared his story. It was soon clear to me that he had given over his power to his diagnosis and consigned himself to his soon death. I shared with him my belief that no one can be sure when they will die, even the doctors who give timelines around a diagnosis. I went on to state the body, like life itself, is a mystery but has an incredible ability to self-heal.

We then talked about connections and how our thoughts and beliefs become live emotional energies moving through the body. I invited him to see his body vessel as a ship where he could become the navigator of his body's moving vessel. I empowered him to use his visualizations and quiet meditative time to bring light and loving energy to his cancer now invading his vessel. We worked together in this way, but I also encouraged him to explore other alternative healing modalities too.

His entire being began to transform as he shifted his perspective, and through months of meditation and powerful imagery, his own healing grace began to emerge as he took back his power to co-serve in his healing. Today, he has been free of cancer for over twenty-five years. He has gone on to be an inspiration to so many battling cancer and their loss of a deeper connection to our greater Source Mystery. He found the creative fire of his soul, loving presence.

My next story is about healing, where the body continues to be diseased, but the creative fire of soul love presence emerges to heal in other powerful ways. When meeting John (not his real name), he also had been given the dreaded diagnosis of cancer. That first day, listening to his story, it became clear how most of his life had been lived through skepticism about any greater source within or without of the separate self. He lived the separation story. Now, here he sat riddled with overwhelming stress and fear. He was dying and void of any means to deal with that fact. His fear of dying, quite evident to me, was due to his powerful belief and conditioning that he was alone. Alone that within him was just a deadly disease and fear.

I shared that our time together was to just help him connect to his deeper soul loving essence, that greater invisible presence of grace that would become his loving companion through the months ahead of chemo and other treatment. Of course he was skeptical of this but was willing to try anything. Thus, we began our journey together, where my role was just to introduce him to the sacred unity within himself. His own loving soul presence enjoined with Beloved Mystery presence.

I knew that once beloved presence and his sensual soul emerged, this powerful source of love would soon be his inner experience, helping him to surrender his long-held beliefs and fears that he was a separate small self. He was told his life expectancy was six months to a year. Yet, he lived almost three years past that time. What is miraculous about John's healing, even though his body did transition, is he died peacefully, unafraid of being alone.

He slowly surrendered to trust and faith of a more sacred loving presence where he felt safe within this cocooning within and with his own soul, loving presence. In those three years, John lived life more alive and more in love with life, and others, than in the almost fifty years prior. He had found not only the connection to greater grace and a sustaining loving presence within himself, but this grace flowed outward to touch everyone. He taught and further fueled my anchor to never doubt the power of the loving sacred unity in dwelling within all things—this powerful interconnectivity that is pure movement in and between all life. He didn't believe for a moment in the end that it was the end. He was almost excited to move into this next mystery of life. From time to time, a deeply felt presence of his soul enters into my soul being…smiling.

Living today with a cancerous tumor in my breast, I've become aware my cancer may heal and my life continue for a long time, or soon death may greet me. Yet, each day for me will be lived fully alive in Divine Love with everyone and in every action in service to be given. Death is not the end. My out-of-body experiences meeting up with my soul gave to me proof to come back and do all my inner shadow work for integrating and embodying my small persona ego mind/body with my soul. Cancer just further reminded me of my surrender to finish whatever cleaning up or growing up to be done. Writing this book is part of my service work to be given. Humble gratitude fills me to have lived each moment in Divine Love to have had these precious experiences upon this Earth. I also know my return is a possibility. Everything is still possible, as poet David Whyte writes.

Physicality gives formless, invisible presence means to experience and expresses through the form. Bodies become like instruments to see through to you and you to me. We learn through each other how to use touch. A soft touch brings pleasure while a harder one often brings pain. We learn how playing through our instruments what sounds another finds soothing and another finds irritating. We learn differences in how so many instruments can play so many notes, but not all notes work together. We learn vibrational sound through the many varieties of notes being played within and without. My note is pleasing to some, but not to all.

This poem gives understanding when surrendering to live within our sacred unity presence.

You open my heart each morning,
filling me with your Presence of
Love. Flowing through my being
like a calm river without ripples.

Yet, I can't see you other than the
trees through the window, the sun

filtering through the leaves, or the
small hummingbirds fluttering their
wings.

I hear the soft sounds and smell
the coffee brewing, but none can
fill the gaps of my yearning for
touching the forehead of your
face.

I want to touch you and feel arms
holding me. I want to kiss you to
melt away all my longings. This is
the most subtle pain between us.

Our unique expressions have an opportunity and potential to become fully grown up into their highest, most loving frequency meeting other vibrations of higher frequency where this formless loving, caring, and sound vibration looks upon its creation as a most beautiful orchestra and smiles it is good…it is true…it is most beautiful. When playing in the denser levels of energy frequencies, we live only through the ego. When we learn to increase our energy vibration through awareness, we move into higher, more subtle soul vibrations and hence the two shall meet to become integrated within the highest vibration mystery love. Wow! Writing this, my vibration is dancing so alive within my sensual, soul, loving presence.

Maria Rilke says, "Have patience with everything unresolved in your heart and to try to love the questions themselves as if they were locked rooms or books written in a very foreign language. Don't search for the answers, which could not be given to you now, because you would not be able to live them. And the point is to live everything. Live the questions now. Perhaps then, someday far in the future, you will gradually, without even noticing it, live your way into the answer."

Our greatest gift encoded within is our sacred Divine Love. When we open our hearts, no matter what is happening and this love is present, then God is present too. When our relationship of him—mind—enjoins with her—soul—we become activated with our sacred Divine Love to have the highest vibration needed in all relationships. Our gift of encoded sacred senses activate all our human senses too as the ego persona has finally surrendered its separation from everything. It is the activation of our sacred senses that begins our soul's awareness and her awakening to live as a higher species beyond just a human small self ego. This becomes our means of great liberation within and without to live as sacred souls through the sensual forms on the Earth planet.

Divine Love is made visible in our actions to give to each other and to give to our beautiful Earth, who has waited with great patience for our higher self to tend her. That which gets triggered must get seen within awareness so to not project its toxicity but instead inject the love from our higher soul, born out of invisible presence, helping us to dissolve the deeper, unconscious pains and stress traumas lived in these soils of our humanness for too long. Our sacred soul Divine Love within awareness activates the keys to our encoding. We then open to Divine loving presence guiding us.

Chapter 7

Many Teachers of Non-separation:

"This is the first, wildest and wisest thing I know, that the soul exists,
and that it is built entirely out of attentiveness."
~Mary Oliver

"Your own soul is your guru, quiet the mind
and listen to your higher self."
~Ram Dass

"All I know for certain is that a good God creates and continues to create
an ever-good world, by enticing it back into the place where it began."
~Richard Rohr

Awareness as Teacher

I've been an observer of my mind and its thoughts for years. It's humorous, scary, and often humble. My sensual soul awareness shows how easy we become addictive to beliefs, distortion, all-out conspiracy, and each's ideology's in the political and religious arenas.

My most amazing discovery is how our alone mind takes an either-or position. This, of course, explains polarization and the concept of duality. It further helps to explain how thousands of years ago, humanity fell into the story of separation.

The story of separation says, *I am here, you are over there, God is somewhere out there as is the universe and the Earth too.* Everything and everyone is separate, and these stories are told with beliefs formed out of these separation stories. We are taught to take sides. We, sadly, don't listen to another's side. When we listen, we come to know a third side. This helps us understand how to be compassionate and to be able to empathize with others. It also opens us to much creativity as we need both sides. We begin the moving once more, the evolving of our development.

Many wars were fought, prejudice was taught, and judging came naturally as God and love came to be whatever side of the heart wall we built to live within.

Thus, today, billions of people, all living in diverse cultures and with different types of skin color and gender are in these ongoing wars of separation inside walls of hate for those on the other side of the wall. And depending on your money, power, and belief, equality is often determined by which "either/or side" is your wealth status.

It's Not Such a Wonderful World We Live Today

What is missing that possibly could unite us? Let's really contemplate this. We all could go tumbling off this divide unless we find a means, purpose, and deep caring and compassion for all of us. What is it that we all need together that's not separate? Because if we don't find the means to live on this one Earth for our short stay, we all will become responsible for its demise—and ours.

For me—and my prayer is you will resonate with me—our sensual soul Divine Love presence is missing. She is our wisdom to our mind gone astray, and it's all-out nuclear. She is the means and end to bring us back home into our garden Earth home. What brings her back within us all is to open back our closed heart wall to allow her

144

wise Divine Love, our innate gift from our One Mystery, and called by many names all over the Earth, to directly live within our heart.

She becomes our greater loving awareness within us to have this vision to witness all the ways so to help us become the most beautiful way to live.

We must today go within for our greatest journey into our own hearts. We must begin the dissolving of all the old walls of distortions and beliefs around our separation story, too long lived, so we each begin to invite our creative fire of soul, loving presence back within our open hearts, helping us to create a more inclusive story with each other to live in more harmony upon the Earth.

Many great teachers have all shared that when we open our eyes of light to see each other in our radiating colors, with all the many perspectives and ideas, then we begin creating together soul partnerships all over the world. We save us and we save the Earth. Today, go sit in nature, perhaps, watching our greatest show on Earth…the sunrise or sunset. It rises and it sets for us all. The oceans, mountains, rivers, earth soils, and streams for us all. The sweetness of the animals and birds for us all. What a divine creation given to us all from a cosmic mystery within universes and galaxies extending beyond us, yet, we are a vital part.

Let's now all give back with the greatest gift given to us all—the innate gift of our Divine Love. Let's open our hearts to invite our wise souls back home. When we do, we see once more with our soul's light. No more separation!

If we could just take a moment to realize we all are plugged into one creation…one Core Love…and this can be likened to many breaths, breathing one air.

145

Becoming more aware and attentive to understanding that we are all likened to lightbulbs, plugged into one current giving us life, we begin to make choices about life for the highest good for all. We become more aware of our sacred unity from this higher activation. We are plugged into our creative fire of soul, loving presence that begins to melt all our learned separation and small ego individualism to become each's own unique soul essence. Our persona then co-partners to become empowered through our soul with our creative fire of Divine Love.

Death-Rebirth of an Alone Mind Ego Embodies Many Teachers

My soul gives whispers, helping me to understand that another great gift we are given is called our inner, innate strength of small will, which when used through our mind/soul/body integration, it gives even greater realization that we must dissolve this wrong separation story creating all our suffering. By becoming inner-attentive, this begins expanding my soul awareness, giving to me her wise counsel how to use my inner, innate small will, empowering me how to change for the higher good, truth, and beauty to live.

Our inner and outer teachers can give wise information or they just ramble junk propaganda. Awareness, being attentive, and using my will to discern opens small will to partnership with my soul wisdom. This helps me to process the stream of emotions to give good understanding or just seeing them as false triggers of junk. My body, also a great teacher, in its small aches or deeper somatic pains, gives great information and signs again of either wise information or tied to the mind and its emotional junk. Let's take a closer look!

First, let's explore awareness and who is aware? Not my thoughts as they often continue regardless of who's watching. Not my emotions as they can also continue even when observed. And not my body's pain as it also has no idea anyone is observing them. This is a partial truth we also must inquire into.

Awareness is my close companion. Who's aware? Some say higher self, some say no self. For me, she is my soul, true self. She, as awareness, just pays close attention to everything now within the mind/body/form, but she also observes everything external. This witnessing, along with her intuitive whispers, slowly shifts the small will mind with all its perceptions, emotions, and deep feelings. How, we ask? The simplest explanation is that awareness is no longer attached or identified in the direct experience as the thought. A gap begins to emerge between awareness and thought. For example: in this gap, awareness watches the mind with its ongoing thoughts, then further observes how these thoughts create the emotions within the body from these thoughts. An embodied understanding begins to arise.

Judging our thoughts often creates anger, guilt, shame, or blame. Loving awareness of our thoughts often create emotions of tender warm feelings flowing through, relaxing the body and wanting to have these deeper connections with our soul awareness and all happening within the form. When we judge out of a small separate will, we contract within, creating tight muscles and a more rapid heartbeat. With loving aware thoughts, just the opposite. The small will begins to listen to this soul loving essence. Something within begins to shift as this emerges out of our true soul self awareness. We begin to feel a higher loving divine presence arising within us, and we seek within to have this loving felt experience more and more. Once Divine Love is felt directly, our awareness says *Yes!*

My awareness and loving presence now feel closely connected. Being attentive brings this insight to me. Surrender and death of feeling separate, in its earlier stages, feels like an existential crisis. We meet up with many dark nights of our soul as she helps bring forth many shadows and ghosts of our past. We stay the course because soul, loving presence is now activated, guiding to slowly move into a greater reality and becoming more integrated within myself as my alone beastly mind feels into her beauty as my wise soul.

When we take time each morning and each evening to become still, quiet, and become open to our own soul awareness within ourselves, a higher felt experience of a greater loving presence will often begin to emerge enjoined with our soul, loving presence.

We stay with this flow each day to where we begin to shift, becoming our higher loving, soul awareness. It's likened to a death and rebirth. This begins to shift us within and changes everything to live our soul essence through this higher state of our awareness. Intuitive guidance will also emerge through from our soul and Mystery Divine Presence. Our teachers will begin showing up internally and externally. Our soul wisdom, through her direct awareness within us, teaches our alone separate, small will mind that it's time to integrate back into sacred loving partnerships within us so to live within our sacred unity, attracting soul partnerships externally.

Just try for a while sitting both morning and evening to see what may emerge for you. The good, bad, and ugly will first arise—our shadows—but it's okay, just witness everything, allowing all to peek through. Try keeping your heart open to allow a greater presence of love to arise too. Keep letting it all flow through within Divine Love so eventually most will also flow out to dissolve. Our thoughts, emotions, and feelings, remember, have been repressed and stored for much too long and all want release. Often, current thoughts and emotions too will come to be witnessed. Be aware to let them too.

Don't hold on to anything. All is needing to flow up so to be held in the arms of your soul, loving presence, enjoined with our one

Beloved Mystery presence. We have much loving guidance within this higher consciousness, loving field, all wanting to bring us back into our freedom. To be free is to be still in Divine Love! This is our surrender of all not inclusive in soul, loving presence within beloved presence. This will take time. Be patient. Remember we are in labor! If my small ego self can do this, so can your small ego self. This is the waking-up process to our soul's emergence, here to assist our alone separate ego's growing up and maturing. What flows from thoughts, emotions, and sensations, just allow so they don't get stuck. Soul, loving presence assists this.

So awareness, we can say, is not the body/mind/emotions. Yet, all is within this consciousness awareness. Awareness, then, is our living essence within and around the human form. This comes from my direct experience, but also from reading of other's direct experience too. We have the science of thousands of subjective experiences to validate pure awareness within consciousness.

For me, this alive awareness is sensual soul me. If I give to my mind/body/emotions an identity called ego, then perhaps this awareness, the real me, is my true identity, as sensual soul, loving presence. My direct out-of-body experience introduced me to my sensual soul, loving presence, and when awakening back into my body form, everything changed.

My gift of direct soul experience removed all separation and fear!

My loving soul emerged one evening when in a trance-like state of in between, not fully asleep or awake. A noise coming from my office just across the hall from my bedroom startled me. Getting up, believing myself awake, my feet went to touch the floor only to discover there was no gravity. My subtle soul energy body began floating out of the bedroom like a butterfly floating through the air.

When reaching the end of my bed, me soul turned to see the physical body still in the bed. Strangely, this didn't concern me at all. Floating across the hall and upon entering the office, a very dark shadow of a person came hurling at me. With great force, my subtle hand pulled back, then thrust it into the shadow, sending it floating out of the office window.

Standing there for a few seconds, it became clear to move forward, then float through the window. As this happened, the window became a fluid transparency like my subtle light body, easily allowing me to pass through into the night sky. Observing myself floating through the window, my cells and molecules just became a non-solid transparency. Once outside, subtle, sensual soul me began to fly.

There are no words to write or offer here to describe that moment of pure freedom and boundless, infinite love. My pure awareness of me soul. Flying higher and around the city, my voice sang the most beautiful song. Telepathically, my inner soul voice whispered *This is our loving soul song.* It was a melody unlike any ever heard, and the words unlike any in my language. Wanting to remember this song and its words, my soul whispered to begin our writings. *Through our writings*, she says, *this will become our love song being sung as our sensual soul love story.*

It became clear that my small persona separate self must humbly surrender to something so much bigger and greater known as pure sacred Divine Love. Presence of love emerging from within and all around me was unlike any love ever known to me. Sacred Divine Love is and always will be the way life is to be lived upon the Earth. This was our song sung! From that powerful, lucid, more-real state—one unlike any ever experienced in my normal dense-like state—my soul's emergence began my transformation. This happened over twenty-five years ago. I died to be reborn.

Even all my out-of-body travels, still happening, and a near-death experience as a child, nothing came close to this experience. My clarity gained from my ability to witness and directly experience Me, Soul Divine Love, beyond my body and small personality, grew within an expanded awareness and higher realization within me. This awareness and witness, soul me, became my life...who I Am...who we all are, as my story is just one of so many stories being shared today, similar in each's unique experience. I'm guided and told this is to be all our story if we so choose. Imagine this:

The Transformative Butterfly Effect

We ask, how do we shift planet Earth from its separation story and its now war raging divisions within our now humanity?

Remember the butterfly effect? When souls begin emerging from their cocoon of small self ego minds into their higher and greater soul aware authenticity, it creates a higher vibrational of light felt frequencies upon the Earth, activating many souls now ready to emerge.

This becomes likened to a butterfly effect to sweep across the planet until the entire lower density of gross frequencies begin vibrating into a more subtle light frequency birthing and arising our soul divine species to now begin living this higher Divine Love and life upon the Earth.

It's all quite beautiful how our Divine Mystery has evolved this Earth from its very beginnings—in Earth time, we believe long and arduous but in cosmic time just hours ago! Be ready, our time of Divine Love and light is now being activated. Tensions already being felt as these two vibrating frequencies meet, creating this great birth but also exposing these lower dark, still-cocooned frequencies unable to survive within higher Divine loving frequencies. Stay focused as best each can in our bigger Divine Love story emerging while doing each's work of surrendering the old separation story!

My awareness began giving to me a vision and directness of knowing I Am not my mind/body form lying in that bed. So who Am I? I am she who is witnessing and floating through the room and seeing the body lying in bed. I am more alive as this creative fire of soul Divine loving presence within this transparency than ever experienced in the dense form. Breathing in…breathing out. This is life for all of us. Many aren't aware…but many are. Being curious around my own breath brings me closer to my subtle, light soul presence breathing me. What, who, and how? Perhaps we may never know why!

Perhaps these questions circle within your mind too. Today, answers still aren't concrete, yet, the true miracle is my loving soul presence is melting so much of my seemingly felt separation from all life. How we all breathe in this one life force is in the same way. Why it happens remains mysterious too—it just does. But I share with you a loving relationship began to form between me and this alive loving presence breathing me in every moment, in every experience, until it became the most natural and loving partnership in my life. My new story beginning! And is teaching and helping me through the cancer in how the body or mind can become diseased but my soul free of any and all diseases. I'm guided how to even divinely love this cancer in helping to heal. It's all quite extraordinary and keeps me ever aware and humble of how the human form is so vulnerable and fragile.

My old pain began dissolving, and old memories slowly faded away. What remains today is living my very ordinary human life in more beautiful, soulful, extraordinary ways, both within and without as my inner presence of Divine Love. This gift is meant for all of us. I write to share my experiences so you know this is possible for you too. We are all unique souls living unique experiences through unique mind/body forms. Inner awareness and attention awakens this realization and is our means to begin receiving our gifts of inner guidance, emerging from our Divine Love's creative fire.

Teachers with their wisdom come in unique ways to guide us all through more intimate and intuitive, moment-to-moment breaths, giving us so many meaningful and purpose-filled ways to live. We become the change by making the choice to change our separation story to a more sacred unity story.

We begin to trust and have faith in this most beautiful way to live. We surrender to our inner path, taking us to live all our moments of life force breaths externally, and we do this with great Divine Love because, truth is, We are Divine Love. All of us are beautiful souls having these amazing human, ordinary experiences in all the many unique ways We each can serve this Love, to make our existence and the Earth a more loving, peaceful place we live.

We just forget, getting caught up in all our human separation stories. But we can all wake up. We can become aware of our alive inner soul essence that breathes us all. All of us then will vibrate out this Divine Love so we co-create together a more loving world with our inner awake soul, loving presence, one with our Mystery Presence, that breathes us all in a subtle stillness, just waiting to love us.

If an ordinary country girl like me can have this most extraordinary loving partnership within me, with this power of Divine Love, so can you. Do I still experience human pains and suffering? Yes! Cancer keeps me very aware and humble about how the human form suffers. What's different is having my partner of soul, loving presence within me to help me through these tough, rough moments. I'm never alone. And if you decide to enter into your awareness within you, to meet up with your unique, soul, loving presence, never will you be alone either. We come from this great mystery of love to live this love as awakened souls, in human form, before taking our final breath to release the form back into the Earth, then we souls return back through our subtle light into our next beginnings. Death is simply a new beginning to begin a new story!

Early one morning, feeling sad, a message from my soul to Beloved was sent, then this Divine Love resounded through me. So powerful, so beautiful, and so intimate and intuitive.

Dear Beloved,
We dance to the rhythm of your Presence of Divine Love.
Yet, I keep stumbling.

Dear Soul,
Remember whenever you stumble, I am always, forever here to catch you.

I am a beautiful, sensual soul, loving presence living in transparent, subtle light energy and the gross body form is within me. As a subtle light soul being, my ability can easily move within and without all form. I am here to bring forth, with other awakened souls, a new story created out of our inclusive soul Divine Love and sourced out of our great mystery's creative fire of core love.

Upon returning from my out-of-body experience, back into the dense body form, with all its mind and body sufferings, there began many long dark nights of mutating old stories and old frozen energies so to help transfigure the human dense body to hold me soul and Beloved within its more beautiful, loving, subtle light energies. My heart grail became the new gravitational field of pure Love, holding me, sensual soul, within the form. My inner work continues right up to today in the year 2022 as me, sensual soul, with Beloved and now-integrated personality are partnering together as a team of core loving energies. If you are reading this, you are also part of our emerging soul love story—our sacred unity!

We are the ones here on this Earth planet, at this most critical time in its history, to help shift consciousness back into its greater resonance of a higher, more unified field, where each of us play our unique part as awakened souls of loving presence. My deep understanding of my out-of-body soul experience must be what it's like at death when we transition from form to a subtle form—a love so sweet and tender in its felt experience that you never want to part from it. And I didn't.

I don't remember returning into my body, but when my eyes opened, tears were streaming down my cheeks, wanting to experience this again. My realization of the dark shadow met in my office was that it was the conditioned, separate personality—all the dark issues and wounds soon for me to dissolve and surrender. I've had several out-of-body experiences, but none that captures this moment of pure bliss and ecstasy. Over the years, this experience continues to hold me in its intensity, knowing me, my sensual soul, loving presence is here living within Beloved Love and all within this mind/body form. And never, never has it dimmed in its ability to bring that loving Grace right into my heart. But even more important, for me, was the direct experience of being in my soul subtle, sensual body, giving to me the faith and proof that we don't really die.

We transition out of the dense form into the lightness of being of our subtle soul love form.

And—this is so important—we have the higher energies here now to plug into this higher source to begin our movement out of a mere ego like chrysalis, conditioned separate personas into a higher self of who we are—a beautiful, sensual soul, loving presence. Awareness is now the key gift to bring forth our sensual soul Divine Love. When we can become ever expanded within our soul awareness, our innate small will morphs into our higher self soul will. Remember, our soul's will is already in oneness with our beloved presence of God, thus, bringing forth to activate our integration of our trinity. One Divine Loving Presence living through the mind/body/soul temple container.

A poem emerges to guide me closely within my awareness:

We are but moments of breath
in time.
Many live for decades, some don't!
My last breath
in a week, perhaps years…

What's now important?
So much time in a fast pursuit of so many things…
How much Love
did I hold in my heart?
Did I care enough? Did I notice enough sunsets,
Smiles, and
how many of my breaths cried?

I am noticing today!
I am gazing into your eyes…
I want to meet your soul! This way,
when my last breath taken,
it's all you beautiful souls I take with me!

Our Souls time travel to meet up again and again...I now look closely for you!

For me now, it's only mystery, the unknown, but a more awake and grown-up personality of me deeply trusts this unknown mystery and has learned to flow with its loving grace taking me to experience my life in such a way of aliveness—alive to life and its precious gift of experience within space/time and the use of the senses to have this most awe-inspiring, humble experience as sensual soul me. Sadly, our development from birth became aborted from its original intent. The Mind/Body Container is for our Soul, loving presence.

This great truth and realization ends separation from God Mystery, each other, and the Earth. We become humble to know we are all here to serve our soul Divine Love, to tend each other and the Earth. We are here to develop and evolve to become each's unique soul, loving presence within forms to have use of the mind/body for using the sensual senses for amazing experiences.

Today, the most important is to experience soul loving partnerships with each other and the beautiful Earth, as an Earth home, and be grateful with grace to be here for our short stay to tend, care, cooperate, and collaborate for the good, truth, and eternal beauty for all. This is our meaning and purpose to be here. So us humans, please, we must wake up into our presence of soul love awareness so we can grow up into our soul maturity, then we clean up our actions so we can start showing up with each other together to begin our co-creating together our soul's new inclusive story. We are not separate!

We mustn't wait too long—for the first time, we don't have much time—the Earth is sick, humans are sick, and soon we may be too late. The tension created from severe toxic polarization will have its tipping point. We must become our higher Presence of Soul Love awareness now so to change our course trajectory!

The big lie is everywhere today in this chaos but, perhaps the biggest big lie is the story of separation from God, each other, and our Mother Nature that none of us could live without. Once we wake up from this big lie, then truth will naturally come to be lived in our inclusive Earth and cosmic world too. We live within our sensual soul, loving presence.

God/Goddess has returned back to the Earth garden with his/her loving family.

The practice is simple—be aware to paying attention in every moment and breath to being in Divine Love with your Soul, Loving Presence within and without. Trust me, this Presence of Divine Love is always, forever there…we must Be Aware…we must Pay Attention!

My judgments can become compassion. Compassion seeks to understand beneath the judgments. My anger can get expressed, then surrendered. We can forgive. Why carry it further? My sadness can become partnered with my joy, each taking turns leading the moment-to-moment living. My dog dies, bringing sadness, but a small sock is found that he chewed, bringing me back into smiles of joy.

Our sensual soul teaches us how to live in spontaneity. She teaches us to become like innocent children again. We see what is in front of us—not behind us—we see with fresh eyes, we hear the wind blowing, we touch the newborn seedling, and we feel intensely the day will soon be over. We trust, as Rilke says, that the answers will come. We live the moments from one breath to the next breath. This is how our sensual soul love story seeks its beginnings.

Death as our great teacher!

Death is another conditioned belief, mostly to deny or not think about it. It may happen to others, but not me. Until, of course, we are faced with the death of someone we love or our death. But, sadly, what we never really consider is that we are all walking around like death zombies daily. We live in fear of anything and everything that's not familiar or in our conditioned, programmed environments. We are afraid of flying, climbing a mountain, rafting down a river, or taking a chance on a new job versus remaining in a job we hate. We fear leaving a marriage or relationship where love is conditioned upon us, changing to meet someone else's expectations or our needing them to change to meet our beliefs and expectations.

I am going to die; I just don't know when, how, or where. There is that fear of opening this door called death for so many, but until we do, life can never be completely lived.

Cancer has opened this door for me. I may die in a year or in twenty-five years. I live within the invitation to not know, always listening and being invited to possibly know someone and a life never before known. This inner doorway beneath, all once believed, is knocking so I'm listening closely. I'm born from the miraculous to hear from invisible whispers uncoiling—invisible arms now holding me.

The only cure for grief is to deeply allow ourselves to grieve! And because we don't explore death to understand that death is an ongoing happening of a moment-to-moment surrender to live life fully and freely, we become trapped in the fear of its movement of change and uncertainty, in and out of one reality into another.

My dear friend Richard Brendan, Hospice Chaplain and former JourneysFire Podcasts, shares, "Let me fall into love with all that is. Let me see all as sacred. Let me see with a loving heart. Let me see that God is in all things. When Saint Francis walked the hills of Assisi, he stopped in front of a cherry tree, and he said, "Oh, little tree, speak to me of God." And the little tree burst into bloom. Soften my eyes so I can see we are all blossoms of God. Make my eyes so tender that whenever I watch the moon at night, or whenever I witness a sunset, or see the heron along the river, or whenever I look on those right before me, I see God looking back at me."

Life gives us many realities such as jobs, marriages, passages of life, and so many other life transitions, but the biggest change and uncertainty around death is the transition of leaving the body. My mom's death taught me so much. She had no fear of dying, but in the end, she felt trapped and controlled as to how she was to live. She was almost ninety-four and lived all her life mentally and physically, for the most part, fully living her life. Her strong spirit and soul illuminated her being. Love flowed from her essence to everyone. One day, she began having lower back pain, and it became harder for her to get up and out of a chair and bed. She walked with a walker, but after falling one day, she could no longer manage by herself.

After a week in the hospital, an MRI revealed she needed surgery if she was to ever walk again. It was determined she wouldn't survive surgery, and she was taken to a nursing home for rehabilitation. She began to refuse food and only did the physical therapy because her insurance wouldn't pay otherwise. My stepdad was unable to care for her at home, or so he felt, and she was determined she wouldn't live with what little time she had left in a nursing facility. By the time I arrived, it was clear to me she was waiting for me to help her leave her body. It was as though since she brought me into the world, I was to help her leave the world.

This would prove to be one of the hardest experiences ever given to me. I wanted her to live, but my soul felt her soul and knew she was ready to make that journey back into Grace. I also knew my stepdad would not be in alignment, at least at first. So both our internal soul forces were guiding, within my mom and myself, for assisting her death, while external forces wanted to prolong her transition through drugs and other means. Every day, her energy dropped as she refused food. On my first day of arrival, the first thing she said to me, "I know you understand. I have lived a great life, and now I am ready to go home." The sadness of losing her in the body form was hard, yet, my soul understood she would never be lost to me. Every day, I sang to her "Somewhere Over the Rainbow" and read to her beautiful passages and quotes she loved. We did this for almost three weeks.

My children came to be with her, and her favorite thing to do with us was to play a card game called spades. She was so weak, but she wanted to get dressed and go out on the porch in the sun and play one last hand of spades. Like the game bridge, you bid your hand according to how many tricks you can win. She bid eight out of thirteen possible tricks to win. We all looked at each other in amazement, but she played that hand like a pro, making her bid and leaving us in awe. She clearly was living her life right to the end.

She then, with equal grace, asked to be taken back to her bed. A week later, she died. The night before her body quit breathing, we lay together, where my sad voice sang and shared with her some of my most painful hidden desires. She listened with her sensual soul. She couldn't talk but blinked her eyes rapidly when asking her questions around taking risk and following my desires.

With profound clarity, she was there listening, her soul giving to me the best inspiration and wisdom without her uttering a word. Just as when we go within ourselves and share our desires and concerns, our wise souls, without saying a word, listen and then find ways to bring surprises in very synchronized moments of realizations.

Around 10 PM, her loving soul emerged from her and hovered all around me for a long time. Just the two of us. Our same loving grace presence, living through me and keeping me safe, was emitting through her sensual soul, giving to me more love than ever known. At that moment, she was leaving me in the form called Mother, for over ninety-three years. Yet, her soul forever with me.

My heart broke into sobs with my arms around her, yet, I knew she wasn't within the body anymore. She stayed with me in her soul presence for almost an hour longer before the room fell empty and dark. Yet, here she was giving to me a direct experience of that same loving grace presence within me, in oneness, co-shared with her same grace presence, now all around and within both our sensual souls. My out-of-body experiences and one near-death experience are the only experiences that can ever give to me, at this time, this sameness. There are no words here to bring how her powerful essence was felt and experienced. The next day, her body shut down. She was no longer present within that body as the night before.

When my brother and stepdad arrived, trying to share the experience was impossible, as words just couldn't capture my very direct experience of my mom's soul enjoined with my soul, both within the Presence of our greater God Mystery. But the experience changed, once again, everything for me regarding death. The body dies, but our immortal soul begins again in a new reality and story. In those last hours sitting by her side, watching her breath slowly stop, was one of the most beautiful and peaceful ever witnessed.

She died the way she lived—pure, core love. In her death, she taught me how to die in love and surrender. My mom's last days will always and forever be one of the greatest gifts our sensual souls gave to each other.

I wrote this after she transitioned: *She was peaceful, her breaths irregular. Eyes closed yet she hears. My lips kiss her. She opens her eyes and looks into mine. My tender whisper says, I love you. She blinks and slightly nods. Her lips indicate to kiss her again. I do. I share a bible verse. I sing softly "Somewhere over the Rainbow." She blinks again. It's hard sharing these last breaths with her. A hole in my heart is being formed. When her last breath is taken my soul says, that hole will forever breathe her love into me. She dies.*

Each day after she was gone, my sensual soul took me for walks in nature as this always has been my way of being so present with beloved presence. Each step taken, touching the earth, my tears flowed steadily while my internal dialogue with Beloved, through my loving soul and my mom's loving soul, was felt intensely. Then almost on cue, a red cardinal bird appeared. An intuitive knowing, my powerful soul connection within was being given an outward expression through the timing of this red bird showing up.

Most of my life, when entering into nature, my soul enters into spontaneous imagery, taking me to experience an inclusive inner and outer world within a consciousness so alive, bursting in a song from the birds in the trees, leaves in colors of the rainbow, seeing deep into their roots into the soils ready to burst forth blooms. Then sitting and resting against a large trunk, me sensual soul listens for your Beloved voice to speak through into my being, a hug is felt like soft tender arms holding me. A hawk flies overhead just when my imagination travels into another time/space where I ride the hawk—much bigger here. It is my protection and my freedom, gliding me higher above the fray below and with a higher vision to see.

Small animals appear, followed by a deer. They all sense being safe in my essence of love. They know—I know too. We begin to hear the winds speaking loudly, rustling all of us to be aware. I want to stay within the woods, just as staying within me with my Beloved is warm, safe, and deeply abiding in love, and being always cared for.

I whisper for my friend Daniel, a name given to my sensual soul friend living deep within me and nature. I look for him everywhere now. My sensual soul knows him from many times and places.

Where are you, Daniel? Please appear smiling...invite me to your cabin for tea...or dinner...or the night. I don't want to return to the physical world right now, filled with so much chaos. Can we just have one dance together or maybe one climb up the mountain, helping me to see with a higher vision how our Earth is being recreated with a higher Divine Love of peace? My sacred walk comes to an end and my imaginal also becomes still. Smiling, gratitude is given for another beautiful time spent in these woods with all my friends and my beloved Daniel! My Daniel whispers, *I will always love you!* My Mom whispers too, *I love you!*

A poetic writing emerged through, helping me to deeply understand Who I Am. My higher sensual soul love self that never dies but continues through all time.

Beloved says home is your open heart where we dance through Love all the human experiences. My Love is the nectar of gravity filling your heart to awaken you, to hold you, my most beautiful sensual soul.

The human senses are designed within a body container as mind, emotions to give ability to journey through the many unique and all different experiences.

Having the many diverse humans and all nature within diversity has always been my gift of creation for the sensual soul/human domain of Earth. The human container is simply your spacesuit allowing sensual souls to venture upon the Earth to have these sensual experiences.

When awakened souls, in oneness with me, find each other, my Love becomes the only means to continue my creative fire. Being human only of the senses can never work. Awaking into your sensual soul essence is the only story meant to be. Sensual Soul Love Presence is the evolution of my Core Love for the Earth garden.

Chaos is now happening to bring back remembrance and begin each souls emerging essence. Many have now emerged from their human chrysalis to help others to awaken so that my Love and essence flows through the hearts, lands, and the Earth to begin to mirror my original creation intent. Love is creativity. I love you, sweet soul.

Often on my walks in nature, this red bird will fly right in front of me, especially when my thoughts are with my mom, again giving to me an outward expression that her soul is present. One day, walking and listening to music on my iPhone, my attention was drawn to a dead tree, yet still rooted in the live soil. A small bush was vibrating quite fast next to it, but there was no breeze anywhere as the day was still and humid with no air movement. I was drawn over and touched the bush, which became very still and then the song "Somewhere Over The Rainbow" began to play. The sun came through the trees so vibrant and illuminating. When my eyes looked into its intensity, a heart formed, then within the heart, thousands of hearts floated out as if to hold me. I laughed, cried, and knew Mom was with me.

It takes great courage to become a hero of our own story. My mom certainly was a hero of her story in the end, but she suffered brutally living her story as so many of us do. How many of us growing up had any power or control over what we believed during the conditional times we grew up? My early childhood and up through all my marriages taught me to use my beauty as a means of surviving in the world. Being smart was not rewarded. My soul, deeply buried, came in many ways, but for a time, my heart shut down to not listen. Many behaviors were taught to me: manipulation, betrayal, and deception, and often when in deep fear or rejection, these became ways to get what was needed.

Being pretty helped me anchor those false means of getting what was believed needed and wanted. But even worse, I didn't really understand what was needed and wanted. Especially in the external world. Yes, loving someone and having someone love me was rooted deep in my sensual soul, but I didn't understand that beloved, sensual, soul relationships find each other through authenticity, trust, and soul recognition. There is no control or manipulation. Our souls emerge to find each other. I know my Daniel will come!

I was taught that men took care of women, and women became subordinate to them by giving over to them their power, beauty, and sexual pleasure. I worked hard at being beautiful so they would love me and give me the material needs I wanted or thought I wanted.

The relationships were based on deception and betrayal; no one understood or knew who the other was in their deepest truth. Love was like everything else—it was conditional love. I will love you on the condition that you give to me_____. We can all fill in the blank with those conditions.

So my story was a surface separation story—a story created by my particular circumstances and the environment that supported those circumstances. Growing up in the deep South, my beliefs taught to me were that God was up in the sky somewhere in a place called heaven and who judged me according to the rules of a book called the Bible. Others have grown up in the world ruled by their God and bible, or the Koran or some other holy book all around the world. We find that these Gods and books dictated the early separation story and learning around God.

My story at the time didn't empower women—maybe not as cruel as in India or Islam, but still very disempowering. What was always missing was directly knowing and experiencing God. God was taught to be separate, judging, and punishing. Consequently, separation became the learned belief. The story lived. I've come to understand the power of true friendship must be experienced first before entering into a more romantic soul loving partnership. What would that feel like?

This poem emerged, giving to me this knowing.

The Depth of Friendship

I want to be the friend
who never stops asking, Who are You!

Please be mine too.
See me each moment we meet with curiosity and open questions.

I want us both to feel
the depth of our friendship
in a trust that we both can be that open vulnerability.

We may never
fully understand each other because we each
change like the winds blowing
through storms that come when least expected.

But we remain

present for each other.
We listen, we cry together, we laugh and hug each other.

We love each other
with no real conditions other than to just Be
with each other when we each need the other.

Reflecting upon a poem, it's like a relationship; it can be with nature, mystery, my sensual soul, my family, a friend, or a simple moment within my awareness. But always it's about relationships. This revelation has deeply changed my interactions with everything.

Whether poems come from my deeper intuitive soul or another, they are deeply personal and intimate and can transform almost all dark trauma from childhood.

Today, becoming partners with my grief and gratitude helps me surrender to feel everything. It's a powerful embodiment of all sides. Joy and grief are enjoined together. My sensual soul awareness gives to me strength to do my waking up work, my cleaning up shadow work to grow up the small immature mind, then my heart portal opens up for me soul so we all show up together where my true authentic identity becomes my higher sensual soul, loving presence self. Life can become the greatest love story ever lived. We each become our true authentic soul self storytellers. What path do we choose? How do we live, love, and find in each moment our inner grace of being alive? We can begin by being kind, being grateful, and being a generous giver. We can be an action of Sensual Soul Love. We become aware how we show up to do this.

Thousands of years of history taught men early in childhood not to show their heart and emotions. Thus began the building of heart walls. They must be strong warriors, trained to kill others, if in wartime, to any culture or ideology showing any differences or that went contrary to one's belief system. Thus began the building of outer walls so to divide and separate from others deemed not like us.

They were taught to shoulder all the responsibility as the breadwinner and protector. Love was shown to them when they conquered and competitively beat out others. And if you were gay, a misfit, or the wrong color, straying away from the status quo, you didn't stand a chance of being accepted or loved by your community. It's a miracle to me that any relationships between men and women survived. And sadly, many, many didn't and don't. Or many stayed in the relationship, living in the same home but different rooms. Divorce rates are high, sadly, around the world.

In his book *Sacred America Sacred World*, Stephen Dinan talks about consecrating the warrior. He says, "A truly spiritual warrior consecrates his or her 'sword' for the liberation or betterment of all beings, not just Christians, or Americans or Buddhists, Muslims or Jews." He goes on to say this is only likely to happen when a critical mass evolves into a different relationship with their warrior side, taking a more middle path forward of embracing the warrior qualities and virtues while using them in service to all."

What are these warrior qualities but a more noble way to serve with an open heart for the peace and good of all? Again, the teachings of Jesus to love thy neighbor as thyself is the highest warrior quality of service for all sexes. We take down our inner wall heart first, then we take down the walls we've built outside too. Even little girls are taught aggressive behavior to compete against each other and the boys as a way to empower. But it doesn't teach true empowerment for either sex, male or female. We are taught it's a dog-eat-dog world out there, and the old rules of survival of the fittest still apply—division, separation, competition, and every man/woman for themselves. We need real in-depth friendships together.

Einstein says, "Human beings are part of a whole called by us the 'Universe,' a part limited in time and space. We experience ourselves, our thoughts and feelings, as something separated from the rest...a kind of optical illusion in consciousness. This delusion is a kind of prison for us, restricting us to our personal desires and to affection for a few persons nearest us. Our task must be to free ourselves from this prison by widening our circles of compassion to embrace all living creatures and the whole of nature in its beauty."

Many believe that Jesus, Lord Yeshua, and his beloved Mary Magdalene were beloved companions. Tau Malachi also says, "The Lord appears as any man and Lady Mary appears as any woman. Completely ordinary in appearance, yet appearing as a strong man and a most beautiful woman."

This to me means a man and woman surrendered of their separation conditioning and both awakened within their soul higher Grace and living their soul way of love. They live in open, trusted friendship.

They have come to recognize the truth and deeper mystery by which they are a part and living now in a form in the limits of time/space reality. They look like you and me, but we must have eyes to see, ears to hear, hands to heal, and hearts that live and teach the way of love.

An awakened man and women search for each other, knowing their beloved consort calls to them, both from within and without. Our minds can hold all the knowledge of Love. Our hearts can express all that knowledge, but it's only when Divine Love can be felt through the arms of Love is its wisdom finally understood and known. The plight of our world suffering with these extreme ideologies where the lives of so many suffer the caged control of beliefs and tribal supremacy. A patriarchal held story where no one is really free. What is missing? Our soul!

"Out of suffering have the strongest souls emerged;
the most massive characters are seared with scars."
~Khalil Gibran

Content to be in this moment with the leaves of green and gold.
My breath moving slowly like a soft wind. I trust now what is needed
will come. Everything else is released like the leaves soon to be floating
in the winds. There is a song singing in my heart; I Am Divine Love!

A Walk With Beloved

In our sacred woods, you hold my hand. My heart bursts open with our sacred love, listening to the quiet stream of water flow its current. Tears flow with the stream for our Earth with floods and fires along all the coast lines. Hurricanes/tornadoes bring harsh destructive winds to homes and all the people so frightened. Wars erupting, taking our freedoms. Tears now flow harder as my love of our Earth and humanity know we are so capable of arising into higher awareness of being more loving and caring. So today, we walk Beloved, and my soul listens to how we must change within.

Chapter 8

The Energetics of Soul Activation

"Enlightenment means taking full responsibility for your life."
~William Blake

The miracles of grace abound. We each pass through love many times—love of a mother, a father, child, or teacher—love of music, religions, a job, or places visited. But what is love? I love you. What do these words mean? Do we say them often? Can they be said without conditions or need of a return?

I release and surrender everything but you, Beloved Presence.

I'm aware of the dynamics playing in my field of awareness. I listen...observe...but do not grasp or allow anything to enter into our inner space where you hold me so close in tenderness.

When you ask me to take an action, this becomes my service to you and to the greater good, truth, and beauty of all.

Divine Love always my action, however, Love chooses to manifest itself. I trust, have faith, and hope. I surrender!

I do believe my experiences, and for many others who also experience more subtle, sensual soul-like transparencies, it is our time of soul activation moving us into a more light-filled existence.

This is the exciting part, but before this truly can transpire, we must face the looming darkness also in polarity to this. What is happening now is the meeting up of the old story of separation where the mind, for so long, has been in dominance without its soul Divine Love presence of wisdom partnership.

The witnessing of violence, hate, disease, and fear looms like dark clouds over the planet, much like the dark shadow meeting me in my out-of-body experience. These shadows within so many today, not wanting to surrender their long histories of patterns and conditions of control, greed, and power over the planet and each other is a true apocalypse, or tipping point, as Thomas Merton says: "At the center of our being is a point of nothingness that is untouched by sin and by illusion, a point of pure truth, a point or spark which belongs entirely to God, which is never at our disposal, from which God disposes our lives, which is inaccessible to the fantasies of our mind or the brutalities of our own will…it is like a pure diamond, blazing with the invisible light of heaven. It is in everybody, and if we could see it we would see these billions of points of light coming together in the face and blaze of a sun that would make all the darkness and cruelty of life vanish completely."

My Surrender—Our Surrender

Beginning around 1998, powerful surges of energy began moving up my spine. They felt like impending death. These always happened, like my out-of-body experiences, just before falling asleep, in a kind of trance-like state. My body became paralyzed as these powerful surges of electric-like energies jolted my body, similar to that day when, only ten years old, my mom backed into a light pole, sending these same electrical like charges running through me.

Here is a transmission of writing from years ago that best describes these experiences that began happening quite often, leaving me in a sea of dark confusion before releasing me back into a more loving presence. My surrender was and is the only means to live these experiences.

Kundalini...Shakti God/Goddess Energy

I don't know! My ego is very frightened of this powerful energy when surging through my body/mind. Why shouldn't it be? Ego only knows emotional energies like anger, sadness, happiness, and superficial love. These higher transformative energies emit through the creative fire of my sensual soul, loving presence, trying to wake me up from this lifetime of sleeping in the human separation story.

As a child growing and developing, the interpretation given to me around Jesus and Mary Magdalene just didn't resonate in my heart—my soul. Nature provided me the sacred temple to directly know them both within me. The container of nature and the container of my own heart provided Jesus's Divine Love and Mary Magdalene's Light to begin my pilgrim journey upon the Earth and flights of my sensual soul's out of body to have experiences into the Light.

Sadly, the separation story gave division from each other as did the Adam and Eve story of kicking them out of the Earth garden to be separated, giving the mind ego power and excluding the sensual soul heart wisdom. We create chaos when living an either-or story where one is always excluded versus an inclusion story where both, always together dancing with each other, for the highest, best truth to live the goodness and beauty so intended in our Beloved's original creation.

Jesus opened my small mind's ego separation from my soul hearts wisdom. My own soul of Mary Magdalene teaching me to enjoin them both....no separation. Jesus and Mary Magdalene must be together as my mind/body and soul must be together. We, dear friends, for thousands of years, have interpreted their story as a separation from them when, in truth, they are inclusive together within us. Archetypes how our masculine mind must be in love with the feminine heart of soul wisdom. They dance, each in balance.

175

No more preaching just presence. We present who we are by our Presence of Divine Love as beautiful souls of this Love. The preacher judges, the presence expresses. The politician rages one-sided truth, just not the whole truth. Presence of Love expresses in how souls of this love live with each other, the Earth, and their inner most Beloved creator of great mystery, always through their direct action of this love. They tend the poor—remember our great teacher Jesus? They show compassion to those suffering—remember our great teacher Buddha? They honor the woman and the child listening to each's voice of their needs and their heart's love. They stop to play with the children learning the child's way. They honor all gender and race.

Presence of Divine Love is the root of all beings and the Earth. This Love is the core fire of all our creativity and how all became created. It is this core, root Love, that is the attraction of life to keep evolving and developing into higher, greater essence of our original mystery Beloved, our Presence, the life force of all living upon the Earth, and Earth herself.

We have reached today a pivotal point upon the Earth where each soul must awaken to its true purpose and meaning of why we are here upon this beautiful Earth planet given to us. We are not these walking robotic programs of separate selves here to war and fight among each other of what way is better than another way. Today, we see this old story of separation is now destroying Earth and much life upon its surface.

Today our prisons are filled with war veterans suffering PTSD, drug addictions and their souls crying to have killed and hurt so many other souls! Why? War weapons make lots of money and war keeps everyone separated fighting for so many things like supremacy or the many religious wars deeming each's God or ideology of God better or more right! We again value guns, a judgmental God and money and ownership of earth and others! Yet once these maimed veterans return no one wants to spend money on their war traumatized minds and souls. They, so many, end up lost and in prisons. Heartbreaking! What if upon returning home each had been given wise mentors to help them enjoin their wise soul with their traumatized minds?

Our great Divine Mystery has hidden powerful energies within us all to be activated and awakened through our soul's emergence.

Our soul will begin to show up when the ego is grown up to surrender its destructive power over the people and land so to enjoin and emerge with her higher soul, loving presence. We emerge as a new species to now move the Earth in a higher, more elevated, and divine direction. Sadly, we are now witnessing the lower energies of an alone ego chaos everywhere killing and harming the planet and each other. Wars, storms, and killings are more frequent everywhere, overflowing our rivers, blowing down our trees, and our beautiful Earth herself trembling beneath in powerful-like quakes to exclaim *Wake Up, Humanity, Now!!!*

"You are a function of what the whole universe is doing in the same way that a wave is a function of what the whole ocean is doing."
~Alan Watts

Nature provides us with its stillness and wonder of love. Out of nowhere can appear deer, white squirrels, hawks, and the tiniest of creatures. Our most loving God moments happen in day-to-day ordinary living with each other and within nature. Fear must not keep us from this higher love. My breath becomes my lifebuoy to everything within and without. My awareness of this ventilation coming from our originator of Divine Love, planted within all life, asks us to keep love alive through our acts and our oneness within our grace presence so we may be like the beautiful butterfly.

We are here for a short stay, fluttering our wings of love to all above, below, within, and without. Is this possibly how we, together, keep our Beloved Presence alive forever in love, slowly letting fear be surrendered into this higher love? We each know the pain, suffering, and loss of people, places, and things. Often in this loss, we believe love is lost, especially if we feel betrayed or deceived in the experience of that love. But is love ever really lost?

Divine Love is the greatest energy, the creative fire of our soul, loving presence, given to each of us from our Beloved Creator of Pure Love. Love pulsates all life in its seeking to connect us through relationships. Can we each become responsible for our vibration of this most important resource, our life frequency of Divine Love, on our planet to keep it flowing and flourishing within and without?

Do we mistake our suffering, loss, and betrayals differently from love? Maybe the intensity of our pain is the intensity of our felt love when experiencing love. Then in its perceived loss, we believe love is also lost. So we must ask, is there sustaining love? A love perhaps emerging mysteriously, not from another or anything outside ourselves but a Divine Love always, already within each of us in its original programming within our own coded DNA. This love thrives our sustainability. This is our core love to be activated.

And could this Divine Love be different, never dependent upon anything? It is powerful in its original state of grace—its chalice, its grail always full. And when we begin to use this love in its original intent of giving it away, then by the power of its gift, it continues to replenish itself through the giving. This is the higher activation of this coded gene within us all. Jesus and so many great sages, saints, and mystics all understood this and sought to teach us that everything is within each of us. We

178

shift from mere human genetics into a more sensual soul love, spiritual Beloved, God genetics. Love becomes the original creative life force of all, firing the caldron of creation. A newborn baby born with disease, when touched daily in its incubator, thrives with this touch of love. From the moment any life is born, it seeks this love—we know this.

Bruce H. Lipton, Ph.D., biologist, along with Gregg Braden, scientist/educator, are both pioneers who share that we are living in the emerging paradigm based on science, spirituality, social policy, and human potential. Both are active in a visionary organization, HeartMath Global Coherence Initiative.

Gregg's book, *The Wisdom Codes*, and Bruce's book, *The Biology of Belief*, both say we are not defined by our genes. The groundbreaking epigenetic research shows biological mechanisms that can switch genes on and off. What this means is we are not defined by our stories. We can switch this gene from the story of mere ego separation to the gene that we are souls of Divine connection with everyone and everything. We are a spirit gene directly connected through our God gene.

We are a holographic image of the loving Divine Mystery itself. As we grow in our sensual soul, love awareness, through the journey within our hearts, we go through many developmental states and stages of consciousness. Each step is awakening us to ascend us into higher and higher frequencies of this Divine Love.

This is energy rising out of its density of gross states into energies of more subtle and causal states. The Creative Fire of our Soul Divine Love.

Remember the kundalini, energetically moving up the spine, opening the body chakras into these higher felt states? These states

179

slowly morph into more sustained permanent stages where humanity becomes a higher, more loving soul species. This is beautiful!

We begin activating our soul gene. Our inner DNA continues to be activated, mutating and negating old conditions and programming from thousands of years of history so each of us can become transformed and transfigured into a more lightness of our being. A more subtle, light sensual, soul body presence emerges a more transparency and intimacy where we see into each other and through each other as beautiful souls into our grace and love of Beloved Mystery.

A powerful transmission early one morning speaks to this...

It's hard learning a
new language and story. We still live among so many still unable to
interpret our sensual soul heart wisdom being spoken. They live from
their language of the small ego mind that believes the old stories of
divide, domination, and a power over others.

Their love is given
to those who believe like them, think like them, and fight like them.
We become lonely, like pilgrims, on our new path with its new
language and story that God, our Beloved Mystery, lives within us
and communicates to us directly through our soul heart.

This becomes a language
of wisdom versus just old knowledge passed down from old outdated
stories. We know that our new language of our sensual soul love
takes time. We learn to listen with patience. We learn to trust our
Divine Love within even when so little love is given without.

180

Even friends and family
keep their own distance so we live two worlds, spoken with two very
different languages, from two very different stories, until enough
sensual soul love is spoken to become the only true language to be
lived and shared.

We know sensual soul love
spoken will one day become an inclusive language for all while ego
love spoken today is an exclusive language for a select few who only
adhere to that language.

Walking this path is
not easy today and very lonely for many of us in the outside
world, yet, very nurturing, tender, and intimate from within us
who directly speak the only language our sensual soul now deeply
understands more and more. This is the language of my sensual soul,
loving presence directly within with my Beloved Presence.

How did the two examples of healing shared earlier switch their mechanism of their gene state from death and being alone to a higher knowing that within each of them was a greater gene—a more loving wholeness of Divine Love and greater healing? They switched to and held a higher belief. How did Jesus heal but through the Divine healing God gene within him, activating the healing God gene within another?

Where two or more are gathered within the One, there shall light and love prevail. We change the conditional, programmed separation state gene into the original sacred unity state gene. Our healing, our within Beloved, and our soul then lights our way with Divine Love, so healing emerges in its many unique ways. We

181

shift and change our long-held beliefs from separation back into our Divine, all-inclusive whole and holy connections within each of us.

We Evolve Love

We begin to take off our false identification with this old separation story to begin creating with each other and the Earth our true identity. We each come to love and embody our love's creative fire within as our sacred unity. Our soul awareness becomes our own light radiating outward of this sacred love and becomes the most profound and vital responsibility we each take to keep our sacred love alive, through each of us, in our Divine connection with our own soul and Beloved Creator within. Then, through our actions taken, we give and give to all.

We begin to witness each other from a higher, more universal Divine Love emerged from our very own Divine natures. The more surrender and negation of old beliefs and patterns of behavior, the more we see rightly through the lens of our true authentic self as an emerging soul, loving presence. We are evolving to ascend ladders towards higher and higher degrees of love and diversity. Each of us comes into the world with a sensual soul essence—our very own genius and gift to share.

In a community, one may have a gift of healing and someone else may have a gift of farming, another a gift of teaching, and another a gift of science, and on and on. Our beautiful gifts become realized from childhood, and they are nurtured through the family and culture for the greater good of the whole community. The color of the skin is honored, as is their language and gender. We marvel at each other how our Divine Mystery has empowered us with these amazing diverse gifts. Imagine this way of living together.

We recognize that our body/personality is simply the instrument, as in a symphony where each of us plays a particular part of the music to form our togetherness of one moving divine sound. Each personality, as an individual, is unique to the whole, but needs the other so that the music of the divine can be played through each of our unique souls. This is sacred Divine Love evolving through the many.

Our natural world is filled with beauty, flowing grace, offering us a moment to reflect and mirror this sameness of love within us. The sun is always there, even when we can't see it sometimes, hidden behind the clouds. But always the clouds flow away, returning the bright beauty and warmth of its natural state, the sun. We also have moments of clouds over our natural state of grace, our aliveness; maybe we lost a loved one or someone we love is struggling with a loss of work or illness, but that cloud of sorrow will always move away, returning our natural state of grace as our aliveness that always is there.

How easy to lose sight of our true nature—who we are. Shadows are like dark clouds hiding our sun, our natural light. Over and over again, we play hide and seek with Beloved Mystery. Our forms, like the clouds, often will cover our sensual soul, loving presence. We become lost playing in the clouds of material toys where our desire for more and more toys, like a child, lures us into false illusions of joy and happiness. Yes, it is so easy to become addicted to believing the toy store of material possessions will give endless love and happiness, either through things or the taught belief that our love and worth will come through another or others.

But it's also easy to seek Divine Love and its radiant light in our very own original home of grace kingdom. Our hearts, where our soul, loving presence patiently awaits to emerge out of our grail chalice, filled with love and its Divine light. We will always be given love as we give it away. That's how easy it is.

A great exercise is to take time to do a walking meditation in nature. Become present to each moment by giving gratitude for nature's gifts. In this way, we allow for our surrender of everything but our present moment. Feel the tension leave as each step on Earth's path is a form of connectivity to grace. Feel how the wind blows, touching your skin, much like your life breath touch's you within. Listen to the rustling of the leaves or branches beneath your feet, drawing you even closer. Watch for an overhead bird or small creature running through the forest.

Everything is coming alive within you and outside of you, a oneness of flowing grace moving and touching your heart, opening you to experience love deep within your being. Allow this love to radiate outward like a beam of light shining in the forest and on all its inhabitants, then on to your family, your friends, then to all life everywhere. Feel this sense of belonging, connectivity, and the freedom and liberation it offers. Then feel your heart open to a moment of listening, feeling into your very own soul presence.

Feel the fullness of your chalice heart cup as love from Divine Mystery pours forth endless, boundless love. Then see it flow out of you like water cascading over the falls into everything and everyone. Give until you are wrapped with divine, tender arms from within saying, "Well done, my beautiful child."

"Soul: where this tree grows and learns to drink without getting drunk.
Soul soaks into existence everywhere, except my rough,
contemptuous personality."
~Rumi

When, even for a moment, we can disengage from our conditional learned personality and emerge our loving soul, we find an instant home with grace. How easy this was for my two grandchildren, ten and thirteen, yet how difficult as we move into our conditioned personality. Forgetting, we fall asleep into this dream-like state, needing to be kissed once again by our internal beloved grace.

As a child being read the fairytales and then reading them myself over and over, it's clear my sensual soul loved this. Who was the sleeping princess waiting to be kissed by the prince? Was this my soul deeply buried away waiting for my Beloved within to kiss me?

But this yearning and longing we each have, buried beneath our dense-like formed personality, struggles to awaken underneath all the trauma and conditions imposed upon it since its birth that have become like frozen barriers in our soul's path, trying to awaken to break free. A soul in her beginnings of awakening responds in how she comes to know itself beyond the personality in this way.

I'm singing in the rain...only it is the rays of sun falling into my heart, opening a window into the vast consciousness space. I am floating through this vast space...Yes...it is Me. Not my body...not my mind...not all the chains, like gravity holding me caged in a world, crying to lift all its dark frozen tears and sufferings back into the lightness of "who we really are" and who is that? Why, it's sensual soul, loving presence...it's Me!

All us "me's" becoming "we's" peering through into the vast dense space of time and the Earth experiences, through all our forms as Beautiful sensual Souls of we. Divine Love is our lightness of being as beaming petals of the sun's rays. We shall now bring forth our creative fire of light into the body forms so that the frozen tears

185

thaw and run like rivers of Divine Love throughout the lands to beam our light outward for a new world arising, to live as beautiful souls together. Please come join me.

When our longing and yearning become greater than our smaller self-personality's ability to maintain, then the journey to follow that yellow brick road home paves the way forward to come home. And, like Dorothy in The Wizard of Oz, many begin to show up on the inner and outer path, helping us to make our journey back home.

We now release our soul. We click our red shoes together, realizing always, forever within us...we are home. Beloved Presence kisses us from within. We wake up!

We mustn't be dismayed by the small ego personality. It is a great gift bestowed to us all. It just needs to grow up, mature, and develop in its understanding of why it's here. It needs to be freed from its history of conditioning and programming. And the good news is we have come to an unprecedented time in our history where the higher energies of Divine Love and light are moving through the shadowy clouds to free us all. But we forget who we are—souls in oneness with Divine grace. We're just in early stages of maturity.

Sri Aurobindo, a great mystic, says, "As the crust of our outer nature cracks, as the walls of inner separation break down, the inner light gets through, the inner fire burns in the heart, the substance of the nature and stuff of consciousness refines to a greater subtlety and purity and the deeper psychic experiences become possible in this subtler, purer, finer substance; the soul begins to unveil itself, the psychic personality reaches its full stature. The soul then manifests itself as the central being which upholds mind and life and body... It takes up its greater function as the guide and ruler of our nature."

So we might say Divine Mystery finally can play with itself through us and never be alone again.

A poem emerges out of my creative fire of soul, loving presence...

*Being alone in
this boat drifting along life, being bumped
up against one current
after another, a light appears in the distance.*

*Someone is guiding
my boat...but who and how? I'm both excited
and frightened.*

*Looking down, my
hands tingle of some power moving the boat
towards this light...*

*My heart begins
to fill with this Love never known or felt, yet, it's
familiar...
I'm part of this fire like power,
an electrical current moving through me.*

*A sweet voice
within
whispers, let go...it's time. Too long you've tried
to fight the ocean and now the ocean
holds you to love you safely
to what your path now reveals...You're a loving, soul presence.*

The mind/body had all it ever needed to grow and develop. The senses given are connected to an array of feelings, where emotions act as a cleansing mechanism, none meant to remain for long periods. Sadness, over time not released, will open to a depression in the mind/body. Clinging to happiness will, over time, lead to inauthentic relationships as it will become challenging to keep bypassing true feelings and their always movement of energies helping the body and mind process. Anger repressed, over time, will project in harmful and reactive ways, leading to some of our most evil acts.

Why this natural process has long been thwarted is because from birth the environment or culture used punishment, ideology, or long-held beliefs of the family to condition the children how to use and when to use their feelings and emotions versus listening to the children why and what they are experiencing. An angry child not able to process his/her anger often becomes the bully. The sad child will withdraw into fear of ever being able to express, thus leading to a lifetime of depression. An overly happy child is often the people pleaser always bypassing any emotion, thus, often becoming the one who isolates, afraid to commit for fear of them being seen.

We can begin to see and understand how these mental and physical diseases slowly develop over time as our projected shadows leaking out into our body organs as our mental constructs. We can also begin to see how distortions and a very closed down inner world thwarted the sixth and higher senses, our intuitive soul, from developing in her natural way. We couldn't process truth and develop trust because we couldn't be true to our soul higher self and to our natural rhythms to feel and flow its information, allowing for the right use of our responses to the outer environments. We began living out of the separation story from the womb.

Responsibility wasn't learned early in our development how to respond rightly without fear and punishment if we made a mistake or had a miss-the-mark moment. We learned to repress and depress, resulting in a projection of our learned ways taught—anger became a judgment to divide us with bullying, blame, and the need to be always right. It takes no responsibility. Sadness became low self-esteem, unworthiness, and often guilt, more and more isolating and leading to suicidal tendencies. Always happy led to a different kind of isolation, bypassing any emotions and a closed heart with boundaries so tight, few are allowed in. Often, humor is used as a distraction as is projection of our other emotions, all from a deep place of loneliness and grief.

We all, every one of us, have lived this untrue story in some form within us. A story of our separation from who we are and who everyone else is too. And worse, we've lived with a deeply repressed grief and rage, our buried souls needing to emerge.

We also became separated from our inner path to experiencing through our never-developed sixth sense of soul intuitive knowing, the essence of our one Divine Source, our true self and the true progenitor of higher truth and information trying to flow through each of us.

Our sixth and higher sense, when highly developed, becomes our intuitive connection to everything and everyone. This is our unity soul awareness.

Today, mystical/spiritual experiences often are a prelude to opening into this higher essence of each of us. Yet, when it happens, it also exposes our long-held shadows so deeply buried. For our higher sensual soul essence to be fully present, aligned with Beloved Source, we need to take responsibility to do the arduous work of releasing all the wrong teachings and conditioning so to free up our buried wounding and traumas. Our soul, loving presence can then release its creative fire to begin melting our human learned stories of separation, filled with old energies of dark molt. This is what will get us back on our right path to trusting our information as it comes through our original six and higher senses given to us.

This is not easy work, often requiring a good mentor or counselor to understand this process of one's wholeness birthing forth a natural unity of mind/body/feelings/emotions and soul/spirit. If our soul voice can become strong enough, we will do this work. One taste of our true, Divine self is enough to not want to live out of our false separate self. Intuitive knowing, our higher senses, become the energy gateways into our soul's loving presence awareness.

We slowly begin our climb up the mountain, but we aren't alone in this climb. Our sensual soul and Beloved God are within to become our empowerment to give us higher will and courage. Signs and synchronized events occur in meeting up with the right people and situations to guide us along the way. This is how we begin to end and mend this darkness now pervading us within and without today.

This is the inner work requiring us to become responsible to take that surrender deep within ourselves to begin each's work to release our long-held shadows of caged children, adolescents, and adults. We grieve openly so we can also be open again to joy. It's not easy, but looking out into the world today, it's also not easy to continue living these chaotic divides where we live all these made-up conspiracies and false stories, and more and more the planet digresses in climate changes and we digress in hate, fear, and deep suffering of disease and separation from our divine selves.

Our Beloved Source, both within us and without, is asking us to *"Please return home to who you are; my Beautiful Souls, only meant to have an experience of yourself through the human mind/body, where you've been given the gift of senses to co-create with me. You are Divine Love to live this Love together in Peace."*

Capturing all this in words here is very challenging. Yet, loving soul me says and knows that what is being transmitted through this writing is the core love, and you reading this will feel and integrate this loving transmission within your being—your soul—and will hear your sensual soul love song and feel this vibrating presence. A higher vibration of Divine Love is moving through the Earth into humanity, giving rise to witness our caged personalities as polarized chaos. Yet, a higher Creation can get chaotic—messy when moving out and dissolving an old outdated, narrative story no longer serving the greater good, true, and beautiful, so to begin a new beginning. Without our soul partnership, we forget Divine Love is our most abundant energy resource to sustain and maintain all the other resources. Perhaps it is time to begin the journey of our new story!

An old story morphs into a higher new story—one where our soul isn't left out—our creative fire activates our sacred soul love to begin our new sacred unity story.

Our soul train of Divine Love is about to depart for all destinations. All ever needed is our heart ticket, vibrating out kindness, smiles, and sacred love. Be ready for many hugs, many stories, and many tears too. Everyone is tired, feeling so separated from each other and life. The conductor greets us with a map to take us on an inner journey to help us let go where we've been. Our light-filled guidance is our own soul traveling with us—each's dear companion for our next destination. Are we ready?

The whistle blows, then the rails slowly begin moving out of an old world story where we've all been separated from each other. Our new story destination awaits us all where we each enjoin our hands and our hearts to live our sacred Divine Love. We've found on this love train we must live this sacred love wherever we each choose to depart in our sacred journey. We realize truth is to live always in our sacred unity within ourselves, with Beloved Mystery of all, our soul, and each other, gathered upon Earth.

Thich Nhat Hanh, a Vietnamese Buddhist monk, in his beautiful poem, reveals so clearly this transparency of our sensual soul when gazing into the eye of another soul. We each become one reflection of our great Creator Mystery of sacred Divine Love through each's diverse form, yet, each's genius of uniqueness helps us see and understand with more compassion and kindness.

You are me, and I am you.
Isn't it obvious that we "inter-are"?
You cultivate the flower in yourself
so that I will be beautiful.
I transform the garbage in myself
so that you will not have to suffer.
I support you;
you support me.
I am in this world to offer you peace;
you are in this world to bring me joy.

What are these felt moments between what is happening within me and that which is happening outside, making me want to land there, like a bird, to just sing? Like a wave rising out of the ocean, a star appearing upon the night sky, or the new life soon to be born. These moments give glimmers of something bigger and greater beating my heart, like a soft drum, into the rhythms of my soul's presence of sacred love who wants to live through me into the world! I now sing for you!

Our Souls are the creative sparks that fire up our human chrysalis with an awareness it's time to birth her into form. We become our higher sensual soul love inhabiting the physical form and Earth re-seeding and re-creating with our greater Beloved Presence of Divine Love! The Earth becomes restored, blooming her garden of us Souls. Beloved becomes the butterfly touching us all with sweet love. As co-creators, we fire each other and the Earth with new novelty, taking Earth to become a most sensuous garden of us lived sensual souls of Pure Divine Love.

Chapter 9

A Higher Science in Unity

"And the time came when the risk to remain tight in a bud
was more painful than the risk it took to blossom."
~Anais Nin

Once We know
our purpose and meaning
is collaborating together to let go
the old story of separation,
we begin readying our caterpillar body/mind
for our soul's emergence
to fly us free to create our new story of inclusion.

It is said that finding what brings us alive becomes our passion, vibrating our cells to thrive this higher love with every breath taken. We can take this further to say when enough healthy cells through enough people are living passionate lives then this becomes an alive energy of cells upon the Earth. Earth cells thrive from human cells thriving, thus, a flowing river of our Divine Love is the result. We become a higher frequency to live our many unique passions that bring us awareness of how we are so much more than human robots working on the battlefields or on machinery lines, living dull and meaningless lives.

May we each listen closely to our own hearts of passion, and may we teach our children to listen very early to their aliveness. Our cells are the inner teachers, human and Earth, how healthy and alive we are. Where did our cells and Earth cells originate from? My soul, loving presence today helps me to listen what brings me alive. What is my passion beating my heart to become more aware so to choose wisely. To surrender all those aspects not in resonance with my passion; Presence of Divine Love guiding my curiosity and wonder with adventure is how my soul is teaching me to live.

C.G. Jung reminds us, "One does not become enlightened by imagining figures of light, but by making the darkness conscious."

Science is also being revealed in its more subtle quantum understandings. A new love story of science in unity with Spirit.

It brings back meaning and purpose to further unite within all of us emerging souls. It is as though the inner physics is being transmuted, transformed, and transfigured while, simultaneously, discoveries of a more unified physics in the physical universe is holographically mirroring this internal light of subtle transparency of our soul emergence. Our very cells lighting up.

My dark cancer cells, contained within a small tumor, came as my final great teaching to be present to these shadow cells speaking. Learning to unify science of chemo treatments with my own spirit of Divine Love, in unity with my own soul forever since childhood, guiding me to surrender, left me to kneel in that final humble surrender. It's been both the most challenging time and the most beautiful experiences of Divine Love with my family, friends, and people everywhere emerging in their Divine soul love. Wow!

"The James Webb Space Telescope is a space telescope designed primarily to conduct infrared astronomy. As the largest optical telescope in space, its greatly improved infrared resolution and sensitivity allows it to view objects too old, distant, or faint for the Hubble Space Telescope." Wikipedia

The Institute of HeartMath has found that as individuals learn how to sustain heart-focused states of appreciation or love, the brain's electrical activity comes into coordination or coherence with the heart rhythms. Changing emotions can alter brain activity.

"The brain's alpha wave activity is synchronized to the cardiac cycle. During states of high heart rhythm coherence, alpha wave synchronization to the heart's activity significantly increases."

One morning, after spending quiet time within my heart, this writing emerged, like most of my writing, helping me see how living in an old outdated story of separation blinds humanity from the truth of our greater unified world and, we, as pure consciousness, within this unified reality.

Let's be honest, no one has ever seen the infinite called by many names. We have felt and seen extraordinary beauty abounding in universes and galaxies. The most recent, images from the James Webb Telescope. And we each have been given the gift of living a short time upon this planet named Earth, through a sameness of breathing from the perfect airways giving us life. We've listened to birds, rivers, moose howling for their lover, or climbed to a mountain ridge to sit, feeling moments of a love unlike any small human emotion.

We've, sadly, mostly lived our lives scurrying like small ants for food or bigger possessions, then we fight if another bug of difference comes close. We have no idea what is beyond our small limited mind lives. We believe in this above place where some higher deity awaits in judgement to see if we obeyed some rules us humans made up.

So, we ask, in which universe or galaxy of the millions in infinite space does this deity await?

We must today contemplate these small mind places we live and we believe, and have been programmed to believe by us humans, that this deity lives to judge there is only one deemed right way in the millions of ways emerged, and still emerging, as gifts of divine diversity throughout time. Kinda silly, isn't it?

Divine Love must be all our way! This love is the creative fire of all that is and ever will be. We are all sparks of this Divine Love, so let's spread our love to each other and to all the beauty that gifts and abounds us. If we live the only truth, to Be Divine Love within us, and we service Divine Love in every out breath back into the world, this just may save us and the Earth from the ongoing wars created by us humans of small minds. We become unifiers of both science and Divine loving Spirit for new novelty and creative endeavors.

We may come to be surprised how our Divine Love through the human senses brings us closer to what we have always yearned for. To know our own beautiful soul within our essence who is always, already Divine Love, to help each small mind surrender back to just being Divine Love within us and with each other. What realization!

We might say science is in its beginnings to give us a greater understanding that there is greater meaning and purpose beyond just the physical world. We find our passion when listening closely to our body's whispers. It loves to walk in nature, be close to the wildlife and wind blowing. Our heart pulsates looking at mountain tops, sunsets, and sunrises. It loves sweet touches, massages, and listening to soothing sounds. A water fountain dripping melodies or a wild crashing waterfall hitting the rocks below. It loves nature because it's made of natural elements. Have we forgotten?

Our soul is starved for the deep love of Spirit, our Beloved Mystery, that we all emerged from, and the ego mind is starved for its soul wisdom to help navigate in the world so not to be overly indulgent. Have we forgotten?

It is true that "What the world needs now is Love, sweet Love... it's the only thing that there's just too little of...No not just for some but for everyone."

Nassim Haramein is a physicist, public speaker, inventor, educator, and the Director of Research at the Resonance Project Foundation, a non-profit dedicated to delivering knowledge and technology to the world, which is based on a holistic and complete view of the dynamics and forces of nature, addressing the critical and systemic challenges humanity faces today.

Through his nearly thirty years of research in physics and writing multiple papers, Haramein has come to a deep understanding of the underlying mechanics of our universe, using his equations and theory to calculate the most accurate prediction of the charge radius of the proton to date. He shows that we live in a connected universe with an inherent feedback network in the structure of space, which has led to pioneering insights in our interpretation of cosmological, quantum, and biological scale systems.

What Einstein gave us as E=MC2, Haramein is showing us a unified connection of everything. Unity is our basic foundation. Soon, we will have this ability to move through the dense gravity of the weighted form as our soul light bodies will move through gravity easily, similar to my own out-of-body experience.

The powerful currents of electrical-like energies that move through my body are both means of dissolving old energies and heralding in the higher energies. This is the new physics, both inner and outer. Our very own millions of protons will light up the less dense mind and body, relieving it of its layers and layers of dense programmings. A new data of light, generated from a direct source, will lighten our subtle soul body to move easily through time-space. The right wisdom will be retained as each's own genius soul gift.

Mark Nepo says, "Pursue the obstacle It will set you free."

The hawk comes to sit just outside my window. Why? Does he message me to pay close attention, becoming more aware? After all, he is the hawk eyes, teaching to pay attention. What, again, is this obstacle? Lately, sadness also comes to sit within my heart. Tears come softly, then pour out like a waterfall down my face. What do they say to pay attention to? Then a walk in the woods brings me closer to this challenging mystery within myself. There is a pond at the end of my walk where a blue heron sits across in the tree. I want him to fly out, allowing me to see him in full flight with his wings outstretched. He doesn't. I leave with feelings of much disappointment. Then something within me wonders, could my disappointment be this obstacle?

The Power of Creative Energies Within Soul Divine Love—-

Perhaps in subtle ways my thoughts create desires or wants to have them happen, then when they don't, some feeling emerges with its emotions ranging from joy to sorrow. Are these creative energies needing my soul loving guidance? Deep contemplation is being asked of me. If our creative fire of passion and possibilities create our energies, then becoming aware and attentive of how we create obstacles versus surrendering to the maybe surprise of the moment is powerful. Being aware of wanting to have the heron fly, but when he doesn't, then smiling, it's okay to surrender my want. Is it possible to do this with any desire that may arise within me or you?

Being in awareness gifts us to become like my hawk friend. We pay close attention to our thoughts, always in some dialogue but with whom often a mystery. Yet, watching them often can slow them down. This also stills our inner energies of emotions, allowing us to be free to be more flowing within our greater soul presence arising from this stillness. Yes, this curiosity to pursue the obstacle behind all our uncomfortable emotions perhaps is the gateway to freedom. Going through this gateway doesn't need to be overwhelming anymore; we can become free to live our life in our journey of love.

Presence of soul love always, forever is within all of us when we each can let go of the insatiable appetite of our ongoing thoughts of desire and wants—some call the ego self—versus our own higher soul self, who is the awareness of it all, and this awareness leads us home through the gateway of our heart to Beloved Mystery Presence.

Our creative inner power flames us into our higher frequencies of Divine Love and light. We become like children again in our soul play and creativity; our body/minds and personality egos can grow up and surrender its wounds and dark learning so to become unified with soul and Beloved Mystery. This gives us the right discipline to live in this more diverse, physical reality as loving guardians of the Earth and each other.

Saint Catherine of Siena, an extraordinary mystic, says, "But as a flame burns higher the more fuel is fed it, the fire in this soul grew so great that her body could not have contained it. She could not, in fact, have survived had she not been encircled by the strength of him who is strength itself."

When reading this from her Dialogue 48, it's clear that my experience of my soul having left the body that night, she felt this burning fire of grace—her powerful love and strength. My soul departed to teach freedom from the body/form and its heavy burdens so contained within the personality/senses and stored in its very cells from years of learned separated conditions. My own internal fire flame, from my soul love, came to help me begin melting my old energies. An exquisite taste of this fire of grace was given to me to help me come back into the form and do the necessary work of mutation and transfigurations for my transformation. My taste of soul, loving presence slowly became my stable way to live. Yet, cancer came too. A final reminder we live in pure mystery within our soul, loving presence while also experiencing humanness within a body/mind susceptible to diseases and final death. What a teaching!

The risk to remain tight in my old story became too great—my sensual soul love needed to emerge for our new story. Entering into a greater field, awareness emerged my soul. A creative fire flamed her energies to be born in her greater power of Divine Love. Our souls have no conditions; her power and strength come from oneness with our infinite source of unconditional Divine Love and light. Yet, it's our soul guiding the personality form to surrender all that keeps us sensual souls, of loving presence, from living through our form in freedom. Being within human form, life will always present its challenges, but our souls give us courage and faith to face them.

Being more aware in our triad partnerships—soul, greater Mystery Source, and each's small self-personality—there is never a feeling of being alone. My hand is always being held walking this path of life. My choices are now made through a higher vision of a non-dual perspective whereby duality is given respectful consideration so to weave all sides together in creating and emerging new novelty. Trusting my sensual soul with faith brings grace to my surrender.

Our personality/mind is a structure operating out of a wrong system that got programmed very early. It is a matter of surrendering that system so our original grace, the Divine Love within, can reconnect, upgrade, and emerge through our unique sensual soul self.

Everything is always already within, waiting to arise once the old system is eliminated. Our higher information, however, often can't be released or is blocked by all the old conditioned programming.

Interestingly, it's not so different from our technology. The old computer systems, ten years ago, aren't able to operate out of the new upgraded systems. Their algorithms just don't work. Now, please, we are not computers...LOL! But our small mind egos can become so outdated, operating out of systems loaded into it from thousands of years ago. Our soul's wisdom of higher information doesn't match up to these old stories.

What we forget and what is quite amazing is within us all, our very DNA messages are encoded, much like an encryption algorithm, but only our sensual souls are authorized, and only when the ego small self has surrendered its old story and is ready, then our soul in oneness with Beloved Mystery activates its release into our informational higher field. Our human genetics get upgraded into our spiritual genetics. Amazing and exciting, isn't it?

"Although the soul is not changeable, it is in a continuous condition of morphing. When we see this continuous morphogenic transformation of the soul directly, in ourselves or in others, we see that it is so amazing and miraculous relative to our conventional notion of ourselves."
~Kirk Dennis

A higher transformed soul loving species will begin to inhabit the Earth, and the Earth soul will grow her higher blooms in its gardens to reflect this. Our creative fire will burn away separation so to ignite our sensual sacred soul, loving presence. It's not the ego personality's fault—it's only doing what it's been programmed to do. But it's on overload through a wrong separation story lived. Our amygdala is never turned off, creating chronic pain and disease due to living in chronic fear, and our souls can't emerge until the ego wakes up, grows up, opens up, cleans up, and shows up to understand its role as a partner to our soul "who we really are."

We Enter into the Shadow Underworld to do Our Work of Surrender

We need to erase everything that keeps us controlled by fear and fear's need to control and all that's attached to this false fear; differences grasping for their righteousness and greed for only material goods without any spiritual grace to guide us in how to live in higher and right abundance. This is why so many of us are now waking up seeking to come together to help our natural world and environment. We see the signs everywhere of how our Earth planet is starting to mirror our behaviors of aggression and abuse of each other by showing signs of its distress in many places. Forest fires, droughts, flooding, global warming in many places, and excessive storms in the form of hurricanes and tornados are happening, as well as new strains of disease-like viruses. A war has erupted, further giving a mirror to our underworld of shadow we've lived too long.

Yet, those still operating out of ignorant, unconscious, dull, conditional behaviors argue and fight for the status quo—more drilling, more cutting down of trees for bigger development, and more fuel emulsions. Big lies are another form of disease. This is becoming all-out dangerous. Fear is a natural state when operating from its intended use. We are signaled to prepare for natural disasters, we don't walk in front of cars, we listen to our body's needs when it has pains, and we are aware to practice safety. Today, fear is out of control, thus, stress is out of control, thus, the body can't handle the intense energies of chronic fear and stress.

It's almost inconceivable to know that what has taken billions of years to create—art, architecture, and even higher consciousness or awareness—is being, in many ways, threatened. Our natural world is being stripped of so much of its beauty while humanity also is slowly becoming dull and robotic. Dark eyes appear out of so much pain and suffering while a few live with an abundance of material goods. But they too have lost the light of their sensual loving soul. And all of this is in the hands of a few who have been given authoritative power to wipe out everything by pushing a button, releasing an arsenal of destruction unlike ever known or seen.

The fundamentalist religious joined with the fundamentalist government joined with the fundamentalist scientists have within their power to do this—and, in many ways, have been doing this in every world war, religious war, and scientific war. It is a hubristic form of control and power, long in use, and grows in its most dangerous today. It's a greedy power, seeing money and control as ways and a means to stay in power over the people and the land. This is the story of separation and control being played out today on the Earth stage. We are being given a crisis to witness this separation story of war, and division must end to begin our sacred divine story.

An Evolved Leadership Emerging Out of Our Crisis

True leadership, and the only leadership that may save us, has a moral, ethical, and higher vision of leading people by empowering people, thus, removing the fear we only grow through war and the dividing and conquering of others, and that equality remains only for a few. True leadership empowerment returns to the people their rights and freedom to become innovators, creators of higher ideas and ideals, all working together from a higher vision that restores Mother Nature, the greatest resource for all creative endeavors.

A true leader, when surrounded by other empowered leaders from all walks of life, understands this is how souls are lit up with ideas and creativity, and how the many higher minds working together can bring forth the higher solutions to resolve all our critical problems. These challenges in environment and climate, food for all, adequate housing, diseases, and our war issues are becoming a threat. There is not one leader but multiple leaders in collaboration and connectivity, all synergistically creating systems for wholeness—not just separate parts. This is how our Earth and humanity begin to evolve and thrive.

Communities will begin to be created locally where people join together to grow their food. Businesses will understand the needs of each local community. Religion will be based on sacred Divine Love within, the love Jesus lived and shared with all people. Each Sunday, churches will be open for all people to share their stories, all singing together and not just one person preaching. This is empowered leadership within religion, and Divine Love will be directly known and felt, giving service to Beloved Mystery directly from each's hearts and soul alive within this love.

Governments will become local and serve the people directly, as our soul and Beloved Mystery serves us directly. War will become obsolete. To kill and war against each other is to kill and war against another soul, in oneness with Divine Love, our loving Source of Mystery. Yet, our Beloved Mystery always directly guiding and informing through each soul's light into the personality body/form. Diversity of nature and sensual soul nature will also be greatly honored.

This is not utopian, but sadly, today's way of life makes it appear that way because we've lived for thousands of years under authoritarian regimes. Our democracy today is being threatened, once again, by this old way of Power Over the People, by a few given that power. And sadly, We the People, have become their robotic subjects doing their bid of status quo, to keep them in power. We the People must become the leaders, each contributors of our unique gifts bestowed by our souls.

Power has been shown and demonstrated to be of two kinds. The outer power of abuse to control people, institutions, and nature. And an inner power of authentic integrity where Divine Love, equality, caring, kindness, and a deep inner connection to our greater mystery and nature seeks to empower all with this same inner power. Judgment is only used when there is an abuse of power, hurting another, and when people of the lie have lost their moral integrity to bring harm to a society and its people. We've come to this edge…this precipice. We must choose now to leap over and into the creative fire of our sacred soul love, co-creating a story where we begin living from our inclusive power within. If not, sadly, we all go falling back down the rabbit hole of the status quo where we continue giving our freedom and power to those who continue to abuse and corrupt our freedoms through their power over people.

We've Reached a Turning/Tipping Point in Our World

We've become like two trains traveling towards each other at high speeds with no brakes. Two political systems refusing to meet up with each other, both filled with differences unable to melt in their frozen stances. Both are headed towards each other, determined to knock the other one off the track. What is to happen to our world and our democracy? Do we brace now for the collision or risk jumping off the train? Our heroes have been reprimanded and ousted. Too many hide their heads, eyes diverted and too afraid.

And all for what? Money? Has this become the end and means to our integrity, moral courage, and willingness to treat others in inhuman ways? Now we can say our health is at risk too. I am sad. We, as a humanity, are better than this—we need our sensual souls emerging through us to end this dark separation story so to begin our loving inclusion story back to sacred love and light.

We need to understand our distorted beliefs all were programed into our very young minds as normal before we even had the opportunity to question or raise an issue that maybe this is wrong. And this is why soul parenting today, by aware soul parents, is one of the most important teachings. Our children mustn't get programmed. It's so amazing how soul me chose to leave the body, then return to debut through transmitted writings. My soul shares so that your soul will be sparked with your own greater awareness as you read, thus, awakening you into your higher Divine Love and grace.

What is to be Crucified, to be Resurrected so to Become Aware?

It was early, the sun not quite awake, when a whisper came to open my eyes. Not my eyes to see the visible but my inner eye to see the invisible. A world of energies pulsating me alive to live differently.

What is God but profound Divine Love vibrating everything into form to live Divine Love.

What is the power of this love but waves of light vibrating it's frequency to create, to heal, and to let go what no longer serves this Divine Love. These sweet whispers each day wake me to becoming aware of how my body form is but a beautiful temple where Divine Love lives and where me soul presence of Love lives to serve the vision of unity to become realized through each's form temple, in each's own unique and beautiful way, to express this love and vibrate out this loving light frequency into each other and all life.

Feeding the dark enough love and light begins to dissolve and shrink it back into its Divine Love. New blooms of story rise up. Our crucifixion! Letting go the long-held stories within the dark now reveals our new story that within us all is the power of Divine Love and its light to heal all. Our unity story! Our Resurrection!

We become this love; we flow this light as a higher frequency to all upon Earth and to Earth herself to begin living our soul's own true story together as a higher presence of love vibrating Earth back into her always unity home.

I Encountered Beloved Today in the Woods and Was Asked to Dance

Raising my left arm to put around my imaginal Beloved's neck, a sweep of wind took me to dance along and through the trees, then back upon the path. Beloved pulled me closer, then this slight breeze kissed my face, then my lips until tears came flooding like a waterfall down my face. On and on we danced until the music stopped. Beloved became still, holding me tight before releasing me to stand in awe of what just happened. Leaving the woods, a snake crossed the path, then a remembrance of when my soul stepped out of my body to fly into the night. My soul continues to dance me within and without, knowing this is our true inclusive love story we create together. Beloved and our soul dance us always, forever as our creative fire within us. Gratitude fills my heart to serve my love.

Our tears, long stored waters deep within the well of our heart, come to touch our pains and suffering. They rush through like the tides building in waves of mine and your betrayals and deceptions to one another, long-believed, but now ask to be surrendered that we become our true soul self love born out of our sacred unity. We feel intensely the Earth's pains too as she sweeps across the lands with her raging fires, thunderous winds, and flooding of her tears. Let us weep with Mother Earth and each other these tears. Let us free our bodies and minds, and gently let us touch and hold each other, allowing our tears to flow together and helping us to surrender so to reveal our transparency and vulnerability.

Yet, mysteriously, once in a while, someone comes through our heart portal, within a loving presence, to give us a temporary key called awareness. Our higher true soul self emerges through her awareness, flying us out of time space and into timeless no space lighting up our senses to experience worlds beyond worlds. This experience breaks us open to surrender everything into a love that holds the fire of all creation. And just like that, it happens that our sacred love emerges, then we became a loving soul presence.

All our thoughts slip into an awareness of silence, then our feelings flow out of sensations of our sacred love, never ever before experienced. An awareness of our sheer gift we are inhabiting this human form where we now have eyes of a lucid sight. Our loving soul voice transmits into all languages, understood as only our sacred Divine Love whenever spoken. Touch vibrates our higher energies, all so tender and intimate, moving our hands as soul, loving presence.

We have come into this time/space to co-create a most beautiful Earth home through each's loving soul, loving presence. Our realization, through our awareness, whispers we let go thoughts of learned knowledge from outdated stories taught and no longer sustainable, to now embrace our higher loving soul wisdom, guiding us on a journey into a more beautiful and more sacred time/space to live our soul's Divine Presence.

Chapter 10

Freedom Dances Surrender Within the Winds of Change

"Nature is slow, but sure; she works no faster than need be;
she is the tortoise that wins the race by her perseverance."
~Henry David Thoreau

Freedom teaches through our dance called life that the winds of change are always blowing. Every experience is different and unique to each of us when to hold on and when it's time to surrender. Living within each's depth is our part of the deep ocean. We each discover our treasure of freedom opens its gems of Divine Love never found upon the surface. Though we dive alone into our depths, what is brought back can be shared with each other. Our hearts become an open chalice filled with these gems of shared love, kindness, and all in an open freedom of our hearts. Now we dance with each other in these challenging winds of change to a rhythm that is our sacred unity. We keep surrendering the old stories no longer bringing us peace to live together in our new found freedoms.

Michel de Montaigne reminds us, "The want of goods is easily repaired, but the poverty of the soul is irreparable." Over the years, my courage has grown stronger as my loving, sensual soul whispers we must ascend the higher freedom path in truth always. She empowers me to know when love in the outer world is withheld, it will always be generously given within me. Its only caveat is to share this higher Divine Love with others, no matter the circumstances. She teaches we are more internally the same once our freedom is restored within this truth. This shared truth opens us to feel our responsibility to be part and whole of the shift from a mere small ego persona of separation back to remembrance that we are sensual souls of loving inclusion.

Our leaves of time blow through the sounds of beloved music as the last blooms of spring in my small garden begin to fall away and the trees in the woods give a joyous burst of vivid colors before their final release to become once more part of the living soils of the earth; my own heart feels into these cycles of life and death. Becoming older now, this mystery called life is both a gift and often too a great challenge. What must it feel like to birth newborn leaves, then have them grow into beautiful green maturity while so many won't make it often released long before the cycle ends in its grand finale? I've too birthed so much and been part of so much loss. My heart now worn with its many cracks of all my many sweet and sad moments learned, and how important to now release my wounds back into kindness and forgiveness; my sensual soul love soil.

Now all my leaves of time are beginning to color; they give me intuitive whispers to spend my moments and days to use my eyes and my hands to hug all with a final gratitude. My heart now feels how all my cracks have been held together by a timeless loving presence always when needed, then released itself to be my inner healing within me. The sounds of beloved music being played through each of our instrument hearts, and we are the notes being played in this grand symphony upon the Earth. Our souls release back into the arms of our Beloved Mystery. How beautiful is this?

My awareness of this subtle creative fire of soul, loving presence within me is my now greatest and most precious relationship of this lifetime. Its teaching is that everything will be gone at a final release; all the dense material things we have been attached to, enjoyed, and also been challenged with, like the leaves, must also be released.

There is only the permanence of sacred Divine Love that we come from and that we return to! Yet, this infinite, always Divine Love is guiding nature and all of us, and we get to take with us into another mystery and adventure. This is who we are—breaths of time as a loving creative fire of Beloved Source to become realized as our soul, loving presence! So now, my loving prayer is to live within this ever-sacred Divine Love as its forever within me, and may my awakened awareness always seek to give this love's sweet nectar into all my relationships within nature and humanity. At final surrender to know that only Divine Love is always, forever.

The beautiful writing below comes through, as my tears flow, giving to me the Divine Love of knowing how my tears are so important in releasing my inner gifts of senses and emotions, like the leaves of time birth and release.

Few understood my tears when we hugged upon arrival or when they left. This is the depth of my Love. This is the depth of my knowing Divine Love. We give many names to this depth of knowing, yet, it remains our greater Beloved Mystery, living within us all, felt and unseen. This becomes how we Live our Soul's Wisdom; a felt depth of inner Divine Love.

Have you ever wondered why we cry when born?
Why others cry when we die?
Tears are the ocean
given to feel so deeply our leaving one realty to enter another.
This is Divine Love within each of us how we connect, how we unite
with each other.

We cry tears of joy, sadness, and feeling overwhelmed in any
given moment.
We release from that which we came yet
we forever remain a part and whole.
Tears become our way through each's most
challenging and most amazing triumphs.
We honor these gifts given to us.
Let us all weep our tears for each other and for our earth too.
Let us swim together within these waters,
cleansing so to resurrect our own souls of
Divine Loving Wisdom within.
Then when the sun comes out tomorrow we
smile again, knowing we are each held and loved
through our own souls and Divine Love.

My Soul Divine Love Emerges Within Poems

When walking in the woods, a gust of wind blew across my hair and face. At the same moment, love blew out of my heart. We can't see the wind or love, yet, its powerful movement topples us over in its felt essence. We can just for a moment remember who we are. Yes, it's you, Beloved, always and forever abiding within me, guiding me, teaching me and I, your humble soul child, bow down to the miracle of us. Divine Love is the rapture flowing through, as you, me, as all.

That Last Passage Lived

Beneath the body pain is the heart pain. Droplets of energies
collected from a small child's tears so long ago. The old tree hears as does
each leaf blowing in the wind...down...down to touch the cold ground.

A child's cry grew into a teen's cry, then its young adult cry.
Each tear like raindrops to fall buried deep into the recesses of the
bones and tissues and soils. Compost grew from old memories stored
and buried until life touched it once more to be released
and dissolved. It's time!

Like a volcanic surge, this last passage blows out breaking open
the icy pain to now melt...the time has come. It's getting late. The
trapped pain becomes a child, long hiding out within the heart,
where now soul Divine Love gives whispers...we are going home.
Take my hand to float up and out of this body.

The body's grown old and tired. Its space full of too much debris of
its long-lived life. The soul knows soon it most depart...yet, before, it
must surrender and release all it has retained of felt and experienced
abuse, lies, deception, and betrayal always just out of its control.
Freedom must come!

The soul must become the light now to shine into the dark
crevices so its release is possible. There is enough Divine Love now
to feel safe and enough light to be healed. The sensual soul love, body,
and mind enjoin together with all the emotions, becoming like a river,
holding memory and felt experience, all in this built dam of suffered
moments in time.

They will break through the barrier of rocks and hard boulders
until the river of every pain is cleared—no longer an obstacle for the
soul or heart.

Once all is emptied and all is surrendered, then the sensual
soul, loving presence may live out its time awake, within the form,
in wonder and with curiosity meeting each moment with eyes wide

open, heart wide open, and mind wide open. Its days to be slower and savored within all its rich experiences of living sensually and divinely in full awareness.

My sensual soul, loving presence knows, like a river in this last passage lived, it must flow free so that when it reaches the ocean it can gently, lovingly become one with its Beloved Love. Home!

"Where there is charity and wisdom, there is neither fear nor ignorance."
~Francis of Assisi

I do this. Do you? Our consciousness is like the mountain asking to be climbed. We remain at its base looking up, but are too frightened to take those first steps. We remain on the surface of our lives versus diving deep within our vast oceans. It's hard because those we love and who love us also remain tight-fisted within the status quo, believing they and we are safe. Yet, all growing weary of this old separation story. But are we safe? Are messages being shown on the giant screen of life today, trying to network us into the higher channel of our sensual soul? Viruses, wars, divisions of tug of war where both sides are losing, and economic disasters are close to hurting us all. We are being asked, each of us, to surrender our old ways and walk upon a new path. Our souls beckon with her wisdom whispers—love its felt truth. No one is an island until themselves; we need each other, remember?

And now our Mother Earth cries to her children to save her so she can continue giving and saving us. Humanity is responsible for taking care of our Earth home, and we are each responsible for taking care of our inner home within us too. When both inner and outer home are in a dance of harmony and balance, both bloom and blossom an infinite variety of loving experiences.

The Great Leap is Upon Us...Take my Hand

It's never too late to listen differently. The edges created so long ago, boundaries to never cross—are they asking each of us today to cross them? In this moment, take a breath, then step out and over.

Our heart may beat rapidly what is to happen. But didn't it also beat rapidly before crossing? Leave behind doubt and fear. There are no tigers and bears. Summon your child again—she will give you your curiosity and courage. She has long awaited to help you come home.

She is your loving soul wisdom always with adventure to live. She will confront the old mind, long heavy with its burdens. She will help him dance across these edges to meet you where you both shall now dance in your new-found freedom.

We need each other in our own space, and we need our allies in other spaces. We need our smiles more than our smears and our hugs more than our fists. We need to share our bread, not steal another's bread. And most important, we need Divine Love—all of us need love. Let's leap across this edge. Please take my hand! You see, without our inner nectar of sacred love, we can so easily turn to fear and hate, then hate becomes the tug of war rope.

Let us now drop the ropes of hate and fear to move towards each other. Somewhere in the middle, we can give a little and take a little. We can find our balance. It is said two wolves live within our minds. One is angry and filled with hate. The other is loving and filled with kindness. We each must decide which wolf we will feed. Our soul wisdom guides how we become aware to make this choice. We drop the tug of war rope.

"When our soul faculty begins to govern our life, our personalities and roles are infused with the real living essence of Love, Creativity, Joy, Generosity, Kindness, Intelligence, and much more than can be articulated in mere words."
~Michael B. Beckwith

What is the Soul of Our World Today Trying to Teach Us?

Who is God but the wind giving breath? The water to quench all bodies, Earth and human. Who is God but the fire alchemically rising our sensual, loving souls to be born within these containers that we may use the mind senses and the heart wisdom to know and love each other and the Earth? Who is God but the minerals of food within soils of Earth and all beings? Who is God but the Earth Goddess herself as a living embodiment of all ever needed to survive? The very food of life. Who is God but the sounds echoing a Divine Love expressed through all unique souls, each here to enjoy love and to be the very eyes for God to see, ears to hear, and hearts to express this love so given in all its myriad ways? Who is God but me, you, and we, all life living and breathing the creative fire of love? My heart bows in humble gratitude to be here. My soul serves you, dear Grace, so generously giving this beauty, abundance, and infinite love. Who is God but the tears flowing from every soul today who sees the pain and suffering but who now take a vow of sacred promise to stop hurting each other and the planet so to begin again to love? Who is God But Divine Love...Come Closer.

Come Closer...Intimacy is our heart opening...the closer we come to listening deeper, the closer we hear a pearl of more subtle wisdom...our soul presence whispers, *Come closer...let me gaze deep into your eyes. Come closer...look and gaze deep into my eyes.* The deeper we gaze, there is a mirroring allowing us both to see each other...our souls emerge with a core love emanating from Beloved. Come Closer...joining our hearts...our souls with our minds change our story of separation. Within our deeper space of consciousness, we are divinely connected...no separation. We are these energy soul, loving presence beings...everything each of us does, says, and holds to be of truth, goodness, and beauty affects now the entire space. Come Closer!

We are not the wave but the ocean
Not the leaf but the tree
We are not the bug but the soil
Not the cloud but the sky
We are not the bud but the flower

I am Aware I'm not the mind/body/emotions
I am the beautiful soul alive within the form
I am the breath breathing the life force
I am the entire Cosmic force...I am Divine Love...

A little bit Socialist...a little bit Capitalist...It's all about Balance...it's all about harmony. This creates resonance.

Might a gentle reminder to us all that our dear Jesus is probably one of the greatest socialists and who taught Divine Love and kindness to be our greatest gift to each other. He broke up the temples where the aligned together preachers and politicians used religion for selfish purposes. I do believe that he would today raise the minimum wage, help the downtrodden, and would insist the very privileged give their fair share too. He might also ask us to give up our assault weapons that may kill another. He would invite us into nature as a reminder that without our natural environment we wouldn't be here.

Both human and Earth natures carry the same inner resources to sustain life. Both need each other to live and survive. This requires taking responsibility for the caring and nurturing of both inner and outer environments.

I abhor the label of liberal-socialist. I am so much more. And I abhor you are labeled too, whether as a conservative or anything in between. You are so much more too. We all are beautiful sensual souls trying to rise above all of this and just be greater, more divine-loving humans. Yes, we must fight for our democracy, our constitution, and we cry for our environment. We hold to the belief that our ecology of democracy, nature, and human nature must be brought together in more unified ways versus our now very polarized ways; a developed soul unity awareness helps us to do this. We all must be careful of our small mind's tendency to take a bias stand to judge the other we deem different. Let's bridge our polarities, bringing social needs and capitalist needs towards the middle because, as Ram Dass reminds us, *"We are all here just walking each other home."*

Today, what is happening is frightening, and it should be. It is why we must, as a collective world, come together to create and care differently for each other and the planet. Contemplate this: why do so many countries stockpile nuclear weapons and biological and chemical weapons? Do, perhaps, our survival needs still override our spiritual value needs? Yet, today one touch by one wrong hand can wipe out our entire civilization. Is it time to stockpile our health, love care resources, and our natural forest resources?

The creative fire of our soul loving consciousness values growth, abundance, and communities all committed to sharing, caring, compassion, kindness, and the pursuit of higher values, virtues, and ethics. The arts, science, education, and all institutions created from our higher souls govern children in ways of cooperation and collaboration for greater synthesis. Meditation is taught along with faith, showing that each has within themselves the grace, light, and love of something bigger, greater than themselves. This is why we surrender to that greater truth, love, and light within us. This is the creative fire flaming through our hearts to become the great leaders.

This empowers real freedom from within every heart to live as our soul, loving presence, guiding the minds of form.

The Longing for Light...Love
I walk into the field to lay next to the Sunflower. How did you do it?
It began deep in the dark soils...like a womb. I felt it...I longed
for it...what was it?

Could I make it to that which would give to me life...light...Love?
I must try, though around me the dark dirt and insects were obstacles
to my breaking free. I must persevere, never give up!
Then it was felt...my movement became faster...a wet tear fell to soak
me with nutrition my own blooms ready...and then it happened...the
light pulled me...held me...kept coming...I am here...you are soon to
awaken...blossom. You are the Sunflower!

Freedom Comes...We are the Soul-flowers Here to Bloom Upon Earth

Every day, we are crucified trying to live someone's else's belief and opinions until we don't live our life but live the conditioned life imposed upon us. This has polarized humanity into a multitude of realities where lives are spent warring and terrorizing each other. No one wins. Everyone is sick, the Earth is sick, and the love so needed to save us all is also depleted.

When we can become resurrected out of these taught dualities of it's my way and not your way, we begin to see…Our Way. Our way leads us out of the toxic waters into the clear, still waters of our own soul, ready to rise up within us all as our saving grace to be free.

Our souls become the wisdom to teach all sides have true value. Diversity gives us a gaze into our own direct presence where our own Beloved God/Goddess dwells as our true inner kingdom.

Watching the sunset at the end of the day often brings tears. Over the years, becoming older, this has increased, seeing this slow-moving ball of fire drop beneath the horizon only to begin slowly moving up from the horizon as sunrise somewhere else upon the Earth. This ball of fire has been making this journey of rising and setting for over 13.7 billion years. Wow! It's the time clock for night and day to wake us from the sleeping dreams to putting us to sleep from the long day. Over and over, humanity is in rhythm to this time clock as is the Earth also in its movement around this ball of fire.

We couldn't survive without this concurring sunset/sunrise in motion by our great mystery that also has aligned our bodies with an ability to be born, then die, but in between we are automated to walk, talk, feel diverse inner emotions, have thoughts, and have cells that can replenish themselves. We often fall and bruise only to self-heal. We have both challenging and great experiences, yet, often our failures lead us to our great successes. Still, few of us stop to even marvel at this amazing life and all the stories each of us live. Why? We must begin having these inquiries.

I must be weird. Maybe my rhythm more attuned to the invitation from the invisible realms to pay attention, to become aware to this marvel we call life and its gifts given with great abundance to seeing all that is ever needed from us humans is to be more grateful, kind, and loving to have this experience and opportunity to be alive.

Living this life must come with responsibility of how to be in service so to give back to keep our abundance regenerating itself. We all are given unique gifts how to do this. Why is this so hard for so many?

My soul heart whispers that we must become aware of what is happening within our body/mind and how its runaway thoughts are leading to runaway emotions and causing runaway behaviors. We must witness how this is destroying each other and Earth. But we can become the winds of change by being co-creative with each other, the Earth, and our great mystery behind the veils of visibility by becoming aware and paying attention to make needed changes.

Today, waking, my first steps are taken. I look outwardly to focus on you Beloved to walk my path. There you are...the tree, the wind, and soft drops of rain falling upon the leaf. I am aware!

"If we surrendered to earth's intelligence, we could rise up rooted, like trees."
~Rainer Maria Rilke

"Love is the bridge between you and everything."
~Rumi

The Science and Spirit of Unified Divine Love...

If two cells in a Petri dish can find a third way to beat together, then two people with differences can find a third way to resolve and solve the difference. We are wired within to do this. We are all created to beat to the relationship of sacred soul love. Our heart is the Petri dish, Beloved presence and my soul presence the two cells pulsating together, now waiting for mind/body persona to enjoin with them, that our trinity becomes the higher new third way to be in relationship to now co-create together our sacred unity becoming a soul loving story.

We are a wave rising out of the ocean, a star appearing upon the night sky, or the new life soon to be born.

Our moments are glimmers of something bigger and greater, beating our hearts like a soft drum into the rhythms of our soul presence of love that wants to live through us into the world!

Nature provides a canopy of how we are more like her and must come to live like her together on planet Earth.

I'm a tree hugger and a believer that we are all trees of many varieties and all part of a great eco system hugging us too. Hug the tree next to you, smile at the alone stranger, deep in pain and suffering. We don't know the stories lived by the trees, of us, all rooted in the same soil but living in the winds of change and uncertainty.

May we breathe in our eternal light giving us all life, then breathe out our eternal love giving us all healing grace to keep hugging.

Living today, July 2022, with a small tumor of cancer slowly shrinking from science treatments of external chemo infusions and internal treatments, of Divine Love infusion, both unified, is teaching science we need internal Divine Love flowing through alchemically changing these infusions for healing the toxic cells while also renewing and creating more alive, healthy cells. Both science and Spirit dancing within the mind/body for healing. For too long, we have separated our mind/body from our own soul and Mystery Source within all consciousness. Just as we have separated Earth, humans, and all external systems created by humans—religions, governments, businesses, medicine, education, and science. We don't want to acknowledge the role Divine Love plays within each of our heart kingdoms, a gift we each are born with yet our responsibility to cultivate by spending time within us through mindfulness practices and deep contemplative prayer. This is our saving grace given, but we activate through our direct partnership and participation with Divine Love and Beloved Mystery. Cancer came as my final surrender to this profound truth! I am grateful!

Chapter 11

Awareness—Activating Our Creative Light of Soul Presence

"You are awareness. Awareness is another name for you.
Since you are awareness there is no need to attain or cultivate it."
~Ramana Maharshi

Arundhati Roy states from his book, *The Algebra of Infinite Justice,* "It is such supreme folly to believe that nuclear weapons are deadly only if they're used. The fact that they exist at all, their very presence in our lives, will wreak more havoc than we can begin to fathom. Nuclear weapons pervade our thinking. Control our behavior. Administer our societies. Inform our dreams. They bury themselves like meat hooks deep in the base of our brains... The nuclear bomb is the most anti-democratic, anti-national, anti-human, outright evil thing that man has ever made. Through it, man now has the power to destroy God's creation."

Perhaps a Mystic...Always a Heretic

This probably best describes me. Always on the edge, waiting to jump into the great mystery of life. Never finding a fit with the status quo-traveled path. My soul likes the adventure and the wonder behind the clouds or above the stars. Gifts of many out-of-body travels cut the thread to any fear.

Yet, my physical form instrument is always playing and learning through many roles—being a mother and Mimi perhaps my favorites.

But also aware my beautiful soul me can never be confined to identity roles; my very heretic nature needs freedom to wonder, imagine, and create. This keeps me in the discovery of my own very sensual, mystical nature—the world never out there but always in here, directly within me. Death always holding hands with life.

A felt presence of some greater love, since childhood, has always vibrated my senses when sitting in meditation or in nature, but it was the powerful moment of meeting up with my sensual soul presence that ultimately brought me intimately closer to Mystery Divine Love Presence. My soul presence became my higher voice awareness, my own true self. She opened an intimacy within me to help guide me in surrendering old stores of feeling so separate and alone to having powerful out-of-body experiences that became an integration of my personhood form, sensual soul love and Divine Spirit all within my ever-expanded consciousness.

This poetic poem tells my story, my own soul loving story, and why we must each die to the old story of separation too long lived.

It was in that moment
when Beloved, invisible Presence of Mystery
became very personal, embodied within my
entire being.
The shift then happened—a direct understanding emerged around
the taught and learned story of separation—

Then she came…
half awake, half asleep
a bolt of an electrical like movement took
me out of my body where floating,
as no need of gravity,

she flew—I flew through the room, out the
window and around the city.

I've done this
since a small child. Yet, each time has taken
me closer and closer to me, soul.
The entire Cosmic Presence of Love entering.

Returning back into
the body gave proof of our Cosmic, invisible
existence, so proof never was needed again.
The Love within just became stronger and
inner guidance became understood. Everything changed.

The teacher and the teaching awaits us all within.
The kingdom is within—remember?

When we are ready, our vast cosmic space opens itself up as our pure soul presence awareness activating our own soul's emergence within our own consciousness. Love becomes the creative light, firing our soul's activation to evolve our sacred love for greater meaning and purpose for the entire planet and all inhabitants.

Kabir says, "Inside this clay jug there are canyons and pine mountains, and the maker of canyons and pine mountains! All seven oceans are inside, and hundreds of millions of stars.

The acid that tests gold is there, and the one who judges jewels. And the music from strings no one touches and the source of all water. If you want the truth, I will tell you the truth: Friend, listen: the God whom I love is inside."

We must challenge our alone mind and its created stories of separation for our survival to continue upon the Earth. We can only do this from a higher, more awake, aware soul presence, where she emerges within each of us to give higher guidance how to dissolve this story that we are separate from anyone and everything so to begin to live our true, original story of unity love.

Richard Rohr says it wisely: "Either we see the divine image in all created things, or we end up not seeing it very well at all."

What we forget is the principle understanding that to survive and to thrive requires all working in collaboration and connectivity with the Earth and all beings upon the Earth. All is innately given within the Earth to live and breathe so to create and evolve. All is given to the fowl above to live the airways with rest upon the waterways, trees, and mountains. As is given to the many animals, plants, fishes to flourish. What a divine gift this life to live.

Understanding How Our Ego Mind Will Became Separated from Our Soul Will Within Our Divine Will

Let's explore another gift given when us humans came upon the Earth. A small will with a conscious ability was given to each of us to begin evolving our own species to become soul awareness; our sacred Divine Love to be this means of evolution. Yet, somewhere in time, a misuse and misunderstanding happened. Our human species, through time and space, reached a consciousness where our small will began to take a separation turn from its inner soul presence and Divine will that was always meant to guide our growth and development.

Here is where we struggle to understand and where today so many stories around this have given a brain fog to humanity. When our human will became disconnected from our Divine will, we became disconnected from Earth, thus began the divisions of land, people, beliefs, and these stories that began their warring of which culture, which ideology, which gender, which color, and on and on, how these many divisions grew, as did our small ego will of human minds grow of an either/or rightness around them.

The lives we each live are so many. A baby grows and develops into his/her adulthood to live their life in its many roles and experiences. Yet, if we don't surrender these earlier lives taking us into adulthood to die so we can each keep birthing our new life, and our always deeper discovery that we are all so much more trying to be born today, underneath all these roles and human experiences, what is to now happen?

Have we reached a precipice in time/space giving to us a vision that we can't keep living these earlier lives and experiences over and over, this same story of separation where each of us, in our perceived separate story of experiences, is in extreme chaos and crisis with each other? Can we begin to see how these experiences have been trapped within our minds and bodies and we've each been playing them out through a small separate ego persona across the Earth?

Are we being asked through this chaos and crisis to shift and change our trajectory of living out of these believed separate stories from eons of time because we all may be facing our own human creation of these divisive wars raging within us and upon the Earth leading to who knows what? Our Divine Creation, we carry as Divine Love within each of us, may need to intercede to bring this now story to an end! How will this happen? Are we the ones to clean up our messes, and are we being asked to now do the real work and responsibility to each begin our deeper discovery of who we really are?

We have this cage within us where we carry and live our old stories and how they interfere with any new life. Our own Divine soul trying to be born out of our true Divine Love, always yearned for, that gives each human form realization of why we are even being born in a form to begin with. We never get to know and experience our true real self within us, beneath all these lived stories of humanness to have our most important birth—our beautiful soul!

Death never gets really understood as an ongoing letting go of experiences to reach a final letting go of the human body/mind form once soul realization has become aware within the human form, so to now excitingly travel in a more cosmic time, infinite with universes and galaxies, to have many new adventures. Our soul awareness never fears death because we know there is no death, just a movement into another birth of new experiences. Yet, is it time for understanding how to choose our experiences? Who chooses—our realized aware soul or the small ego persona living over and over its believed taught and programmed stories?

We have come to name these caged experiences as traumas to now spend so much of our precious time, and even money, to go back and relive over and over, hoping to finally release them. But do we? Even those helping are often living and reliving their own trauma experiences. Do we now shift from mere psychology to greater cosmetology? What an entrapment we've fallen into, yet, just, possibly, when enough beautiful, awakened, aware souls today emerge as our higher guidance, we will recognize and know the work and responsibility today lies within each of us for our greatest birth—the emergence of our souls.

This is not to invalidate our traumatized experiences. Someone losing a child in a horrific war, growing up in a traumatized home, as my experience, where abused, then burying those traumas to become the people pleaser, even though many hours spent in therapy sessions. But even worse, my having amazing out-of-body and a near-death experience only to be told they were a child's fantasy, thus further creating so many of my shadows.

Only when my most recent powerful out-of-body cosmic experience of meeting up with my own beautiful soul did finally these shadows begin to dissolve and dissipate. Cancer arrived to be my last big revelation to understand, not just my shadows, but the dark collective shadows of disease everywhere affecting humanity and earth.

So who are we? Are we just these human experiences we call our life and we call past, future, and present? Just these human time travelers upon a planet to be born and only to live our life in all the many experiences of different places, of different gender and color, then we argue, fight, and war with each other who is right, who is better, until reaching a time we soon will meet what we have been taught to believe as our final death so we die? What purpose and meaning has been served?

If we can come to understand that our true purpose/meaning from our beginnings is to grow/develop beyond just adulthood and into our true soul loving Divine self, then how exciting to know we each are unique souls taking on a human form so to experience the gift of senses in a physical world with other unique souls, and we all are here to find our unique gifts to help each other and the Earth, a very small moving planet in the scope of infinite spaces/places within infinite universes and galaxies, and this gives us the hope and inspiration to wake each day to do our meaningful and true purposeful living. We understand our differences and diversity in a more inclusive shared soul partnership consciousness.

Now we, as immortal souls, can be taught from soul partnerships how to begin life much more aware, and instead of just growing up to develop the form, we realize we must evolve our soul awareness within the form. We are readying the mind/body persona form for us souls. Divine Love becomes the internal energy abundance always within us just needing to be activated by each of us to guide us to do this. Wow! What a world we will now co-create together within our inner Divine Love as beautiful souls of this love!

My heart feels heavy and very, very sad becoming aware of this, yet, my need is to express this so it becomes all our need to express because we must open back our hearts to our soul's wisdom to help us. We need her kindness, compassion, and love holding us all in our hearts. We also need each other in this time of our world breaking herself open in pain too. Let me hold you, you hold me, and let's all hold our Earth home too. We're in this together, whatever is to happen. We can no longer live the binary either/or way. It's so much bigger and complex than this. We need to live our soul's presence guiding!

We also can't just say give it to God because this hasn't worked ever. What or who is God but Divine Love as our living soul presence residing within each of us, our core life force, and is the life force of the Earth and all the cosmos too. Never have we been separated from Divine Love, our own soul, other than through our small mind will who believes this. And now we must see it's up to each of us to emerge our inner presence of Divine Love, and when we do, we emerge the presence of our own soul. This will save us, and this will save the Earth planet. We become bigger and greater than our small psyche will to becoming souls apart of a greater cosmic story.

Yes, we must surrender. But what we surrender is the fallen belief into a false separation story. That we are helpless waiting for this taught God, who's out there somewhere, to save us just isn't the way we are to be saved. Jesus and the many teachers tried to share this. But we weren't ready or mature enough to listen.

Imagine this: the Earth has been rendered depleted of its trees, seeds, and soils like rocks. All the money and all the material wealth of all the richest people and corporations now is gone. Everyone is standing next to each other, regardless of color, sex, gender, and culture, all vulnerable and naked. The only thing of real value, meaning, and purpose is now what's within each of us. Let's ask ourselves: what's within me? What are my valuables to take with me after taking off all my body/mind/emotions of armor that always, since birth, determined all my judgements, values, and beliefs? What will my soul deem to be the most valuable learned while on the Earth to take into my next experience beyond the Earth? We all should be contemplating all these questions today.

Please, let us all take responsibility today—now in this moment. The clock is ticking, the hour is drawing close, and Divine Love within each of us is calling us to come together with our higher, loving soul presence to begin living a more loving creation guided from within each of us.

My vision of living our soul's presence through me, possibly, will be different and unique than through you. This is the beauty of diversity. This is how all our unique soul differences of each's lived unique experiences share an inclusive vision how each of us and our service to living life upon Earth can collaborate, connect, and weave together what is now needed upon the Earth, in its many leadership qualities, to bring the Earth back into stabilization where harmony and balance resumes for all life. This is why Divine Love, our loving creative fire, is within each of us and why our own unique soul is each's means to guide each of us in accordance to what we each are here to contribute through meaning and purpose for the greater cosmic whole.

What we perceive as God/Goddess is always, forever upon the Earth as us many souls within all the different body/mind forms embodying this. How miraculous is this vision of beauty, truth, and goodness? We can do this. My faith, beneath my now sadness, is my courage pushing me through to do my own surrender and must be yours too.

What is this faith but our co-enjoined soul partnerships to know we're not alone? We've always, forever been in here, within our own deep heart, waiting for each of us to reach greater maturity to wake up, grow up, open up, and clean up our messes so we can now show up to begin creating together within and without our sacred unity—our new story of living soul, loving presence upon Earth. We integrate small ego will with our true soul will. Duality/diversity becomes realized as our Divine gift, given to the small human will for higher growth and development within our soul and Divine Love always guiding.

Yet, we also know somewhere in time, our human mind became separated from his/her own sensual loving, soul presence. She got kicked out of the Earth garden and the mind/body. We might frame it another way to say the soul wisdom of the heart got closed off from the alone mind. Thus began separation from man/woman, from Divine Love, and from the Earth. Sadly, this evolved a power over the Earth, people, and anything and everything, and today in frightening epic proportions, and now threatens to destroy life and the Earth. This is how the evolution of the small ego will of man, not partnered with his own higher soul wisdom and with our inner higher Divine Love, has now grown and developed into a more hate/separated consciousness versus what was always intended to be through the trinity integration as an inclusive love consciousness.

Take a moment to reread all this above. Let us breathe deeply to allow our higher vision to embody us. What would our beautiful Earth and planet look like, feel like, and be like if we all live in this beautiful loving way within this inclusive soul love story? Let's take another deep breath to ask, are we ready to take responsibility to change our story of lived separation from the home Earth garden, our own beautiful, sensual, soul, loving presence and our Divine greater Mystery, called Divine Love, guiding us all?

If we can say yes, it's not too late to take our inner journey back home into our wise heart and to ask our loving soul to emerge her presence within each of us and, when she does, so does our Beloved Mystery. Let's take more deep breaths to ask, are we also ready to take responsibility to expand our soul awareness, to feel our true self, as soul sensual love, one with our greater presence within our greater soul awareness of our sacred unity consciousness? Let's keep breathing within this loving higher soul awareness to further seek within to feel all our soul brothers and sisters also wanting and waiting to begin again. Only this time, everyone begins with our integration of small will into sensual soul, loving will and both integrating within with our higher Mystery Divine Love.

Our Divine Love Awakening Gives to us Beautiful Soul Awareness and Realization

That night my soul traveled outside my body, she became my awareness. The body lying in bed wasn't me, just the form instrument housing me soul within Divine Love. She needed to shake up my small mind, always in some strange dialogue. She needed me to surrender all these old separation lived stories bleeding their pain and traumas. She came to heal this beautiful form persona to integrate with her for our remaining time together. My mind ascended into her wisdom and awareness to just observe and witness everything and everyone to gain greater realization of how living soul presence awareness, who we are, and how we are now to live within our infinite consciousness itself is to happen. My awareness became consciousness itself.

This is for all of us to awaken to realize our soul, loving presence. Each moment becomes a blessing of grace and gratitude to be within our mind/body form in direct partnership with our beloved creative fire of love. We need now nothing, nor want anything other than to each be soul, loving presence and to serve this love. We grieve, we rejoice, we laugh, then we weep tears. Our greatest moments become the moments spent in loving embrace of our gifts given while on the Earth for our short stay. We marvel the gift to experience the sun shining and the moon beaming. The gift to walk among the forest of trees with so many species. The gift of arms hugging us through family, friends, or a sweet lover.

Having cancer to realize my death was ever close didn't frighten me as much as realizing my still slumber to not share my story and to not become vulnerable that maybe I'm not living Soul Presence before leaving the mind/body form permanently. It has shaken me up to stand tall with my empowered soul voice to call forth to all my soul brothers and sisters to begin living Our Soul Presence. This is my service, and this is my unique calling. Is this yours too? Thank you, cancer, for waking and shaking me out of this still slumber!

There are two channels of power. One channel is the small ego of humanity living in a small will separation story and always being informed by its conditioning. The other channel is the direct channel of the Divine Love that opens when we surrender our ego will channel to enjoin with our higher soul will already enjoined in oneness with our Divine Love. Thus, our enjoined trinity of oneness through the instrument of the human form. Our trinity, once recognized through greater unity awareness, begins our divine journey for Divine experiences now in our Divine soul partnerships. This is so beautiful to realize and know this is our true story we are to live.

Step one: We become aware of our ego separation story so we begin its mutation.

Step two: We expand our awareness, inviting our soul to awaken back into our heart/body.

Step three: We begin the process of integration, enjoining our trinity of mind/body sensual soul and greater Divine Love Mystery. Remember, we have this encoding within our DNA strains to activate for our awakening. We have our spiritual gene to give us healthy cells!

It is said that we find what brings us alive, our passion, then our cells thrive and give passion to every breath doing what we love. We can take this further to say when enough healthy cells through enough people are living soul passionate lives, then this becomes an alive energy of cells upon the Earth. Earth cells thrive from human cells thriving, thus, a flowing river of soul, loving presence upon Earth is the result. We become awake and alive, living our many unique passions that bring us awareness of how we are so much more than human robots working on the battlefields or on machinery lines, living these dull and often meaningless lives.

May we each listen closely to our own hearts of passion, and may we teach our children to listen very early to their aliveness. Our cells are the inner teachers, human and Earth, how healthy and alive we are. Where did our cells and Earth cells originate from?

The ego, a small self-personality, integrates with its soul wisdom, who always, already is One with the Divine channel. An example is an artist who lets go its small self-ego to enter into the higher Divine flow to have channeled through creative gifts like a great painting, symphony, poetic writing, a great athletic feat, ideas of electricity, technologies, and great scientific advances. Great leaders channel their higher wisdom to the people—Gandhi, Jesus, or Martin Luther King—who led the movement to end so much racism. Our stories of great leaders teach us, yet, so do our stories of dark leaders, like Hitler. Haven't we learned enough through these dark teachers?

Today, we need us leaders transmitting our higher soul love and wisdom of empowerment to the people and not leaders still wanting power over the people. Remember, the nuclear arsenals within the mind and within the stockpiles are very dangerous. Through our conscious surrender, we gain greater awareness that only through the act of surrender can our soul, one with our Divine Source, attend us through our gifts of service. What's equal and sameness? The Divine Love flowing through all our unique creations, each here to express each's unique gifts, and each within our Beloved Source Mystery.

This is where and how we all went astray, believing in only our reason of intellect without our soul heart of wisdom. Our feminine co-heart got sent underground. Without her, he loses his feeling, his intuitive connection to the invisible realm where all higher ideas, innovation, and novelty emerge. Big example: Look at the wars between the Taliban fundamentalist and Afghan nations. Women are kept isolated, wearing clothing hiding everything, and completely dominated and controlled by men. They are like their sex slaves. This is a small mind will of man using their perceived God, they've created, in their small mind image. This begins wrong power!

Michael Singer, in his book *The Untethered Soul*, writes "There should be no cage. The soul is infinite. It is free to expand everywhere. It is free to experience all of life. This can only happen when you are willing to face reality without mental boundaries. Nothing can ever bother you except your edges. You end up loving your edges because they point your way to freedom. That is what it means to go beyond."

We must understand these edges too. If one reality is generating lies faster than one can filter them through truth, this becomes how an authoritarian regime controls. If enough of us are distracted because our inner soul, long-buried of deeper truth, this becomes dangerous. We become easily controlled. But when, as Singer suggests, our edges are lit up to know a higher truth, our higher moral compass will lead us to our higher ethics for bringing together more inclusive truths, more compassion, and a kinder way to relate to others and the natural world, and then the lies will become our edges. Our souls can't be caged within lies.

Our courage will help us to take the risk to go beyond. We will be called into our sensual soul loving guidance within our greater Mystery Divine Love for living together this higher truth for all. Our soul awareness witnesses our mind closely to help direct it when thoughts emerge wanting to judge, be of worry/anxiety, or slide into old conditioning, no longer serving us with how our soul wisely guides us now to live her wise loving presence in all our actions taken for the higher and greater truth.

Our souls tenderly whisper Divine Love is who we are, within our mystery, surrounding all of creation from its first moments of life. This mystery has come to be called by many names across the Earth, but its sacred love vibrates all life the same from our first breath taken out of the womb to the last one taken to return to our soul origins. Behold, there are only three things that will last: faith, hope, and love, and the greatest of these is love. —1 Corinthians 13:13

In his book, *Dark Night Early Dawn,* Christopher M. Bache says, "The great saints and sages have given us glimpses into our evolutionary future. Their spiritual accomplishments are thought to have created the psychic blueprints that are functioning as strange attractors to focus the collective wave erupting within human awareness."

Shall We Each Begin Our Soul Pilgrims Path to Becoming Alive

We believe the church is the sacred temple, and this is beautiful. But what if we become like pilgrims, seeing the Earth and the landscapes another form or church where we walk, sit, become wayfarers of sacred respect for its gifts to us, praying for the water, trees, and for the wildness of its inhabitants?

What if we dare to take another journey within our inner temples, becoming pilgrims to sit within our hearts? What if we become still so to hear a voice or voices from the unknown wanting to become known? What if we begin living our soul's presence? When we become pilgrims of the land, heart, and the higher voices living within the invisible worlds, we don't feel so isolated or separate from our Mystery Source. We all are part and whole from whence we all come and all return.

May we each become still as two seeds uniting within mystery to bring forth life and our sacred unity within mystery we all yearn to return. And the two shall become one, and one shall go out to discover the secret of how to return home again. Our life becomes our labyrinth, as pilgrims, to move each of us through its many dead-end paths to find our center of aliveness. We confront many beasts along our way to find our beauty to begin living our soul presence. We surrender at each dead-end of one life experience into awareness we must allow our soul light, our creative fire of living, loving mystery to guide us back over and over to our living alive our next experience.

We must become humble to look around at everyone tired and lost in their way too. Can we look up into the soul eyes of another to see ourselves, then take their hand? This seeing can bring us to realize we all are breathing and pilgrims walking each other back home. Grief becomes our greatest teacher and companion, revealing our mystery on our always path of Divine Love and its light, as we humbly retrace back our steps out of the labyrinth, our center, to feel our deep-felt pains we all share to surrender them all within our living soul awareness that Divine Love always, forever is our way, and kindness and compassion how we express our Divine Love.

When we become present to our natural rhythms, we allow our soul awareness to observe all-natural rhythms. There's a certain heightened speed to how life now moves, like an out-of-control train soon to derail into its destruction and all of us on board watching, feeling ourselves out of control and helpless to stop it. Our lives are moving so fast, we hardly have time to have any sensual moments to see a lovely sunset or sunrise. We are so caught in the smog or brain fogs of life, barely able to make any contact with each other or the natural world as it rages in its fires and storms crying to us wake up…please slow down…please see today everything is out of its natural rhythms.

Thomas Hubl says, "It seems normal to us that politicians argue and fight with each other. We say that is how politics works. But that is how politics work in a collectively traumatized world. Because the fragmented tension in the government is the fragmentation of the society. That is the voice of the collective - it is a symptom of a wound. It is a pointer to the underlying forces that create the polarization and the fragmentation that we see in many societies around the world, and that we see displayed in many political systems."

Listen closely—Divine Love is whispering your song. It sings you alive…it sings your melody of meaning and purpose. Trust now with faith that I Am here in every breath you take. I activate you to begin living our soul presence! I Love You!

Chapter 12

We End Where We Began—Our Sacred Unity—Our Soul Presence is Born

"Your soul knows the geography of your destiny."
~John O'Donohue

Our souls now emerge as loving awareness living out of both our roots of cosmic soils and Earth soil as both avatar and worm. We live and breathe our life force of Beloved Presence, who lights up our senses with a vibratory energy to see through the lens of oneness where our touch becomes heightened by the soft sounds and smells of a multitude of fragrances. This vibration is Divine Love!

A Higher Divine Vibration Emits a Higher Frequency of Love

Living my soul's presence within awareness has become an expanded attending for me. Everything once seen as you out there, the world out there or anything out there has expanded to being everything and everyone in here, within my soul expanded awareness, within my consciousness. Our separation story and God image is becoming dangerous, and it is our awareness of this false narrative to help begin our new narrative always intended. Our soul presence is born out of our sacred Divine unity.

This old story has prevailed in wars, inequality, Earth crisis, and a story that has separated and divided humanity into race, gender, and culture—my religion over your religion and on and on. We can count the ways we, as a humanity, have used this God image that man has created. Unseen roots give life to everything from plants foul in the air to animals and humans. These roots grow in the rich fertile soils. These soils are within Earth and all forms upon the Earth. They comprise all elements needed to live and grow bodies from sunflowers to humans. Soils and roots must be tended for health and wellbeing of any eco system within and without to survive upon Earth.

Consciousness and soul awareness within consciousness elevates the human mind/body to realize the human form is simply the means for something more alive to live and be experienced within the form and upon Earth. There begins a deeper yearning to know this aliveness. Without our higher sacred Divine Love so yearned for and searched for, we humans remain in our animal-like instincts to rape the soils of Earth and each other. Fighting and war to own the Earth roots and soils is the old god image, but sacred Divine Love, within sacred unity, is our internal flame of our true mystery image.

We must ask at death, does anyone take with them any Earth or human soils comprising any kind of form? No money, no land, no bodies, and no possession. All is left to remain and return back into Earth soils. At death and last breath, do you want to rest in the arms of sacred Divine Love, knowing you did your small part to become aware so to raise your own realization that you are a most soul, loving presence returning to sacred love from whence you came?

Living our soul presence as the emerging Divine energy is our intercessor to guide us in doing this changing of the guards for our survival.

Our holy trinity now becomes understood through all the greatest teachings since time immemorial. There is no separation from anything. Sacred Divine loving unity is our within means for the external relative world to live and know the many different ways

248

to create together. All is divinely a part and whole of sacred Divine Love, the creative fire of life itself. The Earth soils and human soils both permeated with sacred Divine Love to breathe and live through our sacred love, out of our one mystery, never seen but felt, where we each are given the direct means to know within our heart/soul, once becoming aware and realized, so to be lived together.

When this becomes our way forward, a higher vibration of our soul's presence begins her wings of movement, firing her light of higher frequency from me to you, thus, we shift within our consciousness to Divine realization of our true teachings of sacred Divine Love. Sacred love within us all now weaves together all the ways into a more integrated web of unity to save us all upon the Earth. This is our true story to be lived upon the Earth. My sacred soul presence whispers to listen.

As William James, American philosopher, psychologist, and pragmatist says, *"Always the fruit is in the experience."*

My inner direct soul guidance always, forever has been within me, directly experienced and this fruit of experience brought me home to who I am…a beautiful true and higher self soul, one with Beloved ground of all being. I now service this Divine Love and God through my actions, therefore, God lives and becomes known as this love through me. Yet, I do not turn away from pain or suffering, knowing this is mine too. It belongs to all of us as we are all responsible for cleaning up these messes we've created through the thousands of years. There is one ground of being seeking to awaken its higher creative Divine Love within us many. A great teacher teaches and mirrors this one truth. Having cancer and death so close being Divine Love now my only option!

My cancer has become my final surrender to live free of my learned and taught stories! It's brought me forward to speak my soul wisdom and integrate my small voice acting out of people pleasing to obtain a small love! Here is a transmission speaking clearly from Divine Love!

Beloved Mystery hears Our Cries!

Humans cry come save me...
Humans cry why oh why this suffering...
Humans cry why don't you do something...

Beloved keeps answering with this response...

When humans take responsibility to come
within themselves they find me. I am
Divine Love awaiting beneath all their woes...

When humans
begin taking responsibility to see everything
has been given within and without so to save
themselves and earth, and all ever needed is
to take action to Be Divine Love, live Divine Love and that Divine
Love requires each unique human to step up and declare they will
no longer fight another, steal from another, create weapons that kill
another, destroy the earth and finally recognize
I am never separate from them or anything.
I am Divine Love
within them and within the earth nature waiting for them to come into
their higher soul realization each is one with me, as Divine Love!

I am not a religion,
an ideology, a gender, or a color as these are part of the human
diversity and earth diversity and are great gifts to be lived and

understood but humans, in their small will alone mind, have made up these false stories to have false domination and control. These false stories have created chaos and crises each now face.

Humans
must accept responsibility to save themselves
through and what they've created and destroyed, yet, my guidance will always be within and in many signs without, once they surrender to this higher knowing and understanding thus helping humans have now enough awareness, attention and courage to finally see what they have created and destroyed.

Humans
have acted out of infantile behaviors believing in a false story, they created, that they're separate from my divine love and internal always, forever guidance. Humanity now needs to wake up and clean up their messes then begin growing up each's small will self so to finally start showing up with a higher, more developed mature mind, often referred to as an ego....again humans name given...then at last enjoin with each's wise soul to save each other and the earth.

You've been given
everything to get this done. Now it is time to do it so to Be Divine Love in responsible actions!

In other words, until we experience and live this sacred love from a higher sacred soul presence versus a small ego self, we can't taste that fruit. We can't taste the difference between a small ego love presence versus a higher sacred Divine soul love presence. If one day souls are to be awake and realized, within a gravity mind/body form, these experiences become necessary to grow and develop the form to its true purpose.

Each become the instrument and means for living soul experiences and partnerships in these forms with higher elevated senses to live sacred Divine Love within our sacred mystery both aware and realized.

Yet, suffering can be a great teacher, helping us to feel into our's, another's pain, or the Earth's pain in her many climate and war-broken parts too. Suffering doesn't take away the joys and grand adventures we also still experience from walks in nature, being with a great friend, or sitting to gaze into the sunrise or sunset. It becomes our full embodiment of the whole and holy of ourselves, others, and the very Earth and beyond into great cosmic fields too. We are holographic of everything, as our quantum science is now discovering. All so beautiful, true, and good while also can be dark and ugly how it evolves and weaves life in its great web. Creation and destruction! We must come to better understand our wounds!

We have become wounded in different ways today. Disease, addictions, or racism all wounds of the heart/soul. Gender is often confused, yet, we are so challenged to be accepted in our world today. The oldest wound is any person's belief to reign supremacy to own, control, and even take away the rights of women. Why?

We can become the wound or we can help heal each other from the wound. We can take a stand to become what the Earth and all beings upon the Earth need to heal, thrive, and to live in peace. We can open our one heart we've been given, and we can live and love beneath the minds programmed beliefs into a Divine Love we have all been born from and to which we, as souls of Divine Love, shall return.

We take a stand to lock away all guns, to empty our minds of hate, and we become ever bold and brave to speak our truth from our one heart. Divine Love isn't a religion, a government, or some deemed way to get money and control of power over others.

Divine Love is the natural flow of something bigger and more beautiful and what gives meaning and purpose for waking up each day to be amazed at the sunrise, the great comic spaces so infinite and mysterious, the simple pleasures of a cup of coffee, and the gift of today given how we each breathe and experience life and, most important, we can choose how we will service our Divine Love to others.

We can have a mystical experience and be changed by that moment of tasting pure ground of Divine loving being. The absolute pure Divine Love. Then we come back within, where our small self often uses that experience to heighten whatever stage of development they reside. We evolve and develop from archaic, mythical, traditional, science-based, rational, or post-modern stages where everyone is right with whatever stage of truth they live within. This can be most dangerous, as we see this today, with everyone proclaiming his or her truth and righteousness.

Yet, when one has moved into a more integrated stage of their development, where they have awakened to feel and know directly the teacher within, they do their work of growing up their small ego self through higher development, and it takes them to do their cleaning up work of their long held unconscious shadows of early learning and their programmed trauma. We become responsible agents to heal our wounds and to help others heal. Once this is achieved, we show up in the world as a more soul conscious, higher self within the body form, where our Beloved ground of all being, great mystery, lives us in the world. We seek out each other for spiritually awakened soul partnerships in all endeavors, ideals, and innovations, and we take creation into a his/her higher direction.

To understand how our souls travel in and out of the form isn't always simple. Especially if our understanding comes from learned and taught truths about our soul. Yet, once having a direct experience of a near-death or out-of-body experience, we directly experience our soul light bodies. We realize and have a gained awareness that we aren't constrained by the laws of gravity. The laws of gravity enable the human form to be upon the Earth for each's soul to experience for further growth and development to become realized.

We come to understand that death is taking off one form to soul travel to another form experience. Our consciousness is infinite but humanity's awareness within consciousness has remained limited. Today, this is shifting as the small mind is becoming too dangerous with its accelerated technological advancements. Our greater soul awareness today becomes imperative to begin our expansion within the form.

Developing and expanding within our infinite field of consciousness is how we begin living our sacred soul's presence innately to know when it's time for its emergence into the form so to help develop the mind/body with all its emotions into its next highest stage of development and evolution. With its soul partnership, mind can move out of its immaturity of beliefs and patterns, believing it separate from everything versus inclusive with all.

We Are in the Beginnings of Our Soul's Presence Activation to Emerge; This is Wired and Coded Within All Human DNA

Many beautiful souls are emerging onto the Earth planet to be within many human forms. We ask, what is dreaming or lucid dreaming but an out-of-body experience? Really contemplate this! This is a most pivotal time for Earth and all life. When enough sensual sacred souls become enjoined with the small mind selves within the form, this will begin mutation of the old form and transfigure it to transform into its more light, subtle body to encounter higher abilities like time travel into the greater galactic cosmos for an even greater understanding and meaning, and to take Earth and the human/soul into its next higher evolution for all. A higher soul species is born!

How exciting is this? Again, really contemplating this, can you begin to imagine the implications of our ability to time travel, have an ability to teleport, and have telepathic communication with other higher beings in the great cosmic field together? The potential and possibilities of our sensual sacred soul Divine Love/humanity and Earth becomes limitless in its greater quantum creative abilities.

In the world of a human created separate from God, we believe we have been given the Earth to buy and sell its gifts, and we've been given life to buy and sell each other. We believe it's all about profit and gain off the land and each other. Yet, we know Jesus said "it is easier for a camel to go through the eye of a needle than for a rich man to enter into the kingdom of God." As he also said "whosoever shall exalt himself shall be abased; and he that shall humble himself shall be exalted." When the small ego surrenders to Divine Love, within its soul wisdom, this humbles and brings greater realization a higher meaning and purpose is to be lived with others and Earth.

We forgot we are a sacred soul, loving presence within a body to have this beautiful human experience given to all. Now, we have a short time to wake up from our false separation story we created so we may begin again. Otherwise, us humans may be taken from the Earth so Earth can revive and renew itself. We were all sent messages and messengers from eons of time to help all of us to wake up from this false story we've created. Perhaps today, we need to start listening from our heart of sacred soul, loving presence and not just our ego mind of consumption.

Very important: we must also release our use of God/Goddess and Divine Love for our politics, religions, and money, and things to own, dominate, and overly consume. We use the name God or other names to say *my politics, my religion, or my business is the way God supports, and if you don't do it my way, then you will be judged and punished.* How many times have we all heard this? Only small-minded humans could create this kind of separation story of a small image of a God looking down from some place to judge human politics, human religions, and human businesses. Really? What have we done?

We worship our guns and war heads as a way we worship God. We align God with money from these deadly weapons. Pro God is Pro Gun is Pro Money is Pro Life for the few while leaving the many barely able to get by. We take away human rights for all to serve the rights of a few. The good news is we can become soul aware and pay attention to what and how we all have created this and how now becomes all our responsibility to correct so to connect our separated ego mind back with our wise heart/soul.

We, together, shift to a service humanity of each other, the Earth, and in this together Divine service, we honor and service our true God/Goddess by coming back home within our inner kingdom to follow today our simple teachings of living sacred Divine Love. This saves Earth, humanity, and brings forth our higher essence to live as soul, loving presence upon the Earth. Our sacred unity within Divine Love becomes realized!

We become the great artists, creative innovators, and we bring greater novelty for all to live and thrive upon the Earth for whatever time we're given. We become loving mystics, and our Beloved God/Goddess lives through us, having the many loving, beautiful Divine experiences upon the light-filled Earth planet. Truth is, this has been happening since time began—now it can happen on a grander scale. Ask, how did we get this far? From airplanes, telephones, and televisions to smart phones and great teachers of light bodies like Jesus, the Buddha, and so many others. Is our own DNA wired for this great time/space shift from living a small ego mind to living our soul presence and now many of us being activated? Wow! Do you feel this within in your most sacred heart/soul?

Believe me, this has happened and is happening today. My own out-of-body experiences, added to millions of others, give us proof that it's time. We save ourselves, we save the planet, and we meet our galactic neighbors to take planet Earth and all us light, subtle body sensual souls to our next evolutionary level upon the Earth and beyond. We become a higher, loving, sacred soul species upon the Earth. Coming through me now is so much excitement, Divine Love, and higher support from the higher cosmic field—both visible and invisible.

My life is lived on the edge of this visible Earth and the now-thin veil of the invisible realms where these transmissions of writings flow through me. I live my edges of uncertainty today. Courage rises into my form to give me a taste of my strength and my loving soul presence emerges within me. I'm not alone ever. This is being revealed, and this realization makes me aware how my entire life has been lived on this edge of unknown. What becomes important is to trust not the old ways, but to surrender to new potential and possibilities surprising me, never before seen. My cancer always my reminder; yet, it too slowly dissolving as is living any separation!

Soul me has walked this path many times—she walks ahead as my courage, my light, my loving pilgrim self readying the higher path of Divine Love we will live. The alchemy of faith and hope is my creative fire of my soul, loving presence in loving partnership with Beloved Mystery Presence that indescribable mystery words fail to describe.

We're coming to the end of this book with greater loving presence giving a few loving transmissions through me, sensual

257

soul Divine loving presence and sweet human form MaryLinda, both of us together deeply translating in our highest best effort. I am both humbled and in deep gratitude to have this honor. Reading this book, hopefully, you will resonate within your own sensual soul Divine loving presence this truth, beauty, and goodness shared. We're ready for our next great Earth's turning of its axis and humanity's great next transformation from mere small ego personas to partnering, in essence, with our soul's presence to become a most beautiful sacred soul love story living together in our sacred unity.

Throughout this book, many great mystics have been shared. Today, our world is not about one person vibrating out, but about a collective population vibrating these higher ascended frequencies, each having spent hours in the practice of contemplated prayer, meditation, and time in nature, within and without, mutating their lower frequencies of a small ego, all about themselves, to their higher loving, Divine frequencies all about everyone. It's our higher energy of sacred soul, loving presence that Jesus, the Buddha, and so many tried to teach and demonstrate from our long histories.

We are the Artists...We are the Creators...We are the Mystics

A museum is a temple where the art on canvas, sculpted images, or blown glass become displayed for our eyes to feast on color and light. I often sit gazing into the genus's creativity of nothing becoming a great something. This can be said of the great writer who takes out of his/her heart a story or poetic verse, bringing us all to feel this something as a part of each of us. We can go even further to the great athlete, musician, inspired speaker, teacher, or photographer and the landscape or building architects or a creative technology from mere ideas. It includes even our journalists and reporters and our visionary leaders, to the trucks and cars we drive and the foods we eat and clothes we wear. These creations all were internally inspired within at some time.

There is now nothing in this physical existence that didn't begin in the great field of the imaginal somewhere, sometime. Everything began as a thought or idea from our beginnings. In other words, everything out there began in here, in our innermost creative minds/sensual souls, and we must inquire, where did these ideas or images, or knowings emerge from? The narcissistic ego wants to believe it is his/her idea or great vision, but is this true?

There is nothing to compare to the greatest artist always remaining as our great mystery, creating a planet that could evolve through time and space to house all of humanity and nature. Then design and create a human form where within the form all is the same in its river of blood, water, organs, muscles, cells, and so much more. Each with one heart, one brain, and each with a consciousness that through time and space could evolve itself into greater and greater expansion, where many became aware of our great creativity as artists on this great canvas of the planet. We came to know in our great realization that our great mystery artist of creative fire, called by many names, is within each of us. I simply know as the fire of Divine Love. We now morph into our soul, loving presence directly out of our sacred unity. How does this emerge if not wired into our evolution and DNA strands?

Yet, sadly, not enough became soul aware to understand this higher responsibility of creation. Most just saw the means to use the planet and each other to satisfy their selfish hunger. Yet, this egotistical power comes with a price, often leading to a consumption of drugs or abusive substance or its believed lies and distortions to calm the stress so generated to live these false beliefs. The planet now must dissolve its addictive behaviors, created through a separation fear story; all its ferocious appetite to own and consume more and more, thus bringing behaviors to own, drink, eat, do drugs, and live out binge lies to maintain this madness.

Even our sexuality is abused and misunderstood. When our sensual souls take our sexual desire into a higher, deeper understanding of its meaning, from a small mind self, all about my desire, to a mind/body enjoined with its true partnership of sensual wisdom/soul, and both enjoined with Beloved Source Mystery, this opens the heart wilder and deeper into depths beyond body pleasure. Their organism ignites a flame within both, alchemically firing their creativity for more than mere pleasure, child reproduction, and opens them to deeper connections to our great mystery itself of creativity. A Divine Love is felt so intensely that they can only hold on to each other to breathe. A creative fire of love, a kundalini organism, is taken into higher levels of understanding.

"Real love will take you far beyond yourself; and therefore real love will devastate you."
~Ken Wilber

When the mind/ego enjoins sensual soul/wisdom, this takes the sexual desire into a higher soul unity awareness where each enjoined soul/mind/body within each partner seeks this erotic fire of energy release as a moment of pure oneness with the Beloved, within each, and the intimacy felt can never be described in knowledge, but in a sacred Divine Love, each knows they've searched for their entire life. It is this depth of Divine fire released that becomes the sensual soul's love story. We become the way of oneness with our great mystery, soul self, and the enjoined personhood. Love becomes realized through the two as one. Love-making can finally be understood through each's higher realized, sexual, sensual sacred soul loving encounter. We are spirit beings inhabiting a physical body to awaken into our sacred love realization. This sets in motion again our evolution of sacred Divine Love and it's higher movement back into its original intended purpose and meaning.

"Your sacred space is where you can find yourself over and over again."
~Joseph Campbell

Learning to be a bit of a spiritual badass, so as not to bypass my shadow work, is ongoing in trying to understand how most of my life has been given over to being the good one, the perfect one, and the peacemaker. Yet, there is a fire within me that wants to burn the hell out of those crazy, greedy, mean-spirited, and judgmental thoughts of people pretending to be all so holy when they are the betrayers and deceivers, not giving a rat's ass how many are starving, diseased, and living a life where some animals have it better. Who cares if the Earth is burning up? So don't say to me you follow the way of God or Jesus when you turn your backs on children preyed upon, women seen as objects to own and control of people of color, as slaves or less than, or you spend millions on homes, cars, and bonds, but won't support health care, our forest, or our agencies that give to the disenfranchised—very lost.

Yes...I Am becoming a badass and wish many more would join me, and we become the badass sensually sacred soul lovers enjoined with Earth and each other to clean out these messes we've created and then turn the tables of these corrupt dark forces. My sweet soul smiles! You go girl!

"I do believe in the paranormal, that there are things our brains just can't understand."
~Art Bell

Since childhood, I've experienced what some would call these paranormal experiences. While I agree they don't run normal to most experiences, to me, they are gifts and the true revelation that we are these beautiful, sensual, soul, subtle body experiences, and most exciting, what is possible to experience that can be our way out of these old beliefs and programs taught that we're just mere dense bodies of duality playing out life experiences of sometimes good and becoming darker like evil. My greatest understanding now is we are in this time/space shift, living out of these human vessels/bodies of both light and dark, into a greater ability to emerge our more sensual, soul, subtle bodies, much like my own soul's emergence in her subtle leave of my body, then her return that began my transformation. This is for all of us to experience.

What is most important is to begin an inner practice where we each allow ourself to begin a journey within into our own heart where our soul patiently awaits. Since birth, most of humanity lives only from their external life, gaining most of their knowledge from books, religions, and teachings from thousands of years ago. The separation story that has created so much suffering. My friends, the Earth planet, and humanity are evolving. We've gained much since those earlier writings separating us all. It's time to shift from an outer authority to an inner inclusion that we are beautiful, sensual, sacred, subtle souls, one with a far greater wisdom and mystery within us, to activate us all within this creative fire of soul love. This emerges our own souls.

And those like me, having these higher experiences today, within these forms, are getting closer to this higher understanding, as time is shifting humanity and Earth where our subtle, sacred soul bodies are becoming our true form, and the outer dense bodies only for the housing of the bodily senses and structures so that our subtle sensual souls can operate through them. While for many this may appear at first strange, I'm sure eons ago, it was also strange when evolving from a Neanderthal existence.

Has it been easy? It's been very challenging, yet, many, like me, are living today out of our loving sensual, soul, subtle bodies. Very similar, as a child, when no one understood me and so much was hidden, my life became lived out of two worlds—one more subtle, invisible, and one very dense like and physical. Yet, today my sensual soul's awareness gives me courage to live true to my self and enjoin with others to create and live our soul's presence.

Yet, my humanness is still very active too. This writing best describes this early arising of my higher soul presence meeting up with my mind/body human self. Have you ever wondered why some days you wake up to grief almost unbearable? What happened when yesterday you danced like a child in the woods along a path of deer peering and the butterflies floating close? What the blazes happened? The light of my soul forever closely dancing my human shadow so close. Joy and sorrow forever playing hide and seek. Yet, both keep me in a kind of humble balance—can you feel this too?

Resting my head upon the pillow at night, my humble heart asks for abiding soul, loving presence to hold my human hand when my suffering chooses to wake me, but also please not let me forget the joy of love in loving friendships, my family time, and my moments of great inspiring words flowing in and through my heart. My soul, loving presence always so close to my human nature. Not easy, but my awakened awareness now gives light that it is sacred Divine Love within both my joy and sorrow that keep me walking my path home.

We must begin to understand that Earth is but one place in the infinite galactic dimensions. Having my subtle experience of moving in and out of my physical form taught me that we don't die. We just simply outgrow and outlive the physical form to move on to other experiences within the galactic dimensions. Having cancer also is teaching me that my body may become diseased and it may also be healed. What mystery! Yet, me soul, free to only taste the felt experience of Divine Love, which when leaving the body, will remain with me to take forward.

It's an ongoing experience that is unfathomable. And to have now the delight of other dimensions reaching out to me, within my subtle form, with their loving transmissions of information, is an ongoing experience of so much sacred Divine Love within a core lightness of being that is impossible to express here, but please know it's possible for anyone and everyone to experience because it's 'Who We all Are.' We all are these beautiful, sensual, sacred souls within subtle body energies, ready to create our new sacred unity love story together.

Our sacred Divine Love, as sacred souls, asks all of us now to begin emerging our creative fire to live this higher love and inclusion on planet Earth. Please begin your emergence; go within yourself with great loving prayer and intention to become your most beautiful truth, beauty, and goodness.

"I am one with the source insofar as I act as a source by making everything I have received flow again—just like Jesus."
~Raimon Panikker

Our inner kingdom within has been incubating for this new birth time, waiting for us souls to emerge in full awareness to now push this creative higher Divine Love into existence. Let us take the meditative and contemplative prayer route inward; both know the way home to our innermost kingdom where our soul presence awaits. So our big questions: are we now ready? Is it time? Is the hour growing late that we must find each other in all the inner/outer places to begin?

Human Fear Builds Walls. Sacred Love Builds Bridges through all the Divides

Perhaps the biggest wall is the one we have constructed around our heart. This wall is the mind-held voice with its thoughts of held fear, pain, and years we've all felt betrayed and deceived from the subtle deceptions and betrayals we've all committed, enforcing our walls even stronger. Yet, who lives within these walls but us? We are afraid to tear them down and walk free into the open air breathing the stars, galleries of rich landscapes, and feeling all the sacred love flowing in every moment from our one mystical, mysterious sacred love unity, wanting to embrace us and dance us into living this life with open joy, compassion, hugs, and tasting it all.

We must learn to grieve when the heart hurts so its pain can keep moving through to feel and find the injustice, thus allowing our anger to also find its voice. We then allow it to keep moving so we then find our laughter and smiles again or make love to everything when the heart feels so full of sacred Divine Love. But we mustn't cling or get attached to any of it—just let it all keep enfolding and unfolding, moving like un-impeded energy. Flow like night into day, ocean into shore, breath into breath. Relax, then release over and over—again and again—become like the winds of change that life and our higher soul, loving presence through us know, bringing everything to us, whatever we need, if we become aware and awake to receive it.

"Patience is an enormously supportive and even magical practice. It's a way of completely shifting the fundamental human habit of trying to resolve things by either going to the right or the left, labeling things "good" or labeling them "bad." It's the way to develop fearlessness, the way to contact the seeds of war and the seeds of lasting peace— and to decide which ones we want to nurture."
~Pema Chodron

Courage to take down our wall says we surrender our own need to control life. When looking up into the infinite sky—the planets, sun, moon, and billions of stars, galaxies, and universes—we simply ask who, what, and how does this miracle in every moment unfold its movement, it's unfolding of not only this planet but an entire unfolding of life beyond this planet none of us can comprehend? Is my one life better than yours? My country better than yours? Or my anything better if we all, wherever we are or whoever we claim to be, each hold kindness, Divine Love, caring in our one open heart? We must trust with great faith that which moves the Earth moves us!

"Your ordinary acts of love and hope point to the extraordinary promise that every human life is of inestimable value."
~Desmond Tutu

My soul whispers that quiet listening is all about the inquiry deep into Mystery Presence drifting into wonder, flowing into a listening heart where me soul presence, through stillness, opens a portal into an unseen and never-before walked path. A vision seeing with new eyes landscapes all vibrating vivid colors and sounds like soft water falling into my hands of energy waves. Where my soul's words come to give expression to this beautiful world. She says, listen.

Perhaps our greater Beloved God/Goddess is trying to say, Wake Up Humanity! A Covid virus came taking millions of lives, then forced us to close down, isolate, and become aware of our fragile vulnerability. A war came, still raging it's want of control of our democracy. Arising out of our vulnerability, we must now become aware of something bigger and greater. We also are seeing the value of kindness and gratitude for this gift called life and each other. We are opening our hearts and becoming responders to the cries of so many. Our vulnerability is emerging our courage and our soul, loving presence.

Our soul awareness is helping us to see each other from our sacred depths as our surface is being washed away. Yes, many of us are arising with courage, love, kindness, and compassion to become more tolerant of each other. Many souls realizing we are the ones and we are the way to create a more loving and light-filled world.

We know many will cling to the old story and go down fighting for its continuation—the authoritative leaders and their followers not wanting to give up their power over the people or their supremacy beliefs where power and money is the worship to control, own the land, land rights, and own still the people.

But they will not prevail because behind their veils of separation; our core sacred love and light is growing us stronger. We souls arise in oneness with our Beloved Source to bring back our sacred unity from within to back upon the Earth to live and reign in peace, prosperity, and Divine soul partnerships for the many and not just a few. We shall choose our leaders wisely from their soul wisdom, kindness, and caring emerging from their soul essence.

Albert Einstein says, "The intuitive mind is a sacred gift. The rational mind is a faithful servant. We have created a society that honors the servant and has forgotten the gift."

Death awareness in partnership with life teaches me how to balance living for my end time. Cancer also teaching to live this now soul awareness. How do my actions get read at death? My earlier days lived with so many miss-the mark moments. How many decisions were made in integrity, authentic smiles, and sacred Divine Love? Did she live with passion and meaning always greater than mere pettiness of judgment, jealousy, and dislike? Yes…when my mind and my heart become co-partners, then my awareness operates through my soul, loving presence for living in our sacred unity.

Soul whispers, "We walk together and we see the rose ready to birth then to bloom, then we watch the rose lose its last petal, death, and we love them both. This is life lived." Upon my end of life, may those who come to say goodbye say, "She, in the end, lived from her own loving soul presence." May at my death, this sacred prayer be read for those to hold this prayer in their own heart soul.

Beloved Presence everywhere within me sacred is your Divine Love and it's Light. Though the rough waters often beat against my small mortal self and its shores of life, always my heart soul is open to receiving your strength and courage to keep my faith strong and to be still and know never am I alone or without your inner Presence to weather any storms that may blow through. I keep moving to repose in my immortal Soul Divine Love. I let go all that tethers and binds me to anyone and anything not of this higher sacred Love and its higher wisdom. I live in compassion for my brothers and sisters. My actions now are your actions. I act in Divine Love...always, forever filled within with your love. I love you...I am forever grateful.

There is an alchemy of consciousness as we humans begin slowly to awaken. Our higher yearning is like a light beam calling each of us within. Each unique human is encased within their unique soul like the small caterpillar. The soul is always, through sacred love, giving many signs and synchronized happenings to unite as this one sacred love. Two powerful energies coming together to alchemically fire the means for this higher consciousness and her emergence. We must rise in the light of the late Ruth Bader Ginsberg to be the courage of how she used the law of principle to bring the power of truth for equality and using truth to keep our democracy in check.

"Hope is the thing with feathers that perches in the soul and sings the tune without the words and never stops at all."
~Emily Dickinson

"Invite your depression to pull up a chair with you in front of the fire, and sit with it, without looking for a way to escape...When you allow yourself to experience depression, it will leave as soon as it has served its purpose in your loss."
~Elisabeth Kubler-Ross

And just as Ms. Kubler-Ross says, "When it is time, and they have done their job, they leave." And it is how my soul, long in bondage, became free to be me. They left, thus, my new story began.

This book has been a labor of my sacred Divine Love. Not always an easy labor as my small ego mind lived many dark nights in working through its labor pains from early life and possibly many lifetimes of scars imprinted to finally open its chrysalis to become my true sensual sacred soul, loving presence self. Yet, humanely, still vulnerable and fragile too. My cancer is ever present, yet continues to dissolve. I am also eternally grateful for the four men, husbands, as together we each grew and developed through our small ego self, and all of you a forever part of my own waking up to my true sensual sacred soul, loving presence, within Beloved presence. I love you all.

Learning to BE with what is not easy…especially when life is so uncertain and very challenging to stay centered. My way is to Let Go, to just sit with what is surfacing so it is felt, seen, heard, and even touched. Cancer helps me to do this within so much uncertainty.

Breathing in the same air as you gives to me this depth of knowing our breath comes from a Divine life itself. No matter who we are, where we are, or what we possess, our breath is not a given. At any moment, it can be taken away.

What is it that we each can agree to that gives us meaning to live our breathing? I'm asking this today knowing tomorrow is not a given.

For me, it is the practice of what gives rise to each in and out breath. A Presence of Divine Love arises within me that this love gives breath to all life without exception. Everything is and always has been in an ongoing relationship with everything created, through our breathing, in and out of this one airway of sameness.

Is Divine Love always within this airway that breathes us and attracts us to live? Are our forms wired for this love? Must we now evolve love to becoming the most important resource on Earth? Can this be our turning point where we each become our higher Divine Love? Our awareness and attention to choice important!

There is an I-ness within presence, this subtle conscious awareness of thoughts, sensations, feelings, sounds, colors, and all in some ongoing dialogue within these personas of mind/body we all experience. This becomes our soul, loving presence guiding us all.

For me, she is my soul, her loving presence of wise guidance to help the ongoing voice of wave like frequencies of an energy, keeping me, all of us alive, through sameness of breath, and all our forms we all so identify with. Yet, once breath stops, the form also stops, but does my soul I-ness cease? I can answer that as an emphatic—No. My out-of-body and a near-death experience shut that belief down.

So if you want to meet who you really are, then take time every day to let go into your own present inner self to just sit and begin to listen, watch, pay close attention to what's going on. Then inquire who is aware, who is conscious, who is always behind a seemingly scenario of an ongoing dialogue, feelings, and emotions within you? The big question is, who's inquiring?

Here is another helpful understanding. When you are dreaming at night, who is dreaming and observing all these stories within the dream? When we awake from the night travels and begin dreams into the day travels, we believe the day dreams feel more real, but are they? Is our soul, our I-ness, or true self, just having adventures, within form, upon the Earth?

Becoming aware of our true self—our I-ness or soul self— we can change how we want to be in the dream, and we can begin to create a more loving, peaceful, and exciting adventure upon the Earth while we are in this dream-like reality, within mind/body forms. The small little mind/body for too long has been living and breathing in a belief of separation from its true self. The small self needs wise, loving guidance from its higher soul self to change the trajectory of separation stories back into unity stories where all becomes integrated into right loving relationships with each other, Earth, and our Beloved Divine loving mystery wired within us all. Again, just contemplate all this, then take yourself inward on an adventure to know you!

A Beautiful Transmission for us with a Most Loving Poem to End

Once Upon a Time—

Living Our Soul's Presence, we became someone never before known. We surrendered what separated us from our Divine Love. We understood ourselves as cosmic soul travelers through the universes, galaxies, and the Earth, a place we visit and live through the physical form for earthly experiences.

But somewhere in time/space, upon the Earth, we fell from our cosmic existence, once unified, into a false, fearful story that we are alone, small separate selves, and to not believe in this story, we would be punished after death from an above authority. This false story has reigned for eons of time and has come to give this same authority to others to control and manipulate the fearful people. This domination, for their false power, has grown into ongoing wars, deep divisions, and is slowly destroying the Earth.

This false story has taken our Divine Love, innately within all beings, to be buried deep beneath the small self. This story has remained hidden and buried throughout our history as many became known as heretics and even witches. Deep fear came as millions of people have been killed for living their soul presence authenticity.

Today, we are being faced once again with this dark control stripping away women's rights and gender and racial rights. We must not go backwards in time. We mustn't allow the beast of a few to become again the power over the many, slowly taking the beauty of our Earth and each soul's wisdom, now ready to rise up, to finally give partnership, once again, to the alone beastly mind so we end this separation story.

We have help! Today, the Cosmic Light returns to expose these darkly beasts and to give back to us many, our own unified remembrance so we each can return back to living our soul's presence.

We become once more the someones never known in our small mind, yet, always known in our depths as souls of Divine Love. We surface in our greater awareness and awakening. We return to live again, unified upon Earth, where we restore her balance and harmony. We begin living our soul presence as a higher soul species within the physical form for abiding sensual experiences.

The Earth plane becomes once more a beautiful place each unique soul can visit and where all souls can uniquely create together through each's gift given. Once Upon a Time begins again our true unity story of Divine Love.

Fairytales can come true! Believe and listen to your soul's whispers!

Fields of Soul Flowers—

Peace can never be obtained through our alone separate mind.
Our alone mind collects data and information from the external library.
Humanity has long yearned for our missing partner within our inner
wisdom. When chaos becomes the everyday weather, we all must
seek shelter. Our heart is this shelter. Within our heart is the mind's
missing partner. She is sacred Divine Love, and she lives within our
heart as our home of sacred unity!

She whispers in an intuitive, wise language understood by all our
minds. She is our Soul, and she comes today to end the wars within
our minds. She comes to unite us as sacred partnerships within to
live as peace upon Earth.

She becomes our wise loving counsel to our alone separate mind;
we must listen! She is the seed planted within all heart soils ready to
burst forth her creative sun.

She says it's time to unite. She says our sacred love united with our mind flames the soul flower of 'who we are' to help erase our mind of all its learned divisive separation.

Peace within brings peace without. Above the sun, below all life's green abundance for living. Our Soul flower seeks to meet in the open field to lay next to each other in sacred unity.
We accept our responsibility...We all are here to tend the Earth garden and ourselves for our gifts given to live our sacred partnerships in sacred loving unity with each other, Divine Love, and the Earth.

We've come to the top of the summit. A long arduous climb.
Looking up, outward, and down only one way calling—
one way open to now venture. My soul whispers it's time to fly—
Divine Love will become our wings lighting our way.

Epilogue

I end this book with the good news that I am cancer free. My journey through cancer became my final surrender to Living my Soul's wisdom so often denied through my own alone mind distractions. Perhaps, my own direct experience of living with death and life, close in partnership, took me to my own edges where dying and surrender opened my small mind to surrender, coming into true partnership with my own souls emergence.

These are beautiful transmissions that emerged through upon hearing that I was cancer free.

Divine Love comes
softly like a bird
perched upon the leaf.

It asks nothing
yet it fills the heart like
the sun fills the blooming rose.

Once we feel
this Love, unlike any love
ever felt, We know!

We want this
Love again and again so

like the sons and daughters we go out
into the world in search.

We drink the
wines, smoke the grass then kiss and
hug many around us. Still
something is missing. We haven't found it!

We become weary
in our outer search and sadness comes.
We ask why? We become a bit angry-
what purpose to have me taste
this Divine Love- if now its elusive and gone?

We go to sit
upon the edge of our life wondering-what's
it really all about? Money didn't make
me happy-trying to control my life never worked
as disease came, disasters came and
many I loved died too soon.

Then it happened!
My heart burst open, this surge of surrender,
like a giant earthquake, rattled my bones
then threw me to the ground in sobs
uncertain and uncontrollable wishing myself
dead and gone.

I died!

I opened my eyes
to the beautiful sun shining and the bird flew in
chirping- only the sound like a melody
unheard.

My breath was
slow like a river flowing into the large sea.
Divine Love flowed through my being-yes the same
Love felt so long ago-my body began to dance
my laughter became loud-unable to stop.

Divine Love
never left me. I left this Love believing it was to
be found in the external world. And truth is
it was-but first it was to be found within me-so
Divine Love can be understood as why the
bird chirps, why the water flows, why the sun
comes out every morning and the moon every night!

Why the dark soils
need a rooted life-our dark soils within us and the dark
soils in the earth for growth and development
to one day come back home
remembering We are all Divine Love!

We are the Way
to bring forth Divine Love that earth and all living
upon the earth, like so many, must surrender
to this Love and it's abundance to live our very precious lives
together…not separate fighting…but loving each other!

277

We surrender
our small alone separate mind of all its learned ways,
in its alone external search, to come back home
within ourselves to find waiting is our own very unique,
wise soul, already in oneness with Divine Love.

Wisdom of Soul
enjoins with lost mind of persona to partner with our
Divine Love, thus begins upon the earth a higher
species, where each's unique purpose is found how to
live together, serving Divine Love, for all and all to come!

Welcome Home
all prodigal son's and daughter's! You are equally loved!

2nd transmission!

How fragile
our bodies to pain-even death.

How strong
our resilience to heal- live life.

How minds
become the survival voices to
bring reaction-caution helping us be safe.

Our Soul's
wisdom we forget to listen for guiding
our minds- it's not just about
survival but surrender to live our edges.

Our edges
keep rubbing up against pain, sufferings
to go through into surrender where
fear and survival lose their control over us.

Passion fires
our purpose to live life by loving life in all
it's gifts given through each other in
each's shared unique ways.

Creativity
within each's passion and unique gifts is
how We each contribute to bringing
Divine Love, firing the heart soils and the
earth soils, for living our soul's wisdom.

Unity
is a world and divine humanity together
in harmony and balance; all aware
and attentive to each's passion and purpose!

CPSIA information can be obtained
at www.ICGtesting.com
Printed in the USA
BVHW052026150623
666019BV00005B/92

9 781513 697550